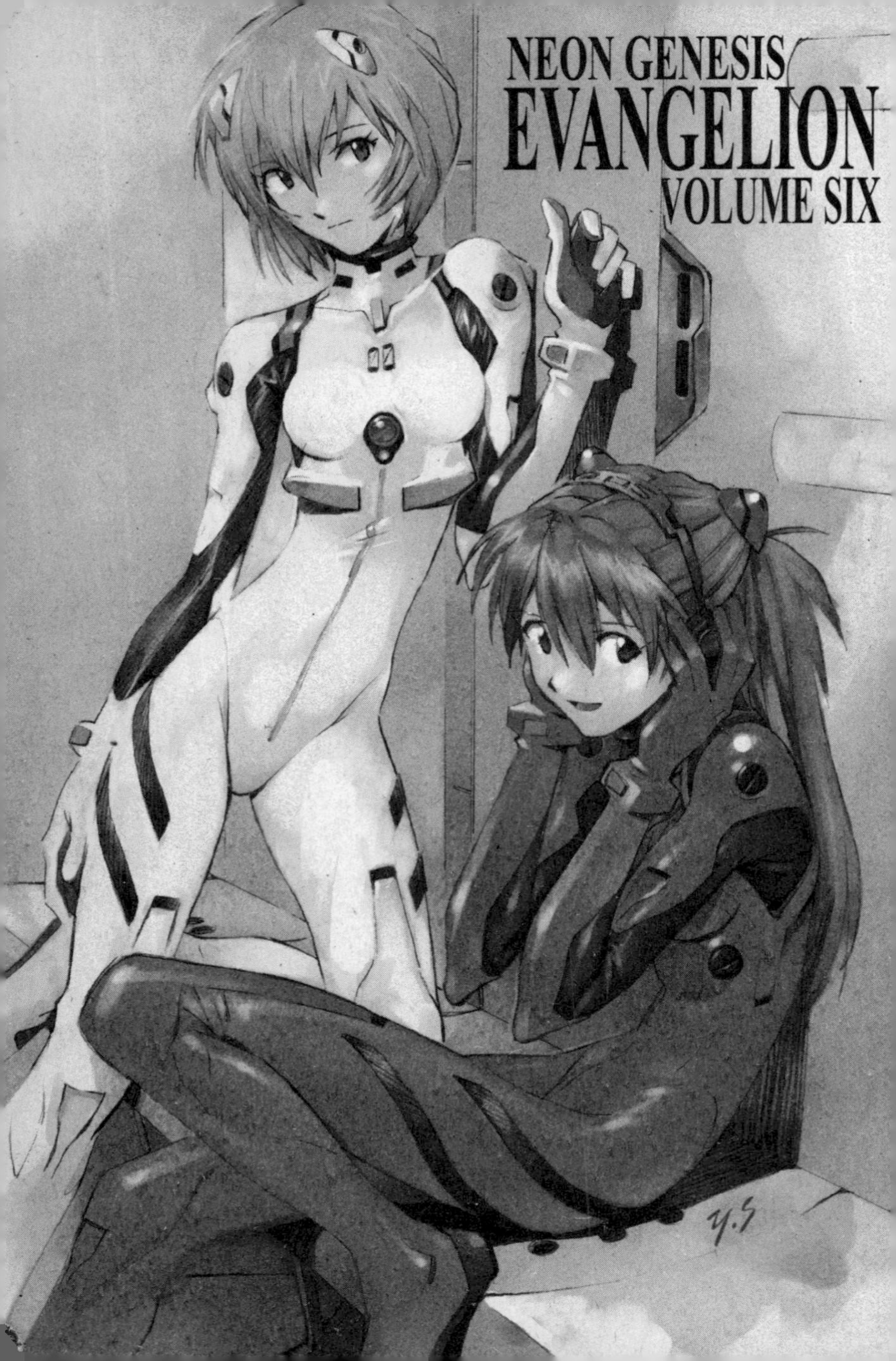
NEON GENESIS
EVANGELION
VOLUME SIX
Y.S

C O N T E N T S

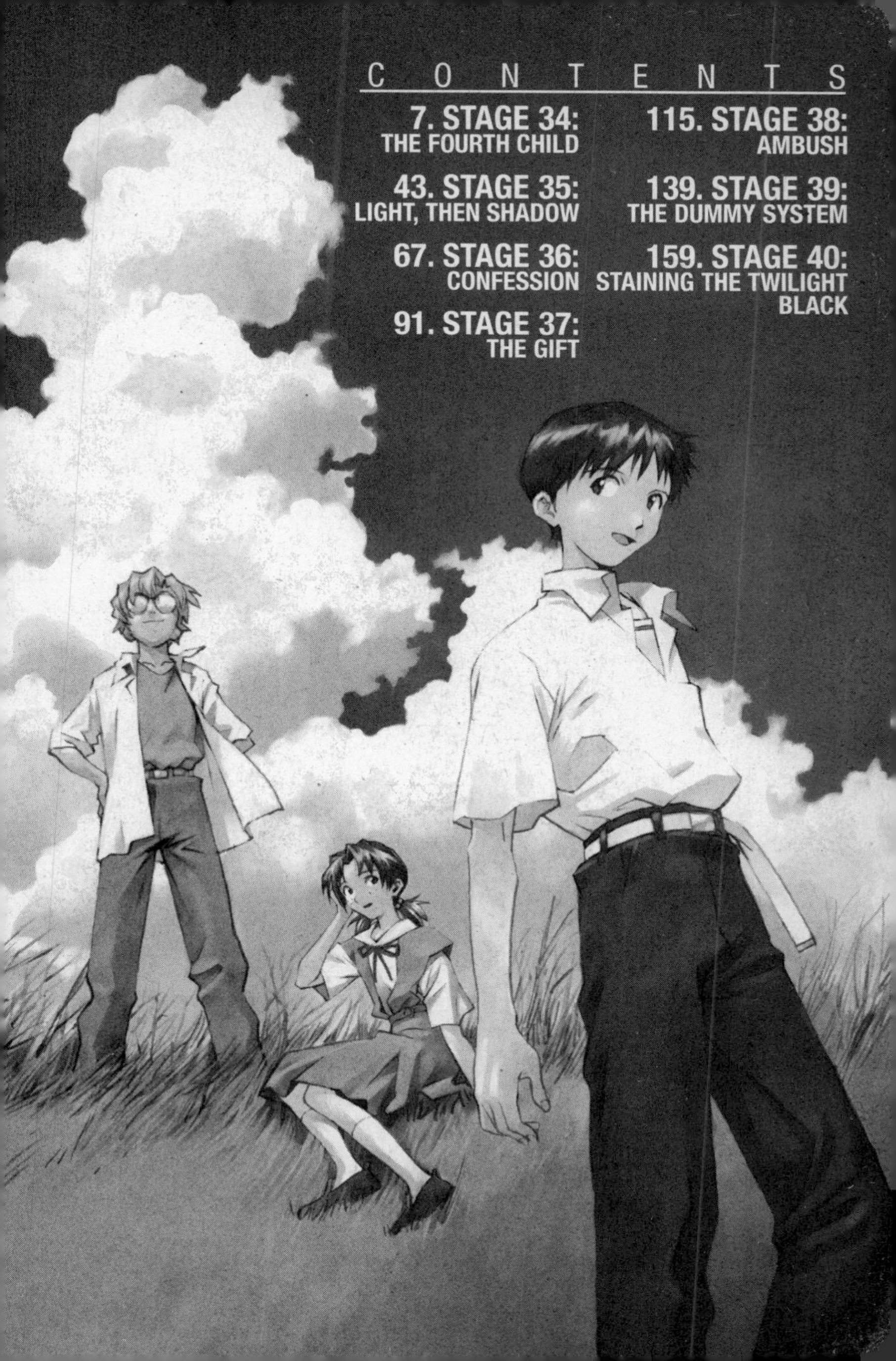

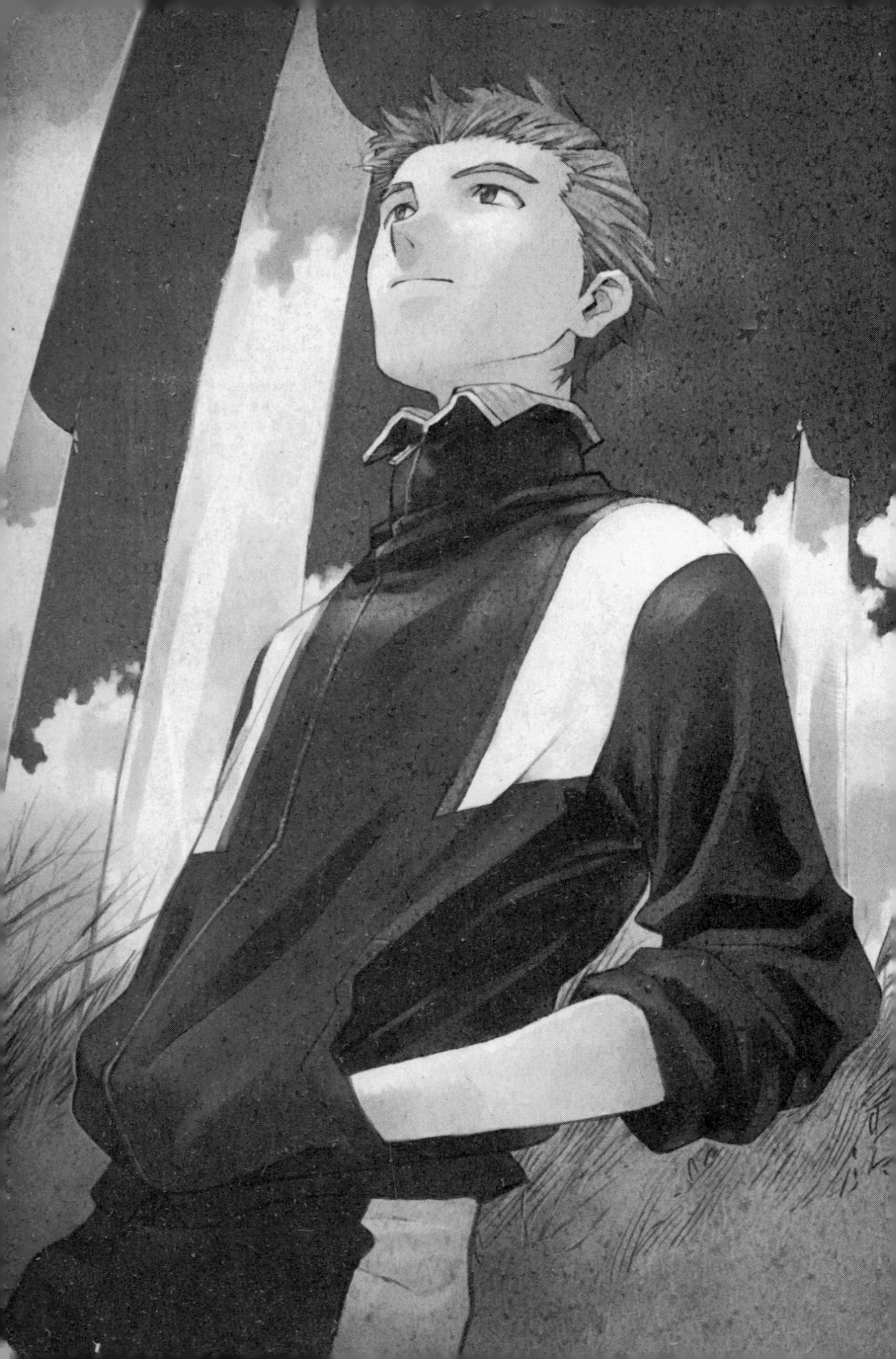

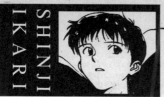

SHINJI IKARI

EVA PILOT, NERV
MIDDLE SCHOOL STUDENT Age: 14

Shinji was the "Third Child" chosen to pilot the monstrous Evangelion series: biomechanical units developed by the clandestine UN paramilitary agency known as NERV to fight entities code-named "Angels." Both resentful of his father, supreme commander Gendo Ikari, and desperate for his approval, Shinji has already defeated four Angels despite having no previous knowledge of NERV or combat.

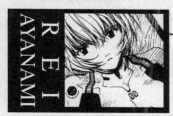

REI AYANAMI

EVA PILOT, NERV
MIDDLE SCHOOL STUDENT Age: 14

Rei is the "First Child" to be chosen to pilot an Evangelion, and first to use it in combat, sustaining severe injuries in Unit-01 while fighting the Third Angel. Although Rei barely expresses emotion, she at first regarded Shinji as an interloper. Since she and Shinji fought the Fifth Angel together, they have grown closer, yet Shinji is still mystified at how Rei relates to Gendo in a way he himself cannot.

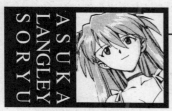

ASUKA LANGLEY SORYU

EVA UNIT-02 PILOT, NERV
MIDDLE SCHOOL STUDENT Age: 14

Asuka is a United States citizen of mixed Japanese and German ancestry. A boastfully "superior" product of eugenic breeding, Shinji knows that she tries to hide both her bratty nature and pain over the loss of her mother. Asuka is the "second Child" to be identified as qualified to pilot an Evangelion by the obscure Marduk Agency, and was assigned to Eva Unit-02. Attracted by Ryoji Kaji.

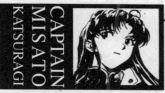

CAPTAIN MISATO KATSURAGI

OPERATIONS CHIEF, NERV Age: 29

Even though Capt. Katsuragi is third in command at NERV, after Commander Gendo and Sub-Commander Fuyutsuki, and oversees the Eva pilots in combat in her role as tactical planner, there are many things about the organization that have been kept from her. A carouser and slob in her off-hours, Misato has become surrogate family for Shinji, with whom she shares an apartment.

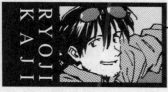

RYOJI KAJI

DOUBLE AGENT: NERV/JAPANESE
MINISTRY OF THE INTERIOR Age: 30

Escorted Asuka to Tokyo-3 from Germany bearing the embryonic "Adam." Senior NERV personnel are aware he is also spying for the Japanese government. Yet both he and Gendo consider the arrangement satisfactory—for now, although Kaji suspects his own personal loyalty to the truth may yet cost him his life. Wishes to renew his old college love affair with Major Katsuragi.

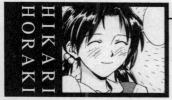

HIKARI HORAKI

MIDDLE SCHOOL STUDENT Age: 14

Believed to be the permanent class representative of Shinji's homeroom, 2-A; responsible for encouraging good order and decorum among her fellow students, including supervising clean-up chores…

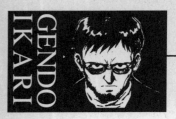

GENDO IKARI

SUPREME COMMANDER, NERV
Age: 48

Shinji's father; this ruthless and enigmatic man is the guiding force behind the development of NERV's Evangelion system. He is also the man entrusted to carry out the even more secret Instrumentality Project. Gendo was an absent father, entrusting Shinji's upbringing to his uncle and aunt.

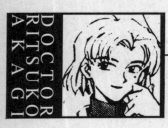

DOCTOR RITSUKO AKAGI

CHIEF SCIENTIST, NERV
Age: 30

Technical supervisor for NERV's "Project E (Evangelion)," Dr. Akagi is a polymath genius who rode the wave of scientific revolution that followed the cracking of the human genetic code at the end of the 20th century. Her disciplines include physics, biotechnology and computer science. Dr. Akagi was a friend of Misato's in college.

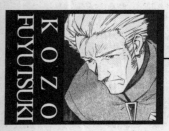

KOZO FUYUTSUKI

SUB-COMMANDER, NERV
Age: UNCERTAIN—ABOUT 60

Gendo's second-in-command and right-hand man. Before the Second Impact, Fuyutsuki was a biology professor in Kyoto, Japan, during which time he first met Gendo, who married his prize student. He and Dr. Akagi may be the only ones at NERV besides Gendo to know the complete story behind Evangelion and the Instrumentality Project.

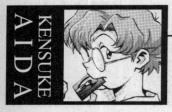

KENSUKE AIDA

MIDDLE SCHOOL STUDENT
Age: 14

A devoted fan of military affairs, Aida plays war games in army costume out in the country, habitually carries a Sony camcorder to capture shots of hardware or combat, and engages in computer hacking to acquire information for his "mania." He has expressed the wish that someone like Misato would "order him around."

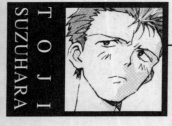

TOJI SUZUHARA

MIDDLE SCHOOL STUDENT
Age: 14

Best friend of Aida; speaks with a pronounced accent from his home town, Osaka. His father and grandfather are both part of NERV's research labs. At first he blamed Shinji (and punched him out) for injuries his sister suffered due to "collateral damage" from the first battle in Tokyo-3 against the Angels; now both Aida and he are friends with Unit-01's pilot.

NEON GENESIS EVANGELION
VIZ MEDIA EDITION VOLUME SIX

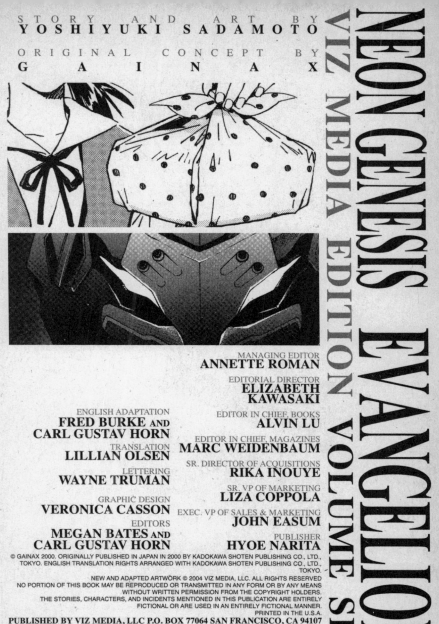

STORY AND ART BY
YOSHIYUKI SADAMOTO

ORIGINAL CONCEPT BY
GAINAX

ENGLISH ADAPTATION
FRED BURKE AND CARL GUSTAV HORN

TRANSLATION
LILLIAN OLSEN

LETTERING
WAYNE TRUMAN

GRAPHIC DESIGN
VERONICA CASSON

EDITORS
MEGAN BATES AND CARL GUSTAV HORN

MANAGING EDITOR
ANNETTE ROMAN

EDITORIAL DIRECTOR
ELIZABETH KAWASAKI

EDITOR IN CHIEF, BOOKS
ALVIN LU

EDITOR IN CHIEF, MAGAZINES
MARC WEIDENBAUM

SR. DIRECTOR OF ACQUISITIONS
RIKA INOUYE

SR. VP OF MARKETING
LIZA COPPOLA

EXEC. VP OF SALES & MARKETING
JOHN EASUM

PUBLISHER
HYOE NARITA

PRINTED IN THE U.S.A.

PUBLISHED BY VIZ MEDIA, LLC P.O. BOX 77064 SAN FRANCISCO, CA 94107

VIZ MEDIA EDITION
10 9 8 7 6 5 4 3 2
FIRST PRINTING AUGUST 2004
SECOND PRINTING DECEMBER 2006

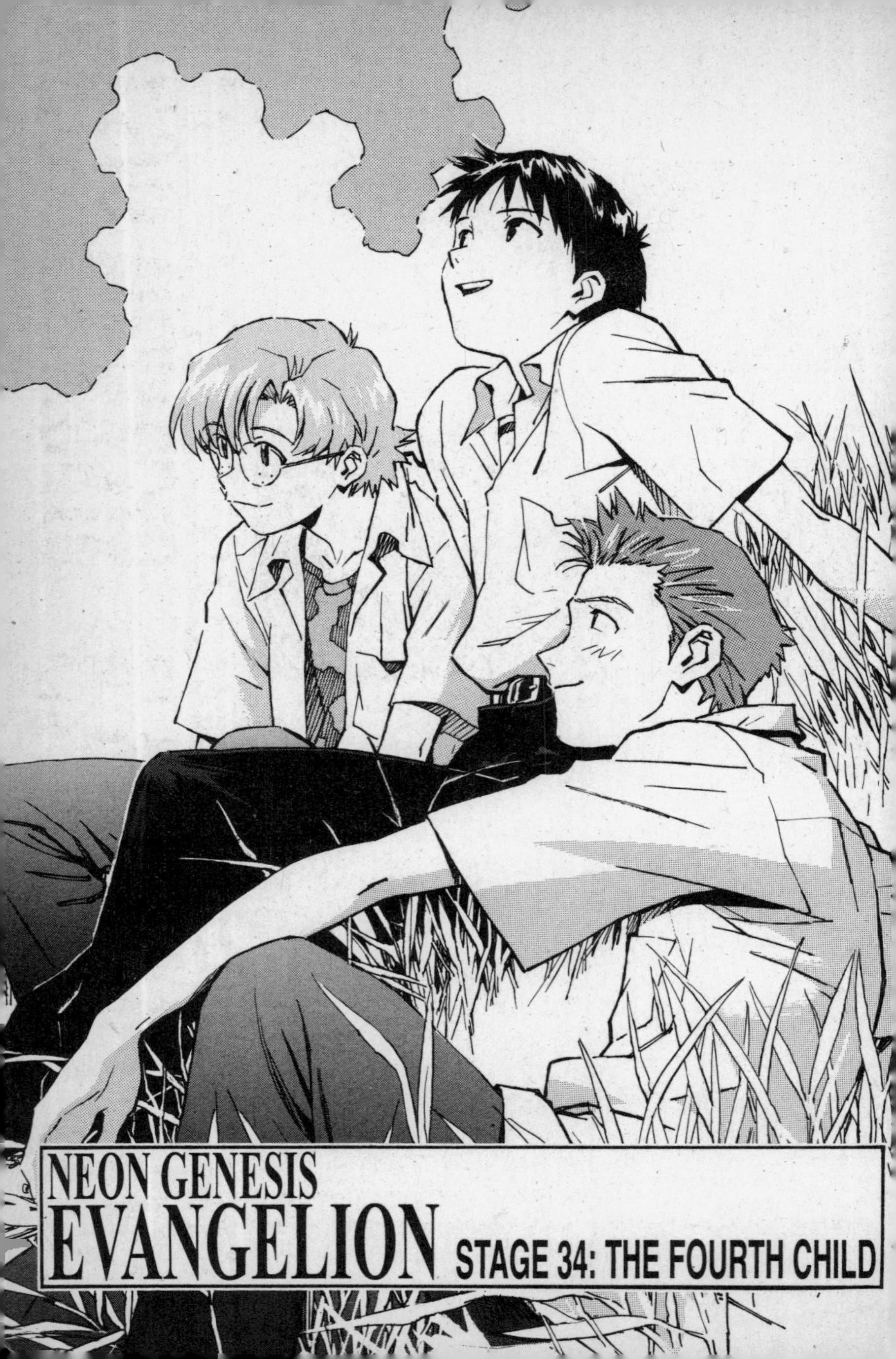
NEON GENESIS
EVANGELION
STAGE 34: THE FOURTH CHILD

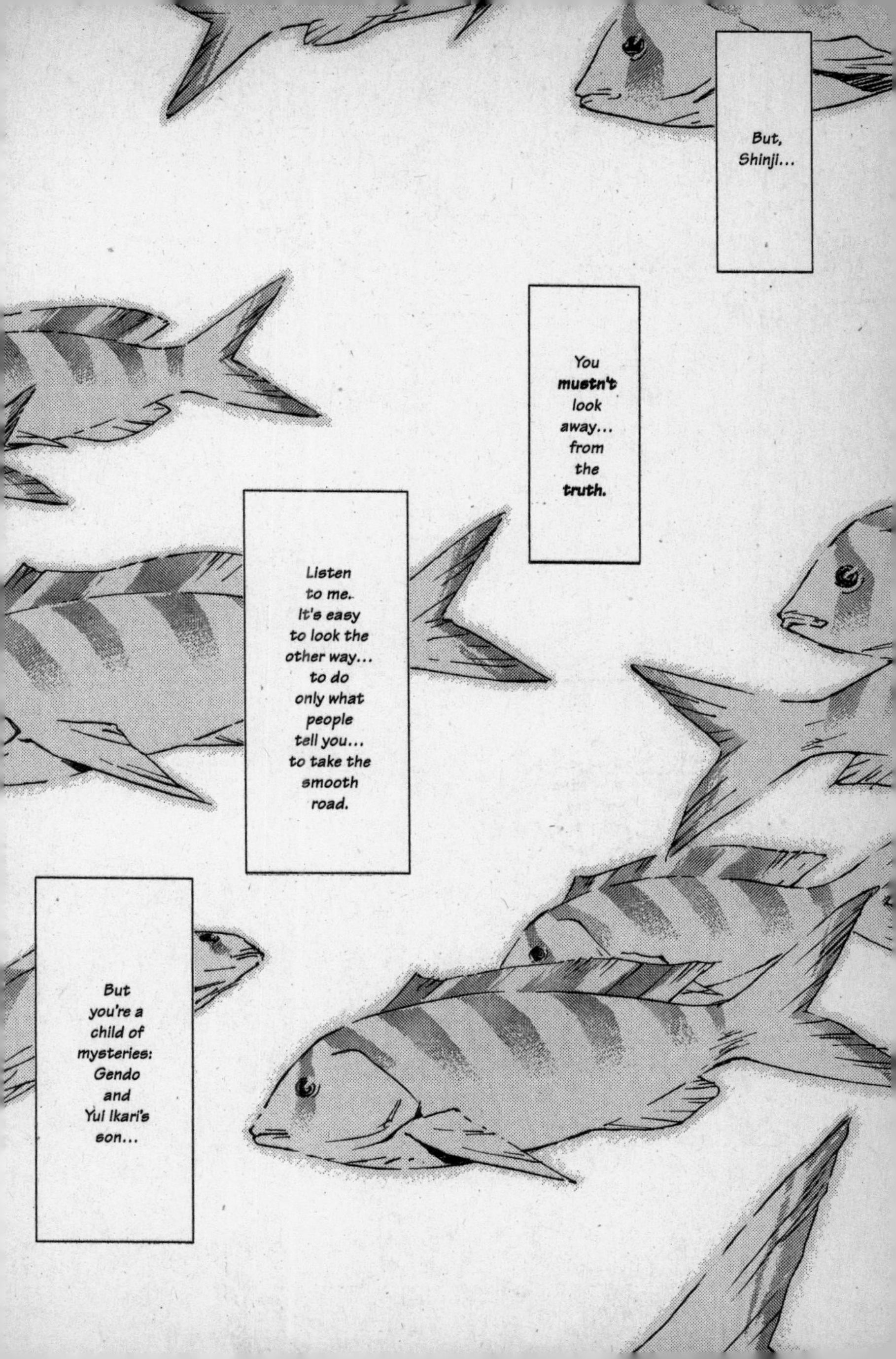
But, Shinji...
You **mustn't** look away... from the **truth.**
Listen to me.. It's easy to look the other way... to do only what people tell you... to take the smooth road.
But you're a child of mysteries: Gendo and Yui Ikari's son...

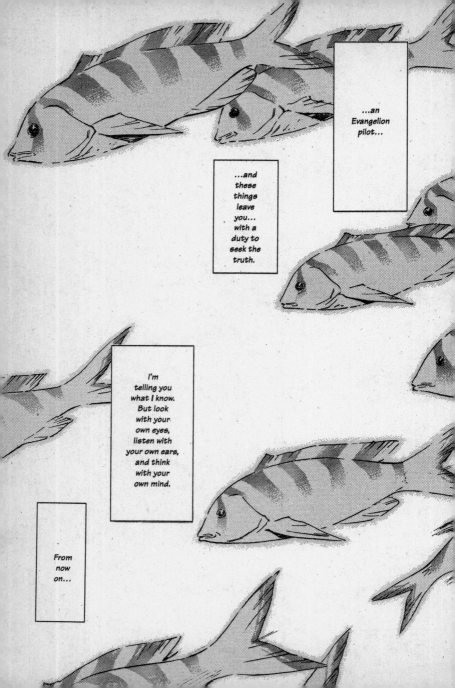

...an Evangelion pilot...

...and these things leave you... with a duty to seek the truth.

I'm telling you what I know. But look with your own eyes, listen with your own ears, and think with your own mind.

From now on...

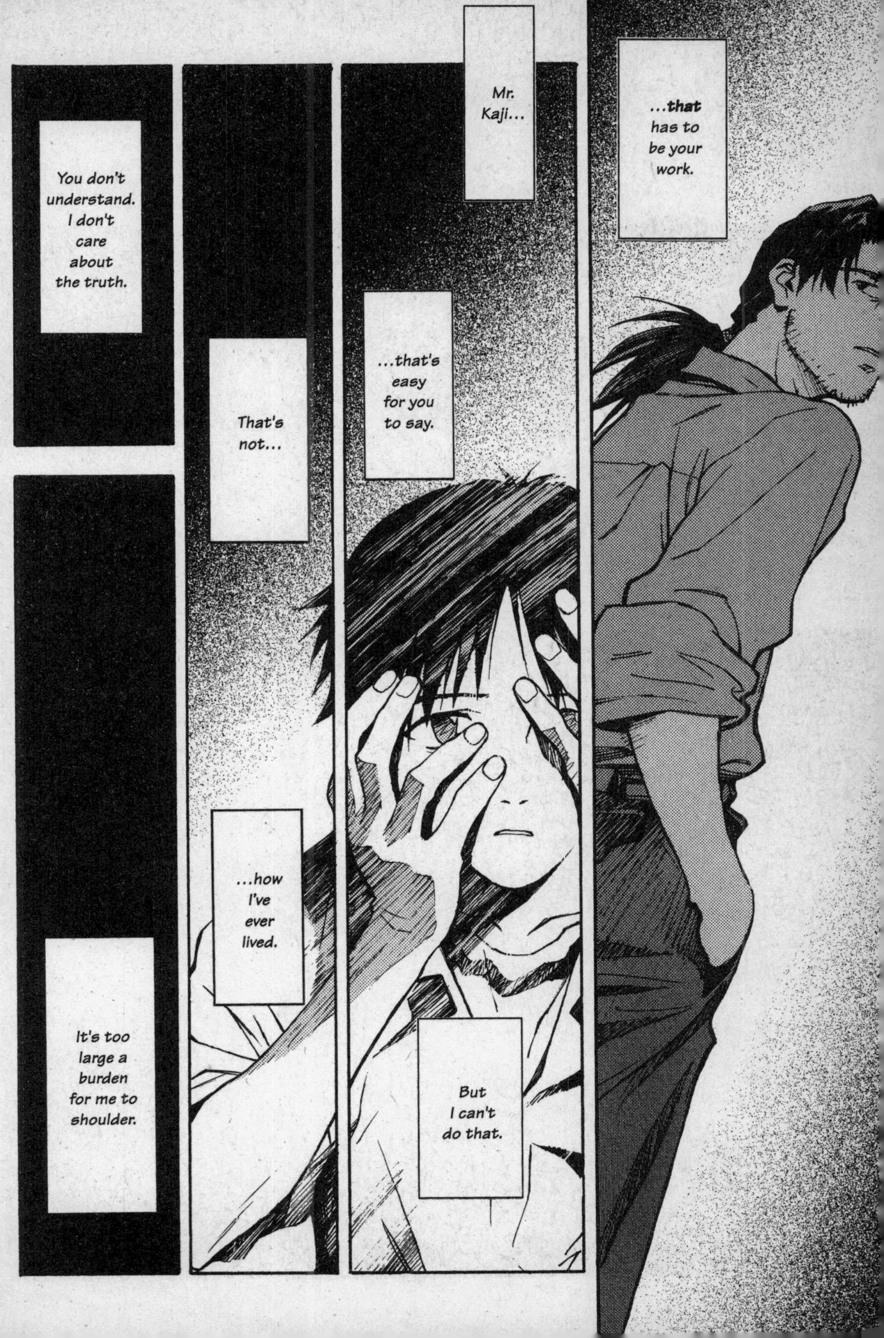
...**that** has to be your work.
Mr. Kaji...
...that's easy for you to say.
But I can't do that.
That's not...
...how I've ever lived.
You don't understand. I don't care about the truth.
It's too large a burden for me to shoulder.

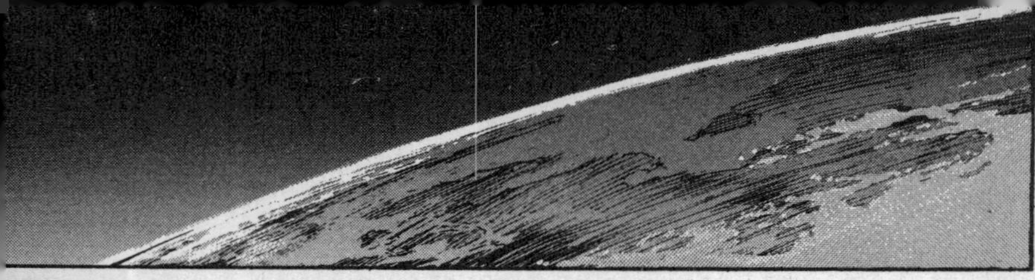
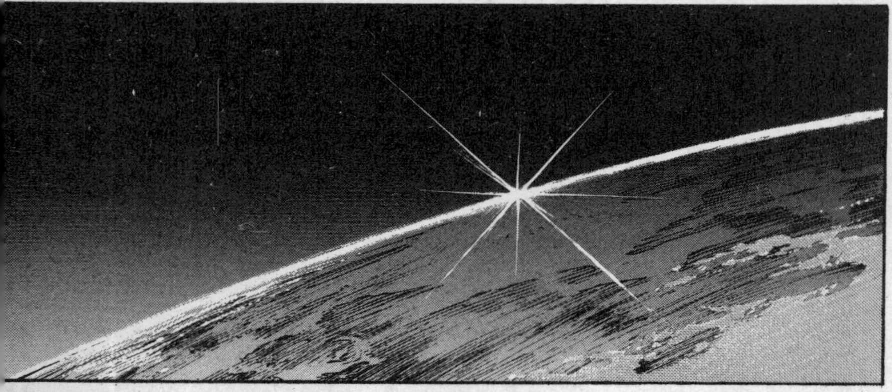
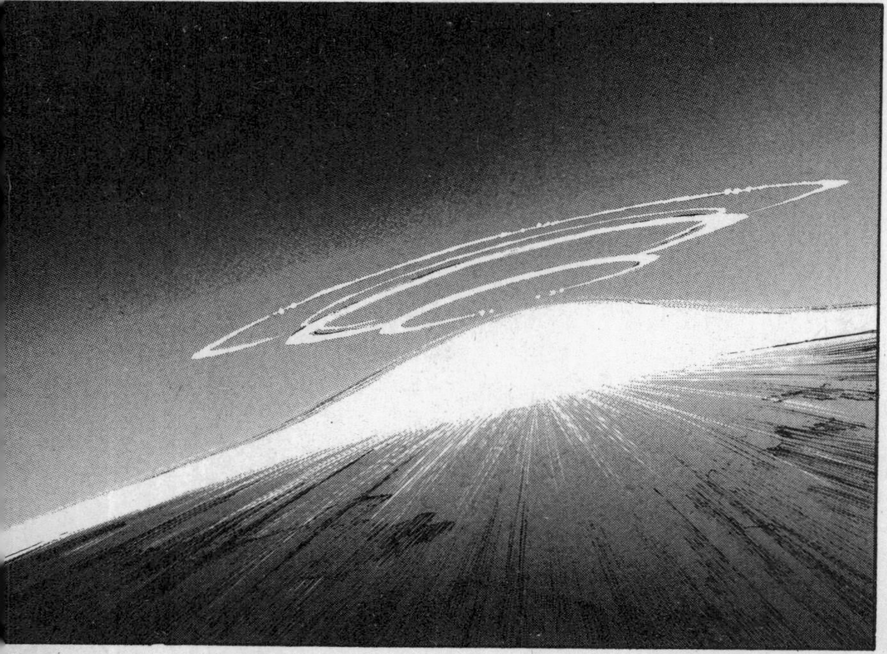

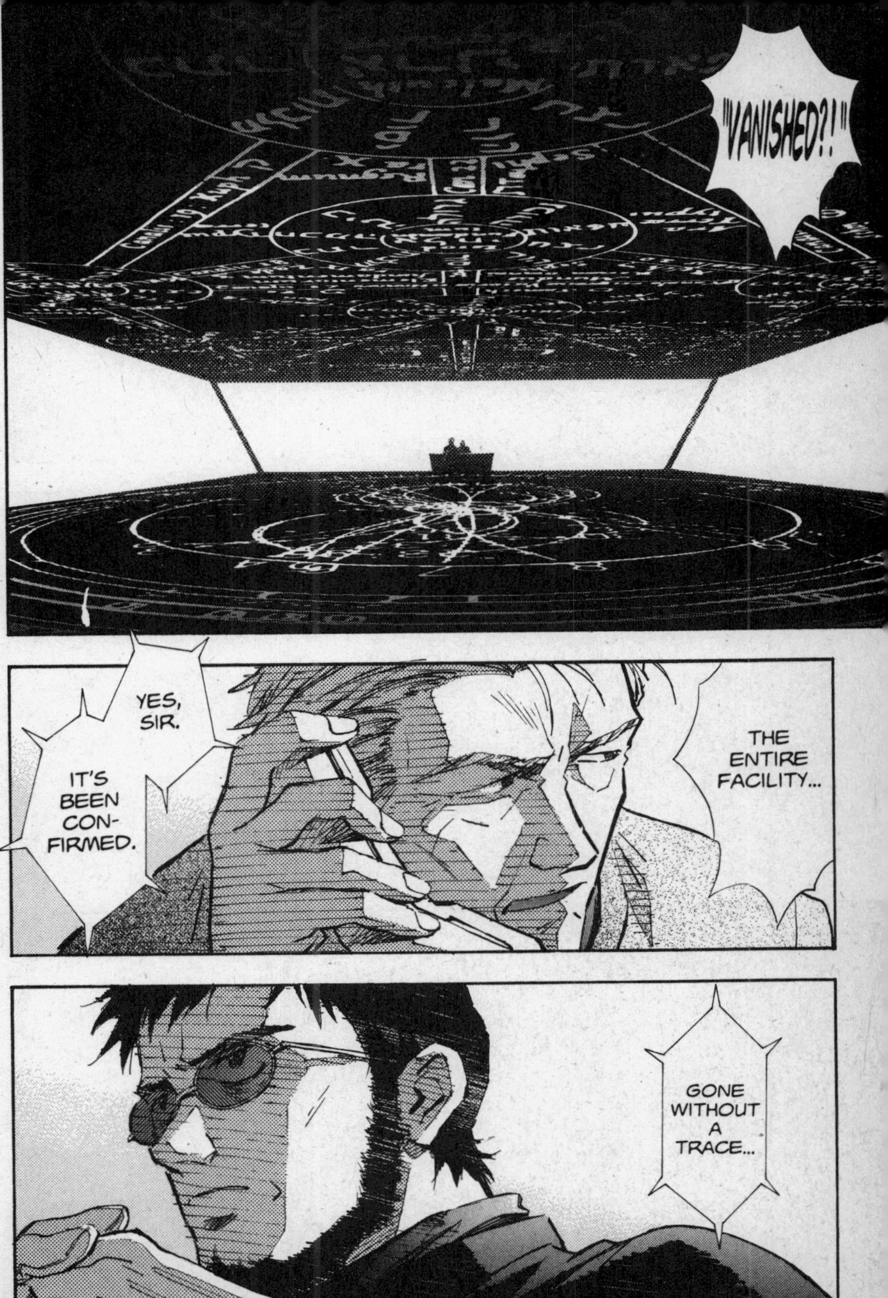
"VANISHED?!"
THE ENTIRE FACILITY...
YES, SIR.
IT'S BEEN CON-FIRMED.
GONE WITHOUT A TRACE...

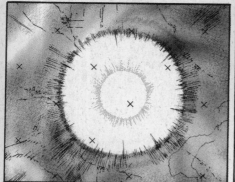

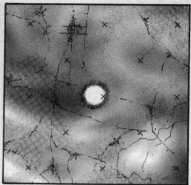

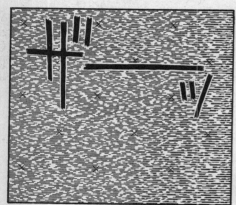

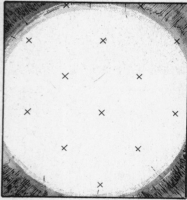

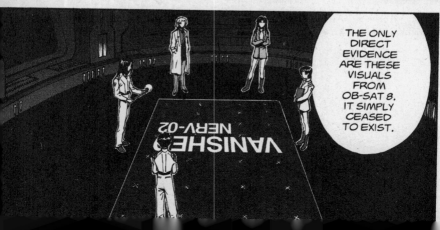

THE ONLY DIRECT EVIDENCE ARE THESE VISUALS FROM OB-SAT 8. IT SIMPLY CEASED TO EXIST.

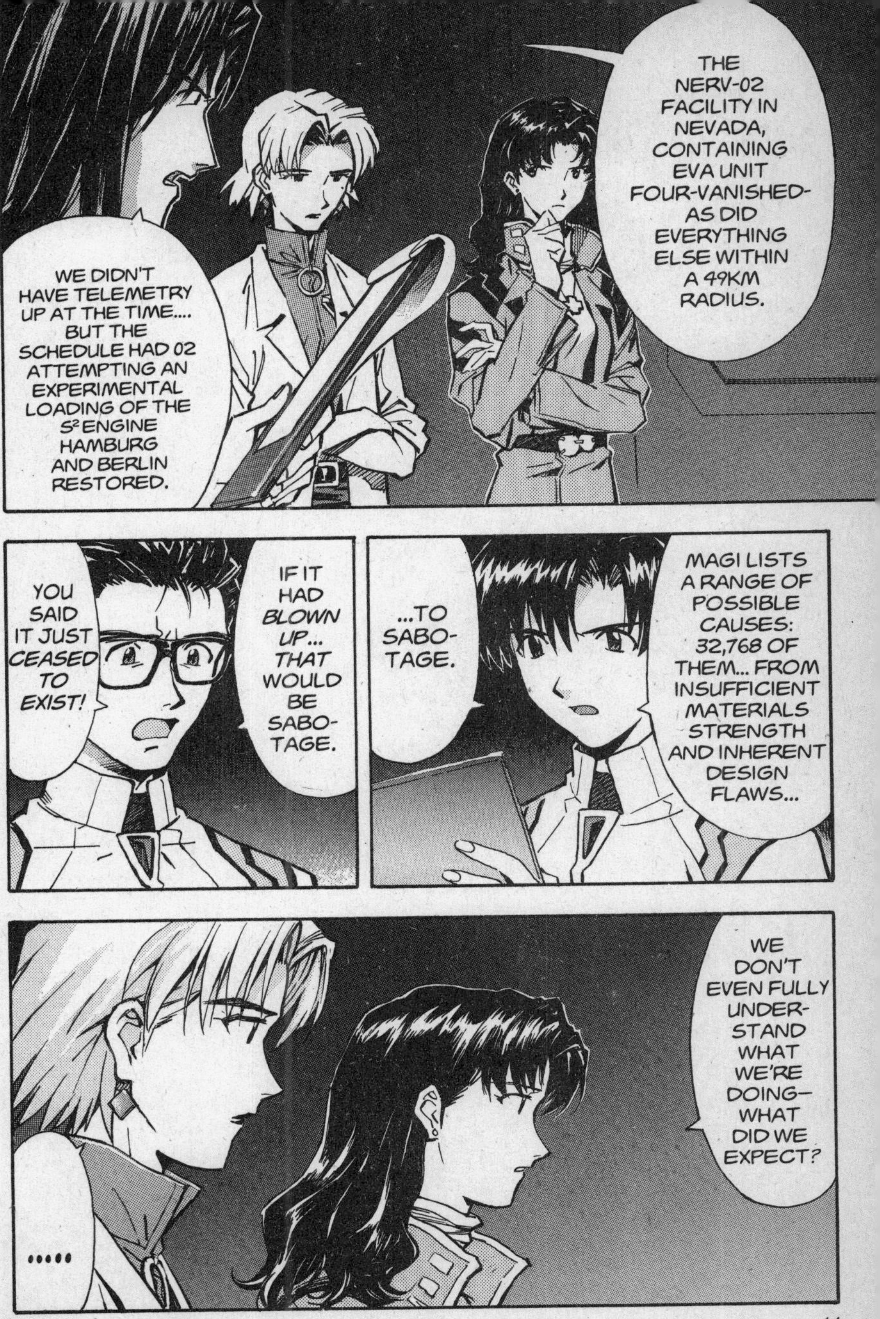
THE NERV-02 FACILITY IN NEVADA, CONTAINING EVA UNIT FOUR-VANISHED-AS DID EVERYTHING ELSE WITHIN A 49KM RADIUS.
WE DIDN'T HAVE TELEMETRY UP AT THE TIME.... BUT THE SCHEDULE HAD 02 ATTEMPTING AN EXPERIMENTAL LOADING OF THE S² ENGINE HAMBURG AND BERLIN RESTORED.
MAGI LISTS A RANGE OF POSSIBLE CAUSES: 32,768 OF THEM... FROM INSUFFICIENT MATERIALS STRENGTH AND INHERENT DESIGN FLAWS...
...TO SABOTAGE.
IF IT HAD *BLOWN UP*... *THAT* WOULD BE SABOTAGE.
YOU SAID IT JUST *CEASED TO EXIST!*
WE DON'T EVEN FULLY UNDERSTAND WHAT WE'RE DOING-WHAT DID WE EXPECT?
......

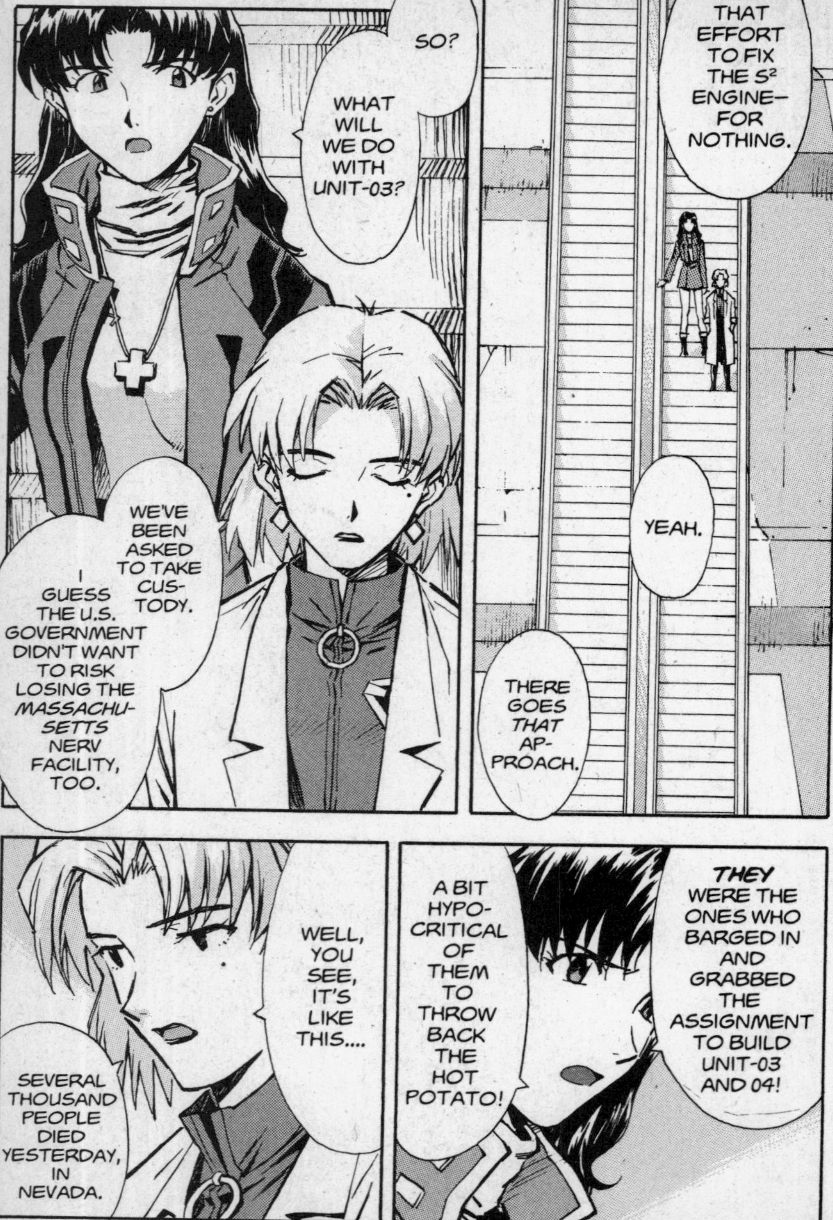
ALL THAT EFFORT TO FIX THE S^2 ENGINE—FOR NOTHING.
YEAH.
THERE GOES *THAT* APPROACH.
SO?
WHAT WILL WE DO WITH UNIT-03?
WE'VE BEEN ASKED TO TAKE CUSTODY.
I GUESS THE U.S. GOVERNMENT DIDN'T WANT TO RISK LOSING THE *MASSACHUSETTS* NERV FACILITY, TOO.
THEY WERE THE ONES WHO BARGED IN AND GRABBED THE ASSIGNMENT TO BUILD UNIT-03 AND 04!
A BIT HYPOCRITICAL OF THEM TO THROW BACK THE HOT POTATO!
WELL, YOU SEE, IT'S LIKE THIS....
SEVERAL THOUSAND PEOPLE DIED YESTERDAY, IN NEVADA.

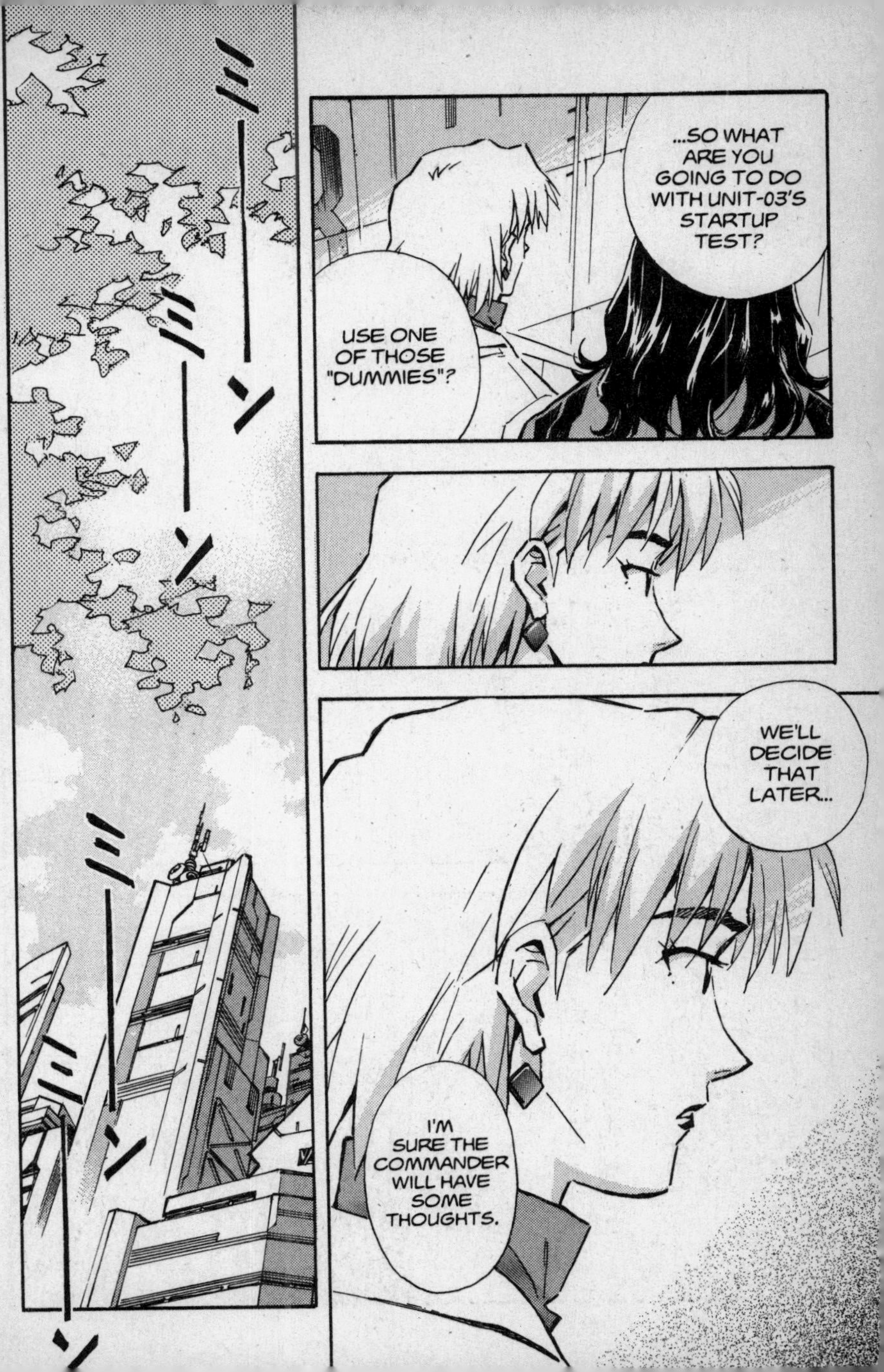
...SO WHAT ARE YOU GOING TO DO WITH UNIT-03'S STARTUP TEST?
USE ONE OF THOSE "DUMMIES"?
WE'LL DECIDE THAT LATER...
I'M SURE THE COMMANDER WILL HAVE SOME THOUGHTS.

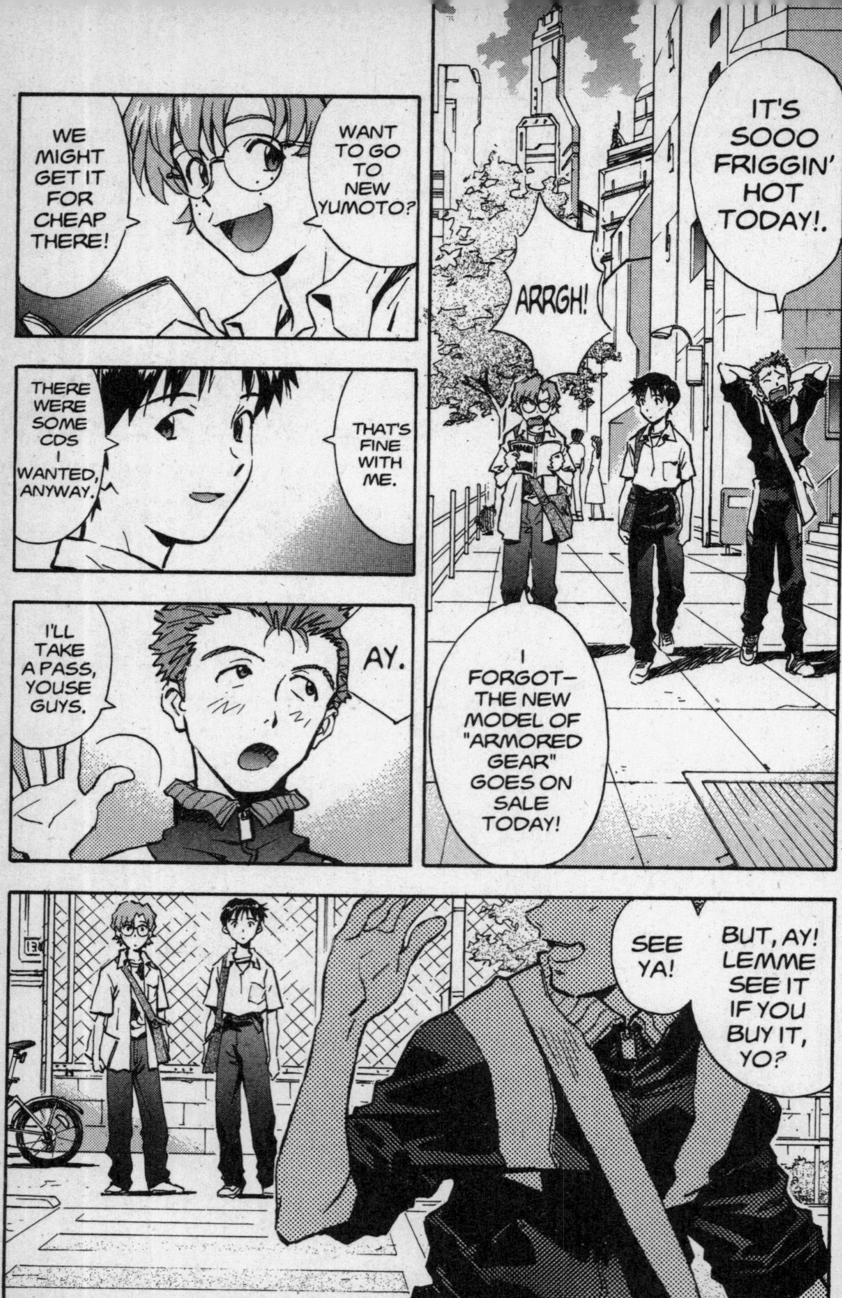
IT'S SOOO FRIGGIN' HOT TODAY!.
ARRGH!
I FORGOT—THE NEW MODEL OF "ARMORED GEAR" GOES ON SALE TODAY!
WANT TO GO TO NEW YUMOTO?
WE MIGHT GET IT FOR CHEAP THERE!
THAT'S FINE WITH ME.
THERE WERE SOME CDS I WANTED, ANYWAY.
AY.
I'LL TAKE A PASS, YOUSE GUYS.
BUT, AY! LEMME SEE IT IF YOU BUY IT, YO?
SEE YA!

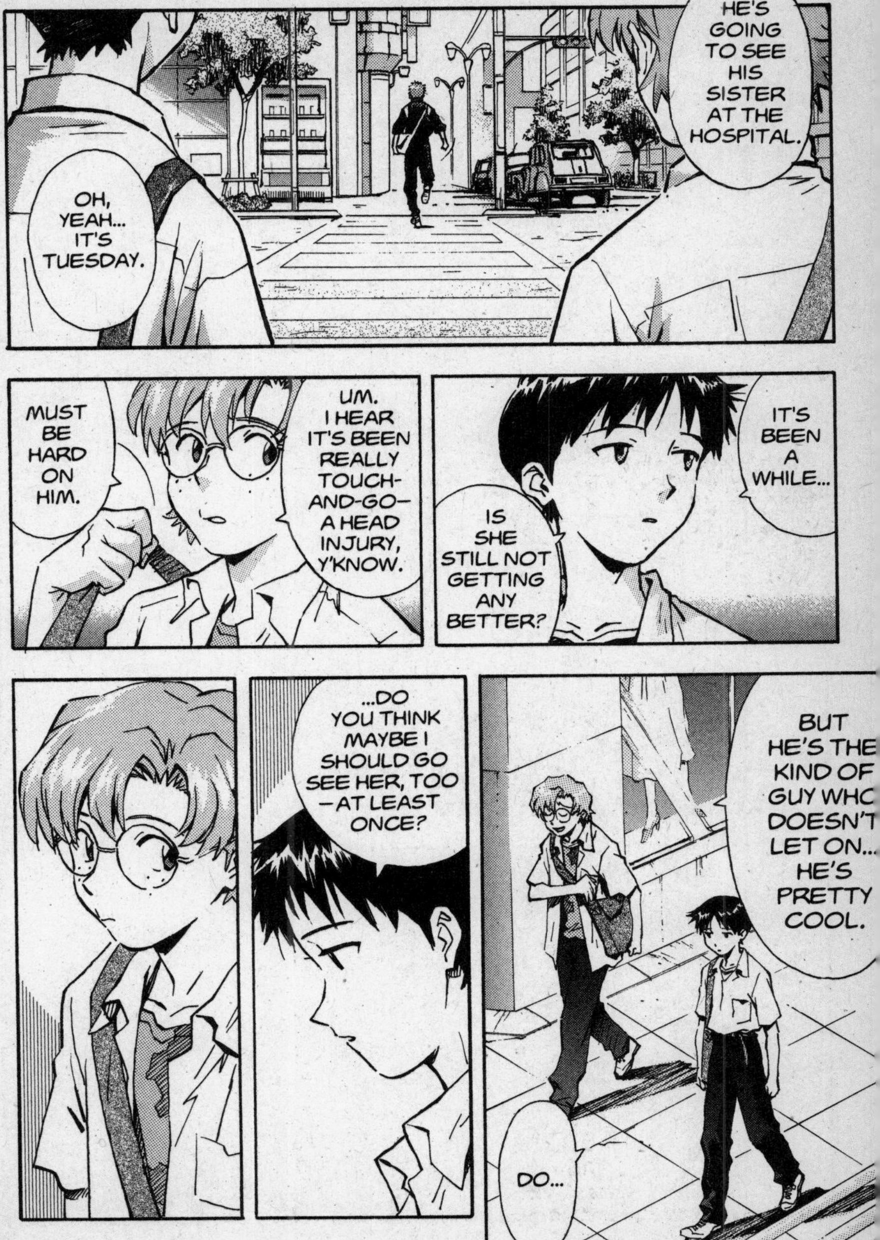
HE'S GOING TO SEE HIS SISTER AT THE HOSPITAL.
OH, YEAH... IT'S TUESDAY.
IT'S BEEN A WHILE...
IS SHE STILL NOT GETTING ANY BETTER?
UM. I HEAR IT'S BEEN REALLY TOUCH-AND-GO—A HEAD INJURY, Y'KNOW.
MUST BE HARD ON HIM.
BUT HE'S THE KIND OF GUY WHO DOESN'T LET ON... HE'S PRETTY COOL.
DO...
...DO YOU THINK MAYBE I SHOULD GO SEE HER, TOO—AT LEAST ONCE?

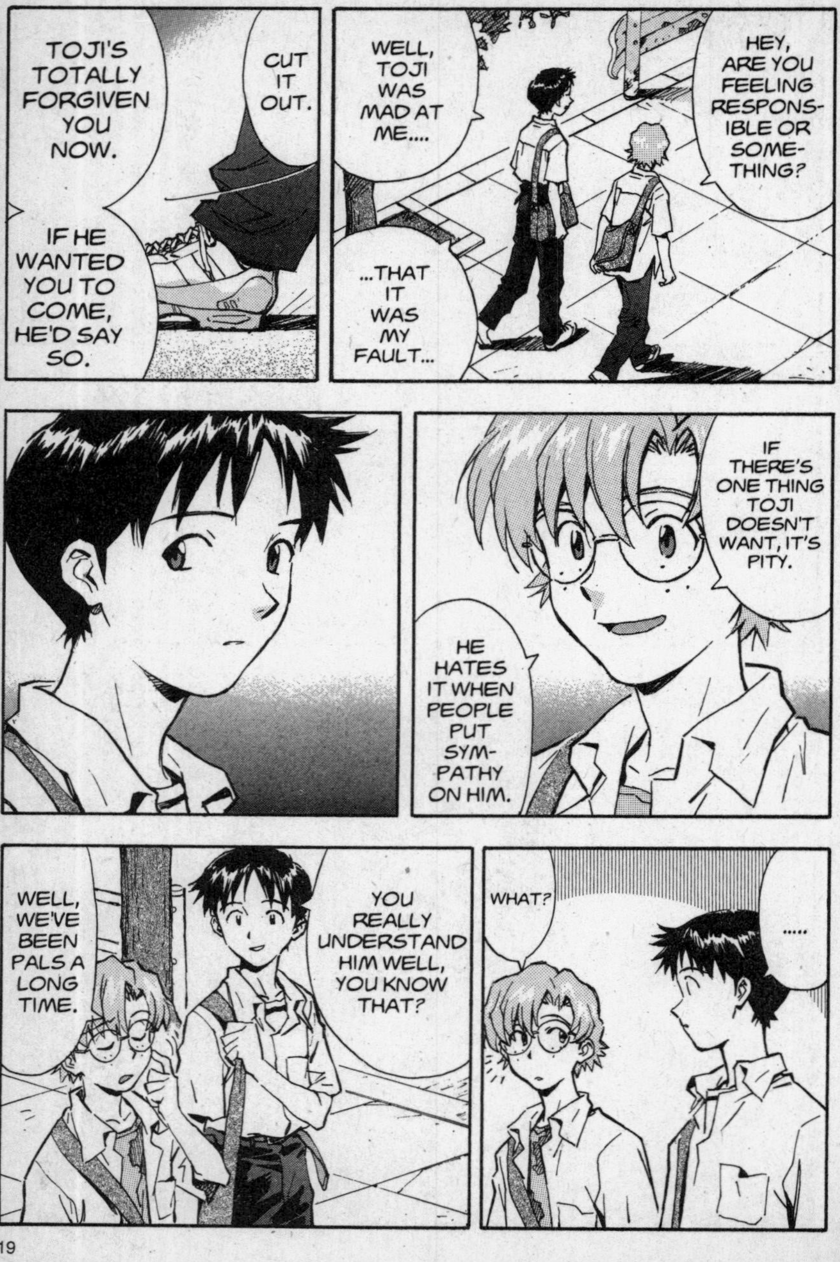
HEY, ARE YOU FEELING RESPONS-IBLE OR SOME-THING?
WELL, TOJI WAS MAD AT ME....
...THAT IT WAS MY FAULT...
CUT IT OUT.
TOJI'S TOTALLY FORGIVEN YOU NOW.
IF HE WANTED YOU TO COME, HE'D SAY SO.
IF THERE'S ONE THING TOJI DOESN'T WANT, IT'S PITY.
HE HATES IT WHEN PEOPLE PUT SYM-PATHY ON HIM.
.....
WHAT?
YOU REALLY UNDERSTAND HIM WELL, YOU KNOW THAT?
WELL, WE'VE BEEN PALS A LONG TIME.

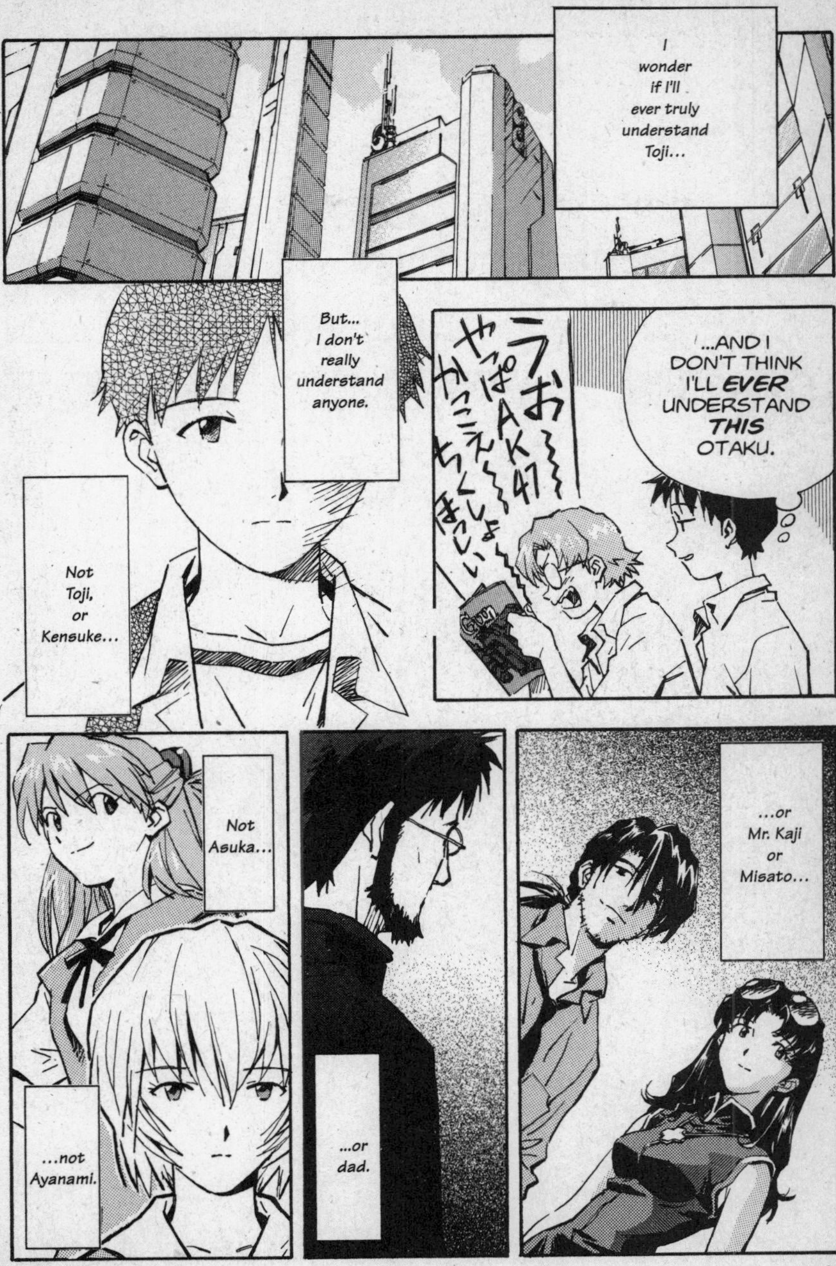

I wonder if I'll ever truly understand Toji...
But... I don't really understand anyone.
Not Toji, or Kensuke...
うお～～
やっぱAK47
かっこえ～～
ちくしょ～
ほしい
...AND I DON'T THINK I'LL ***EVER*** UNDERSTAND ***THIS*** OTAKU.
Not Asuka...
...not Ayanami.
...or dad.
...or Mr. Kaji or Misato...

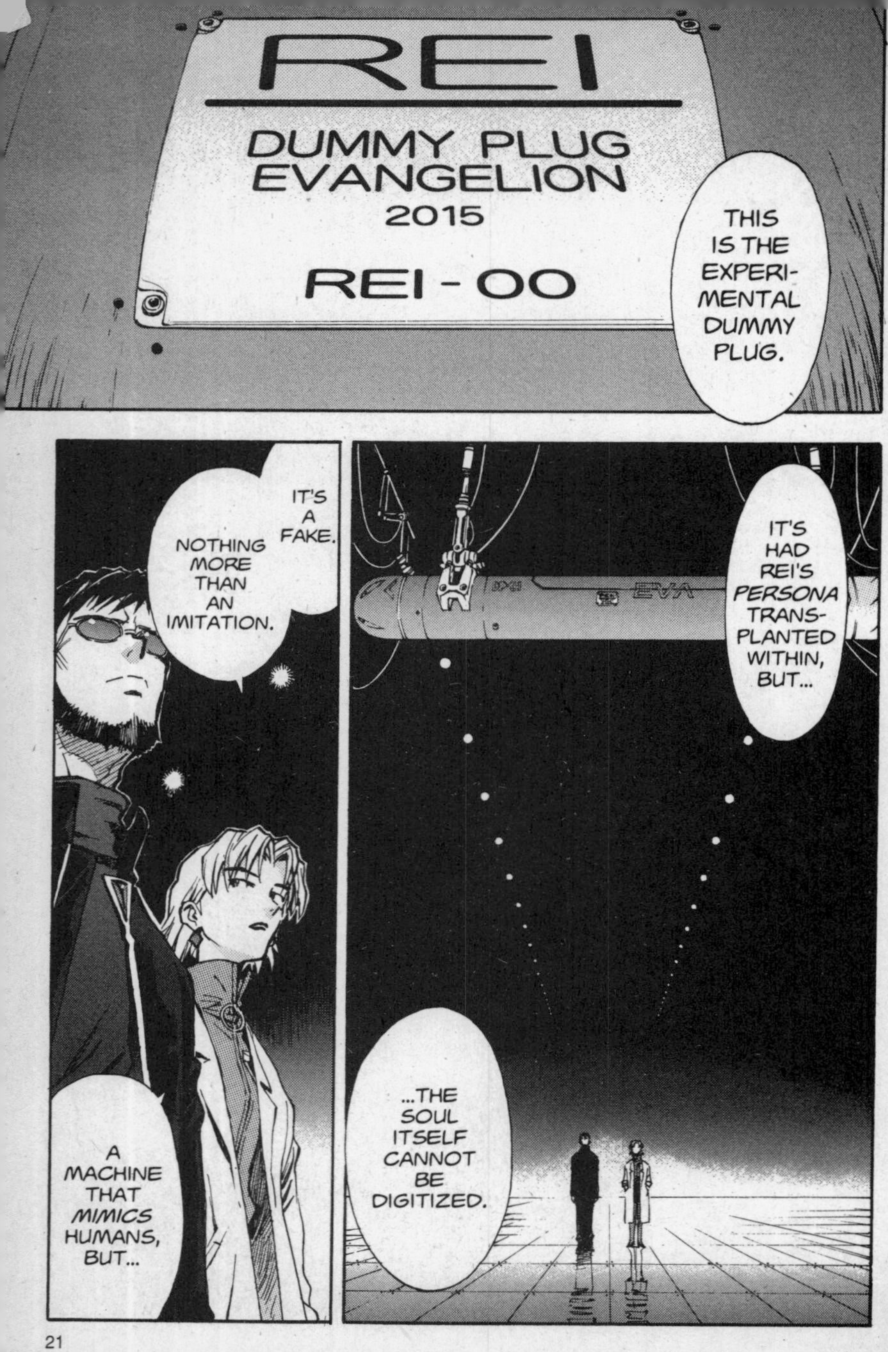
REI
DUMMY PLUG EVANGELION 2015
REI - 00
THIS IS THE EXPERIMENTAL DUMMY PLUG.
EVA
IT'S HAD REI'S *PERSONA* TRANSPLANTED WITHIN, BUT...
...THE SOUL ITSELF CANNOT BE DIGITIZED.
IT'S A FAKE.
NOTHING MORE THAN AN IMITATION.
A MACHINE THAT *MIMICS* HUMANS, BUT...

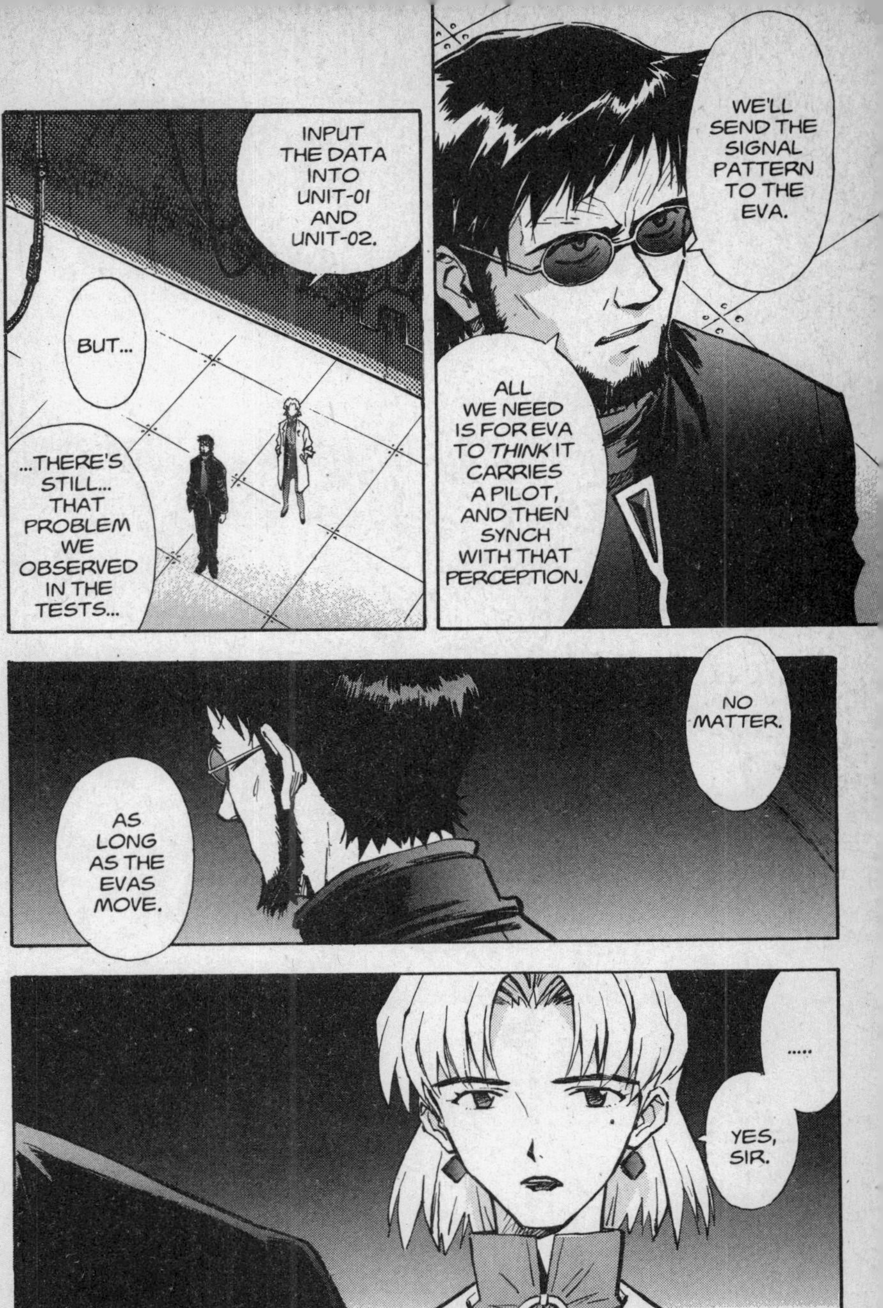
WE'LL SEND THE SIGNAL PATTERN TO THE EVA.
ALL WE NEED IS FOR EVA TO *THINK* IT CARRIES A PILOT, AND THEN SYNCH WITH THAT PERCEPTION.
INPUT THE DATA INTO UNIT-01 AND UNIT-02.
BUT...
...THERE'S STILL... THAT PROBLEM WE OBSERVED IN THE TESTS...
NO MATTER.
AS LONG AS THE EVAS MOVE.
.....
YES, SIR.

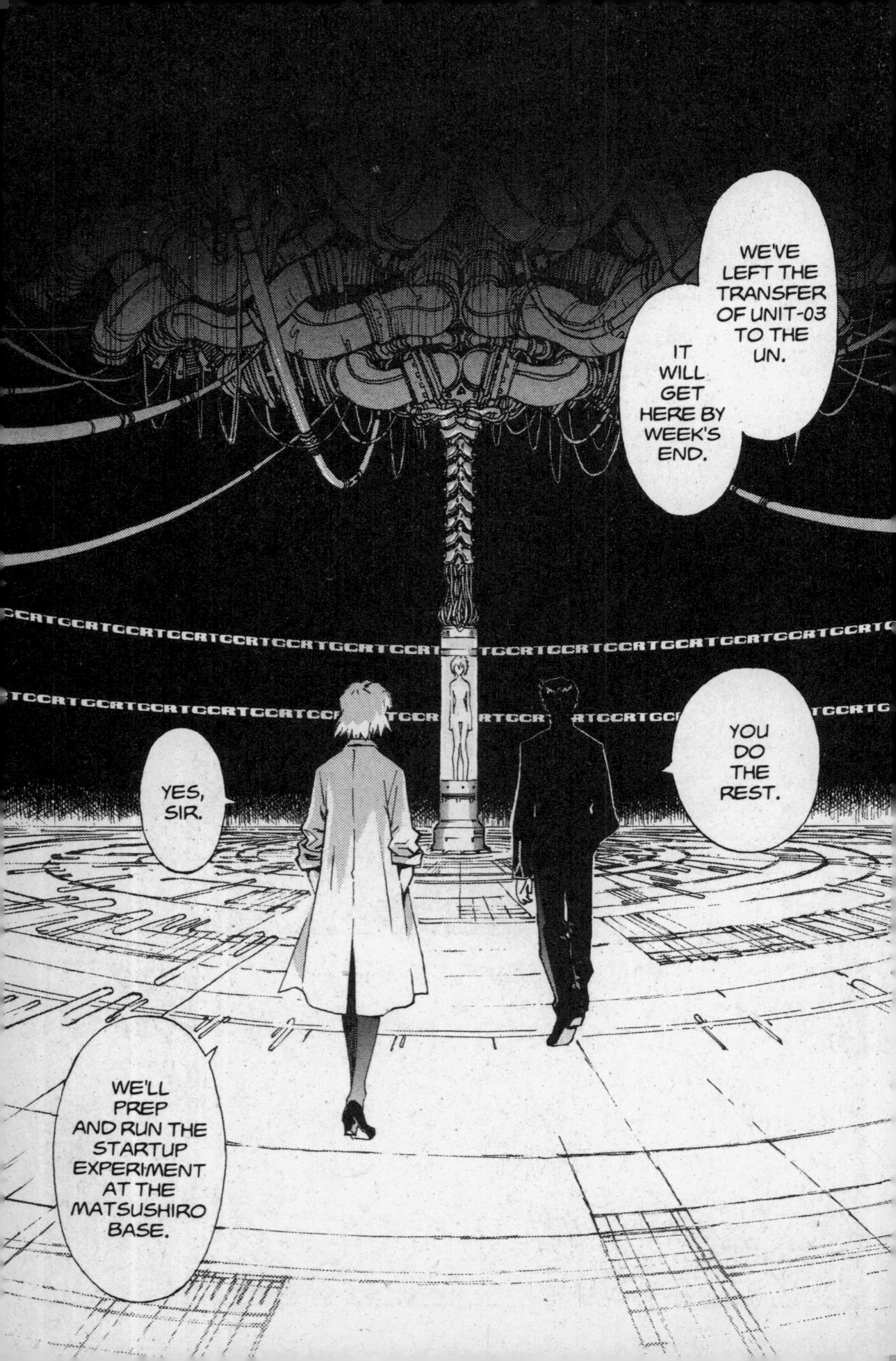
WE'VE LEFT THE TRANSFER OF UNIT-03 TO THE UN.
IT WILL GET HERE BY WEEK'S END.
YOU DO THE REST.
YES, SIR.
WE'LL PREP AND RUN THE STARTUP EXPERIMENT AT THE MATSUSHIRO BASE.

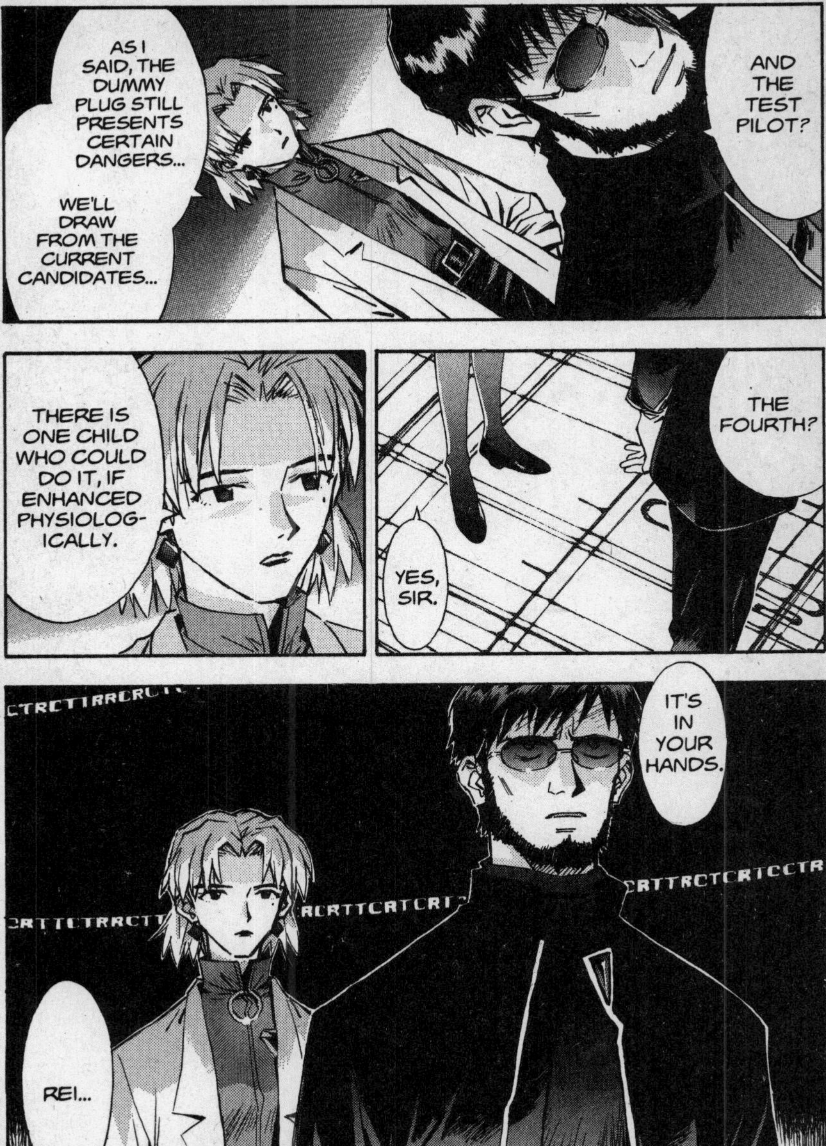
AS I SAID, THE DUMMY PLUG STILL PRESENTS CERTAIN DANGERS...
WE'LL DRAW FROM THE CURRENT CANDIDATES...
AND THE TEST PILOT?
THERE IS ONE CHILD WHO COULD DO IT, IF ENHANCED PHYSIOLOG-ICALLY.
THE FOURTH?
YES, SIR.
IT'S IN YOUR HANDS.
REI...

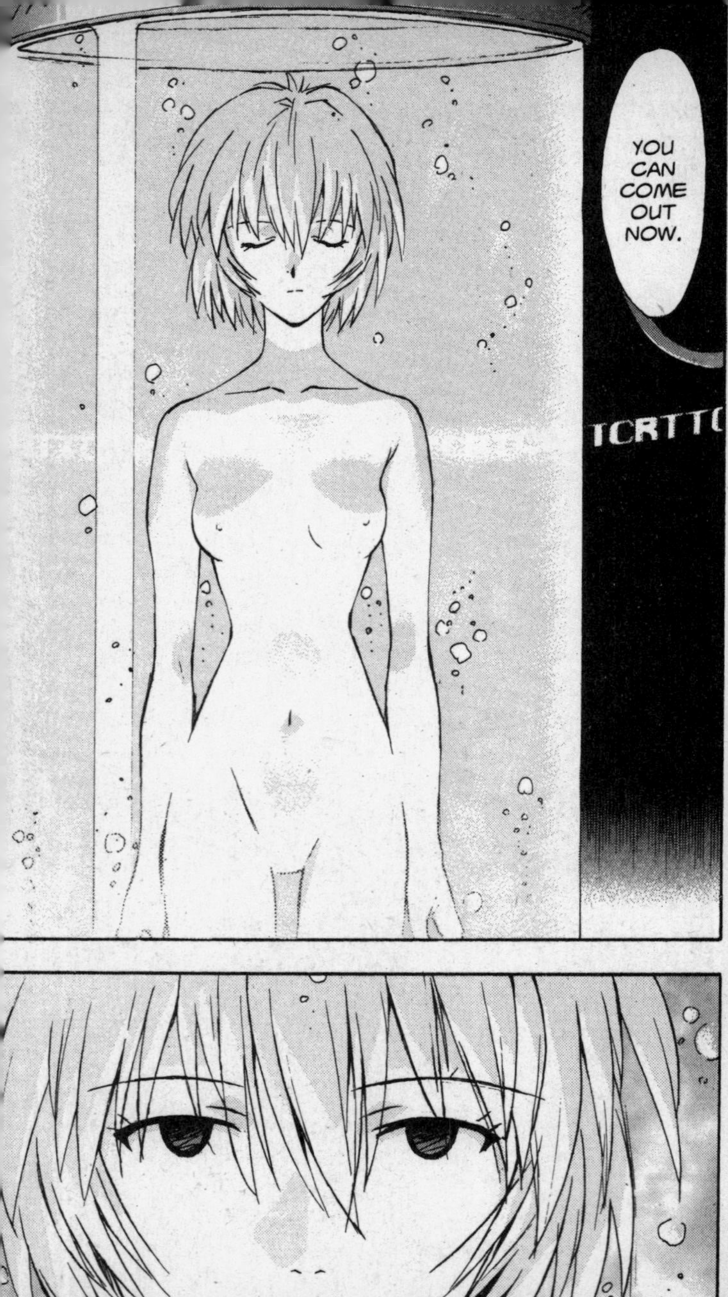
YOU CAN COME OUT NOW.
TCRTTC

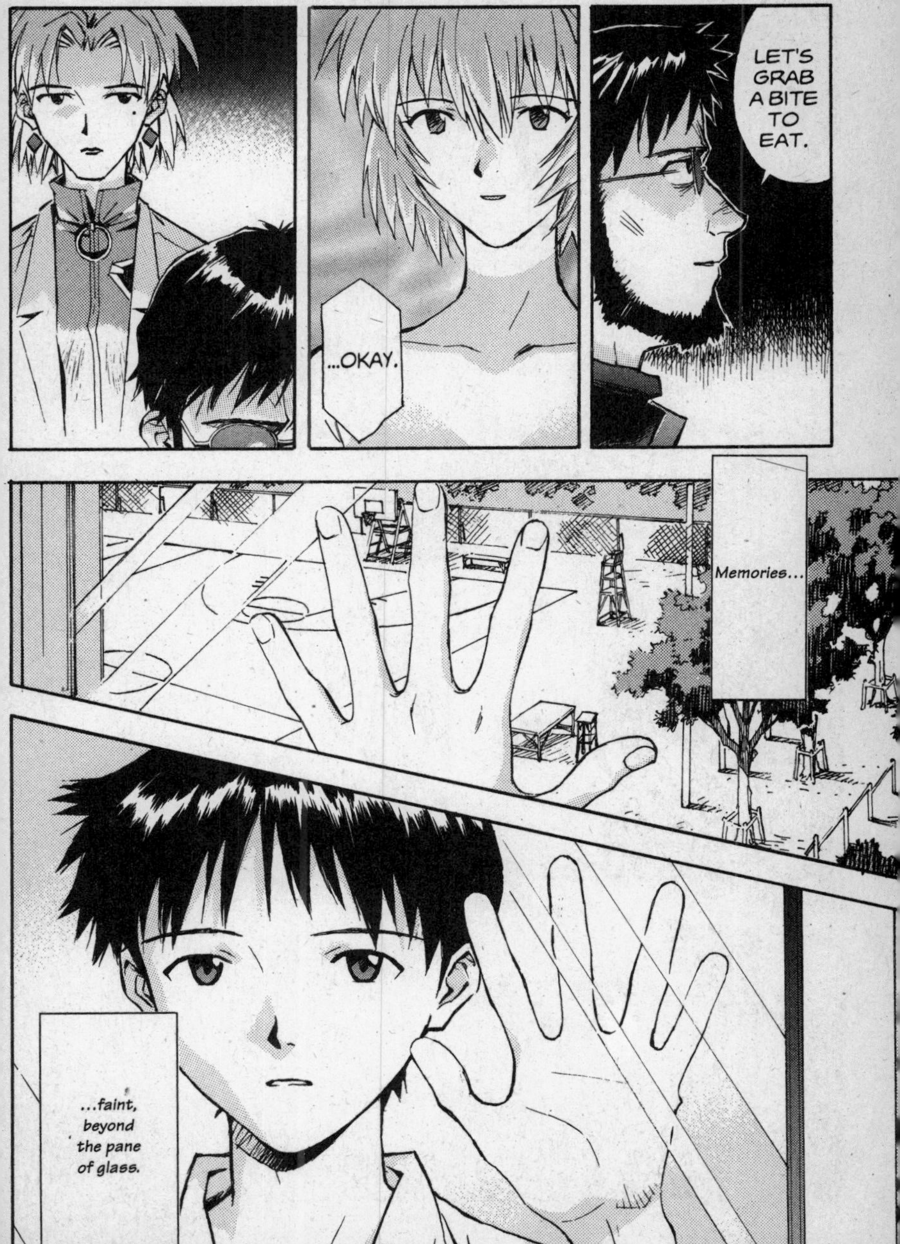
LET'S GRAB A BITE TO EAT.
...OKAY.
Memories...
...faint, beyond the pane of glass.

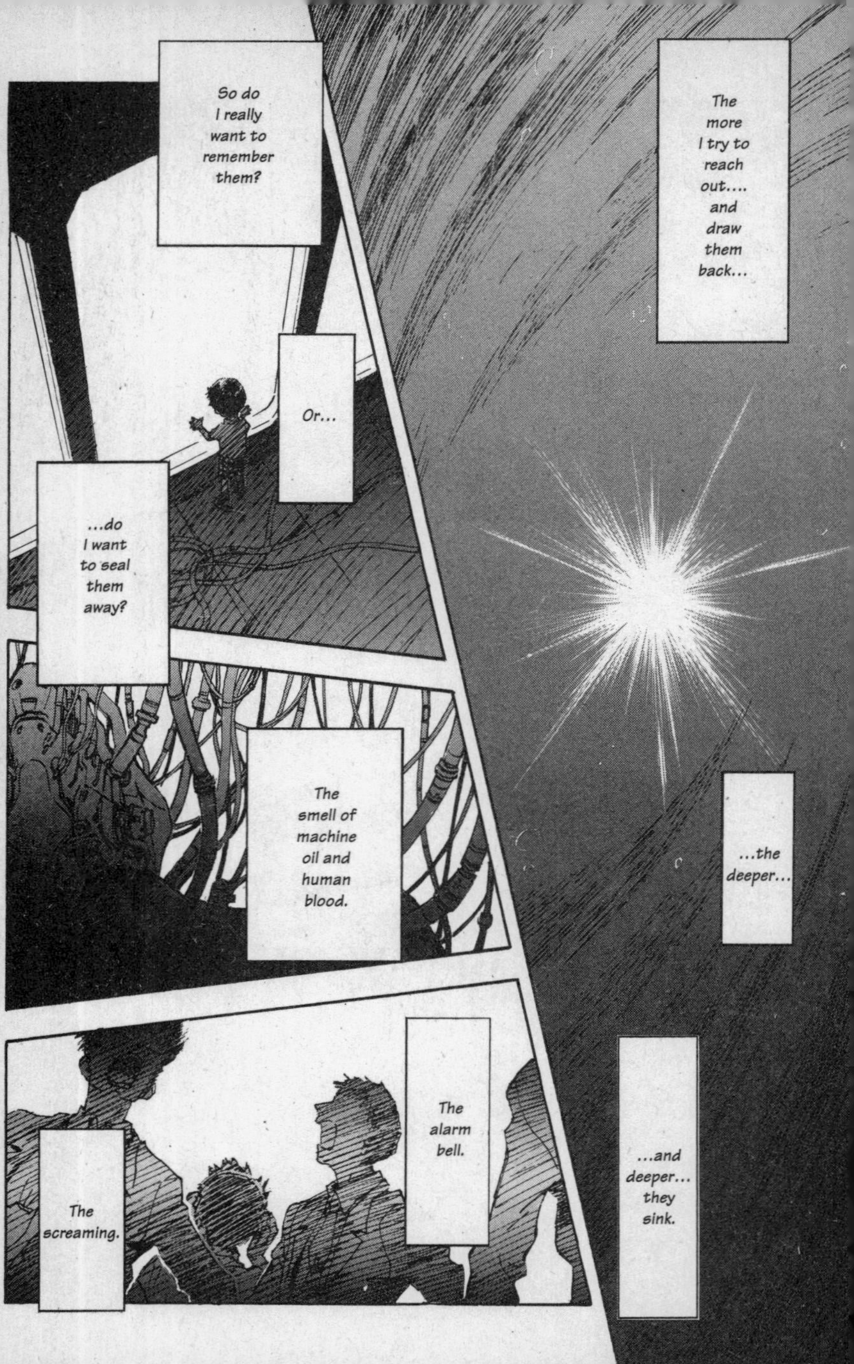
The more I try to reach out.... and draw them back...
...the deeper...
...and deeper... they sink.
So do I really want to remember them?
Or...
...do I want to seal them away?
The smell of machine oil and human blood.
The alarm bell.
The screaming.

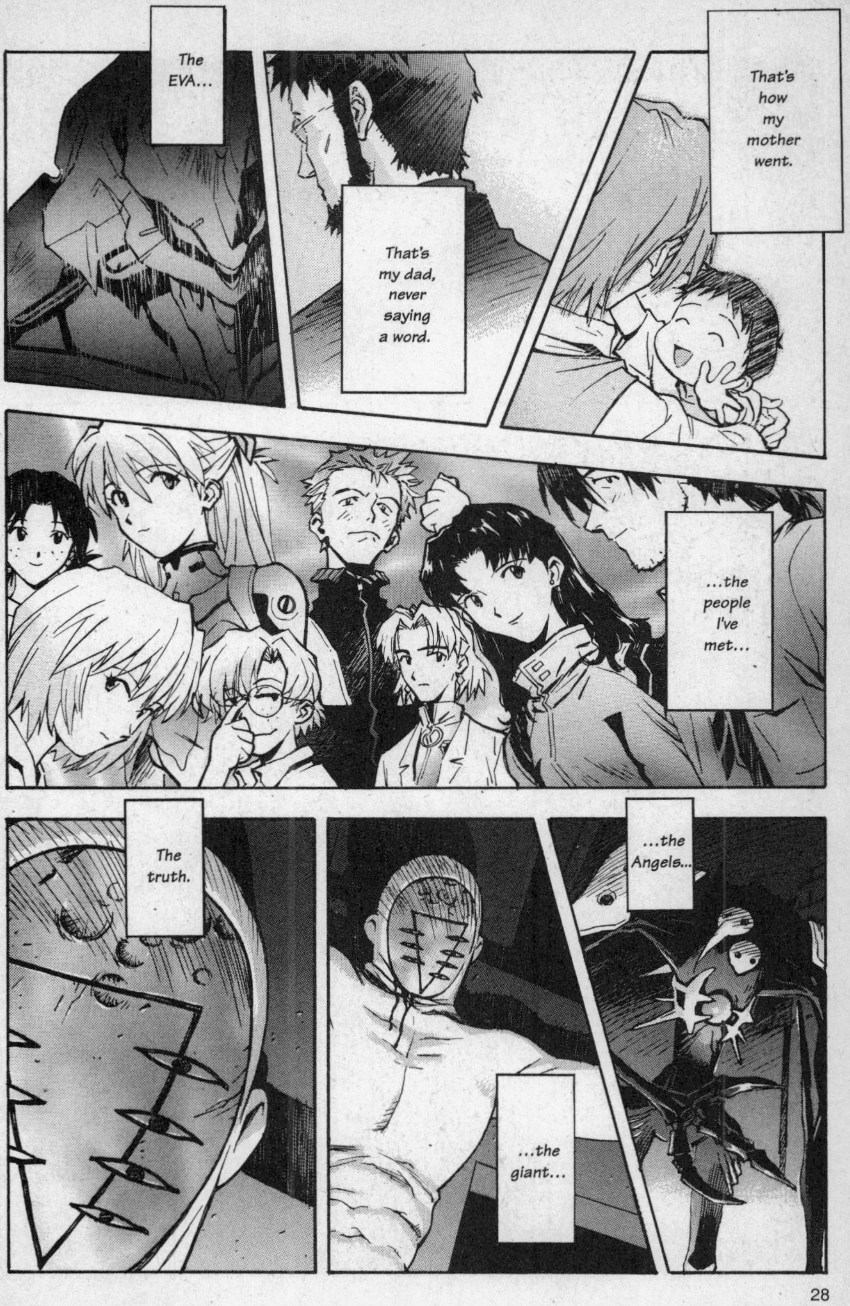
That's how my mother went.
That's my dad, never saying a word.
The EVA...
...the people I've met...
...the Angels...
...the giant...
The truth.

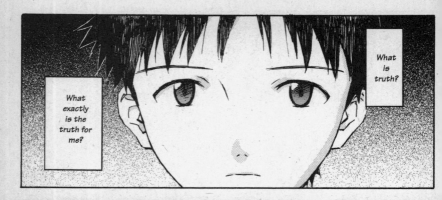

What is truth?

What exactly is the truth for me?

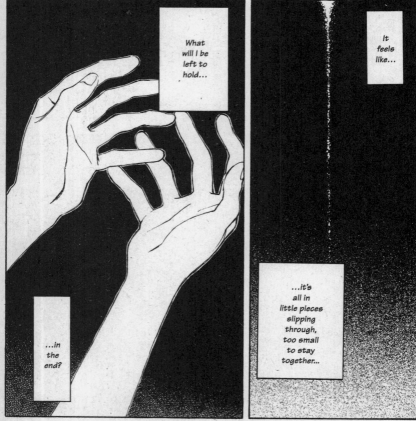

What will I be left to hold...

...in the end?

It feels like...

...it's all in little pieces slipping through, too small to stay together...

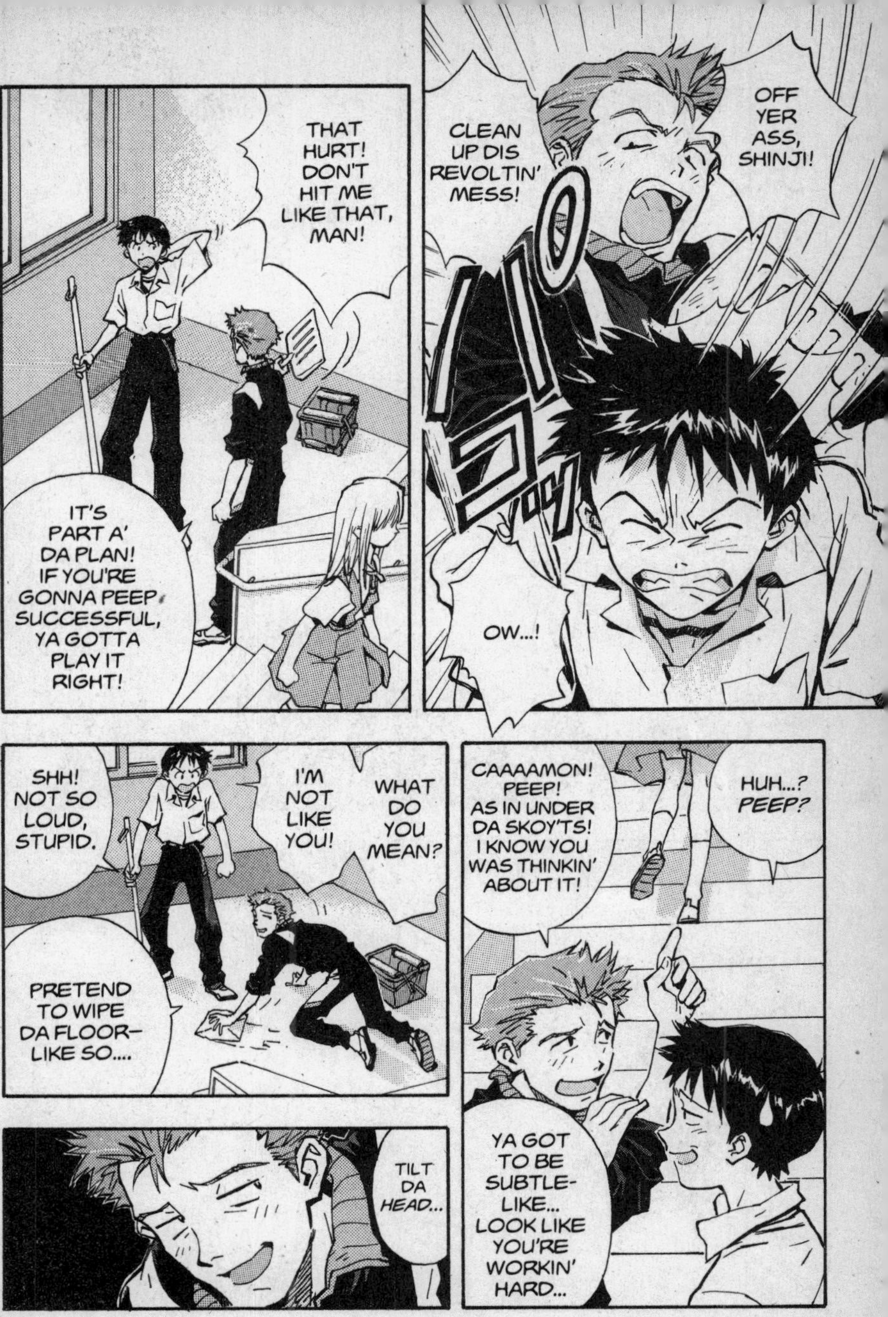
OFF YER ASS, SHINJI!
CLEAN UP DIS REVOLTIN' MESS!
OW...!
THAT HURT! DON'T HIT ME LIKE THAT, MAN!
IT'S PART A' DA PLAN! IF YOU'RE GONNA PEEP SUCCESSFUL, YA GOTTA PLAY IT RIGHT!
HUH...? PEEP?
CAAAAMON! PEEP! AS IN UNDER DA SKOY'TS! I KNOW YOU WAS THINKIN' ABOUT IT!
YA GOT TO BE SUBTLE-LIKE... LOOK LIKE YOU'RE WORKIN' HARD...
WHAT DO YOU MEAN?
I'M NOT LIKE YOU!
SHH! NOT SO LOUD, STUPID.
PRETEND TO WIPE DA FLOOR—LIKE SO....
TILT DA HEAD...

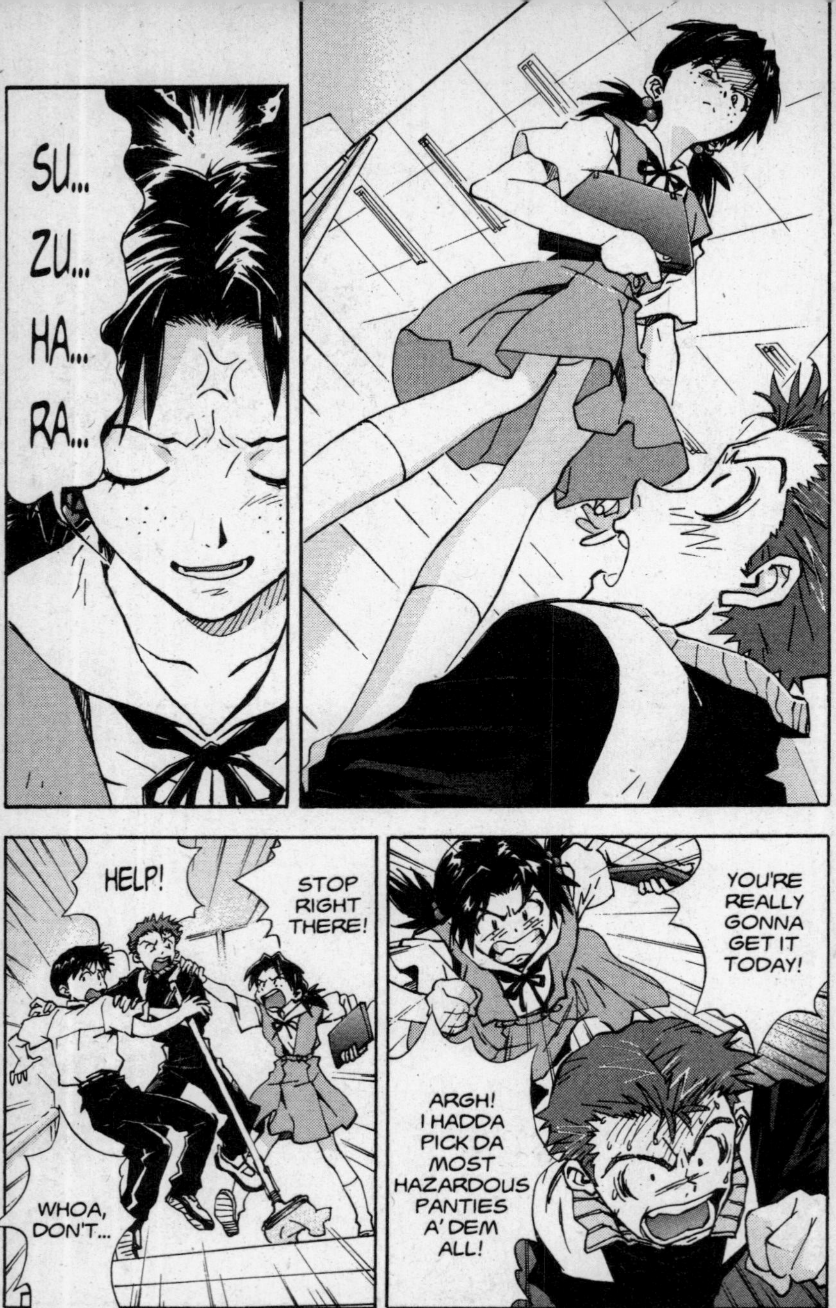
SU... ZU... HA... RA...
YOU'RE REALLY GONNA GET IT TODAY!
ARGH! I HADDA PICK DA MOST HAZARDOUS PANTIES A' DEM ALL!
STOP RIGHT THERE!
HELP!
WHOA, DON'T...

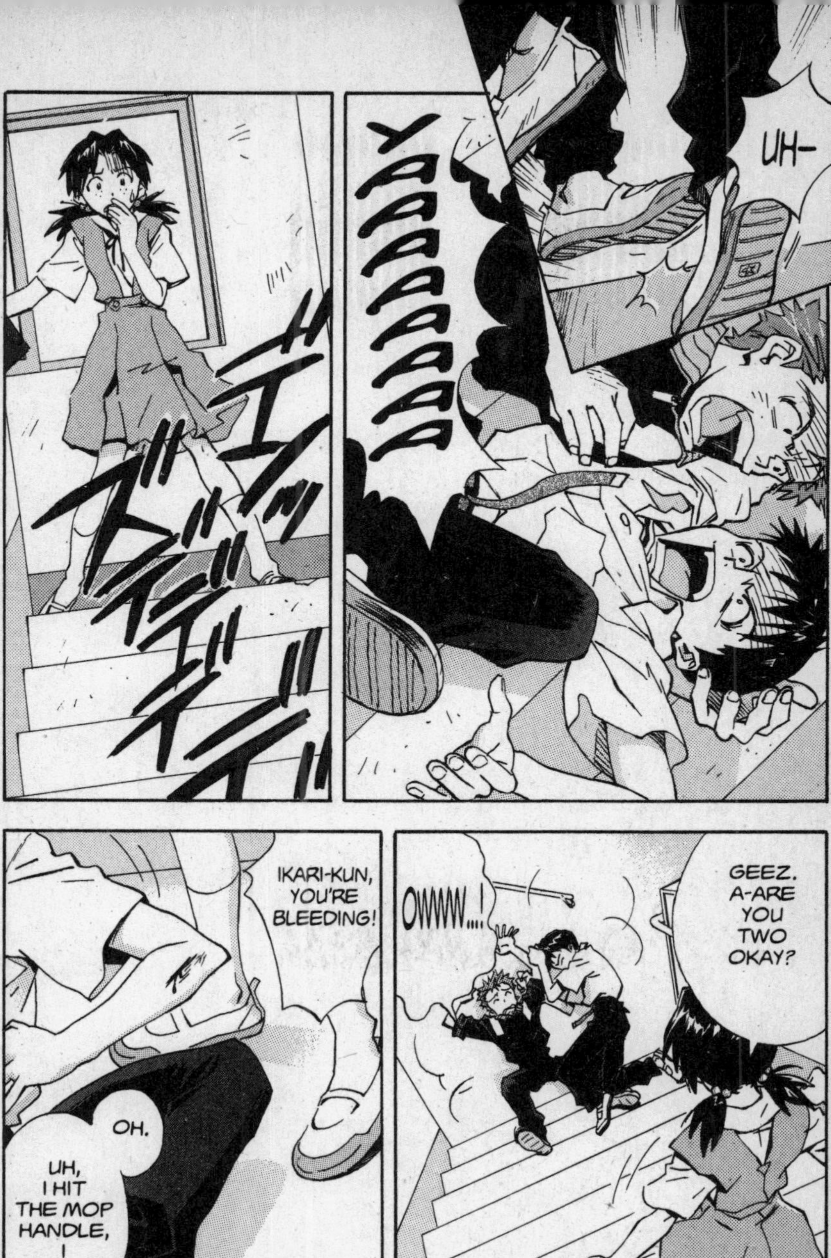
UH-
YAAAAAAAAAA
GEEZ. A-ARE YOU TWO OKAY?
OWWW...!
IKARI-KUN, YOU'RE BLEEDING!
OH.
UH, I HIT THE MOP HANDLE, I THINK.

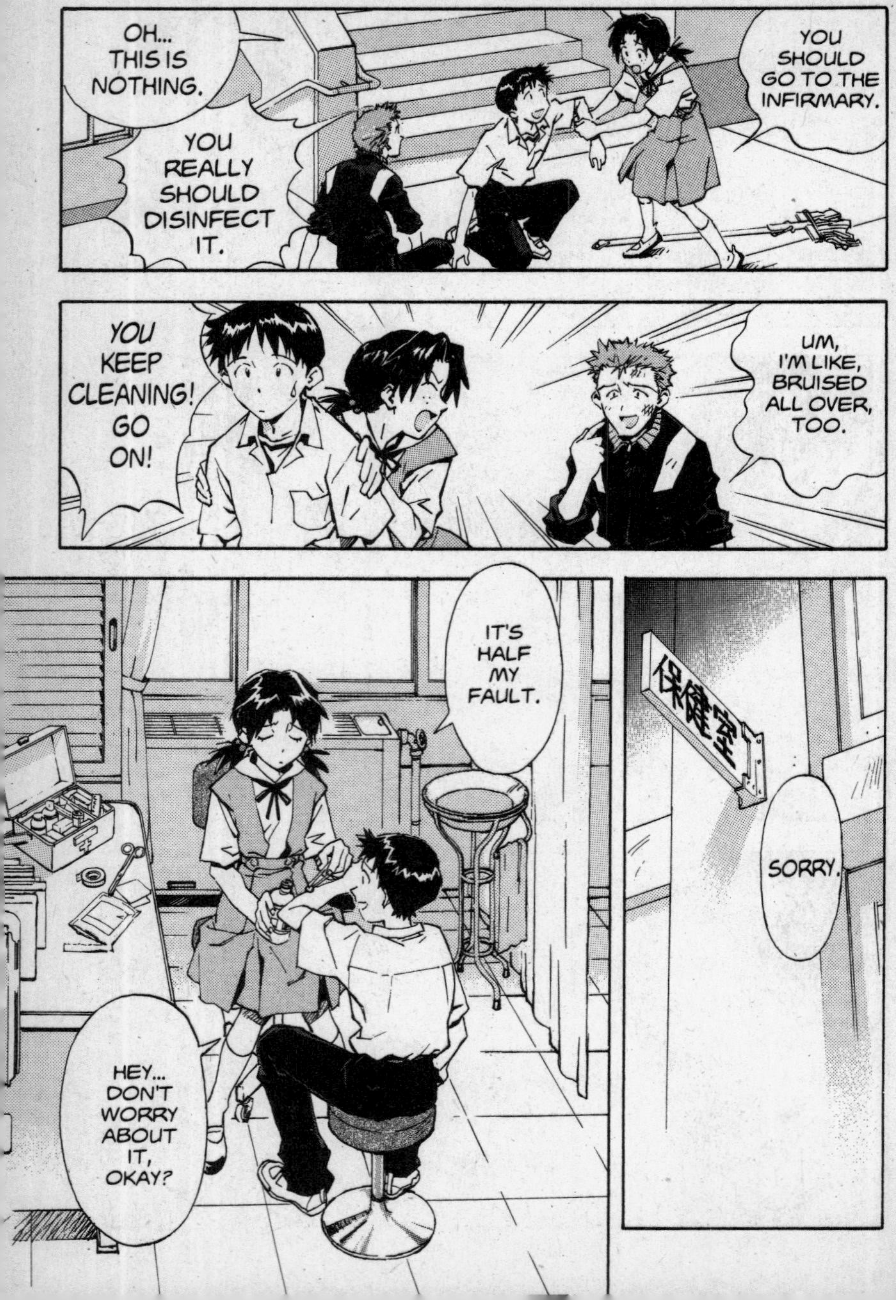
YOU SHOULD GO TO THE INFIRMARY.
OH... THIS IS NOTHING.
YOU REALLY SHOULD DISINFECT IT.
UM, I'M LIKE, BRUISED ALL OVER, TOO.
YOU KEEP CLEANING! GO ON!
保健室
SORRY.
IT'S HALF MY FAULT.
HEY... DON'T WORRY ABOUT IT, OKAY?

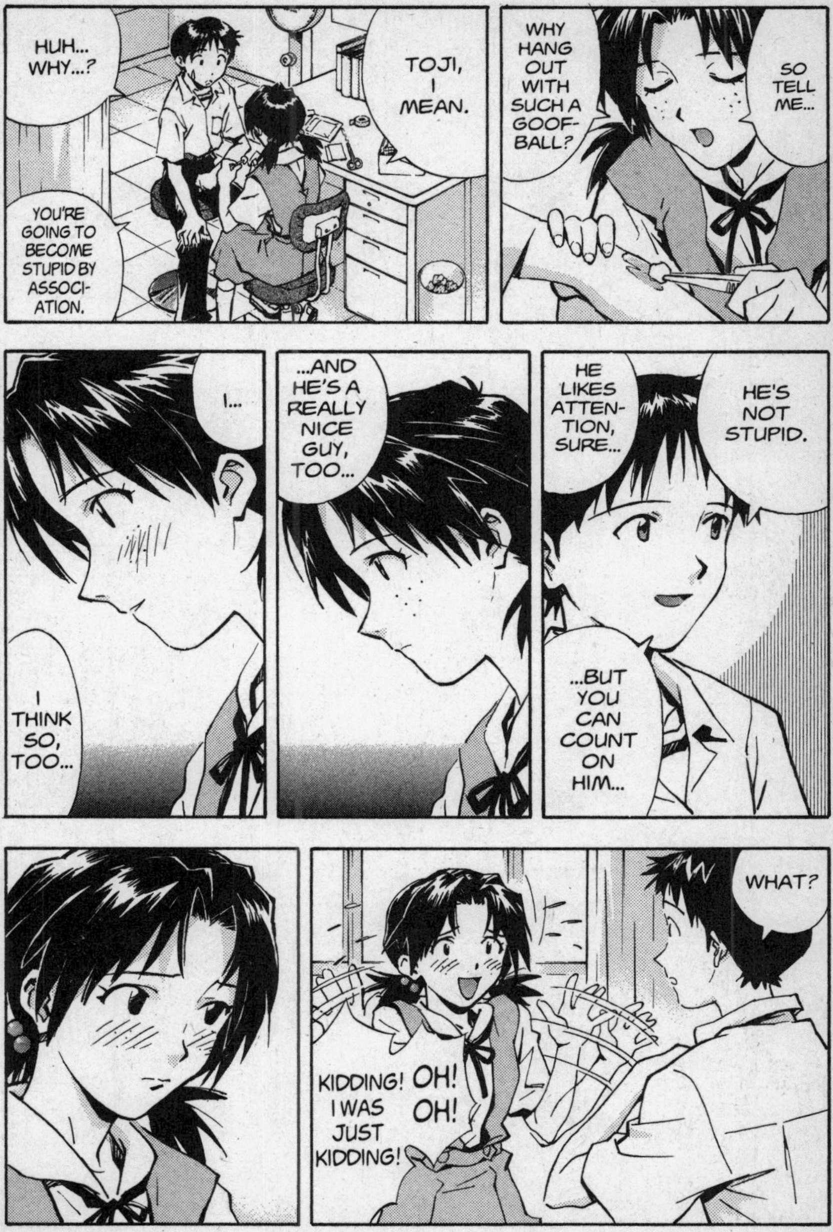
SO TELL ME...
WHY HANG OUT WITH SUCH A GOOF-BALL?
TOJI, I MEAN.
HUH... WHY...?
YOU'RE GOING TO BECOME STUPID BY ASSOCI-ATION.
HE'S NOT STUPID.
HE LIKES ATTEN-TION, SURE...
...BUT YOU CAN COUNT ON HIM...
...AND HE'S A REALLY NICE GUY, TOO...
I...
I THINK SO, TOO...
WHAT?
OH! OH!
KIDDING! I WAS JUST KIDDING!

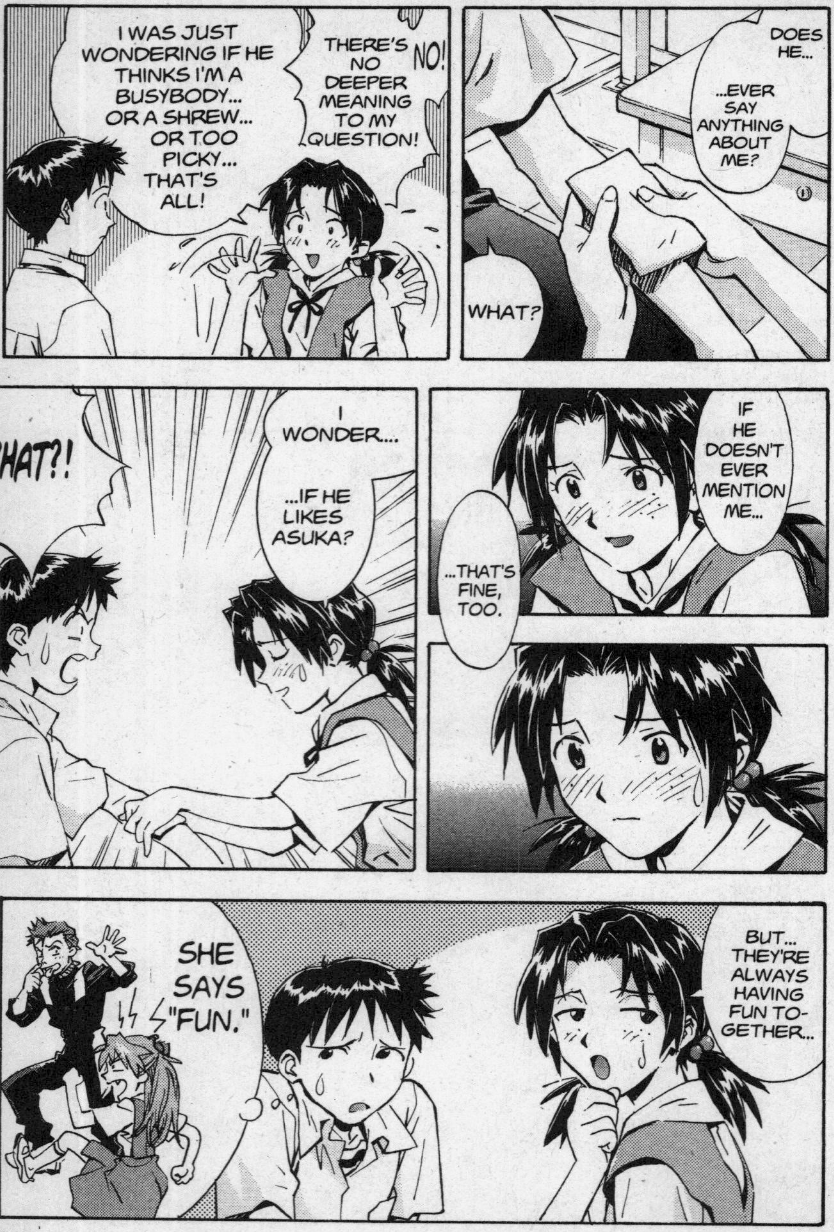
DOES HE...
...EVER SAY ANYTHING ABOUT ME?
WHAT?
NO!
THERE'S NO DEEPER MEANING TO MY QUESTION!
I WAS JUST WONDERING IF HE THINKS I'M A BUSYBODY... OR A SHREW... OR TOO PICKY... THAT'S ALL!
IF HE DOESN'T EVER MENTION ME...
...THAT'S FINE, TOO.
I WONDER....
...IF HE LIKES ASUKA?
WHAT?!
BUT... THEY'RE ALWAYS HAVING FUN TOGETHER...
SHE SAYS "FUN."

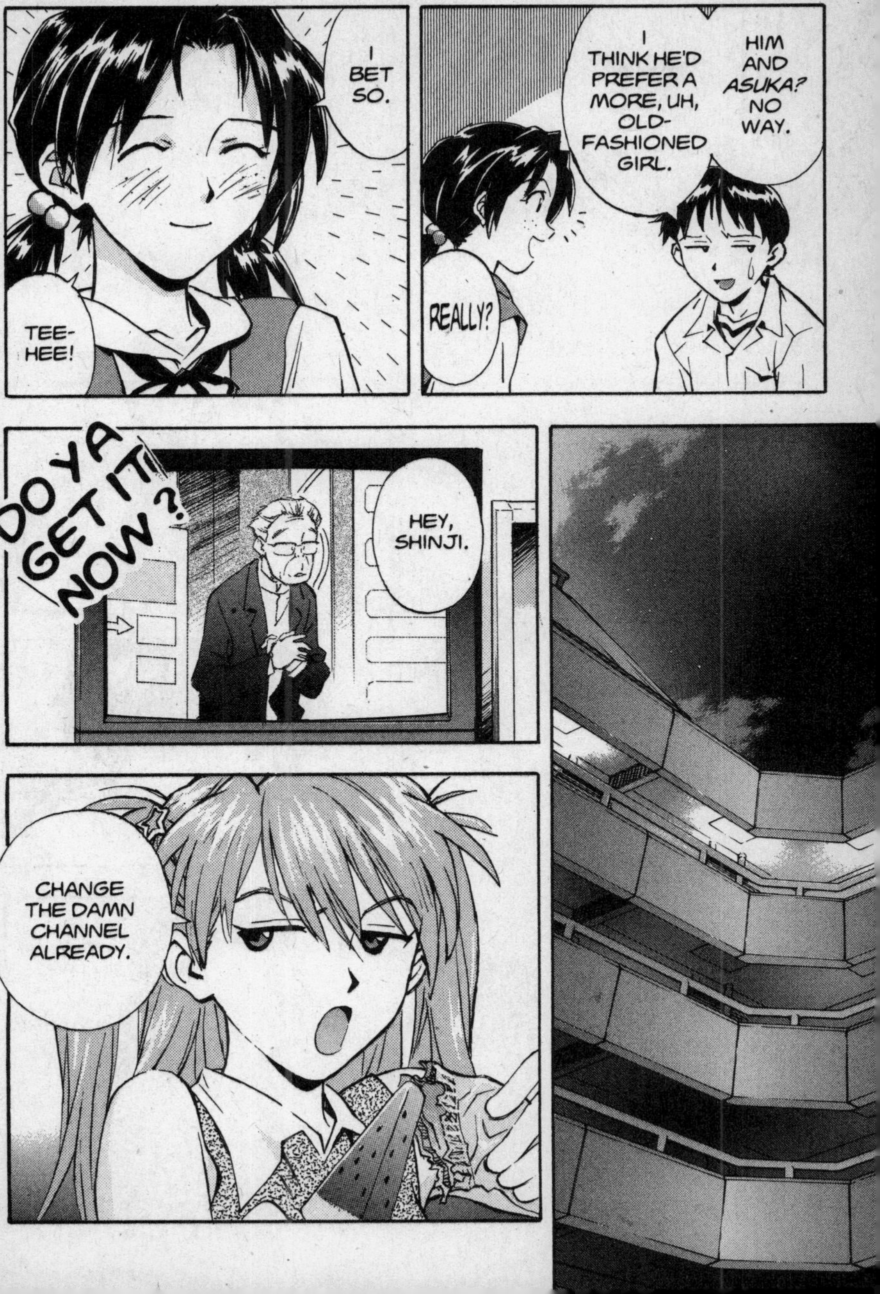
HIM AND ASUKA? NO WAY.
I THINK HE'D PREFER A MORE, UH, OLD-FASHIONED GIRL.
REALLY?
I BET SO.
TEE-HEE!
HEY, SHINJI.
DO YA GET IT NOW?!
CHANGE THE DAMN CHANNEL ALREADY.

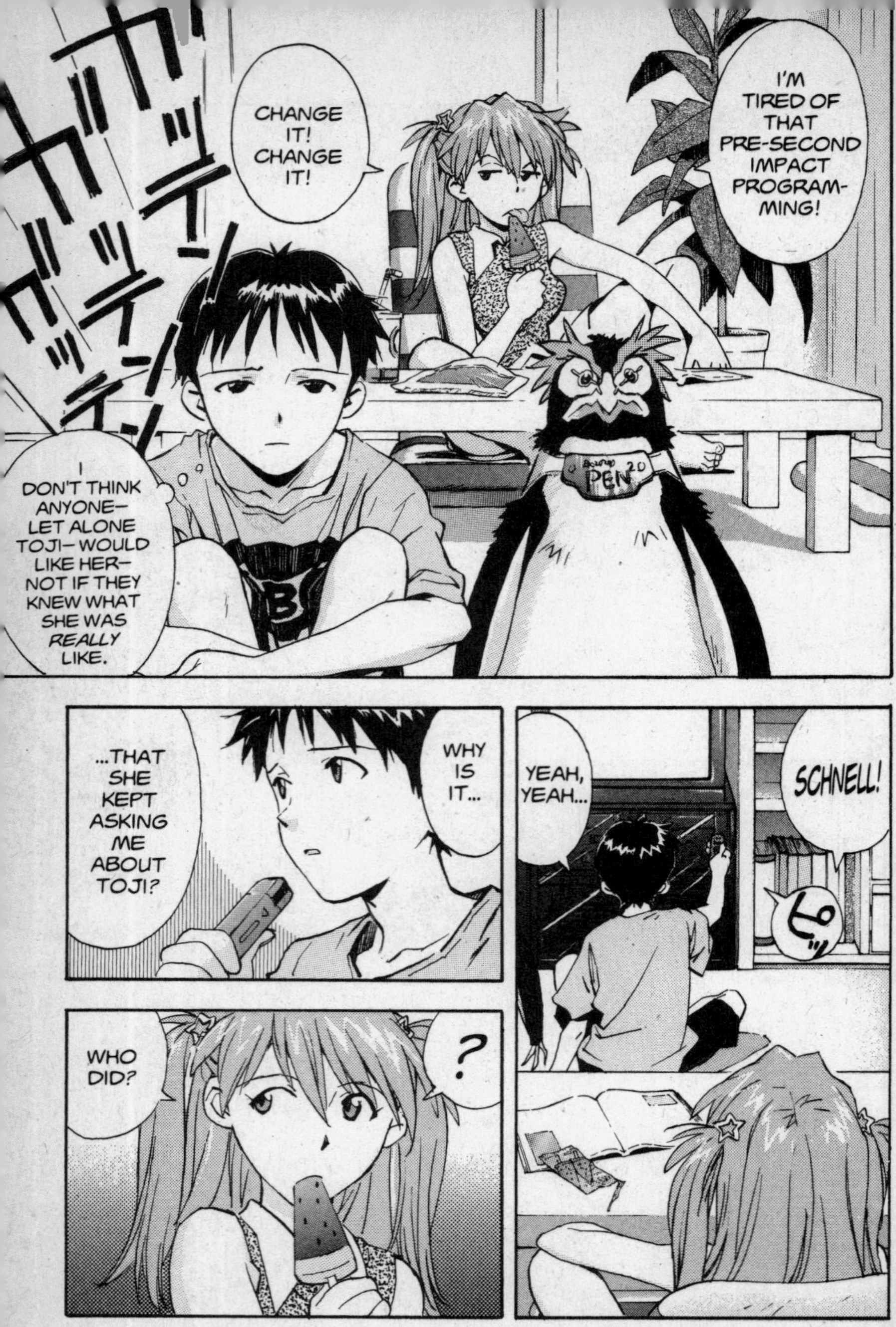
I'M TIRED OF THAT PRE-SECOND IMPACT PROGRAMMING!
CHANGE IT! CHANGE IT!
I DON'T THINK ANYONE—LET ALONE TOJI—WOULD LIKE HER—NOT IF THEY KNEW WHAT SHE WAS *REALLY* LIKE.
SCHNELL!
ピッ
YEAH, YEAH...
WHY IS IT...
...THAT SHE KEPT ASKING ME ABOUT TOJI?
?
WHO DID?

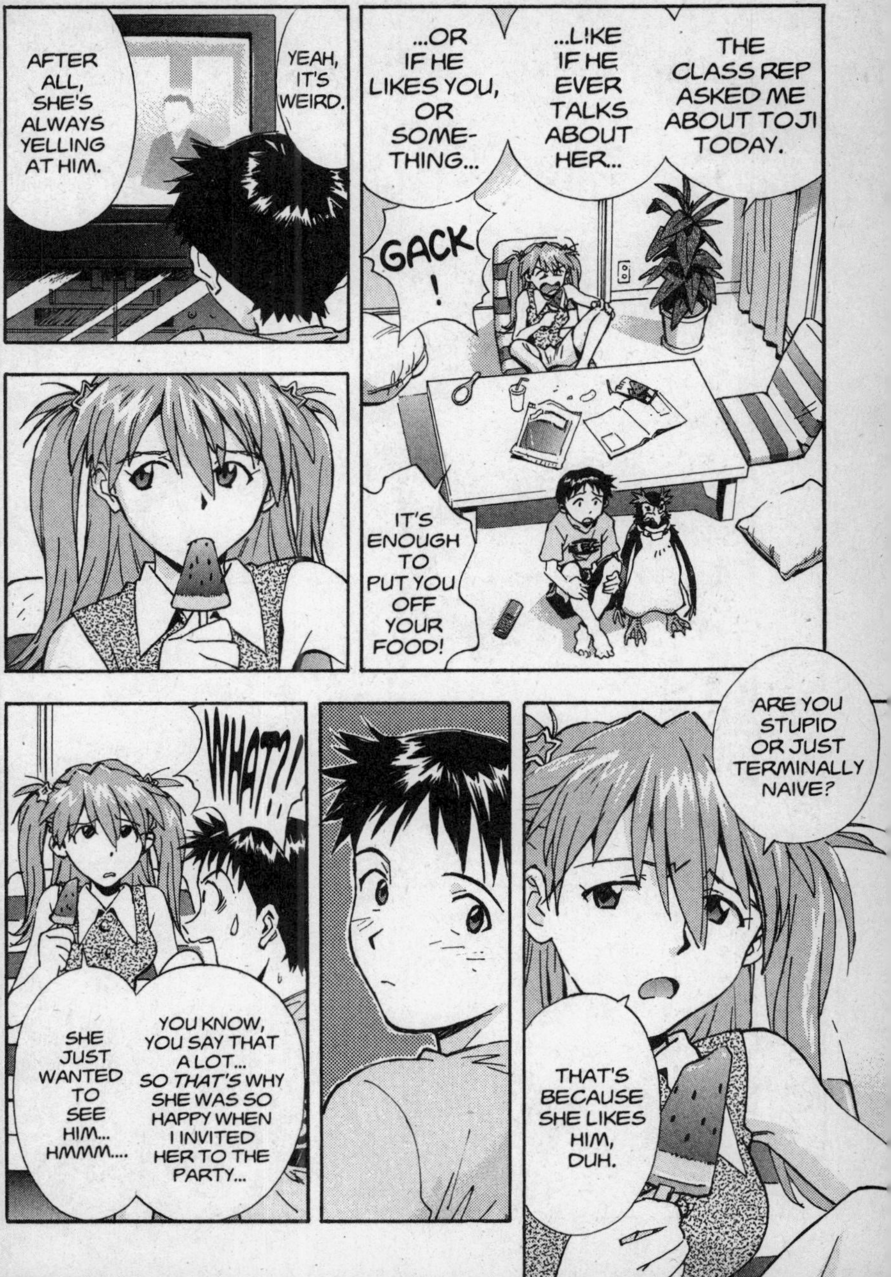
THE CLASS REP ASKED ME ABOUT TOJI TODAY.
...LIKE IF HE EVER TALKS ABOUT HER...
...OR IF HE LIKES YOU, OR SOMETHING...
GACK!
IT'S ENOUGH TO PUT YOU OFF YOUR FOOD!
YEAH, IT'S WEIRD.
AFTER ALL, SHE'S ALWAYS YELLING AT HIM.
THAT'S BECAUSE SHE LIKES HIM, DUH.
ARE YOU STUPID OR JUST TERMINALLY NAIVE?
WHAT?!
YOU KNOW, YOU SAY THAT A LOT... SO *THAT'S* WHY SHE WAS SO HAPPY WHEN I INVITED HER TO THE PARTY...
SHE JUST WANTED TO SEE HIM... HMMM....

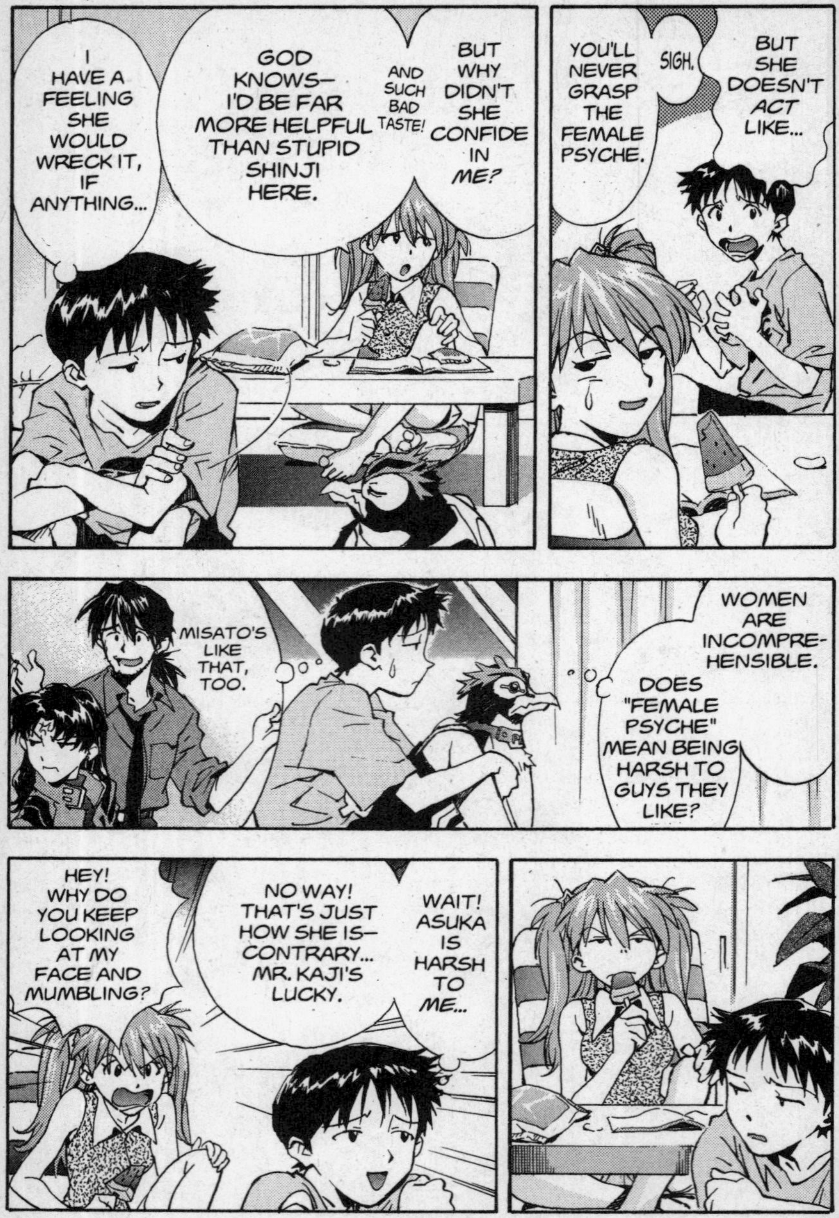
BUT SHE DOESN'T *ACT* LIKE...
SIGH.
YOU'LL NEVER GRASP THE FEMALE PSYCHE.
BUT WHY DIDN'T SHE CONFIDE IN *ME?*
AND SUCH BAD TASTE!
GOD KNOWS— I'D BE FAR MORE HELPFUL THAN STUPID SHINJI HERE.
I HAVE A FEELING SHE WOULD WRECK IT, IF ANYTHING...
WOMEN ARE INCOMPRE-HENSIBLE.
DOES "FEMALE PSYCHE" MEAN BEING HARSH TO GUYS THEY LIKE?
MISATO'S LIKE THAT, TOO.
WAIT! ASUKA IS HARSH TO *ME*...
NO WAY! THAT'S JUST HOW SHE IS— CONTRARY... MR. KAJI'S LUCKY.
HEY! WHY DO YOU KEEP LOOKING AT MY FACE AND MUMBLING?

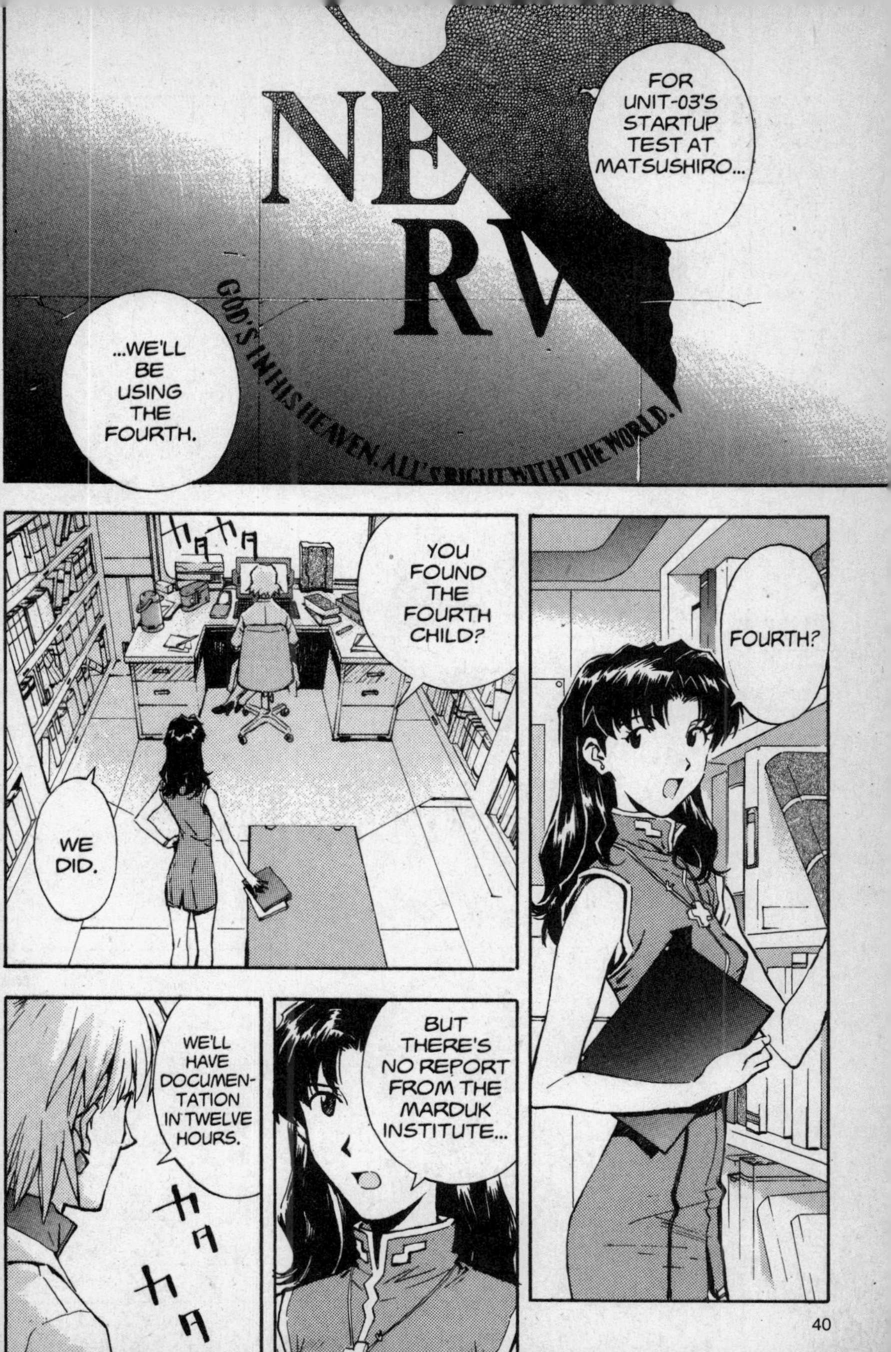
FOR UNIT-03'S STARTUP TEST AT MATSUSHIRO...
NERV
GOD'S IN HIS HEAVEN. ALL'S RIGHT WITH THE WORLD.
...WE'LL BE USING THE FOURTH.
FOURTH?
カタカタ
YOU FOUND THE FOURTH CHILD?
WE DID.
BUT THERE'S NO REPORT FROM THE MARDUK INSTITUTE...
WE'LL HAVE DOCUMENTATION IN TWELVE HOURS.
カタカタ

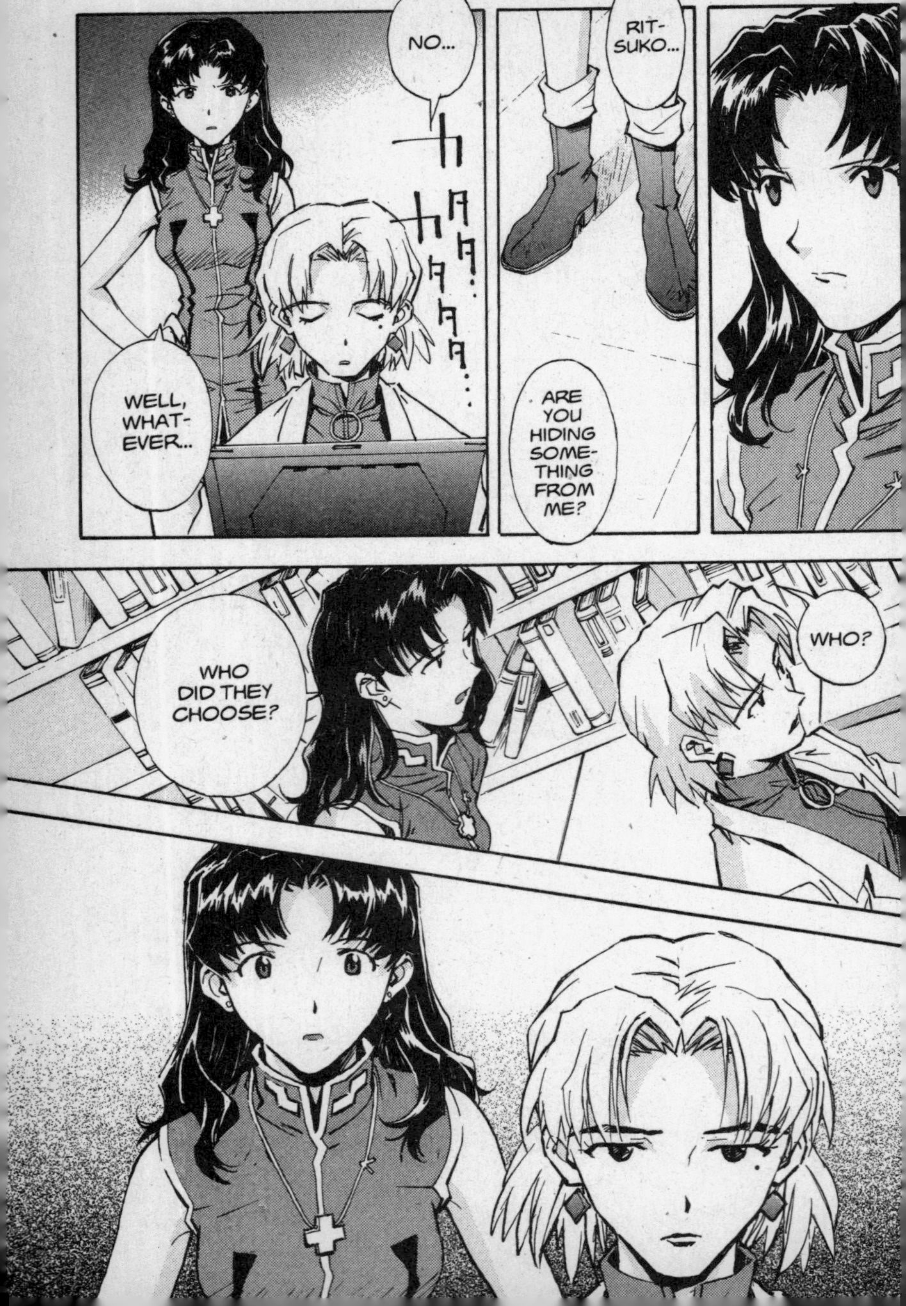
RIT-SUKO...
ARE YOU HIDING SOME-THING FROM ME?
NO...
WELL, WHAT-EVER...
WHO?
WHO DID THEY CHOOSE?

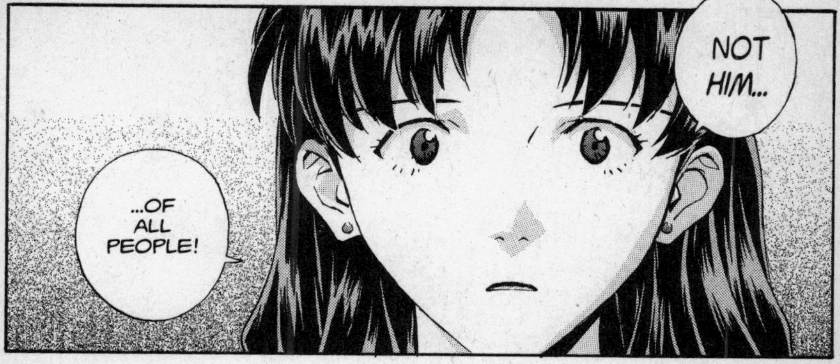
NOT HIM...
...OF ALL PEOPLE!

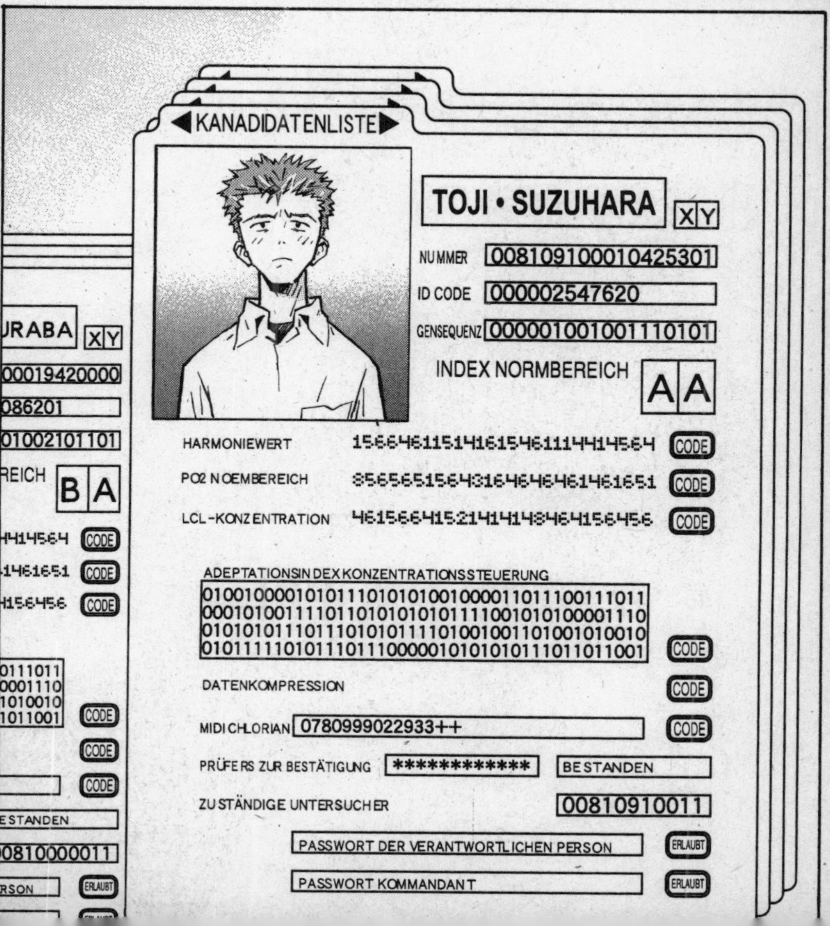
KANADIDATENLISTE
TOJI • SUZUHARA
XY
NUMMER 008109100010425301
ID CODE 000002547620
GENSEQUENZ 000001001001110101
INDEX NORMBEREICH
AA
HARMONIEWERT 156646115141615461114414564
CODE
PO2 NOEMBEREICH 85656515643164646461461651
CODE
LCL-KONZENTRATION 46156641521414148464156456
CODE
ADEPTATIONSINDEXKONZENTRATIONSSTEUERUNG
0100100001010111010101001000011011100111011
0001010011110110101010101111001010100001110
0101010111011101010111101001001101001010010
0101111101011101110000010101010111011011001
CODE
DATENKOMPRESSION
CODE
MIDICHLORIAN 0780999022933++
CODE
PRÜFERS ZUR BESTÄTIGUNG ************
BESTANDEN
ZUSTÄNDIGE UNTERSUCHER 00810910011
PASSWORT DER VERANTWORTLICHEN PERSON
ERLAUBT
PASSWORT KOMMANDANT
ERLAUBT

NEON GENESIS EVANGELION

STAGE 35: LIGHT, THEN SHADOW

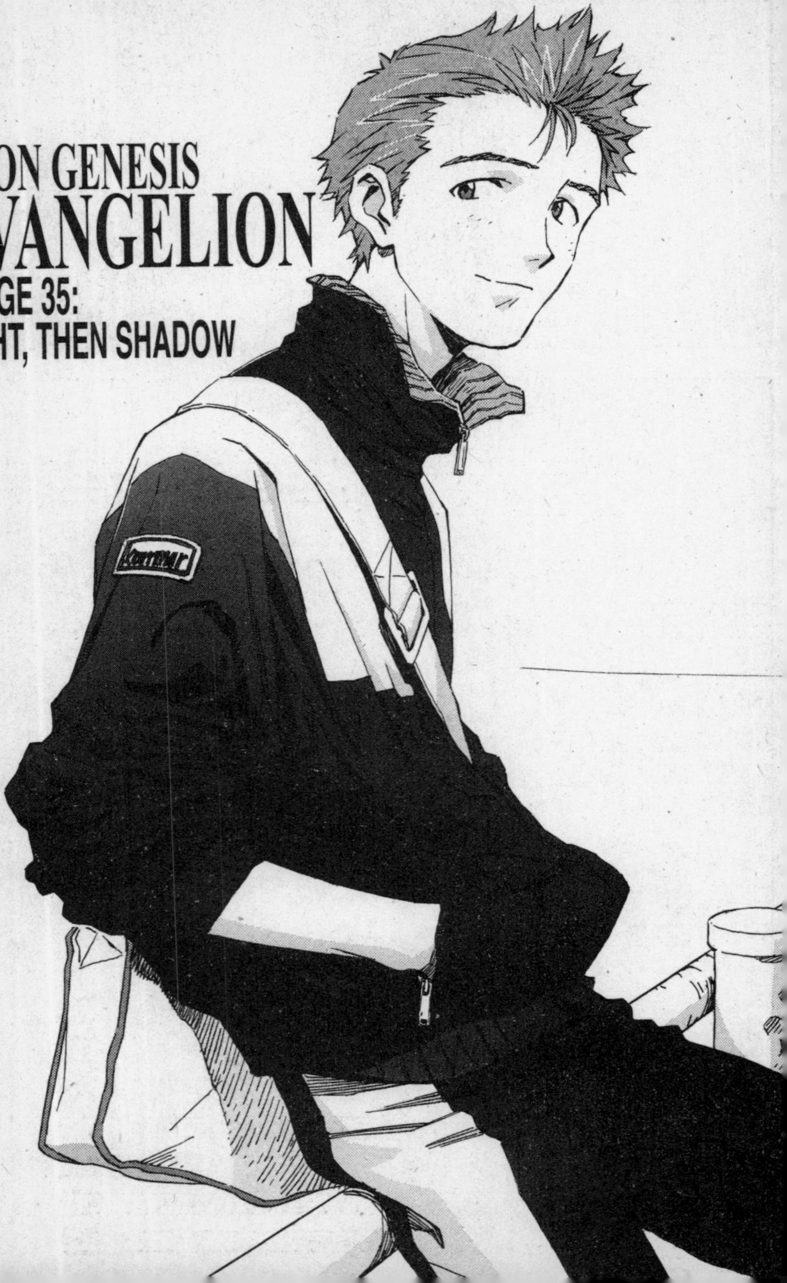

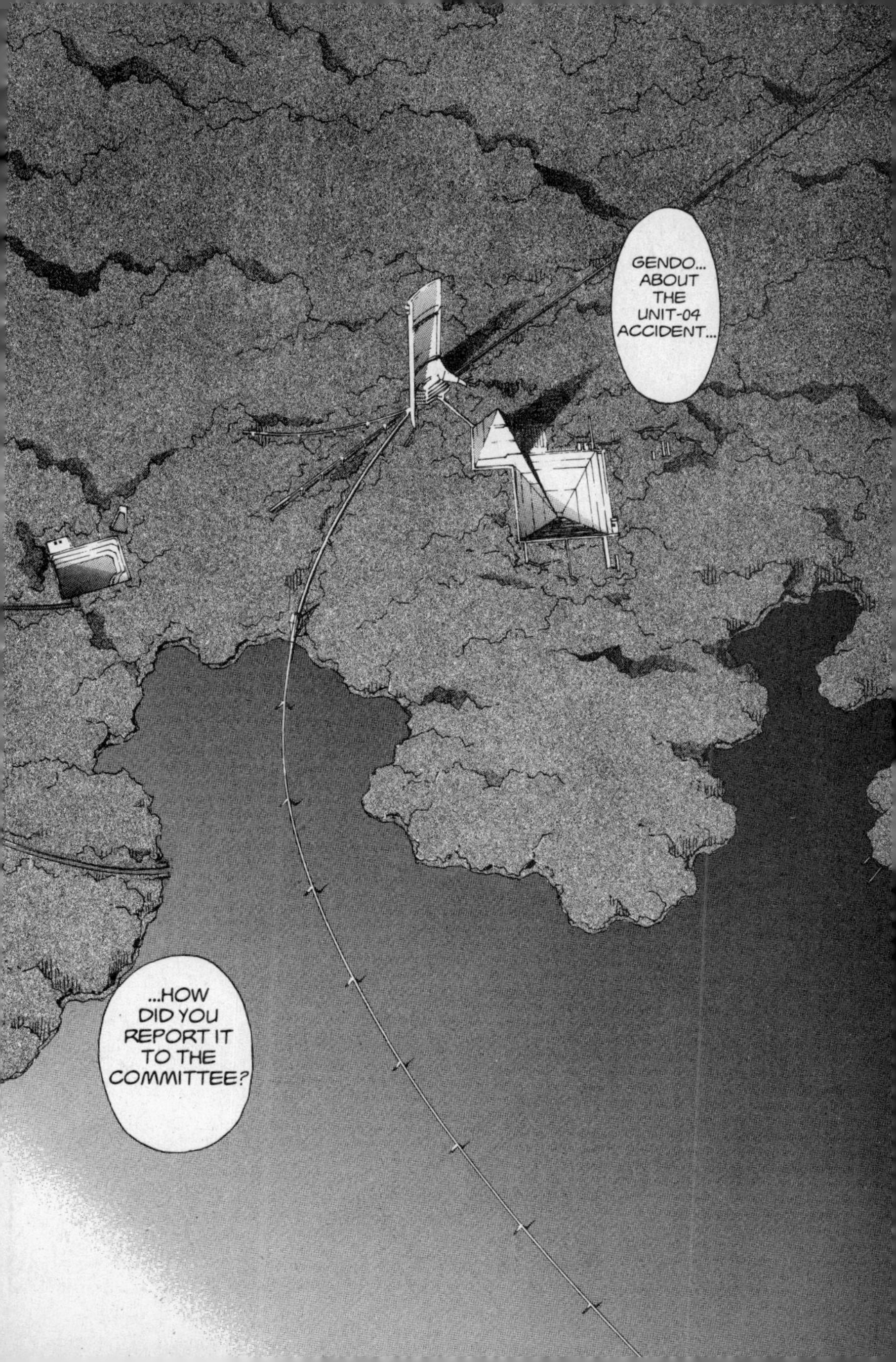
GENDO... ABOUT THE UNIT-04 ACCIDENT...
...HOW DID YOU REPORT IT TO THE COMMITTEE?

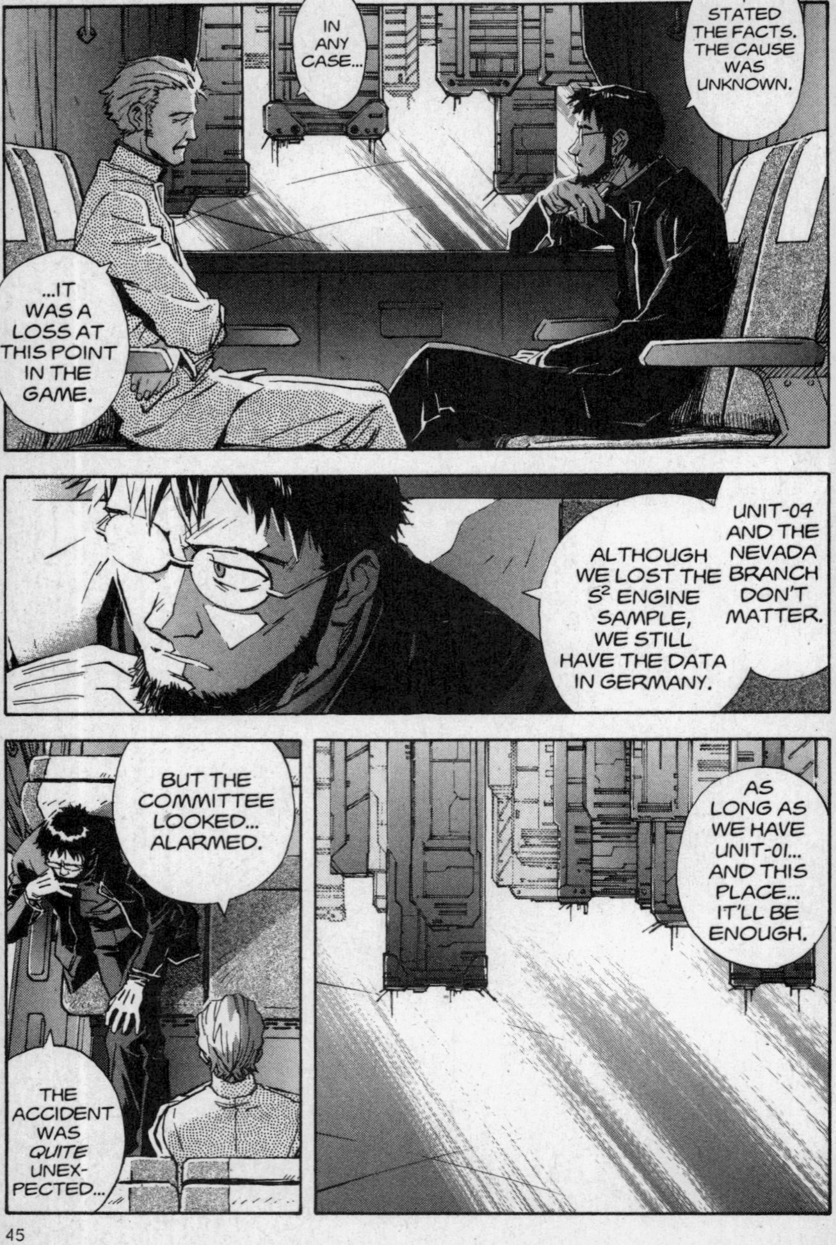
I STATED THE FACTS. THE CAUSE WAS UNKNOWN.
IN ANY CASE...
...IT WAS A LOSS AT THIS POINT IN THE GAME.
UNIT-04 AND THE NEVADA BRANCH DON'T MATTER.
ALTHOUGH WE LOST THE S^2 ENGINE SAMPLE, WE STILL HAVE THE DATA IN GERMANY.
AS LONG AS WE HAVE UNIT-01... AND THIS PLACE... IT'LL BE ENOUGH.
BUT THE COMMITTEE LOOKED... ALARMED.
THE ACCIDENT WAS *QUITE* UNEXPECTED...

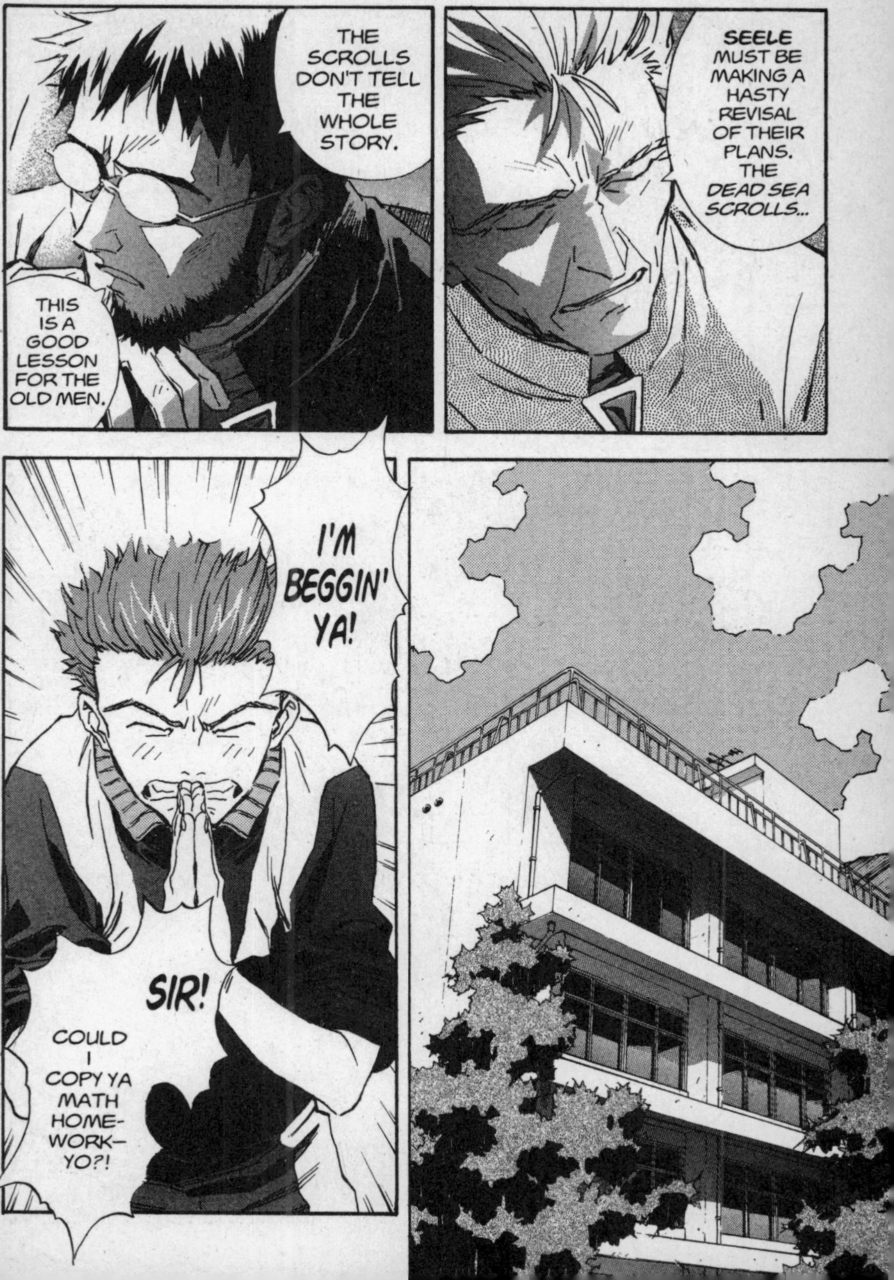
SEELE MUST BE MAKING A HASTY REVISAL OF THEIR PLANS. THE DEAD SEA SCROLLS...
THE SCROLLS DON'T TELL THE WHOLE STORY.
THIS IS A GOOD LESSON FOR THE OLD MEN.
I'M BEGGIN' YA!
SIR!
COULD I COPY YA MATH HOME-WORK-YO?!

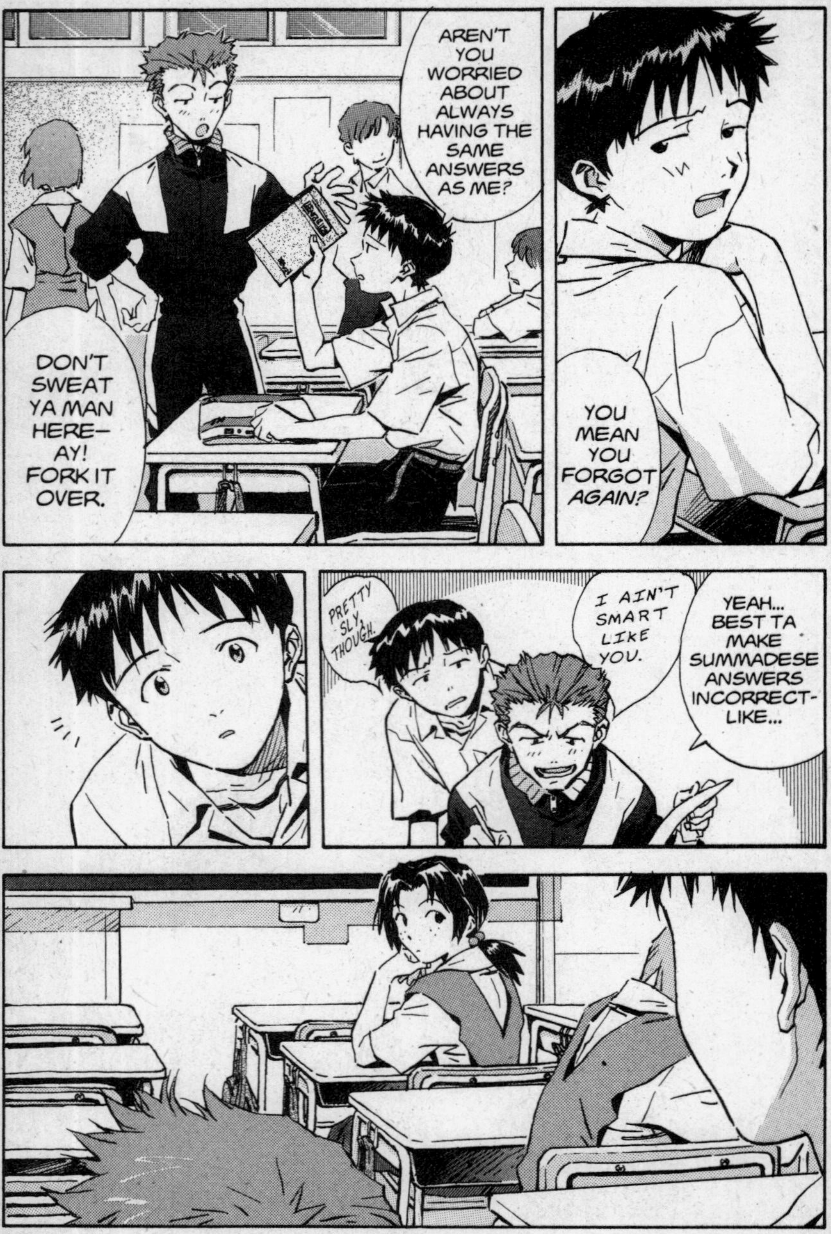
YOU MEAN YOU FORGOT AGAIN?
AREN'T YOU WORRIED ABOUT ALWAYS HAVING THE SAME ANSWERS AS ME?
DON'T SWEAT YA MAN HERE— AY! FORK IT OVER.
YEAH... BEST TA MAKE SUMMADESE ANSWERS INCORRECT-LIKE...
I AIN'T SMART LIKE YOU.
PRETTY SLY, THOUGH.

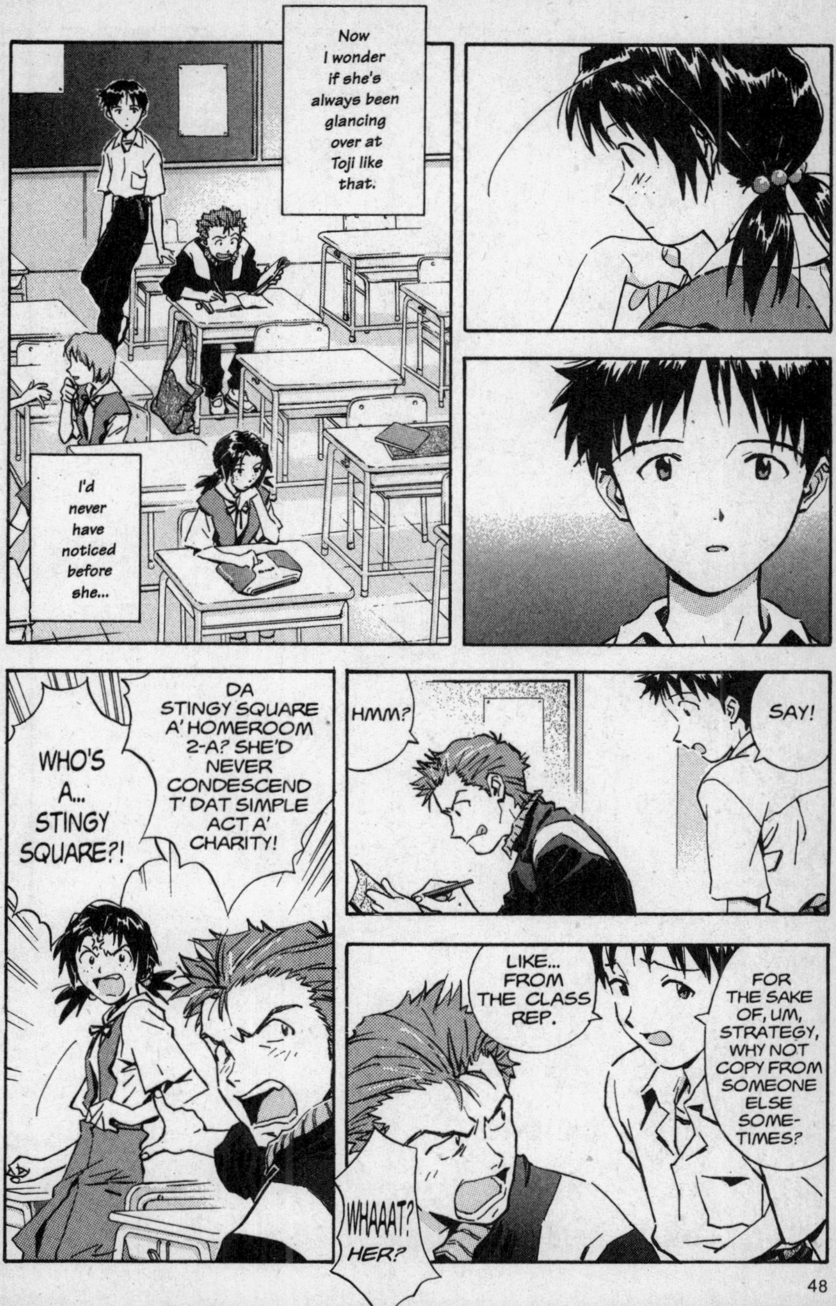
N!
Now I wonder if she's always been glancing over at Toji like that.
I'd never have noticed before she...
SAY!
HMM?
FOR THE SAKE OF, UM, STRATEGY, WHY NOT COPY FROM SOMEONE ELSE SOME-TIMES?
LIKE... FROM THE CLASS REP.
WHAAAT? HER?
DA STINGY SQUARE A' HOMEROOM 2-A? SHE'D NEVER CONDESCEND T' DAT SIMPLE ACT A' CHARITY!
WHO'S A... STINGY SQUARE?!

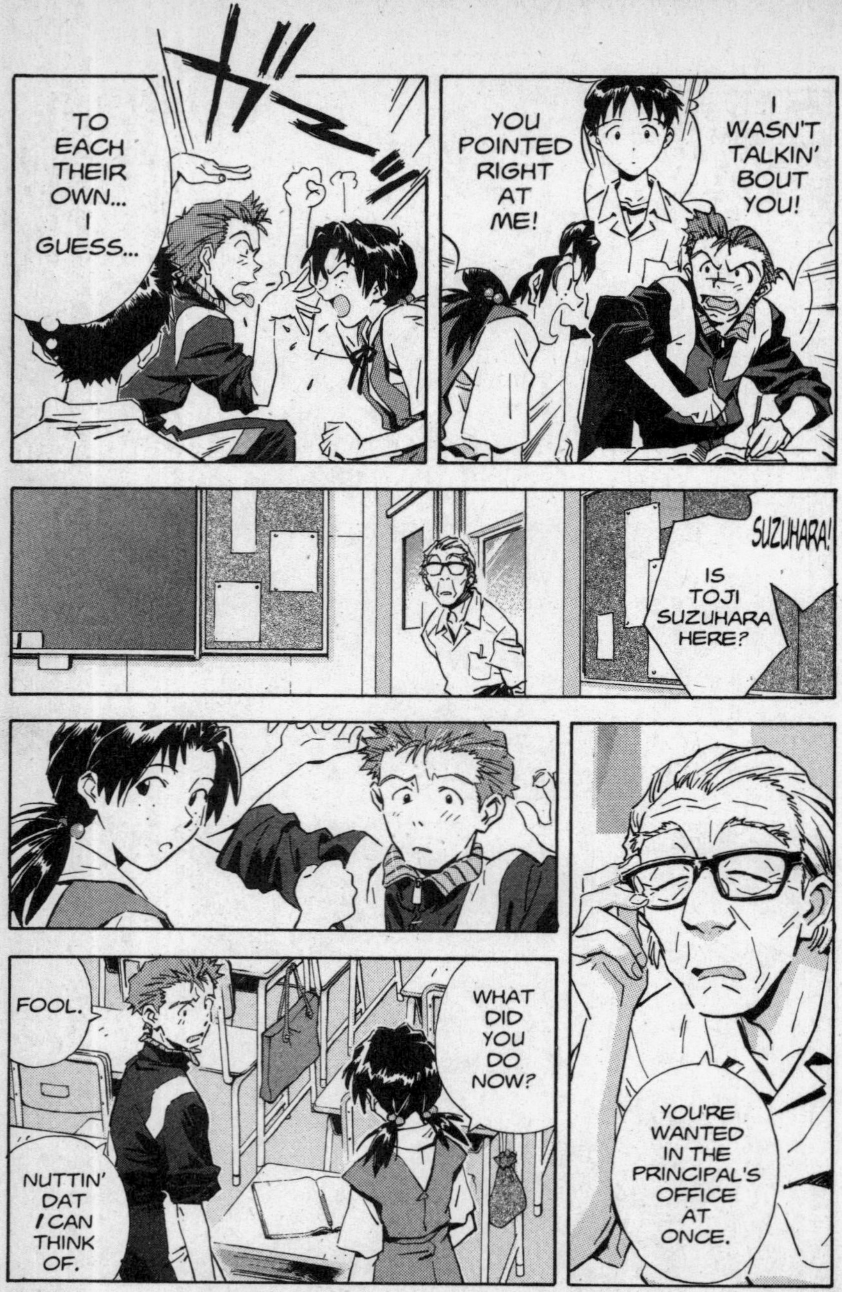
I WASN'T TALKIN' BOUT YOU!
YOU POINTED RIGHT AT ME!
TO EACH THEIR OWN... I GUESS...
SUZUHARA!
IS TOJI SUZUHARA HERE?
YOU'RE WANTED IN THE PRINCIPAL'S OFFICE AT ONCE.
WHAT DID YOU DO NOW?
NUTTIN' DAT I CAN THINK OF.
FOOL.

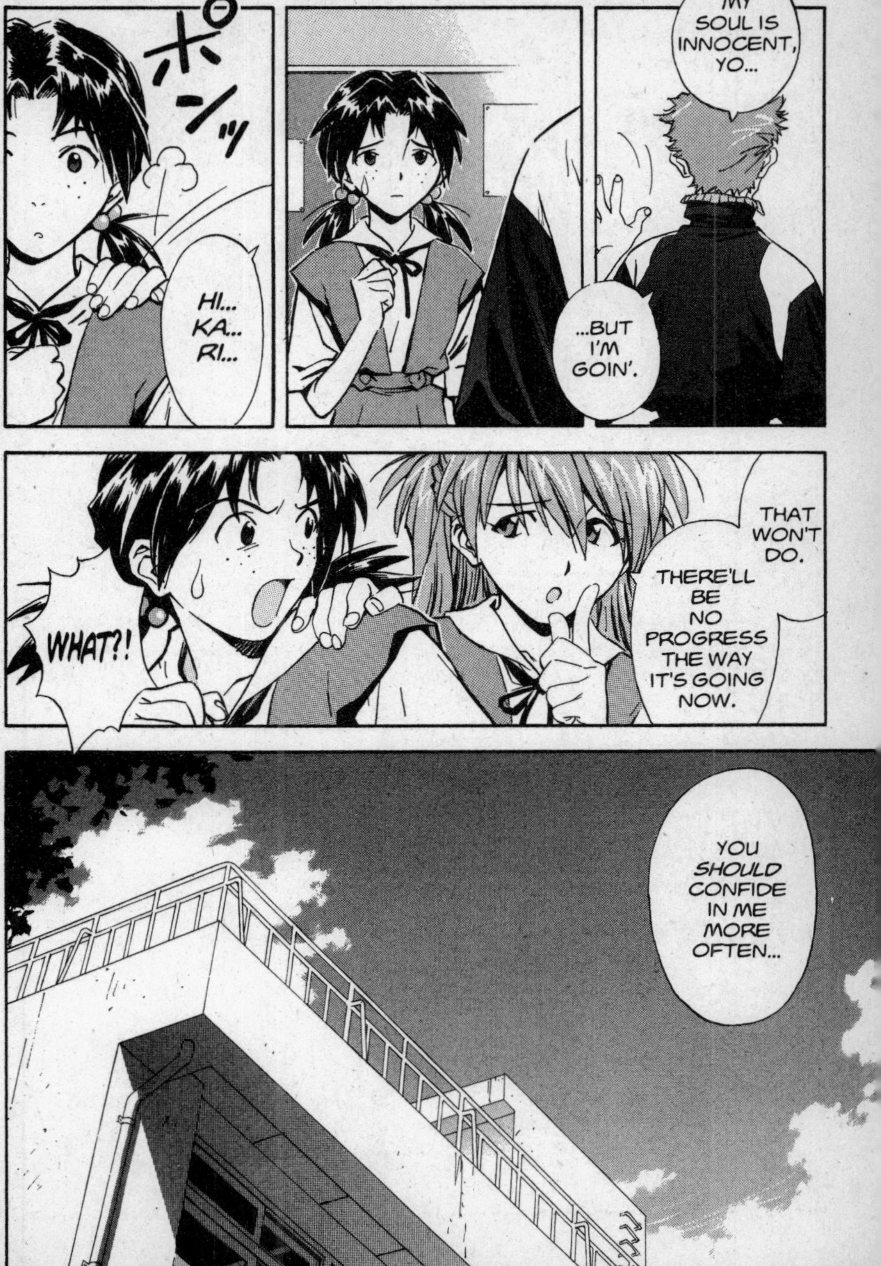
MY SOUL IS INNOCENT, YO...
...BUT I'M GOIN'.
ポンッ
HI... KA... RI...
THAT WON'T DO.
THERE'LL BE NO PROGRESS THE WAY IT'S GOING NOW.
WHAT?!
YOU *SHOULD* CONFIDE IN ME MORE OFTEN...

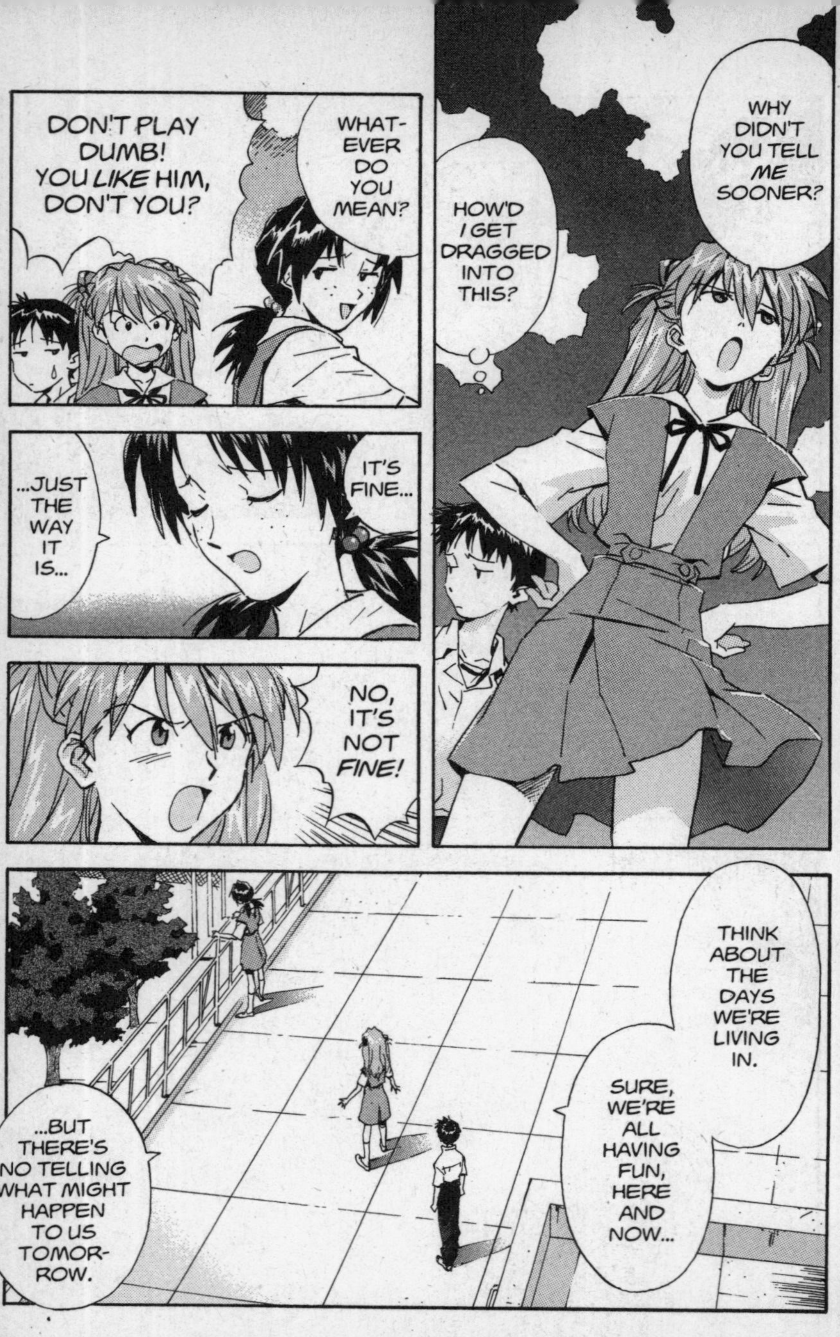
WHY DIDN'T YOU TELL *ME* SOONER?
HOW'D *I* GET DRAGGED INTO THIS?
WHAT-EVER DO YOU MEAN?
DON'T PLAY DUMB! YOU *LIKE* HIM, DON'T YOU?
IT'S FINE...
...JUST THE WAY IT IS...
NO, IT'S NOT *FINE!*
THINK ABOUT THE DAYS WE'RE LIVING IN.
SURE, WE'RE ALL HAVING FUN, HERE AND NOW...
...BUT THERE'S NO TELLING WHAT MIGHT HAPPEN TO US TOMOR-ROW.

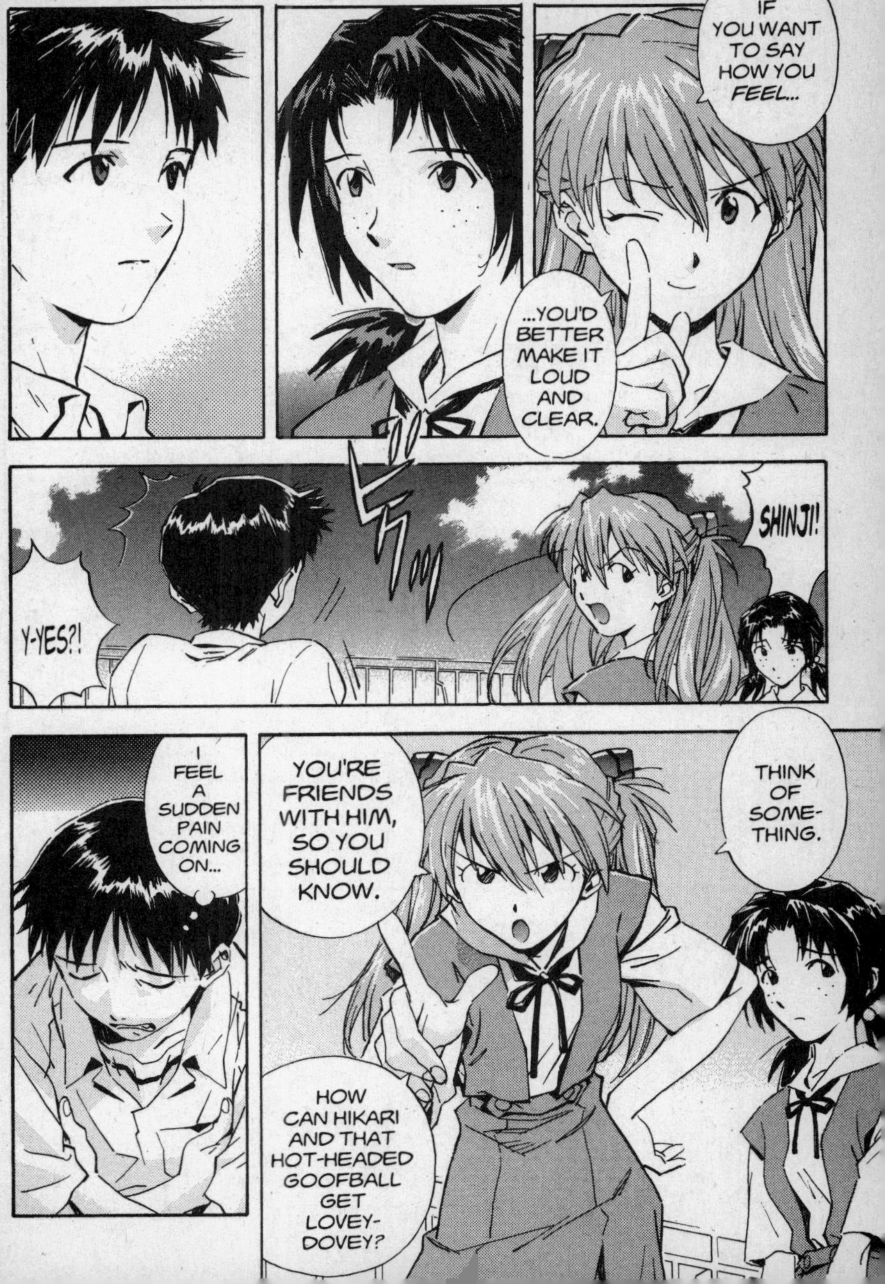
IF YOU WANT TO SAY HOW YOU FEEL...
...YOU'D BETTER MAKE IT LOUD AND CLEAR.
SHINJI!
Y-YES?!
THINK OF SOME-THING.
YOU'RE FRIENDS WITH HIM, SO YOU SHOULD KNOW.
HOW CAN HIKARI AND THAT HOT-HEADED GOOFBALL GET LOVEY-DOVEY?
I FEEL A SUDDEN PAIN COMING ON...

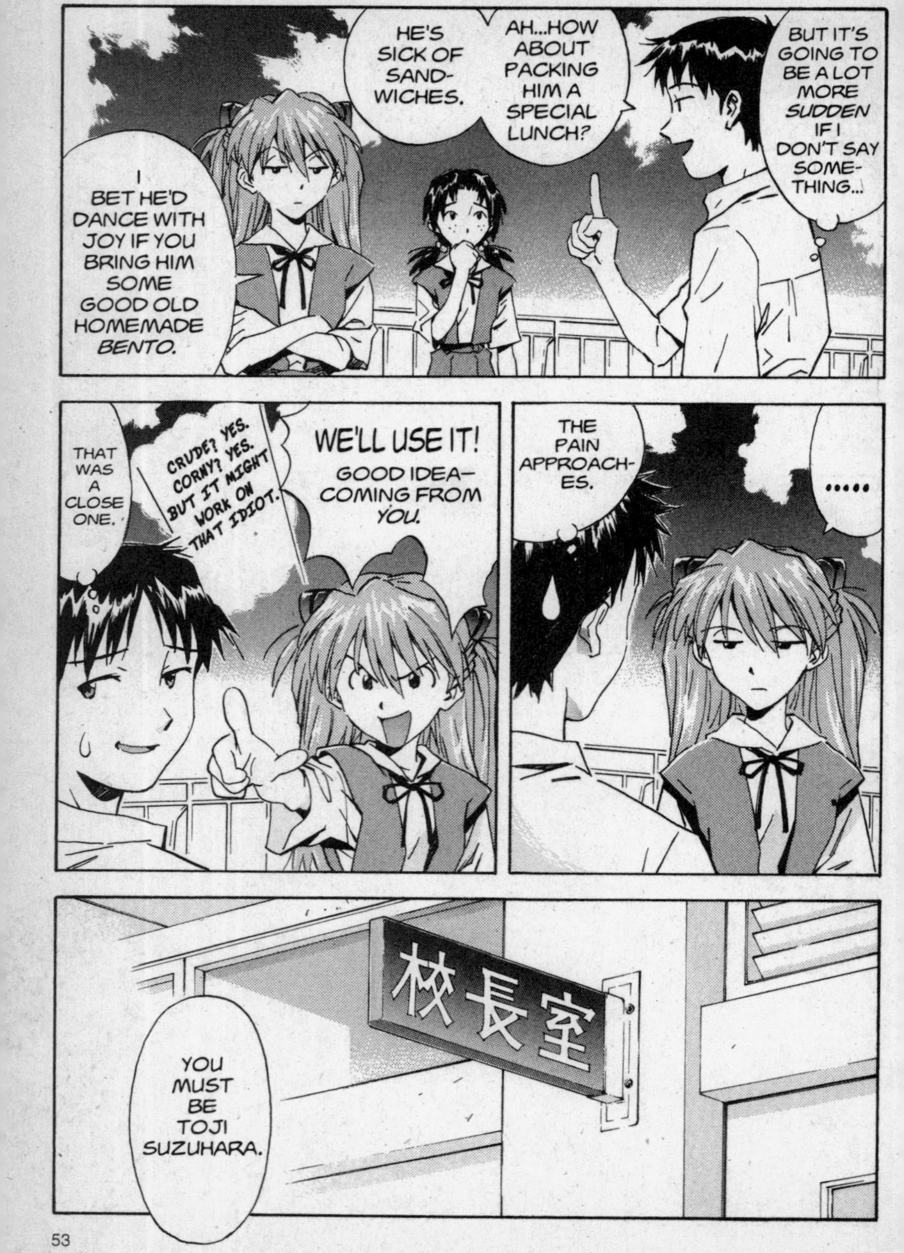
BUT IT'S GOING TO BE A LOT MORE SUDDEN IF I DON'T SAY SOMETHING...
AH...HOW ABOUT PACKING HIM A SPECIAL LUNCH?
HE'S SICK OF SANDWICHES.
I BET HE'D DANCE WITH JOY IF YOU BRING HIM SOME GOOD OLD HOMEMADE BENTO.
.....
THE PAIN APPROACHES.
WE'LL USE IT! GOOD IDEA—COMING FROM YOU.
CRUDE? YES. CORNY? YES. BUT IT MIGHT WORK ON THAT IDIOT.
THAT WAS A CLOSE ONE.
校長室
YOU MUST BE TOJI SUZUHARA.

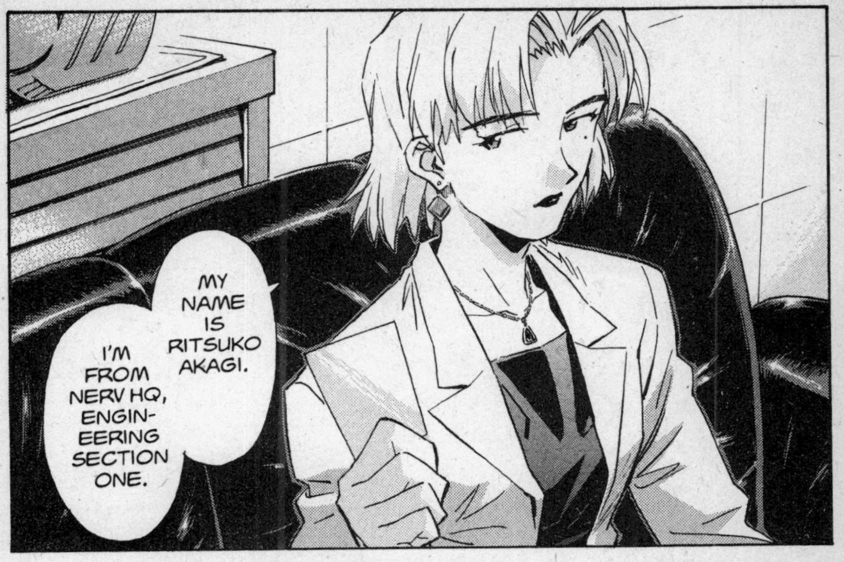
MY NAME IS RITSUKO AKAGI.
I'M FROM NERV HQ, ENGIN-EERING SECTION ONE.

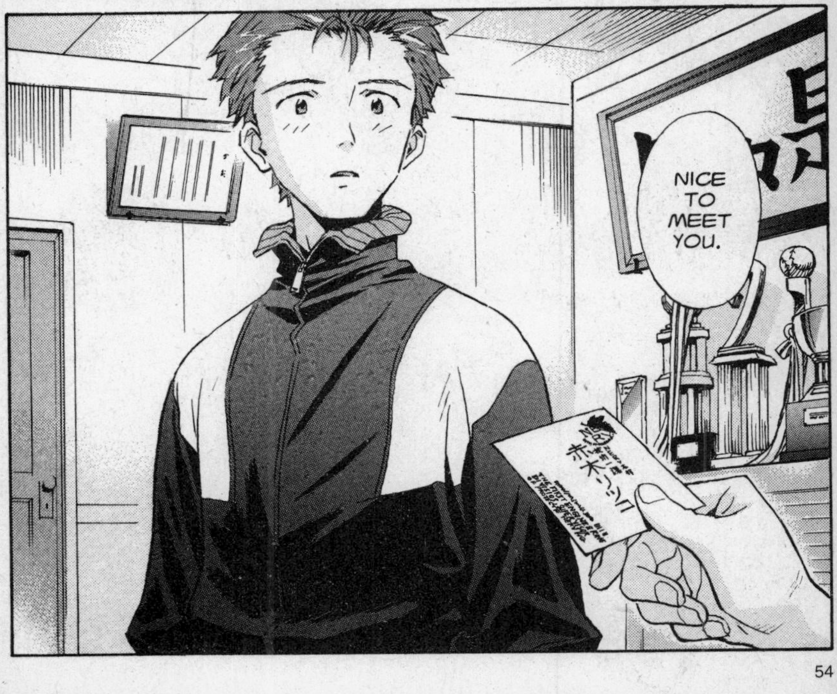
NICE TO MEET YOU.

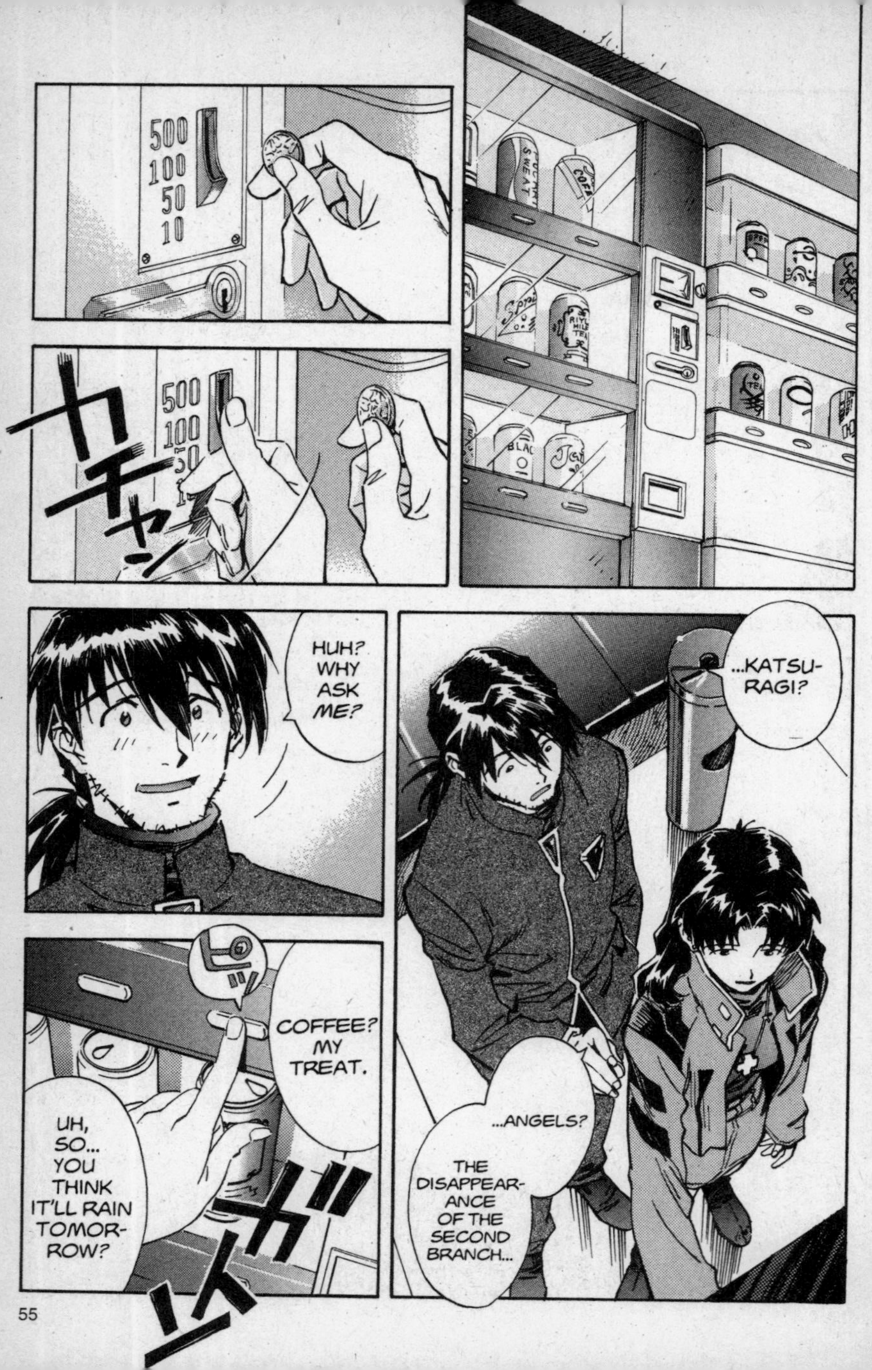
500
100
50
10
カチャーン
...KATSU-RAGI?
...ANGELS?
THE DISAPPEAR-ANCE OF THE SECOND BRANCH...
HUH? WHY ASK ME?
ピッ
COFFEE? MY TREAT.
UH, SO... YOU THINK IT'LL RAIN TOMOR-ROW?

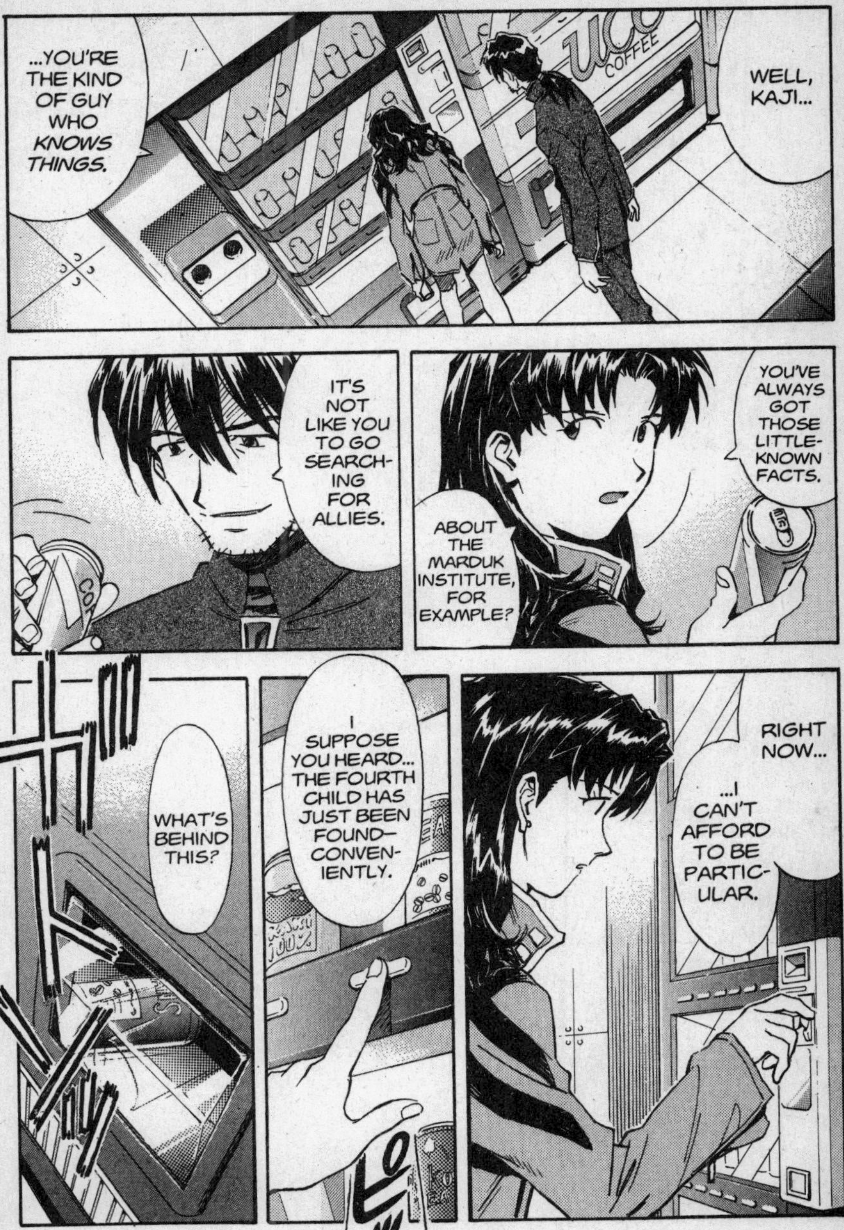
WELL, KAJI...
...YOU'RE THE KIND OF GUY WHO KNOWS THINGS.
YOU'VE ALWAYS GOT THOSE LITTLE-KNOWN FACTS.
ABOUT THE MARDUK INSTITUTE, FOR EXAMPLE?
IT'S NOT LIKE YOU TO GO SEARCHING FOR ALLIES.
RIGHT NOW...
...I CAN'T AFFORD TO BE PARTICULAR.
I SUPPOSE YOU HEARD... THE FOURTH CHILD HAS JUST BEEN FOUND—CONVENIENTLY.
WHAT'S BEHIND THIS?

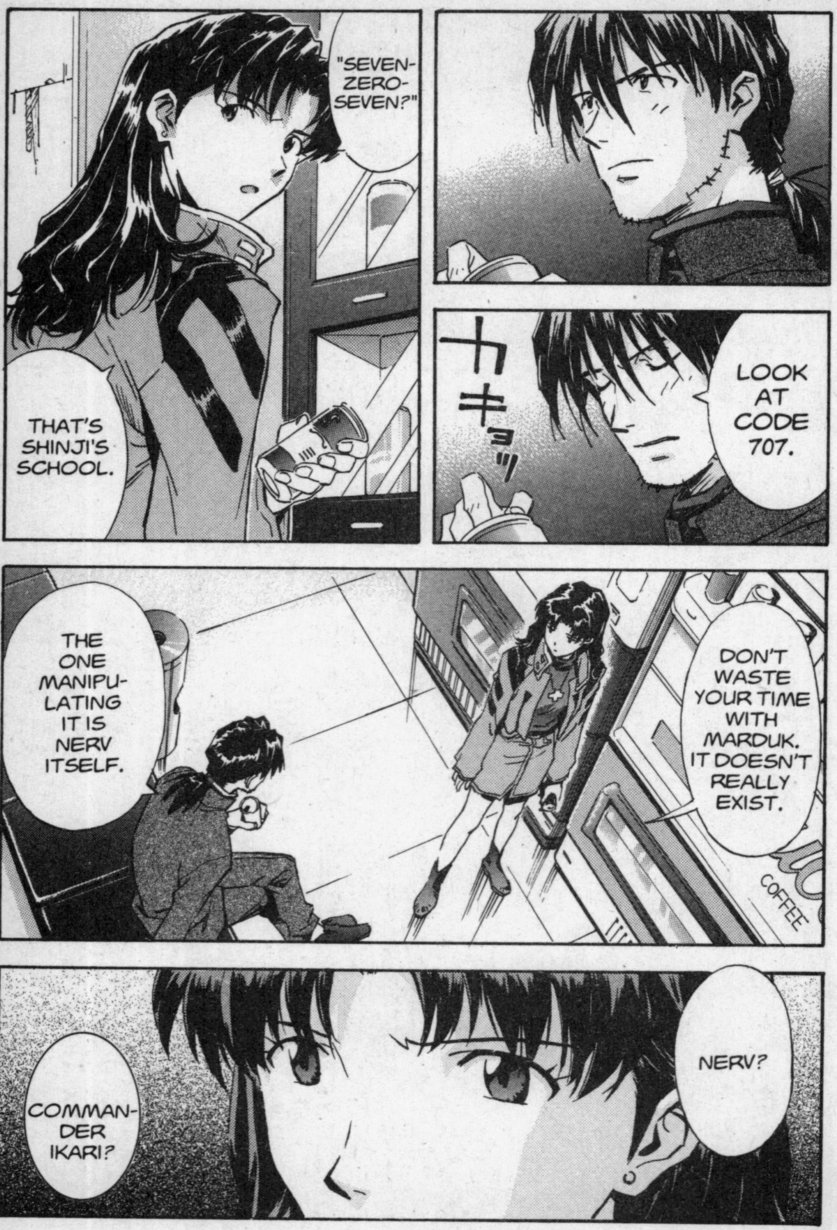
カキョッ
LOOK AT CODE 707.
"SEVEN-ZERO-SEVEN?"
THAT'S SHINJI'S SCHOOL.
DON'T WASTE YOUR TIME WITH MARDUK. IT DOESN'T REALLY EXIST.
COFFEE
THE ONE MANIPULATING IT IS NERV ITSELF.
NERV?
COMMANDER IKARI?

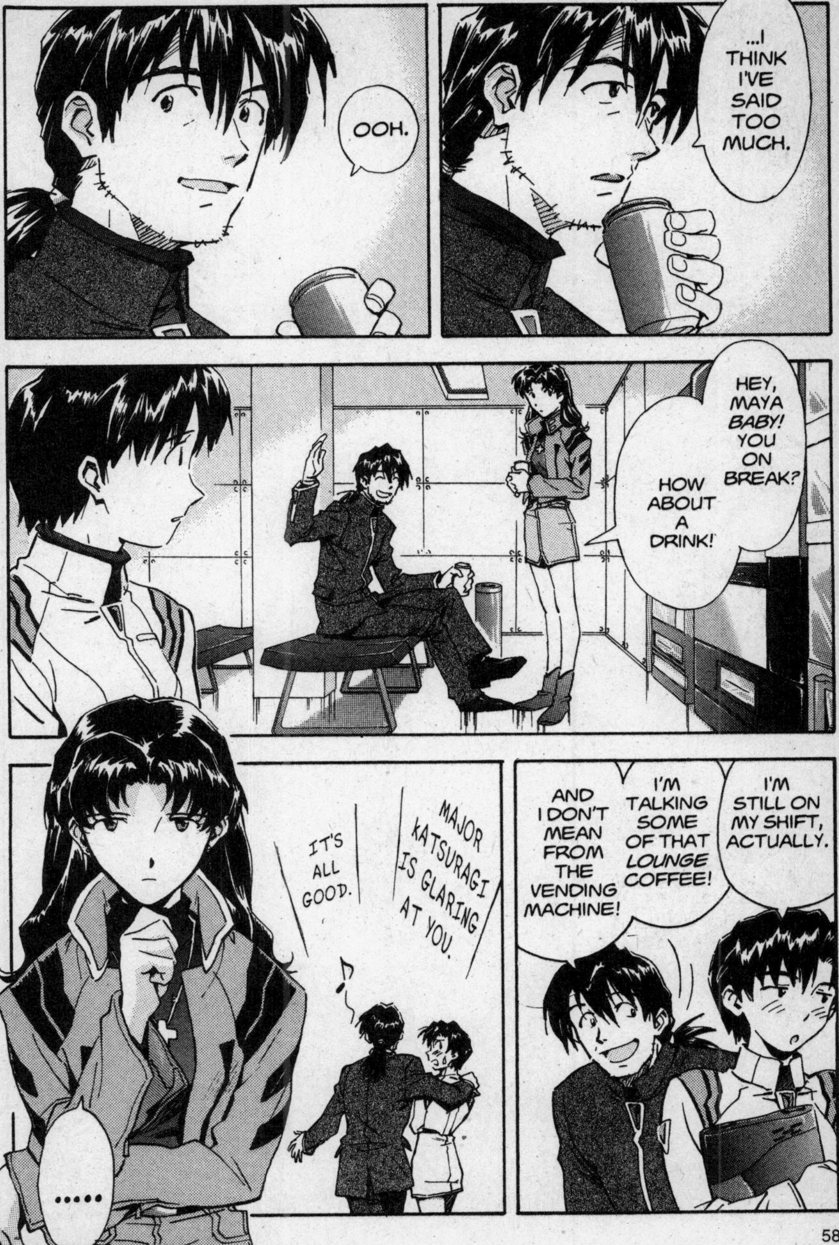
...I THINK I'VE SAID TOO MUCH.
OOH.
HEY, MAYA *BABY*! YOU ON BREAK?
HOW ABOUT A DRINK!
I'M STILL ON MY SHIFT, ACTUALLY.
I'M TALKING SOME OF THAT *LOUNGE* COFFEE!
AND I DON'T MEAN FROM THE VENDING MACHINE!
MAJOR KATSURAGI IS GLARING AT YOU.
IT'S ALL GOOD.
.....

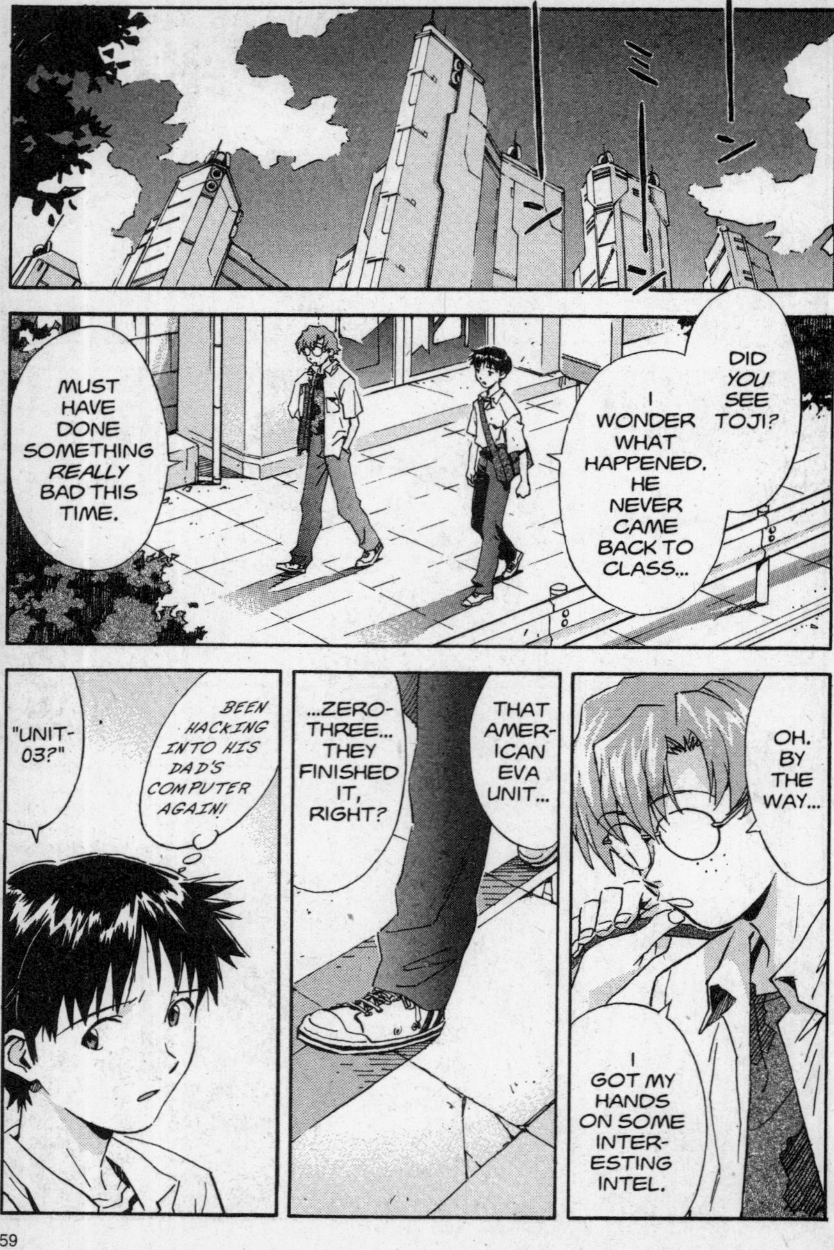
DID YOU SEE TOJI?
I WONDER WHAT HAPPENED. HE NEVER CAME BACK TO CLASS...
MUST HAVE DONE SOMETHING *REALLY* BAD THIS TIME.
OH. BY THE WAY...
I GOT MY HANDS ON SOME INTERESTING INTEL.
THAT AMERICAN EVA UNIT...
...ZERO-THREE... THEY FINISHED IT, RIGHT?
BEEN HACKING INTO HIS DAD'S COMPUTER AGAIN!
"UNIT-03?"

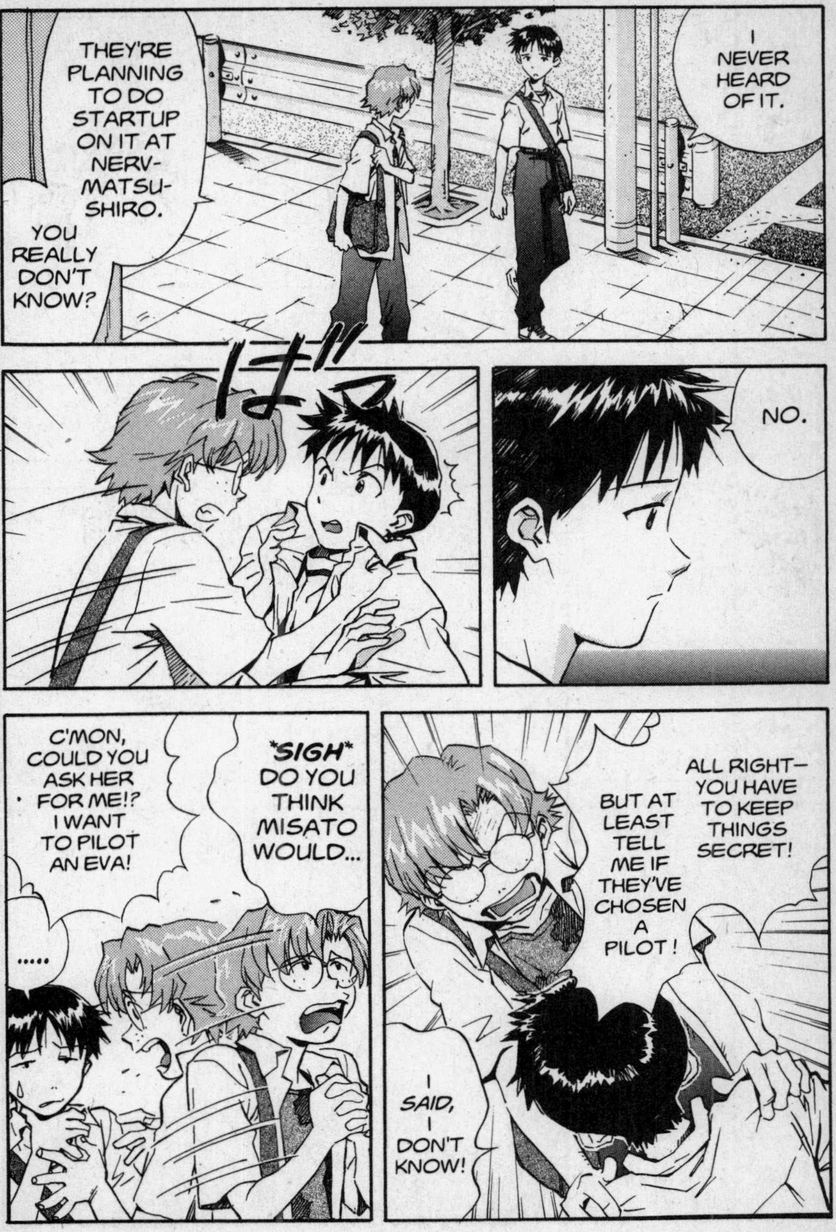
I NEVER HEARD OF IT.
THEY'RE PLANNING TO DO STARTUP ON IT AT NERV-MATSU-SHIRO.
YOU REALLY DON'T KNOW?
NO.
ばっ
ALL RIGHT— YOU HAVE TO KEEP THINGS SECRET!
BUT AT LEAST TELL ME IF THEY'VE CHOSEN A PILOT!
I SAID, I DON'T KNOW!
SIGH DO YOU THINK MISATO WOULD...
C'MON, COULD YOU ASK HER FOR ME!? I WANT TO PILOT AN EVA!
......

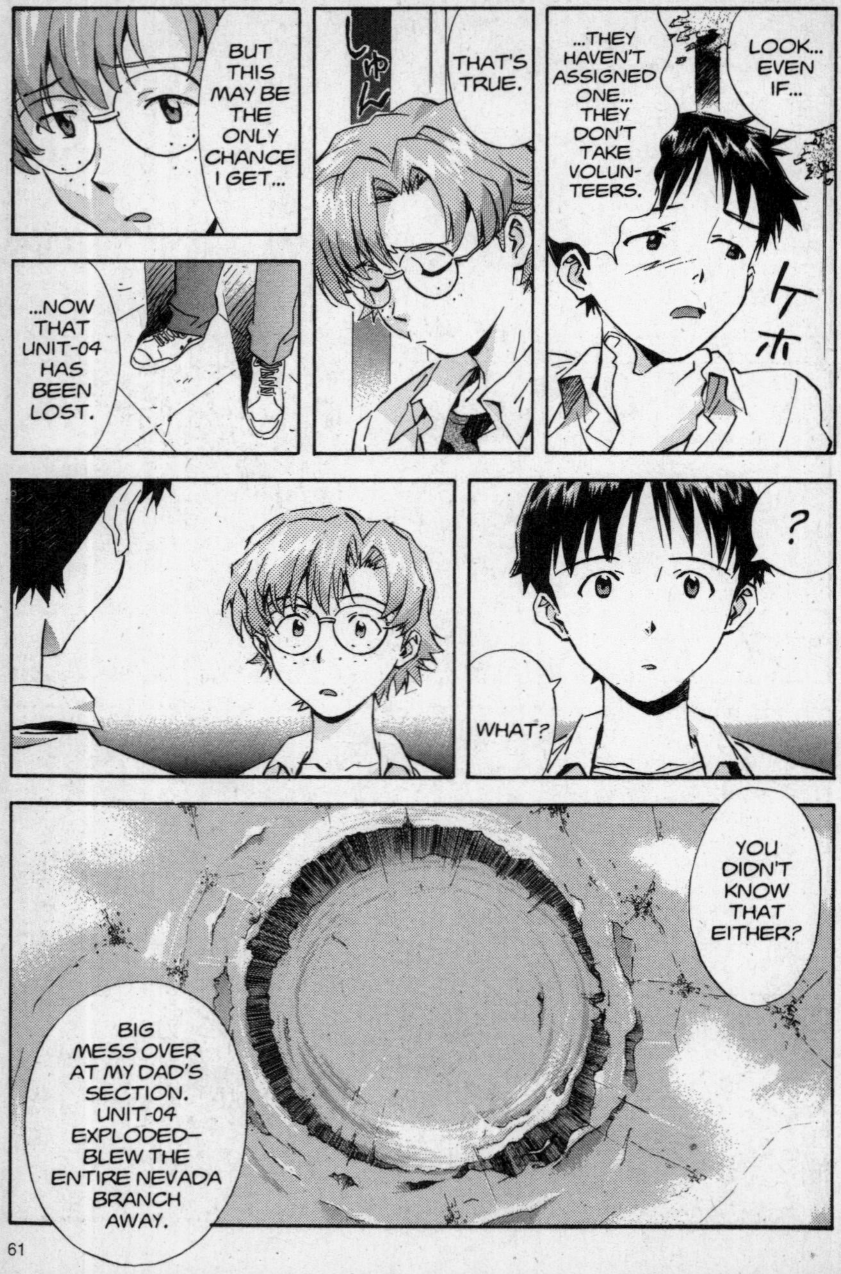
LOOK... EVEN IF...
...THEY HAVEN'T ASSIGNED ONE... THEY DON'T TAKE VOLUNTEERS.
ケホ
しゅん
THAT'S TRUE.
BUT THIS MAY BE THE ONLY CHANCE I GET...
...NOW THAT UNIT-04 HAS BEEN LOST.
?
WHAT?
YOU DIDN'T KNOW THAT EITHER?
BIG MESS OVER AT MY DAD'S SECTION. UNIT-04 EXPLODED— BLEW THE ENTIRE NEVADA BRANCH AWAY.

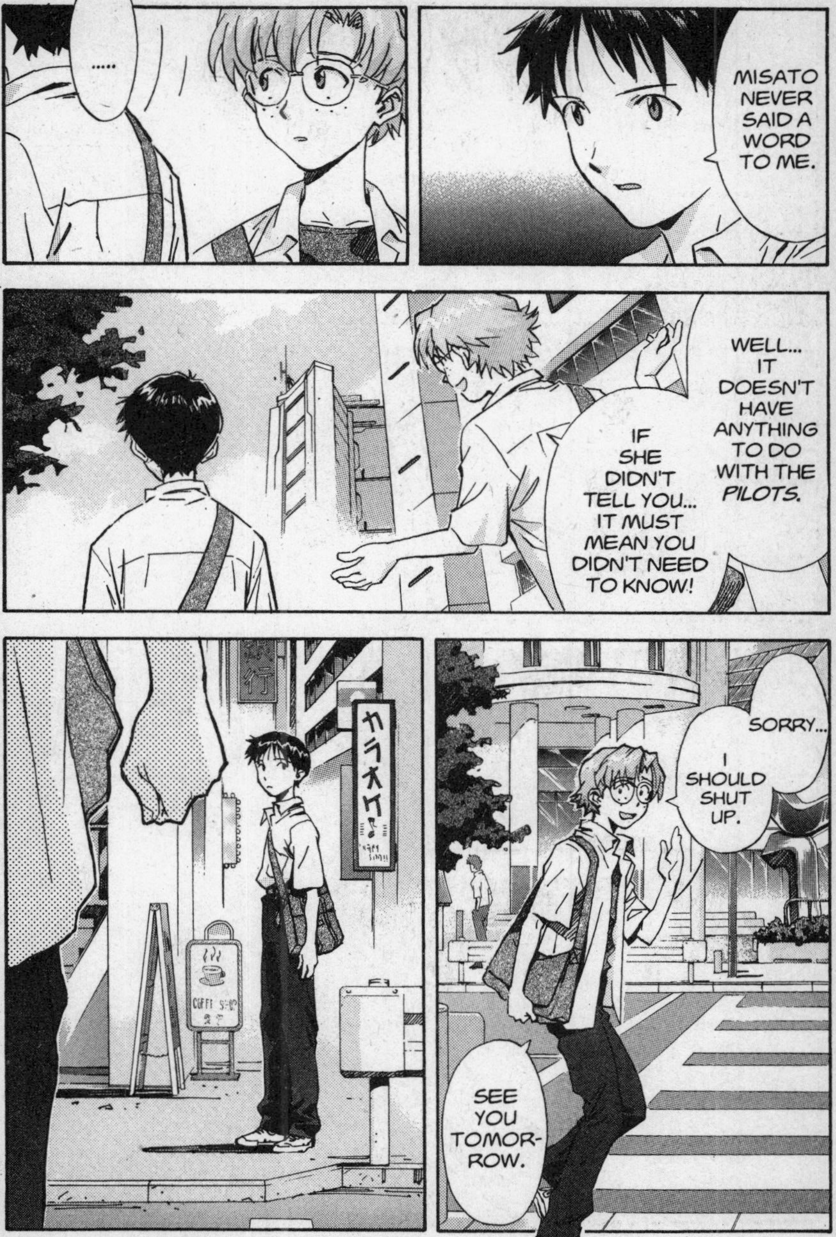
MISATO NEVER SAID A WORD TO ME.
......
WELL... IT DOESN'T HAVE ANYTHING TO DO WITH THE *PILOTS.*
IF SHE DIDN'T TELL YOU... IT MUST MEAN YOU DIDN'T NEED TO KNOW!
SORRY...
I SHOULD SHUT UP.
SEE YOU TOMOR-ROW.
カラオケ

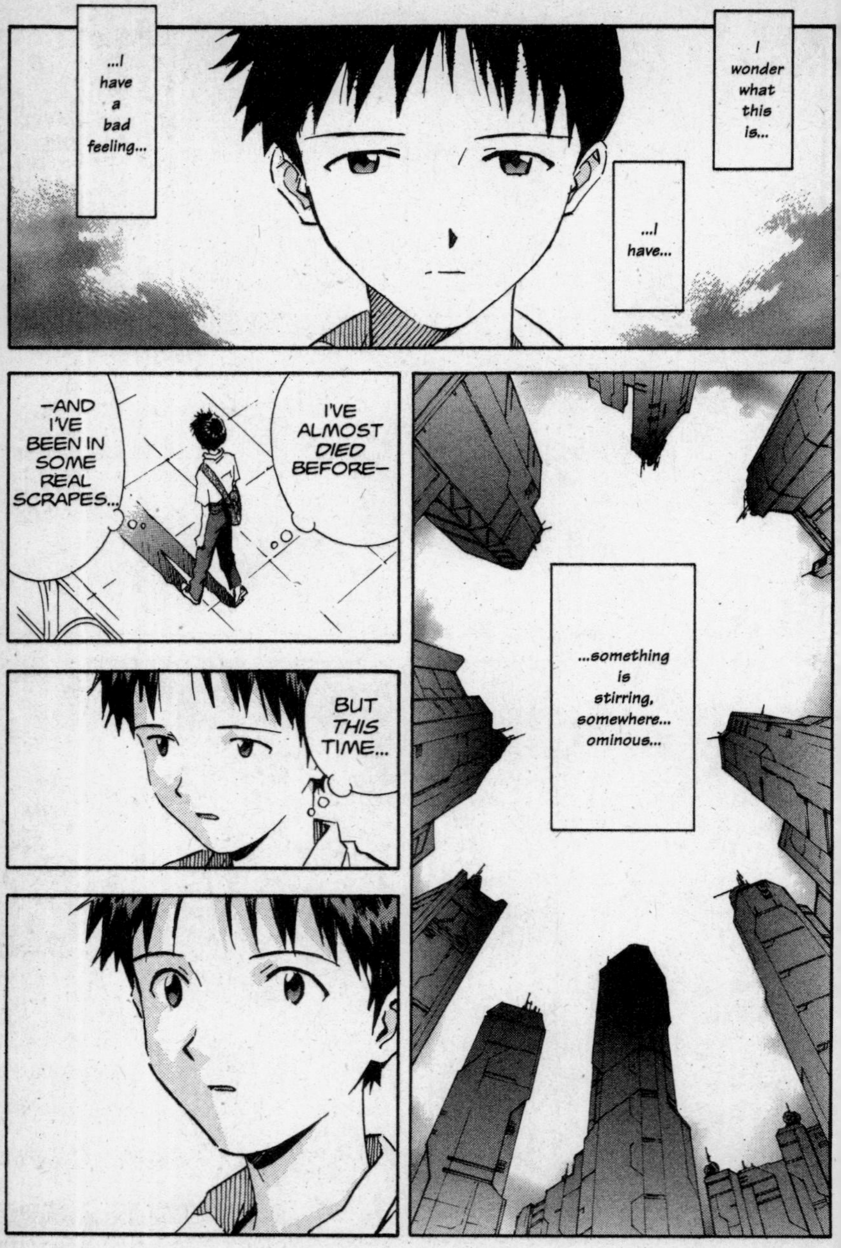
I wonder what this is...
...I have...
...I have a bad feeling...
I'VE ALMOST DIED BEFORE—
—AND I'VE BEEN IN SOME REAL SCRAPES...
BUT THIS TIME...
...something is stirring, somewhere... ominous...

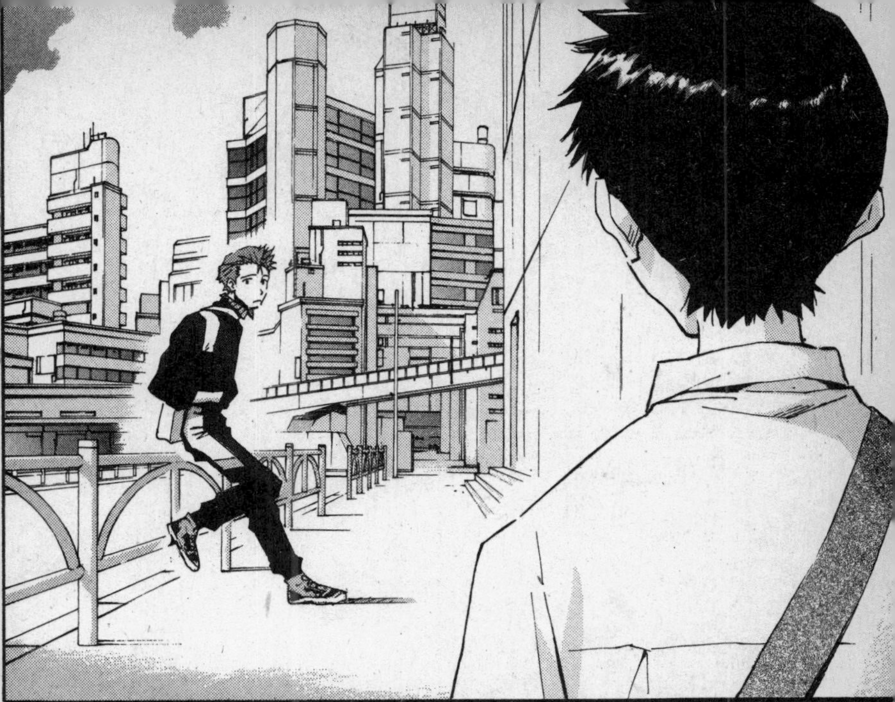
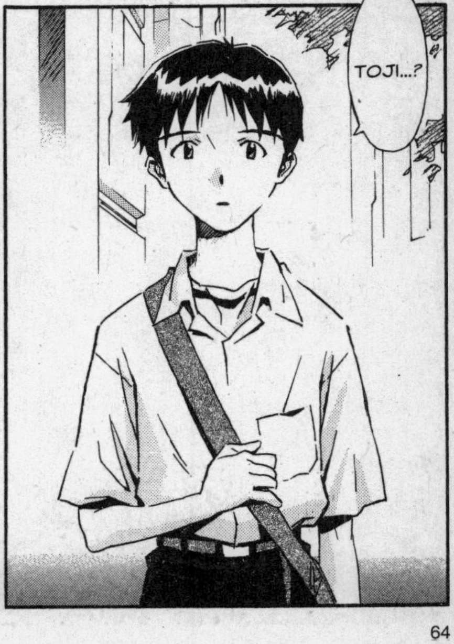
TOJI...?
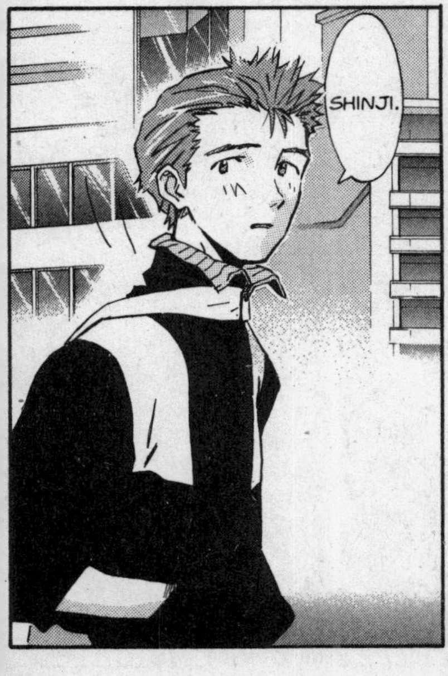
SHINJI.

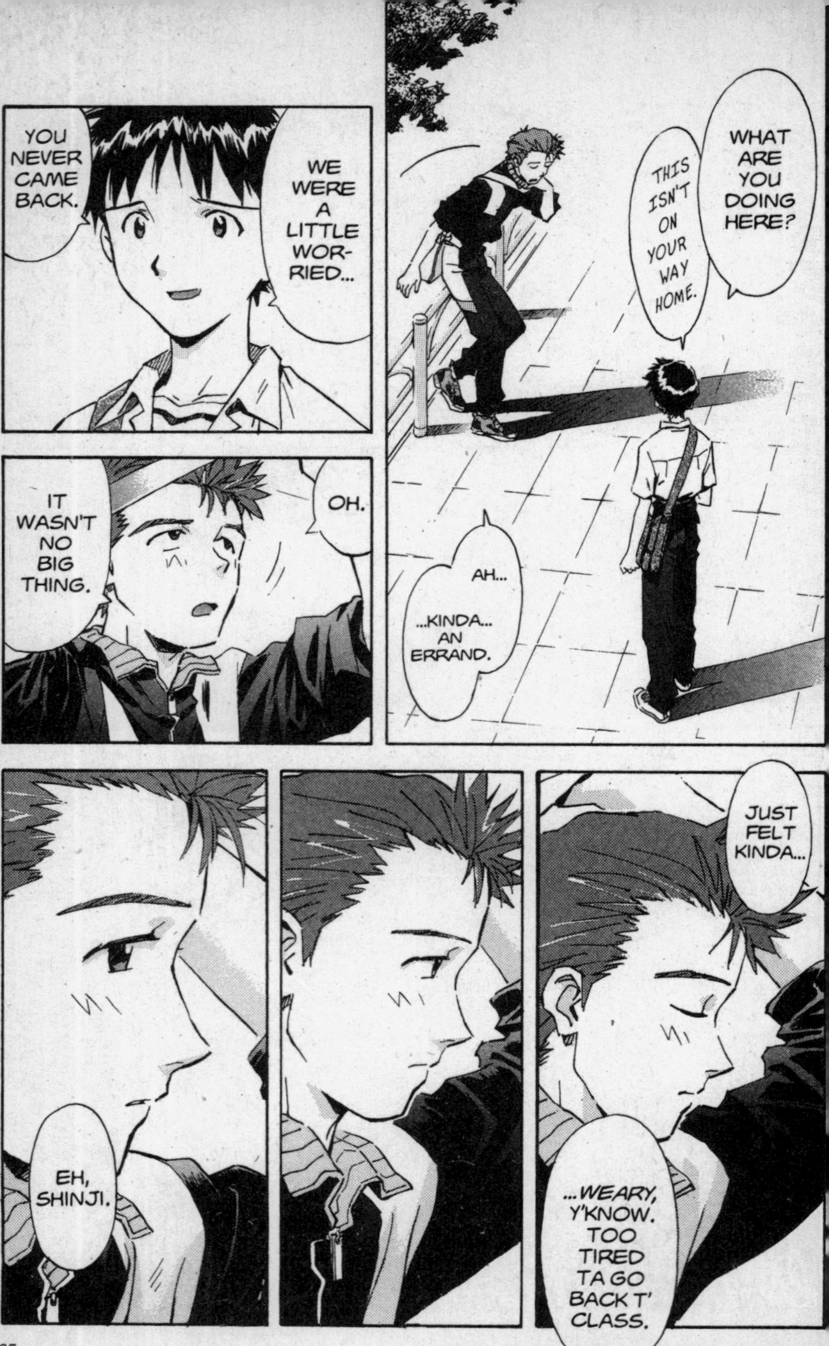
WHAT ARE YOU DOING HERE?
THIS ISN'T ON YOUR WAY HOME.
AH...
...KINDA... AN ERRAND.
YOU NEVER CAME BACK.
WE WERE A LITTLE WORRIED...
IT WASN'T NO BIG THING.
OH.
JUST FELT KINDA...
...WEARY, Y'KNOW. TOO TIRED TA GO BACK T' CLASS.
EH, SHINJI.

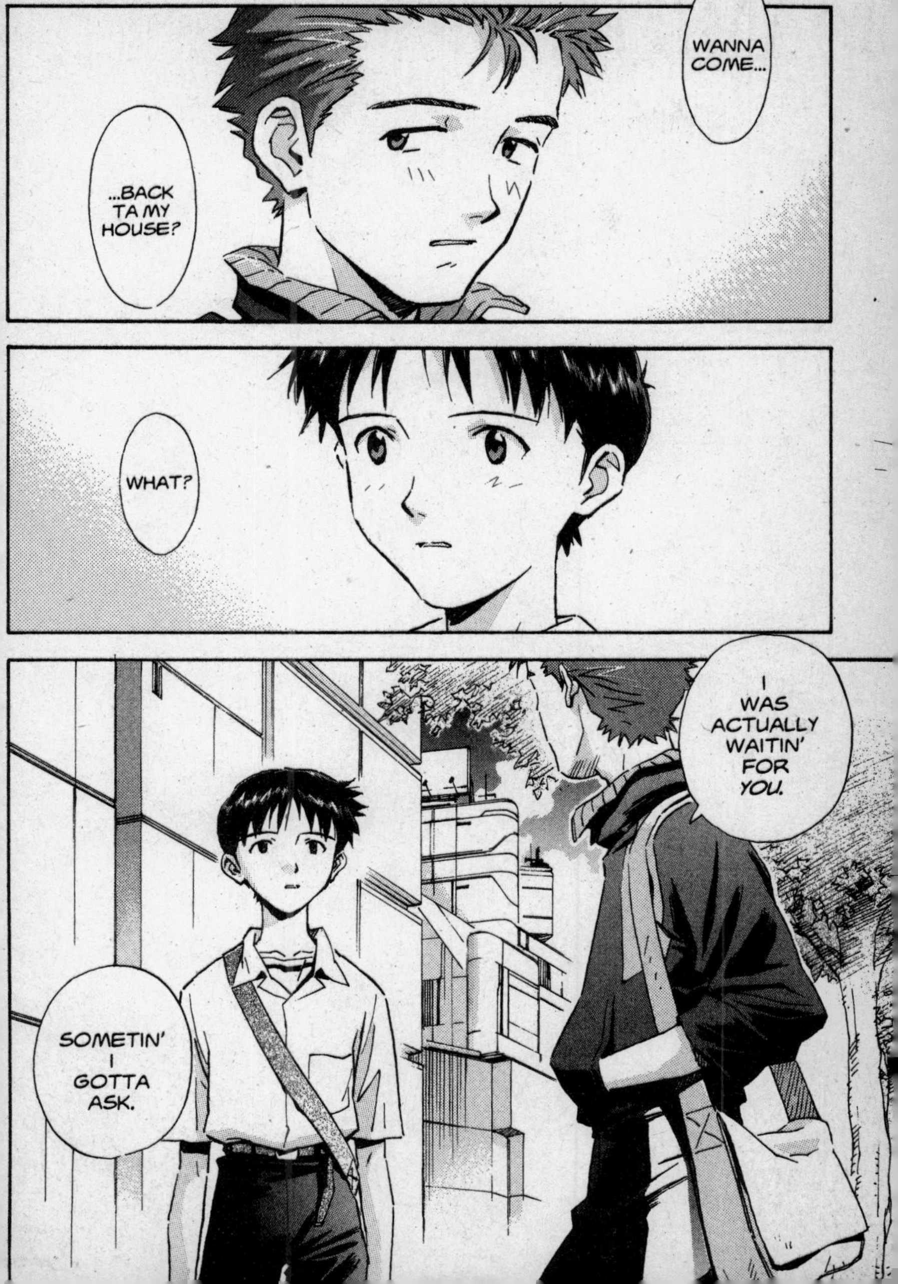
WANNA COME...
...BACK TA MY HOUSE?
WHAT?
I WAS ACTUALLY WAITIN' FOR YOU.
SOMETIN' I GOTTA ASK.

NEON GENESIS EVANGELION

STAGE 36: CONFESSION

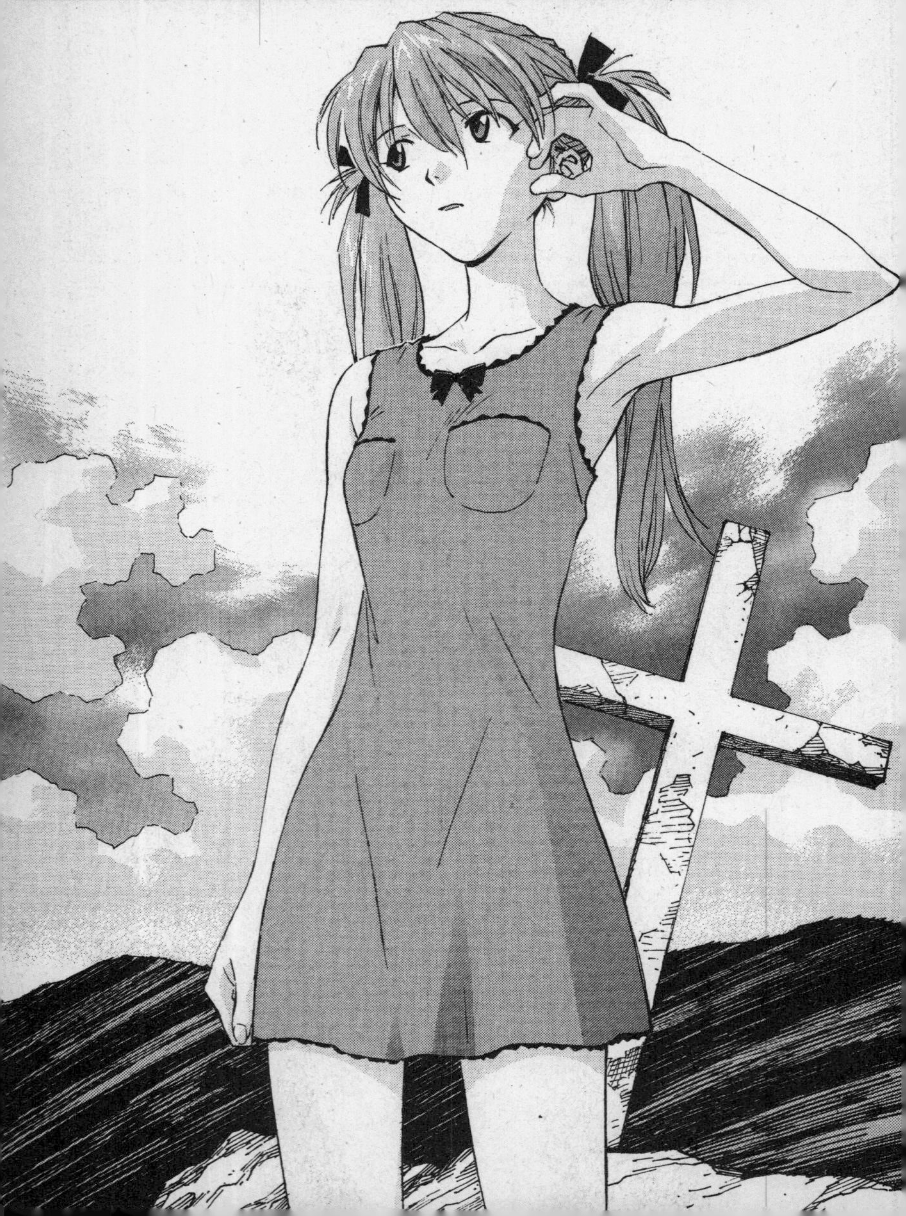

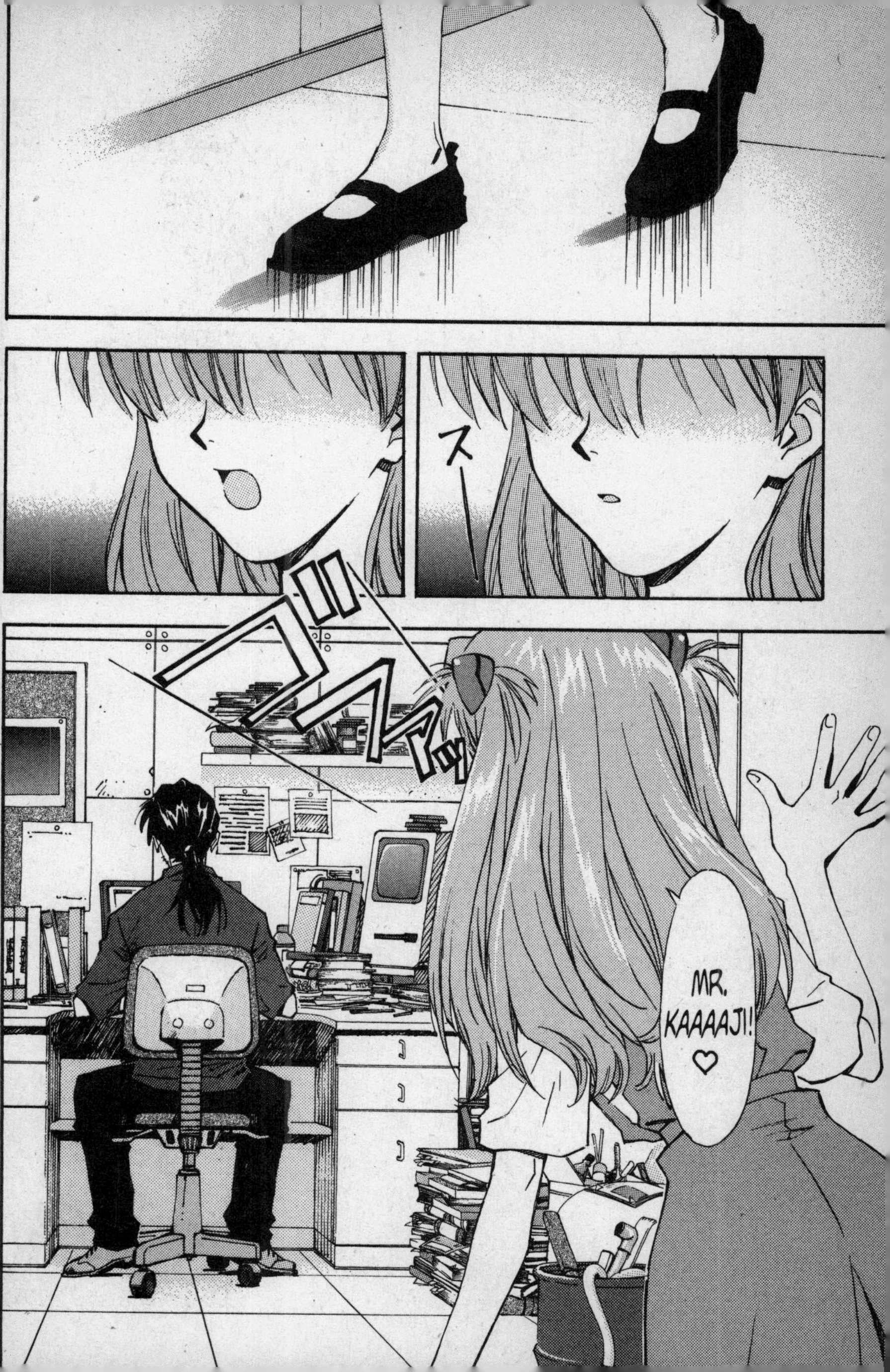
スー
MR. KAAAAJI! ♡

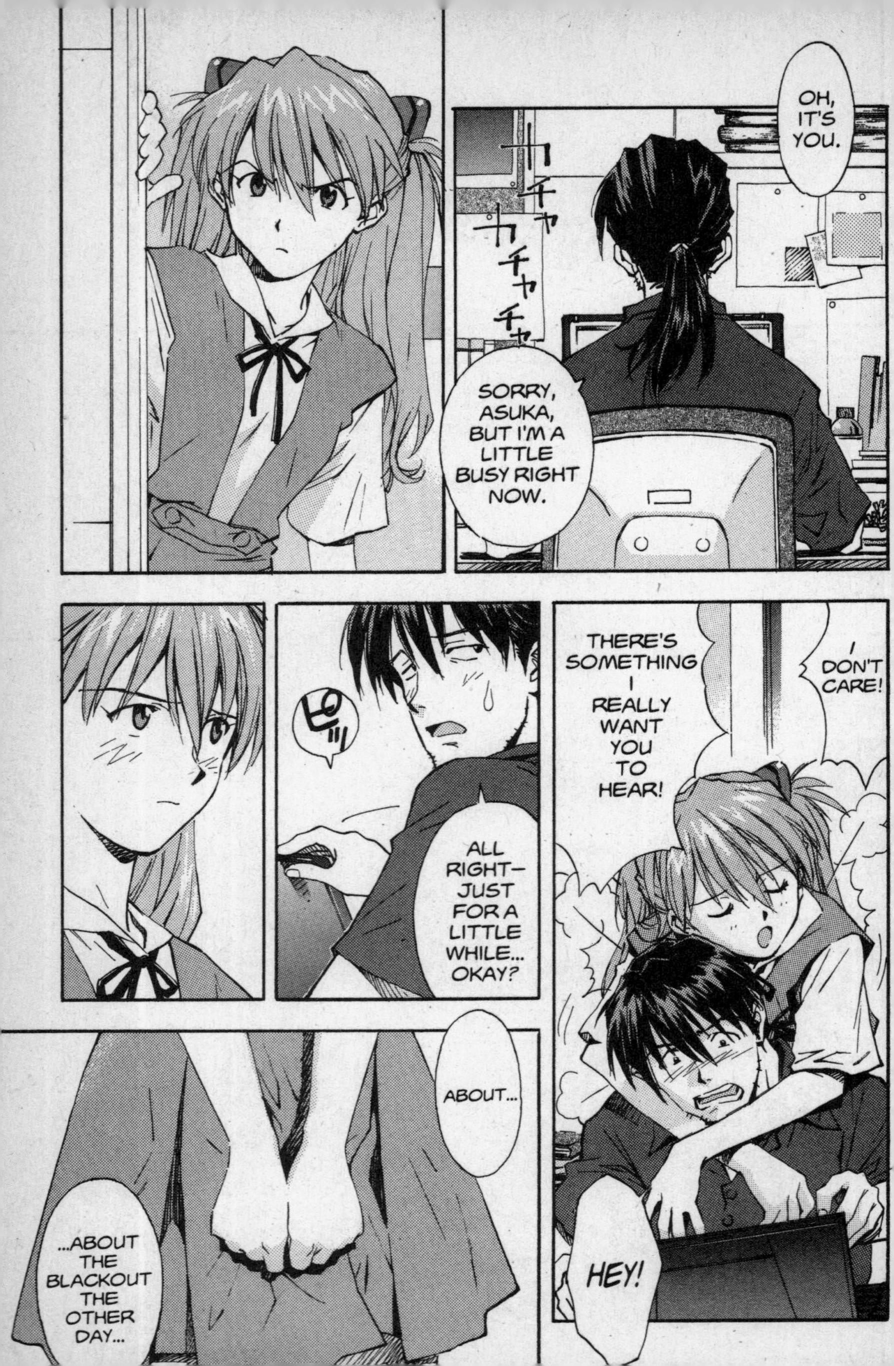
OH, IT'S YOU.
カチャ
カチャ
チャ
SORRY, ASUKA, BUT I'M A LITTLE BUSY RIGHT NOW.
I DON'T CARE!
THERE'S SOMETHING I REALLY WANT YOU TO HEAR!
HEY!
ピッ
ALL RIGHT— JUST FOR A LITTLE WHILE... OKAY?
ABOUT...
...ABOUT THE BLACKOUT THE OTHER DAY...

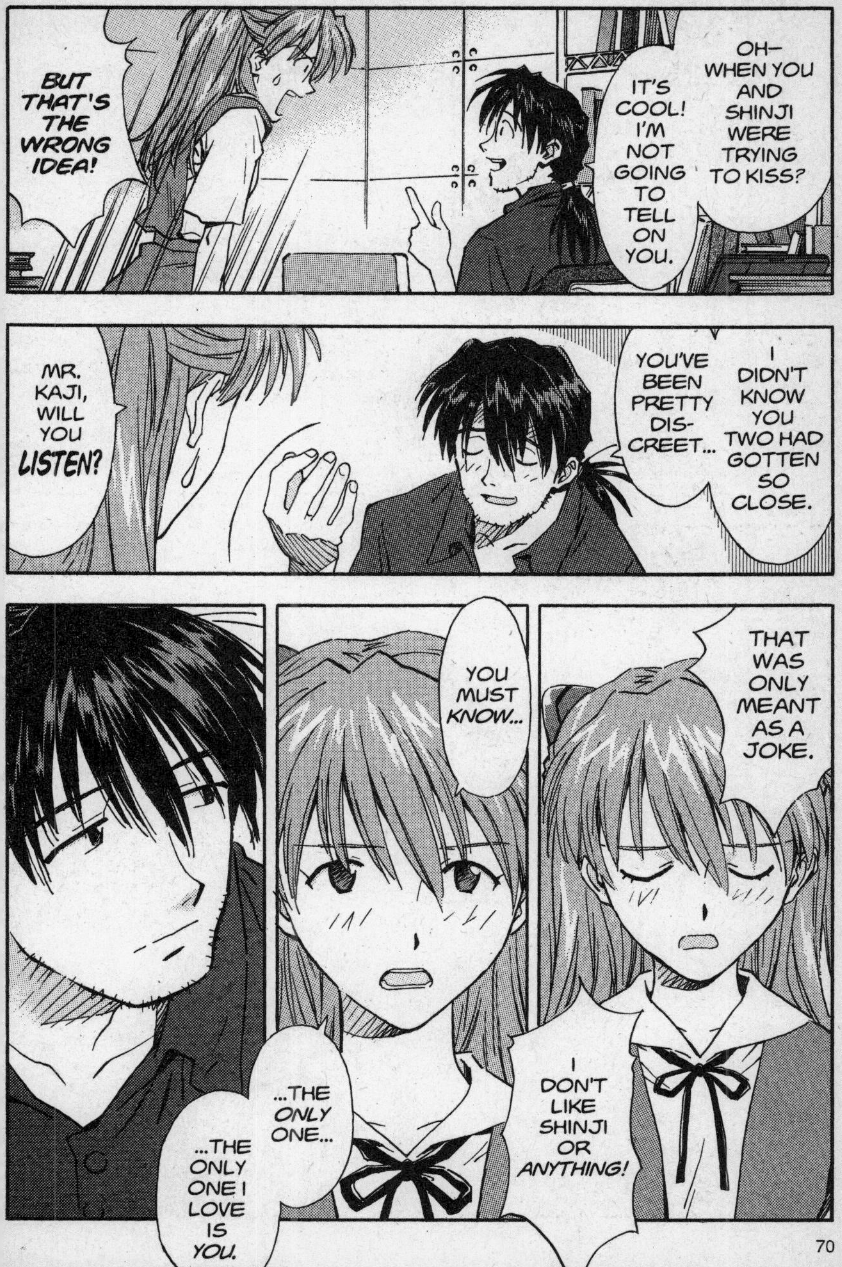
OH— WHEN YOU AND SHINJI WERE TRYING TO KISS?
IT'S COOL! I'M NOT GOING TO TELL ON YOU.
BUT THAT'S THE WRONG IDEA!
I DIDN'T KNOW YOU TWO HAD GOTTEN SO CLOSE.
YOU'VE BEEN PRETTY DIS-CREET...
MR. KAJI, WILL YOU LISTEN?
THAT WAS ONLY MEANT AS A JOKE.
I DON'T LIKE SHINJI OR ANYTHING!
YOU MUST KNOW...
...THE ONLY ONE...
...THE ONLY ONE I LOVE IS YOU.

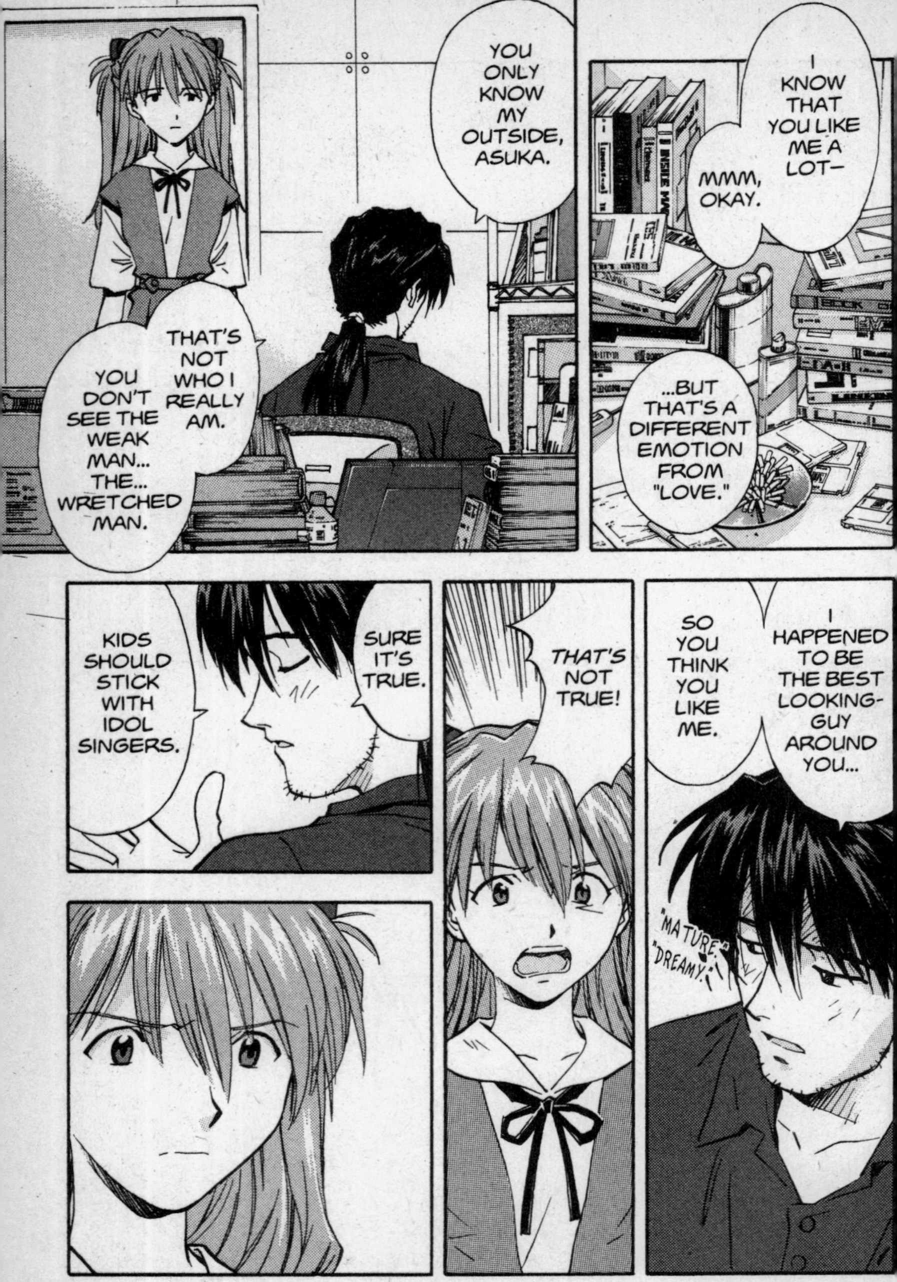
I KNOW THAT YOU LIKE ME A LOT—
MMM, OKAY.
...BUT THAT'S A DIFFERENT EMOTION FROM "LOVE."
YOU ONLY KNOW MY OUTSIDE, ASUKA.
THAT'S NOT WHO I REALLY AM.
YOU DON'T SEE THE WEAK MAN... THE... WRETCHED MAN.
I HAPPENED TO BE THE BEST LOOKING-GUY AROUND YOU...
SO YOU THINK YOU LIKE ME.
"MATURE."
"DREAMY."
THAT'S NOT TRUE!
SURE IT'S TRUE.
KIDS SHOULD STICK WITH IDOL SINGERS.

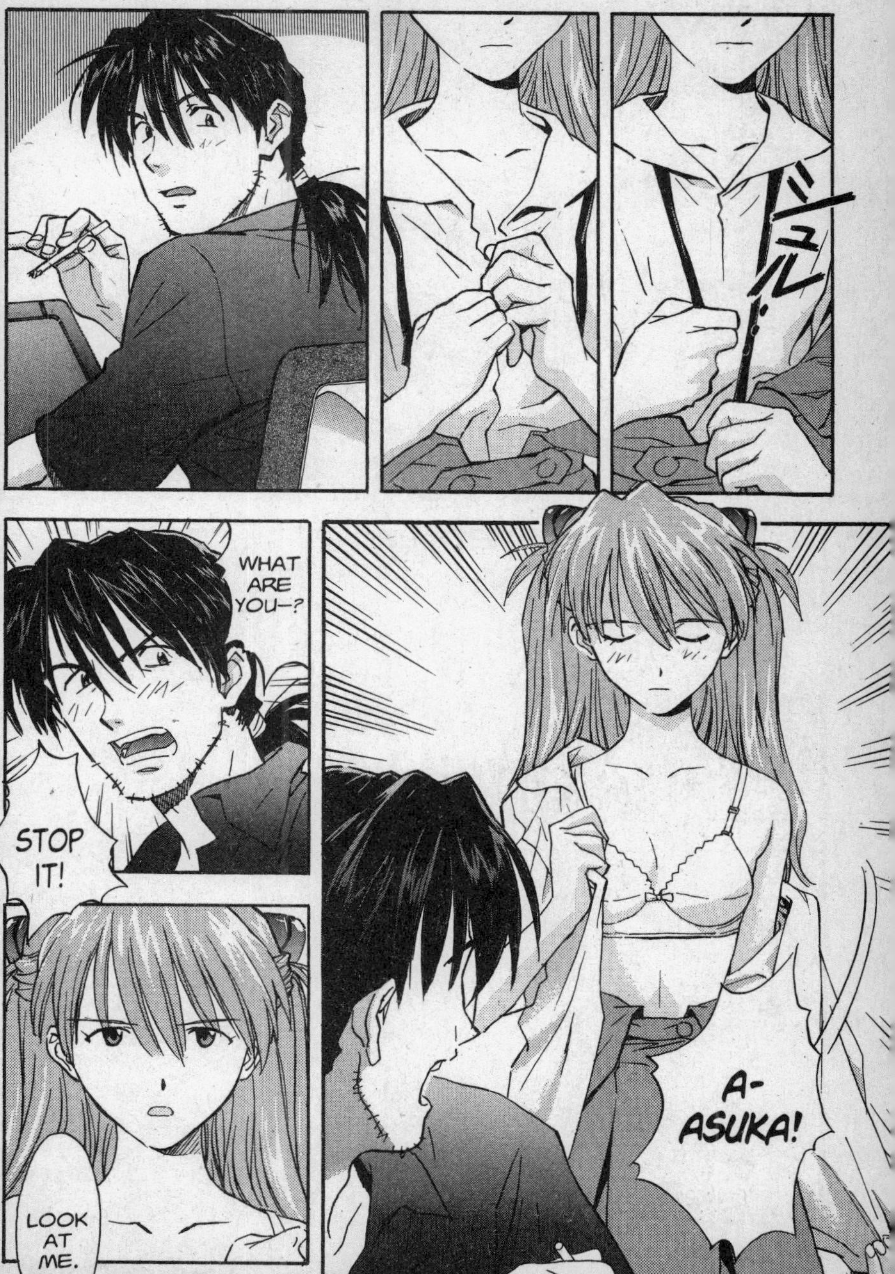
シュル
A- ASUKA!
WHAT ARE YOU—?
STOP IT!
LOOK AT ME.

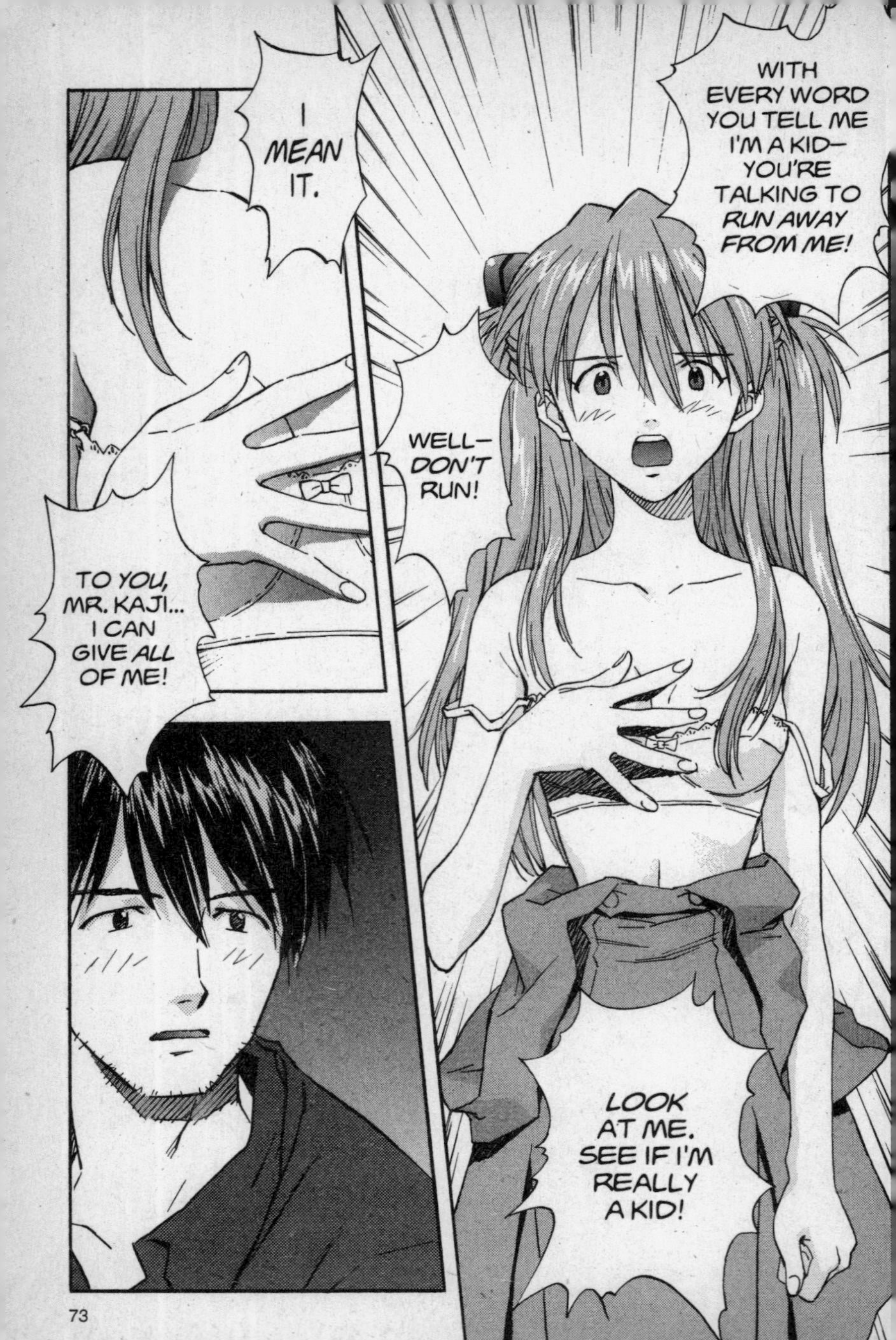
WITH EVERY WORD YOU TELL ME I'M A KID— YOU'RE TALKING TO RUN AWAY FROM ME!
WELL— DON'T RUN!
I MEAN IT.
TO YOU, MR. KAJI... I CAN GIVE ALL OF ME!
LOOK AT ME. SEE IF I'M REALLY A KID!

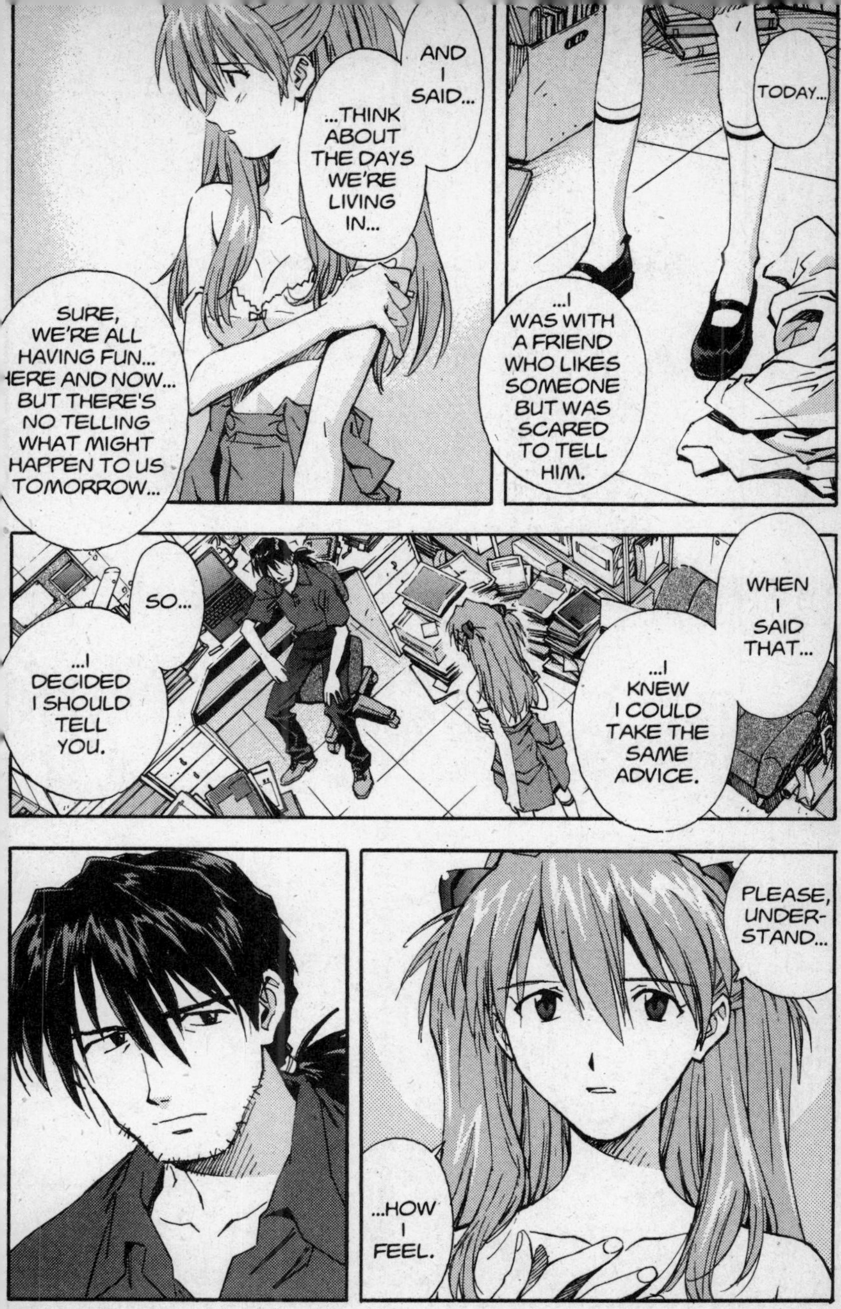
TODAY...
...I WAS WITH A FRIEND WHO LIKES SOMEONE BUT WAS SCARED TO TELL HIM.
AND I SAID...
...THINK ABOUT THE DAYS WE'RE LIVING IN...
SURE, WE'RE ALL HAVING FUN... HERE AND NOW... BUT THERE'S NO TELLING WHAT MIGHT HAPPEN TO US TOMORROW...
WHEN I SAID THAT...
...I KNEW I COULD TAKE THE SAME ADVICE.
SO...
...I DECIDED I SHOULD TELL YOU.
PLEASE, UNDER-STAND...
...HOW I FEEL.

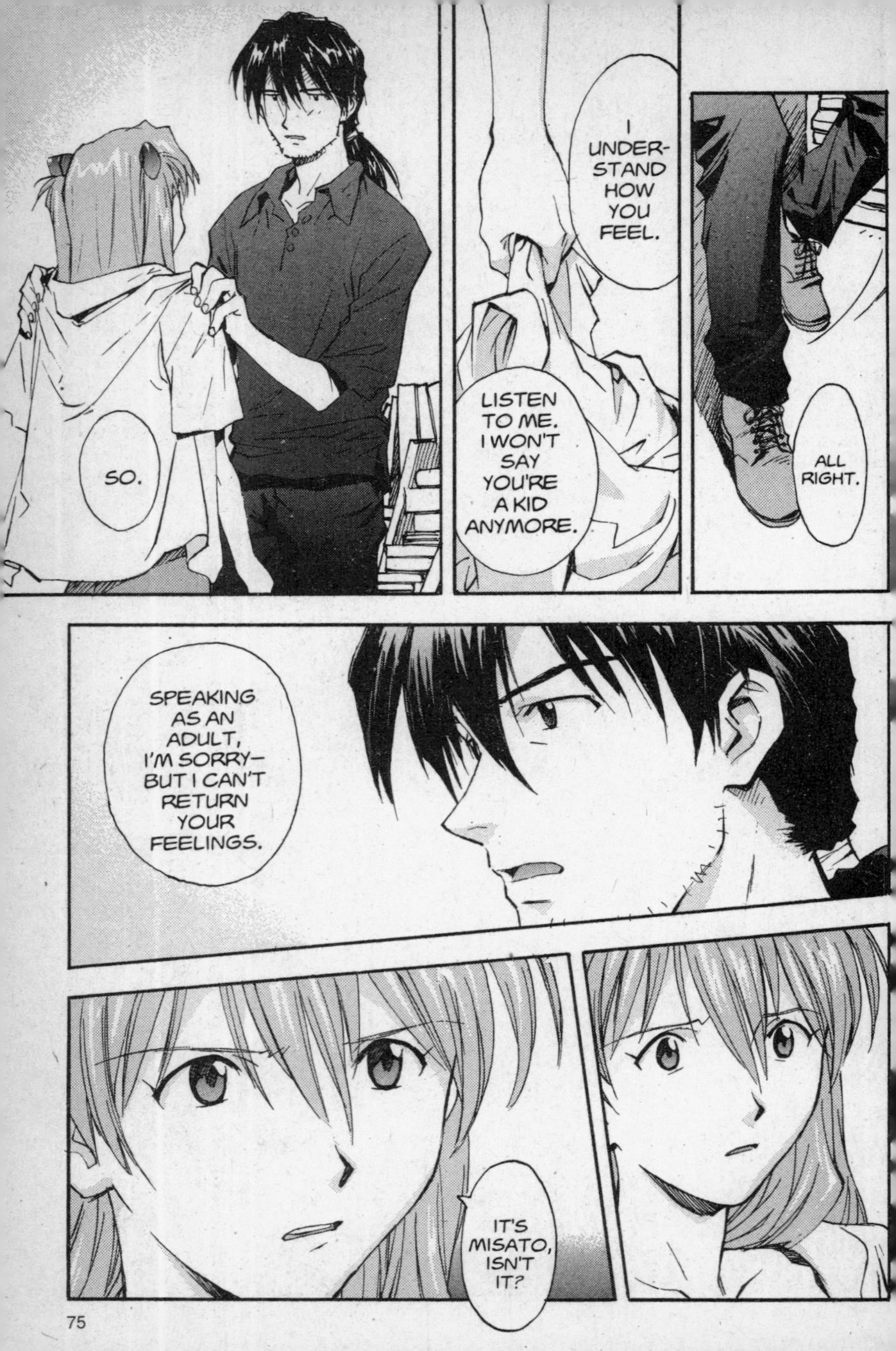
ALL RIGHT.
I UNDER-STAND HOW YOU FEEL.
LISTEN TO ME. I WON'T SAY YOU'RE A KID ANYMORE.
SO.
SPEAKING AS AN ADULT, I'M SORRY— BUT I CAN'T RETURN YOUR FEELINGS.
IT'S MISATO, ISN'T IT?

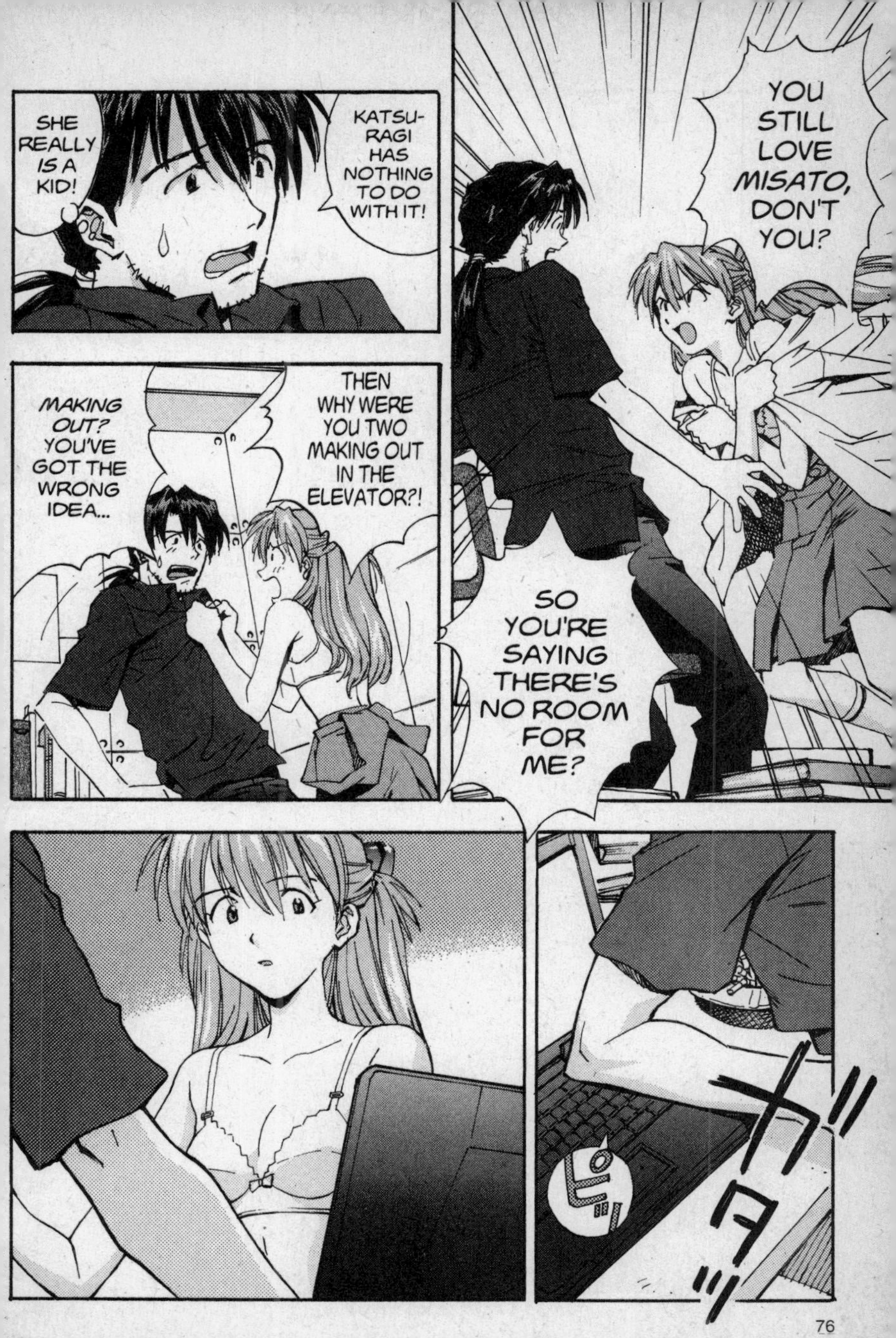
YOU STILL LOVE MISATO, DON'T YOU?
KATSU-RAGI HAS NOTHING TO DO WITH IT!
SHE REALLY IS A KID!
THEN WHY WERE YOU TWO MAKING OUT IN THE ELEVATOR?!
MAKING OUT? YOU'VE GOT THE WRONG IDEA...
SO YOU'RE SAYING THERE'S NO ROOM FOR ME?
ガタッ

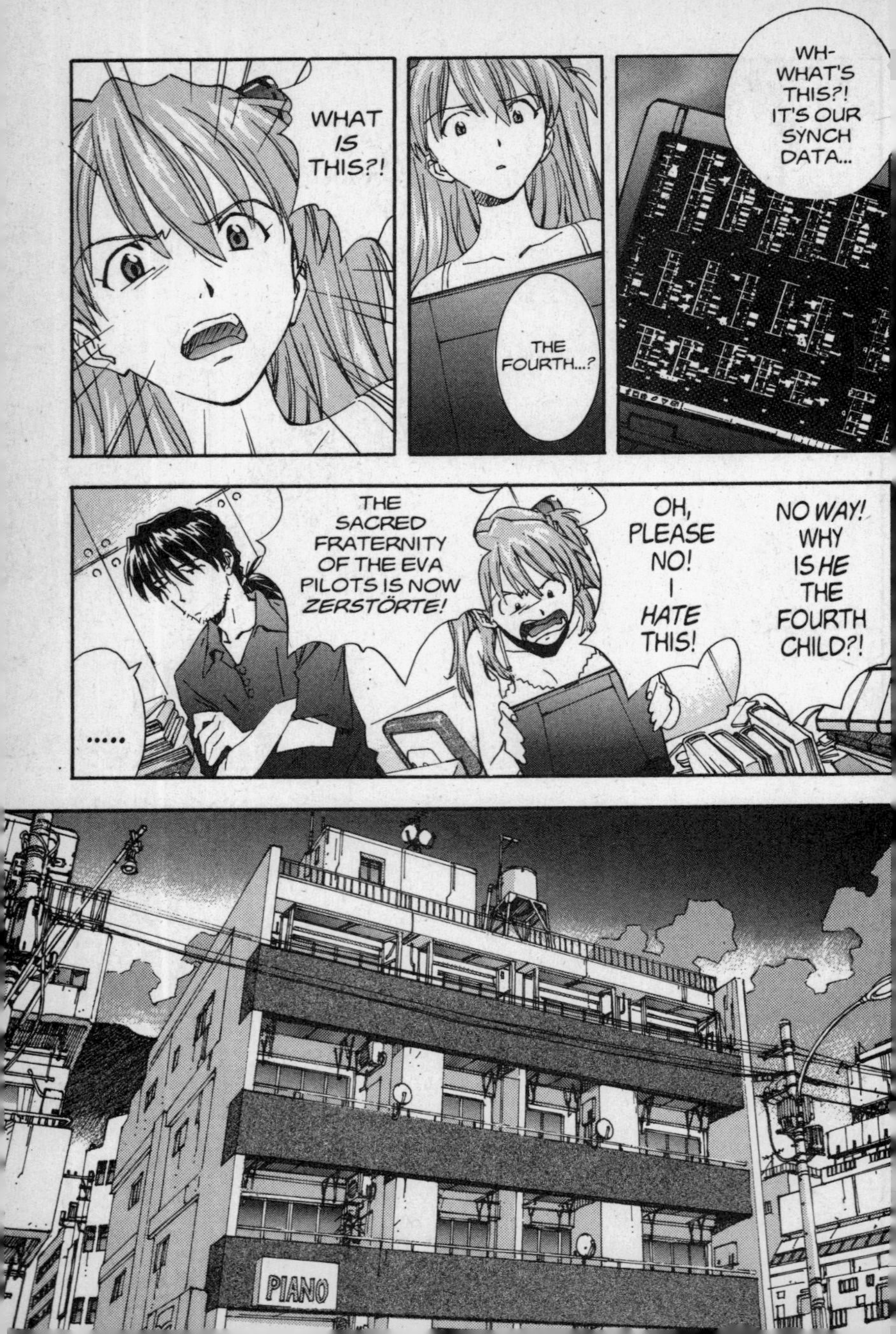
WH- WHAT'S THIS?! IT'S OUR SYNCH DATA...
THE FOURTH...?
WHAT IS THIS?!
NO WAY! WHY IS HE THE FOURTH CHILD?!
OH, PLEASE NO! I HATE THIS!
THE SACRED FRATERNITY OF THE EVA PILOTS IS NOW ZERSTÖRTE!
.....
PIANO

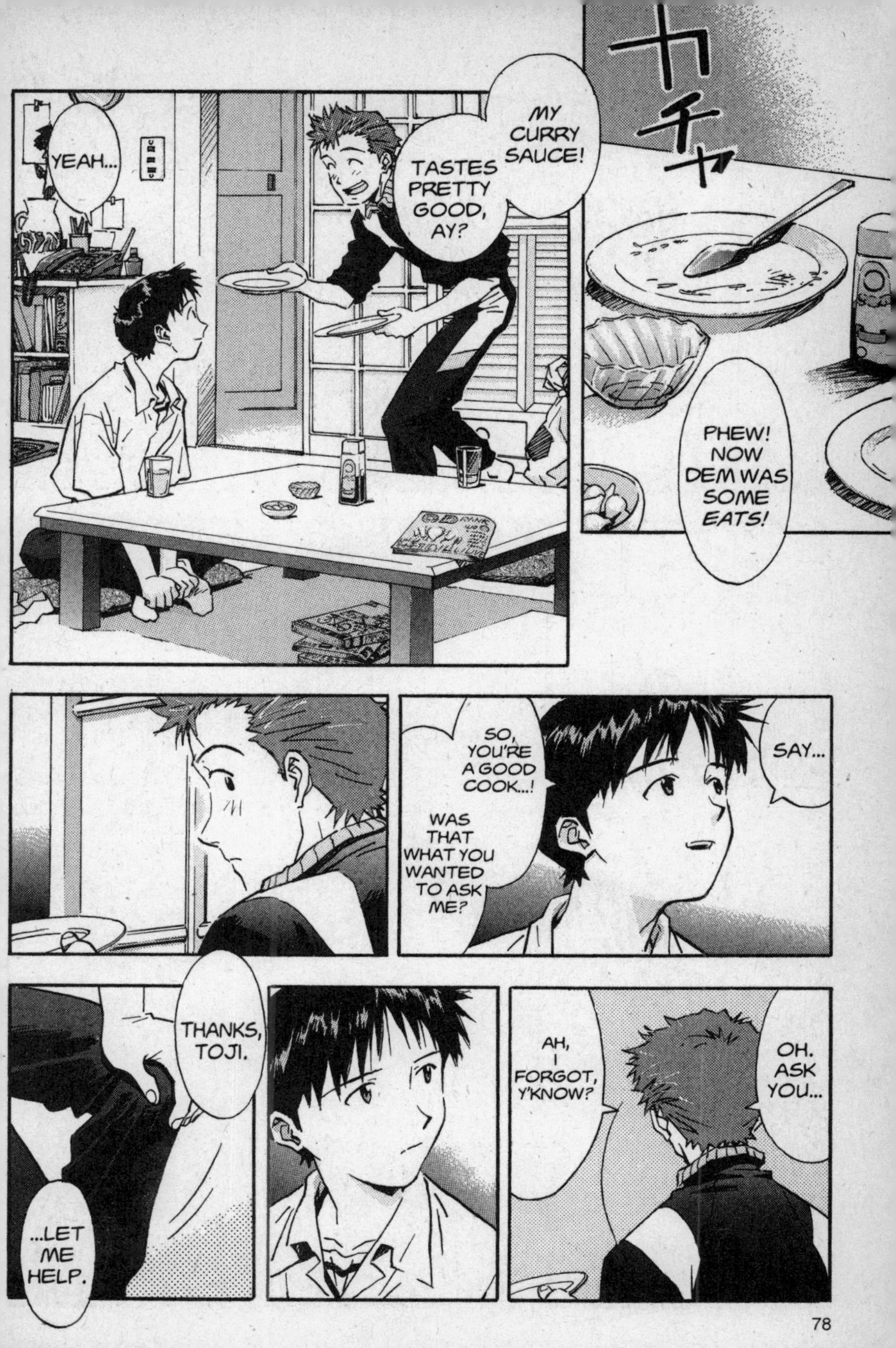
カチャ
PHEW! NOW DEM WAS SOME EATS!
MY CURRY SAUCE!
TASTES PRETTY GOOD, AY?
YEAH...
SAY...
SO, YOU'RE A GOOD COOK...!
WAS THAT WHAT YOU WANTED TO ASK ME?
OH. ASK YOU...
AH, I FORGOT, Y'KNOW?
THANKS, TOJI.
...LET ME HELP.

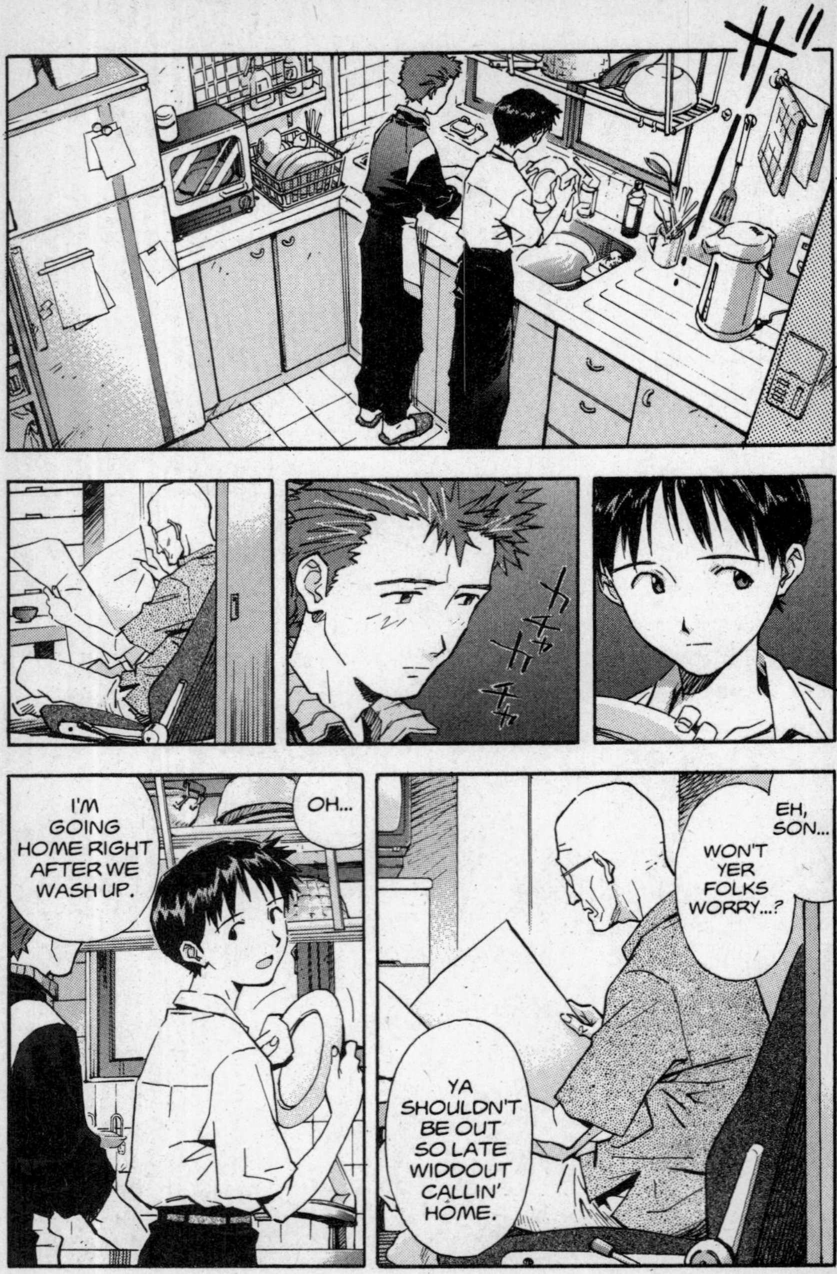
EH, SON... WON'T YER FOLKS WORRY...?
YA SHOULDN'T BE OUT SO LATE WIDDOUT CALLIN' HOME.
OH...
I'M GOING HOME RIGHT AFTER WE WASH UP.

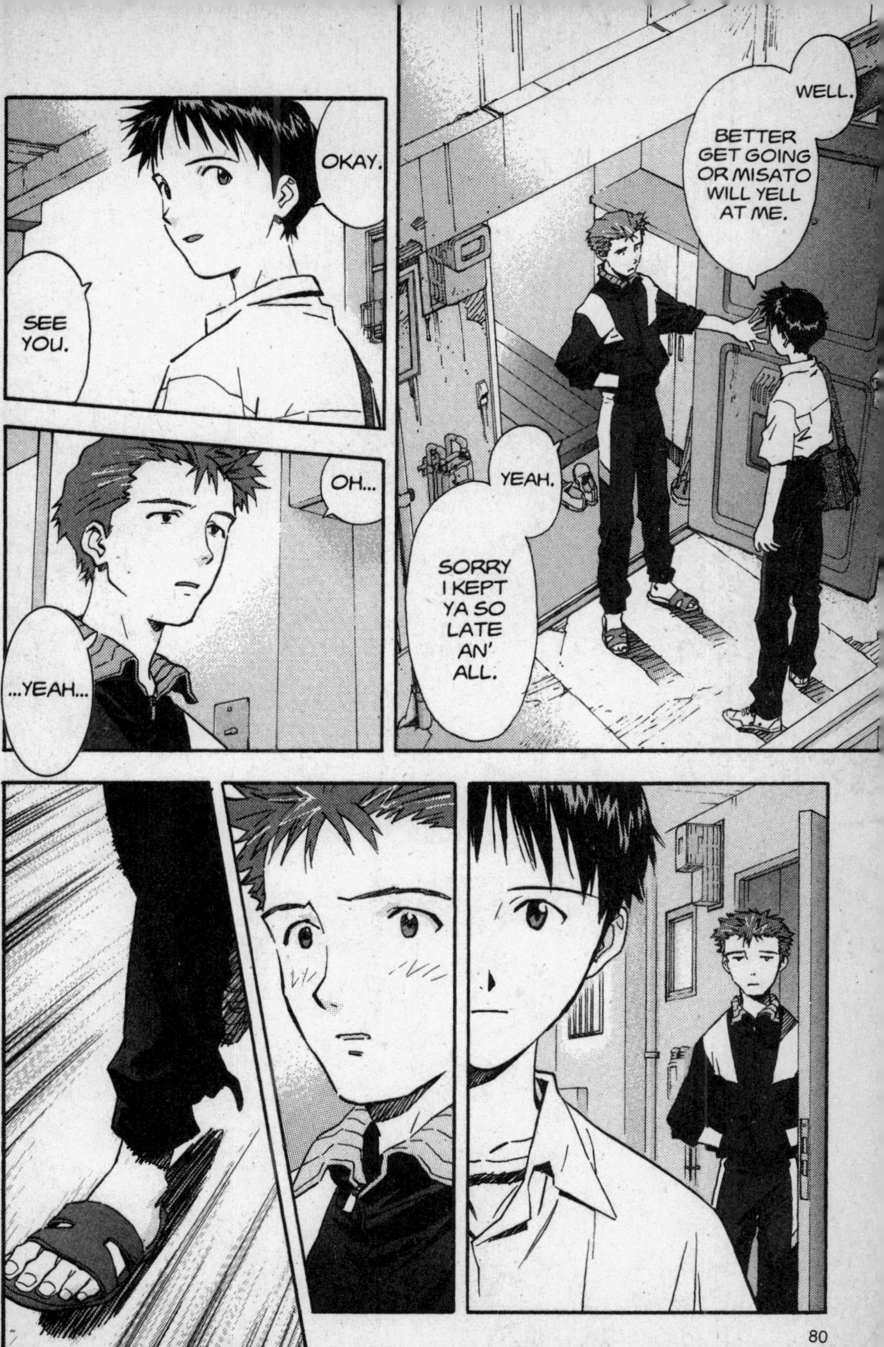
WELL.
BETTER GET GOING OR MISATO WILL YELL AT ME.
YEAH.
SORRY I KEPT YA SO LATE AN' ALL.
OKAY.
SEE YOU.
OH...
...YEAH...

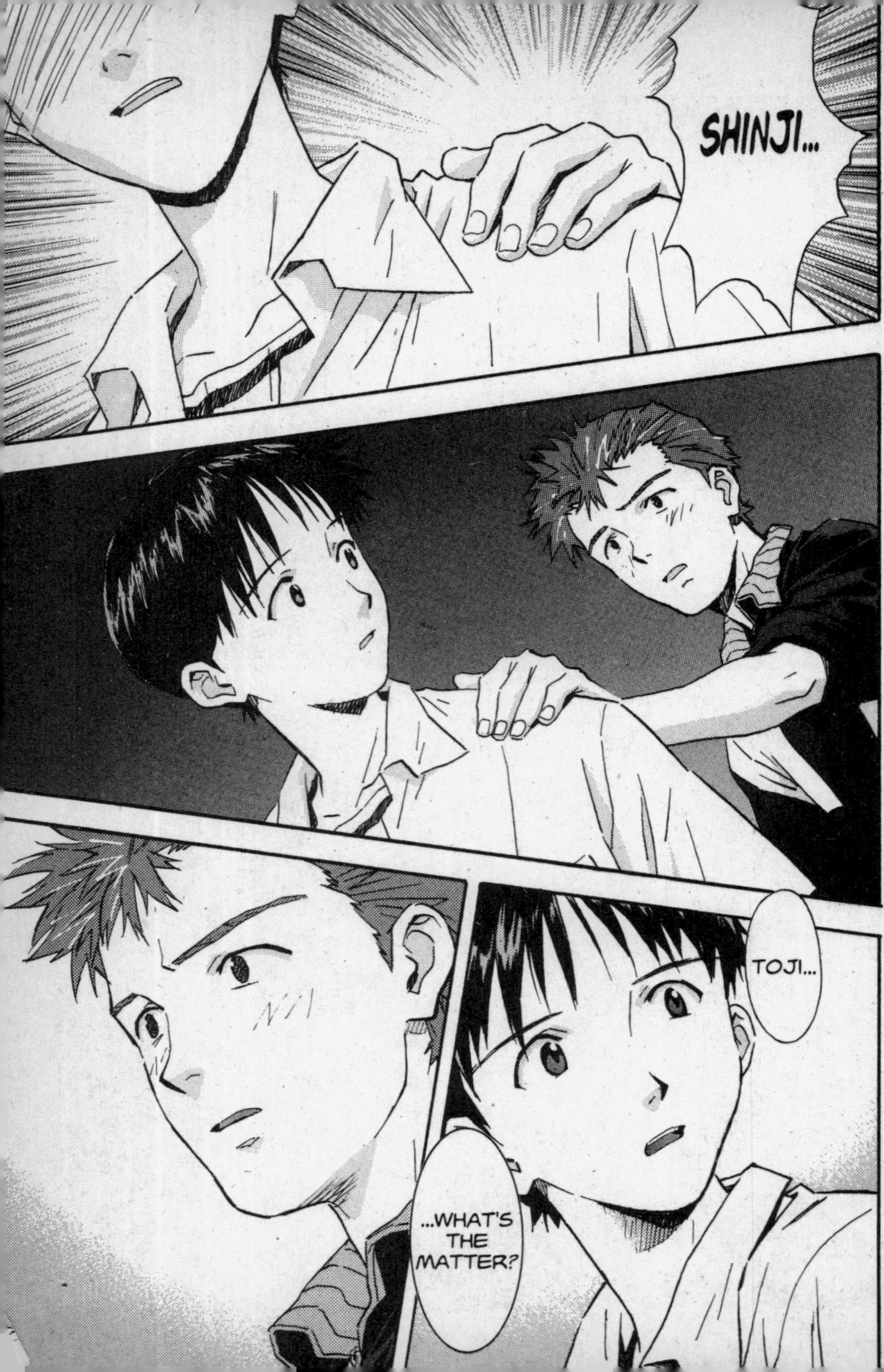
SHINJI...
TOJI...
...WHAT'S THE MATTER?

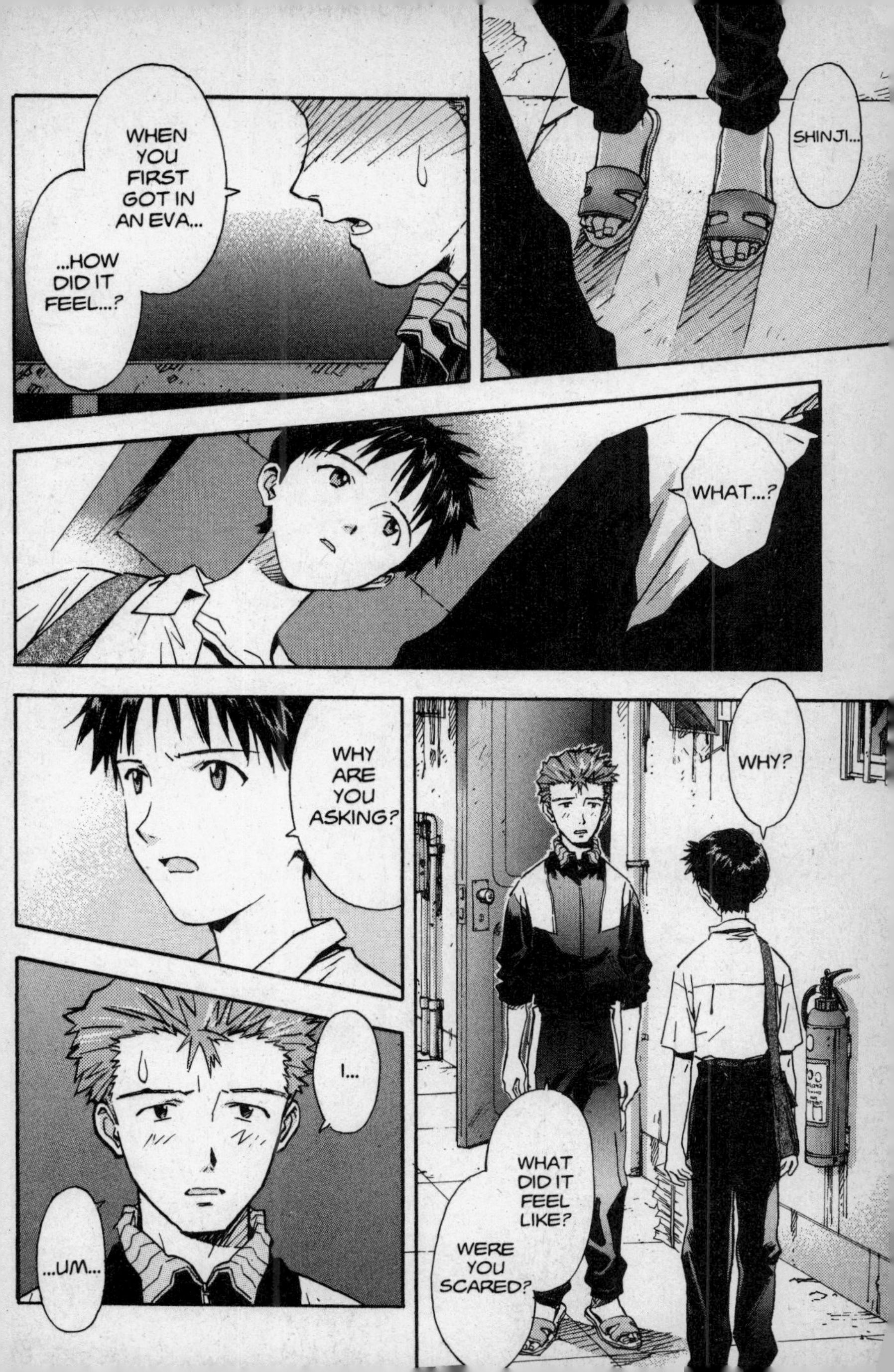
SHINJI...
WHEN YOU FIRST GOT IN AN EVA...
...HOW DID IT FEEL...?
WHAT...?
WHY?
WHY ARE YOU ASKING?
I...
...UM...
WHAT DID IT FEEL LIKE?
WERE YOU SCARED?

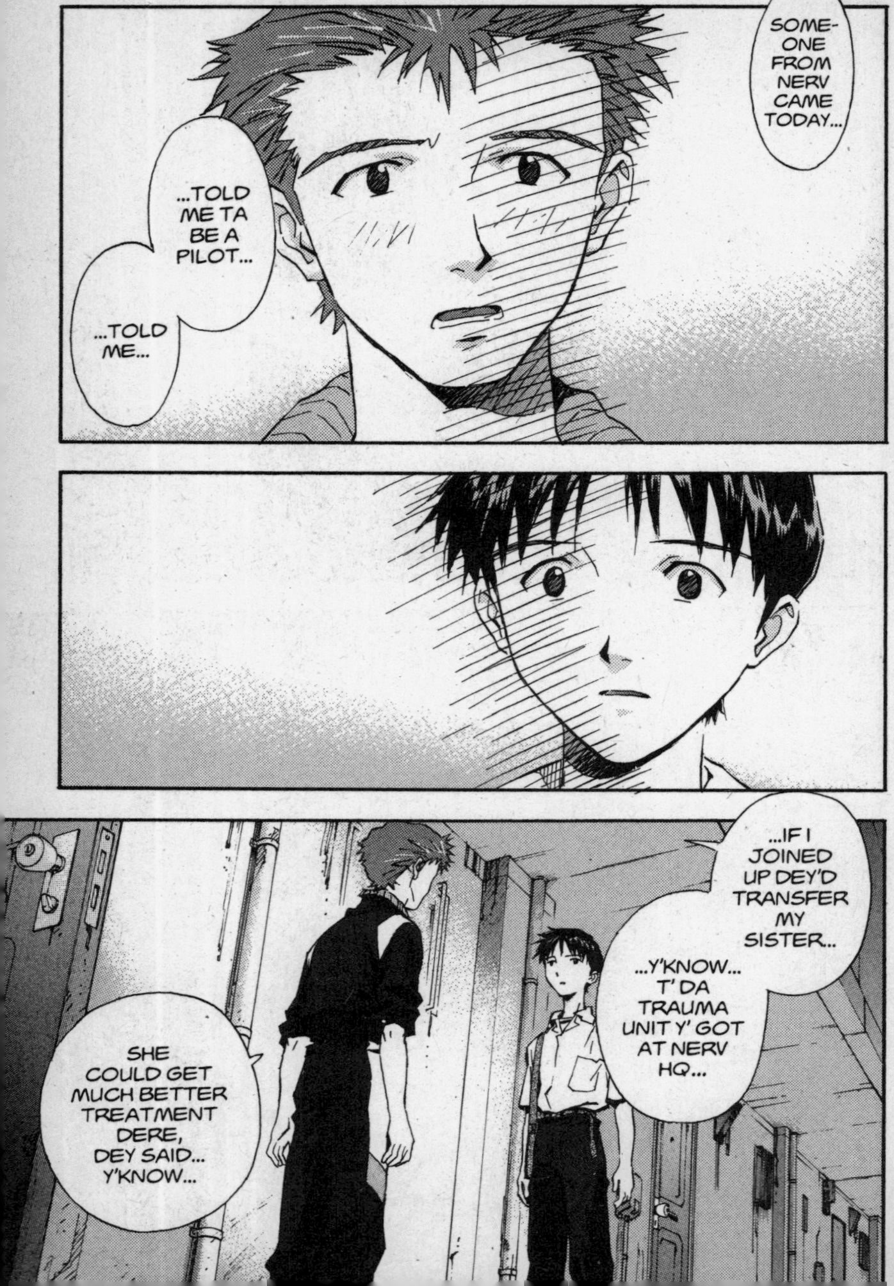
SOME-ONE FROM NERV CAME TODAY...
...TOLD ME TA BE A PILOT...
...TOLD ME...
...IF I JOINED UP DEY'D TRANSFER MY SISTER...
...Y'KNOW... T' DA TRAUMA UNIT Y' GOT AT NERV HQ...
SHE COULD GET MUCH BETTER TREATMENT DERE, DEY SAID... Y'KNOW...

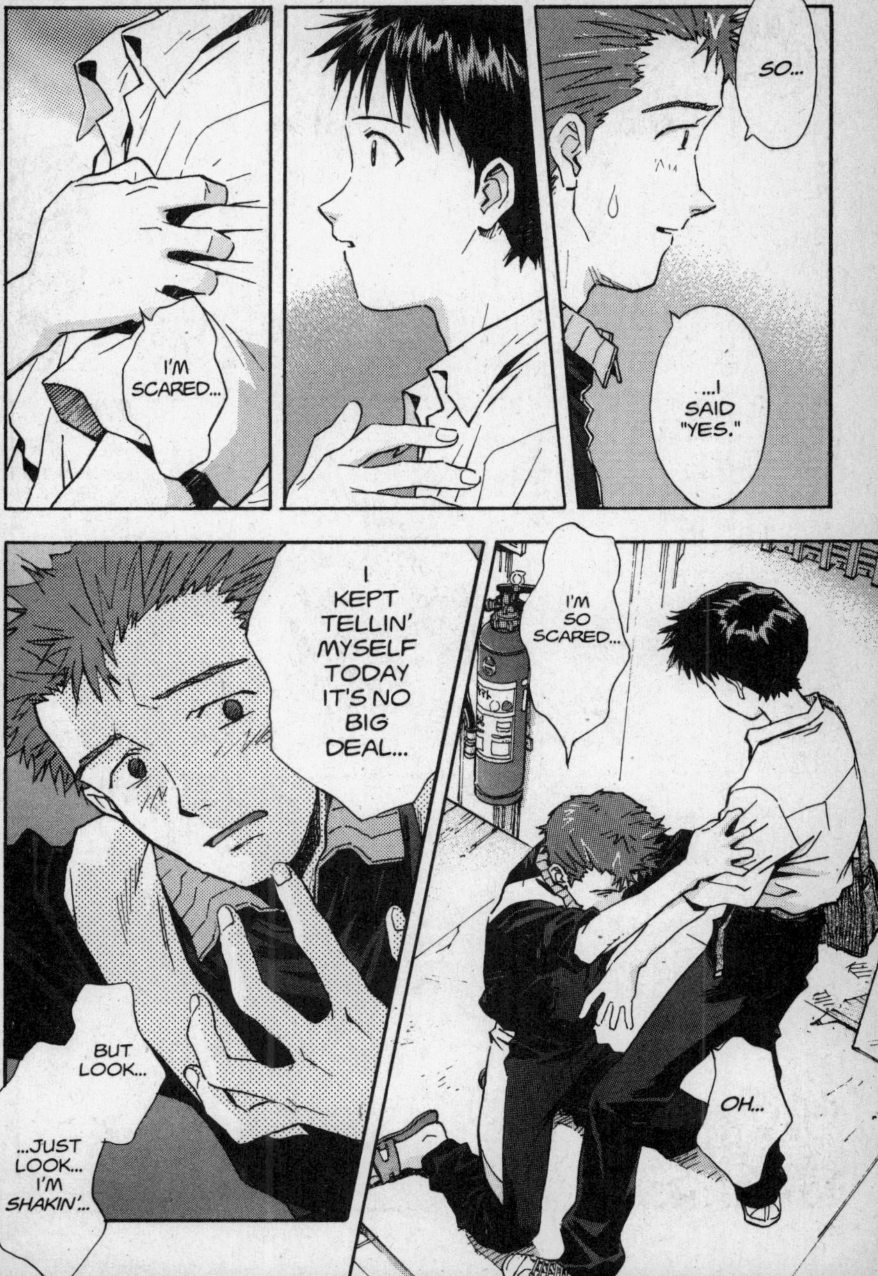
SO...
...I SAID "YES."
I'M SCARED...
I'M SO SCARED...
OH...
I KEPT TELLIN' MYSELF TODAY IT'S NO BIG DEAL...
BUT LOOK...
...JUST LOOK... I'M SHAKIN'...

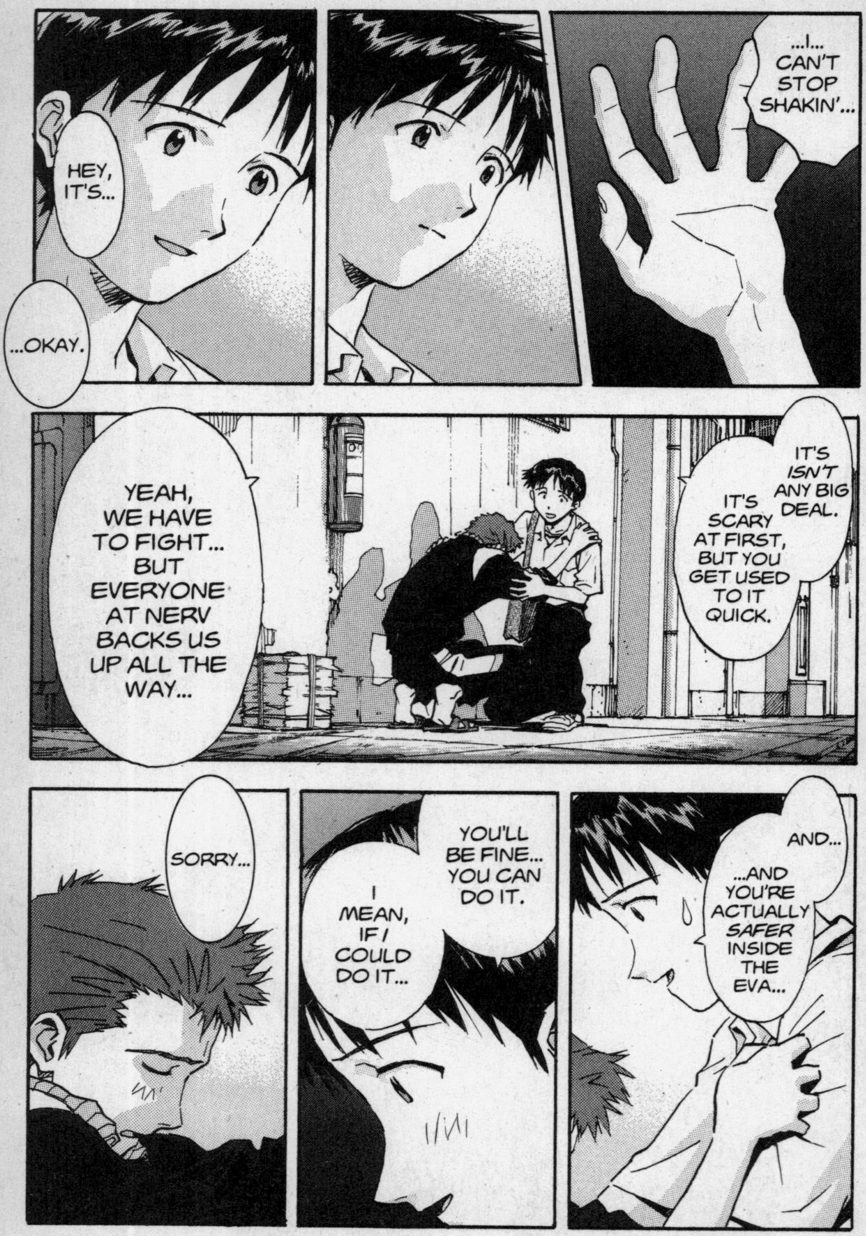
...I... CAN'T STOP SHAKIN'...
HEY, IT'S...
...OKAY.
IT'S ISN'T ANY BIG DEAL.
IT'S SCARY AT FIRST, BUT YOU GET USED TO IT QUICK.
YEAH, WE HAVE TO FIGHT... BUT EVERYONE AT NERV BACKS US UP ALL THE WAY...
AND...
...AND YOU'RE ACTUALLY *SAFER* INSIDE THE EVA...
YOU'LL BE FINE... YOU CAN DO IT.
I MEAN, IF I COULD DO IT...
SORRY...

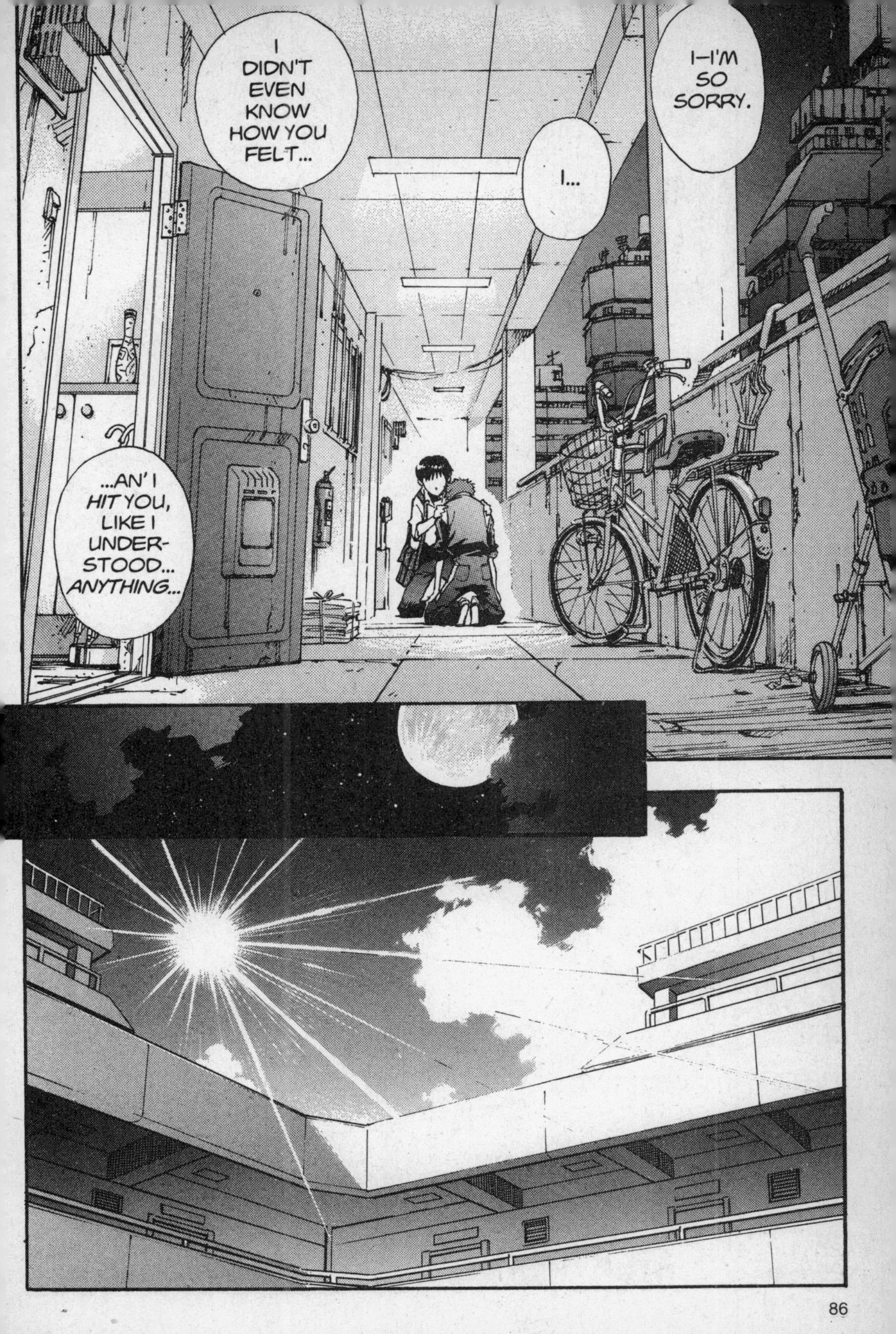
I-I'M SO SORRY.
I...
I DIDN'T EVEN KNOW HOW YOU FELT...
...AN' I *HIT* YOU, LIKE I UNDERSTOOD... ANYTHING...

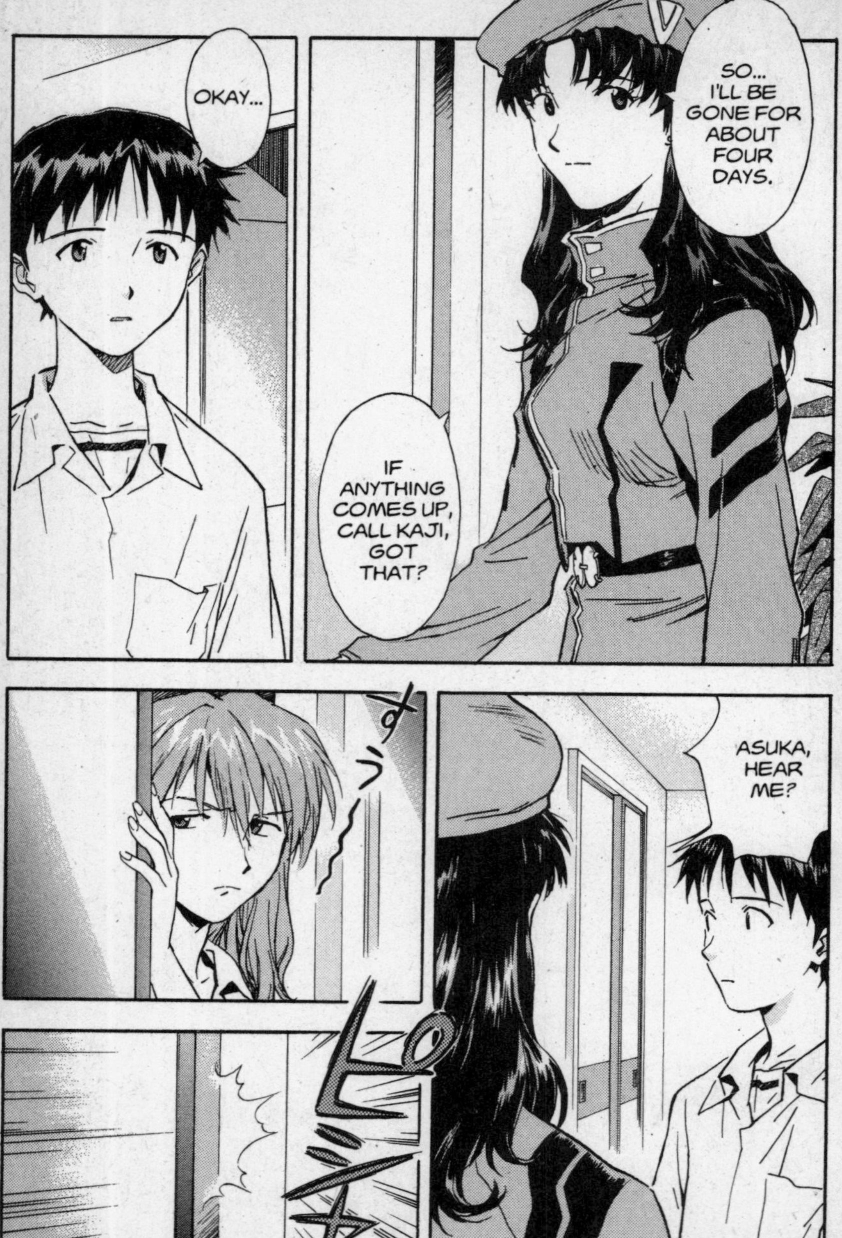
SO... I'LL BE GONE FOR ABOUT FOUR DAYS.
IF ANYTHING COMES UP, CALL KAJI, GOT THAT?
OKAY...
ASUKA, HEAR ME?

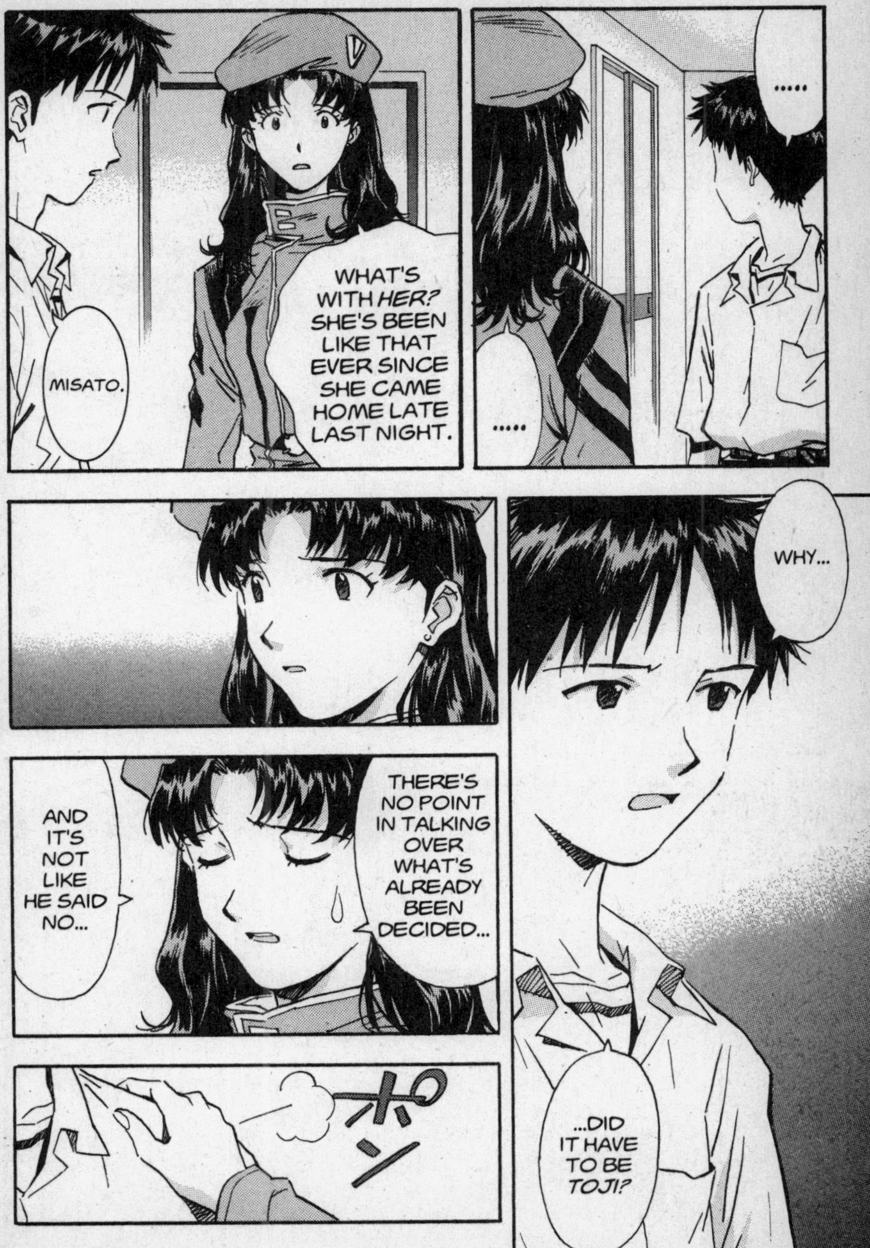
MISATO.
WHAT'S WITH *HER?* SHE'S BEEN LIKE THAT EVER SINCE SHE CAME HOME LATE LAST NIGHT.
.....
.....
WHY...
THERE'S NO POINT IN TALKING OVER WHAT'S ALREADY BEEN DECIDED...
AND IT'S NOT LIKE HE SAID NO...
ポン
...DID IT HAVE TO BE *TOJI?*

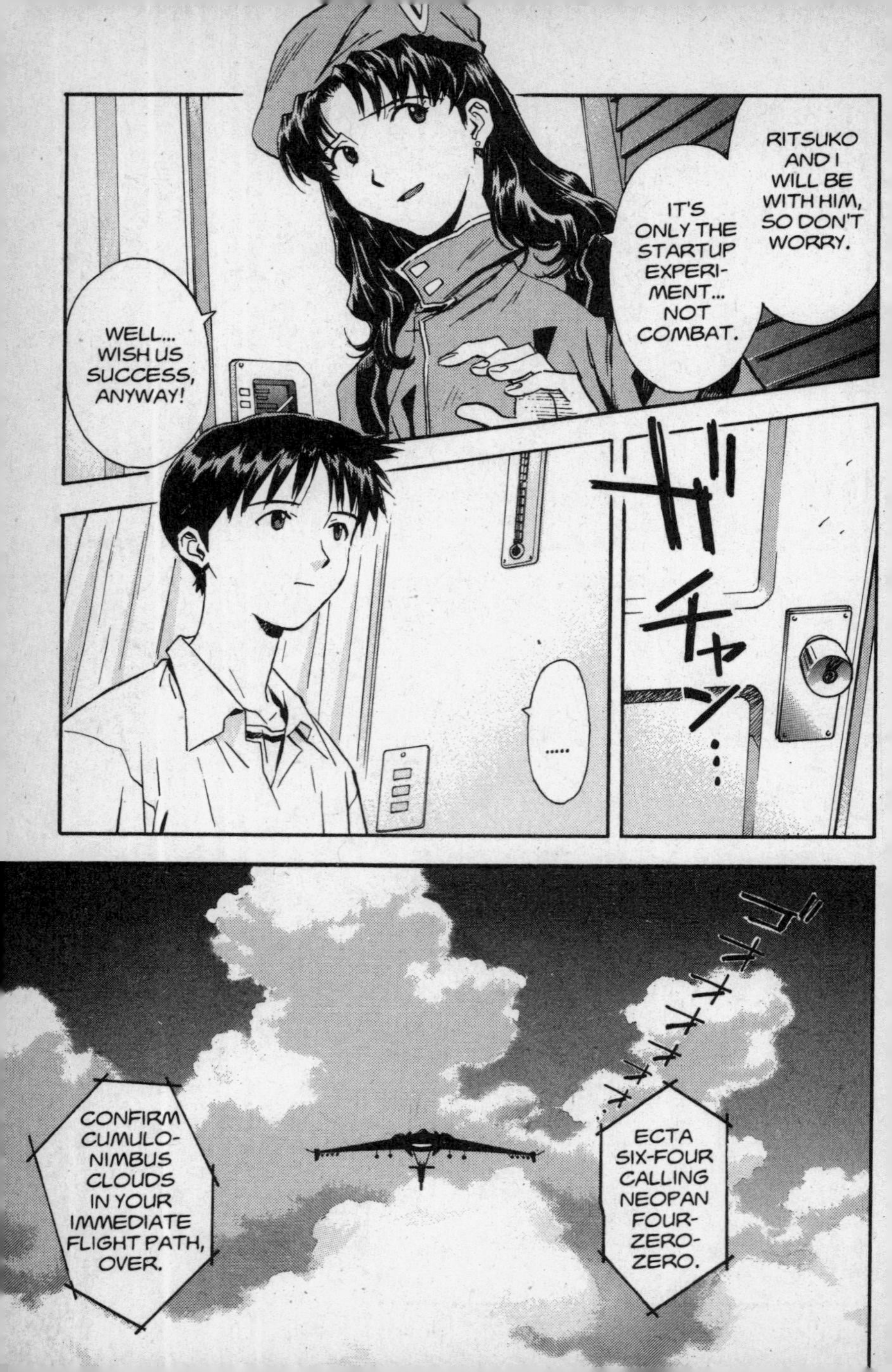
RITSUKO AND I WILL BE WITH HIM, SO DON'T WORRY.
IT'S ONLY THE STARTUP EXPERIMENT... NOT COMBAT.
WELL... WISH US SUCCESS, ANYWAY!
ガチャン…
......
ゴオオオオオオ…
ECTA SIX-FOUR CALLING NEOPAN FOUR-ZERO-ZERO.
CONFIRM CUMULO-NIMBUS CLOUDS IN YOUR IMMEDIATE FLIGHT PATH, OVER.

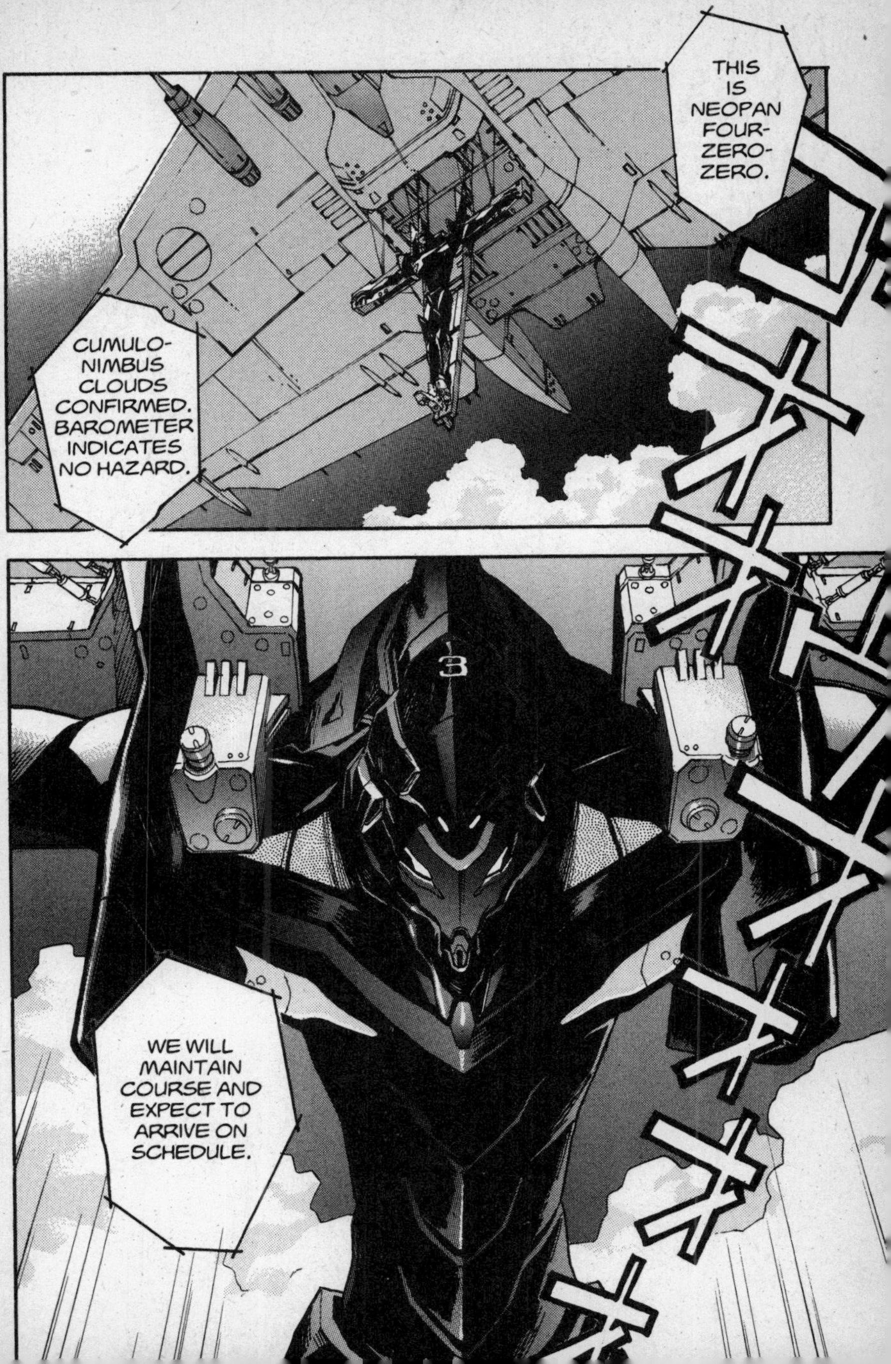
THIS IS NEOPAN FOUR-ZERO-ZERO.
CUMULO-NIMBUS CLOUDS CONFIRMED.
BAROMETER INDICATES NO HAZARD.
WE WILL MAINTAIN COURSE AND EXPECT TO ARRIVE ON SCHEDULE.

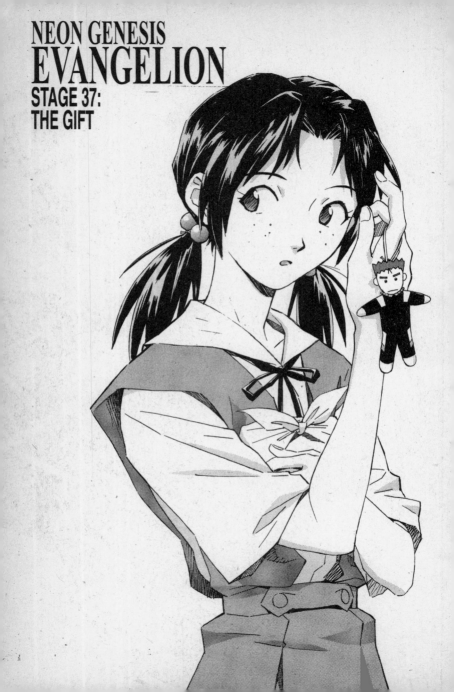

NEON GENESIS EVANGELION

STAGE 37: THE GIFT

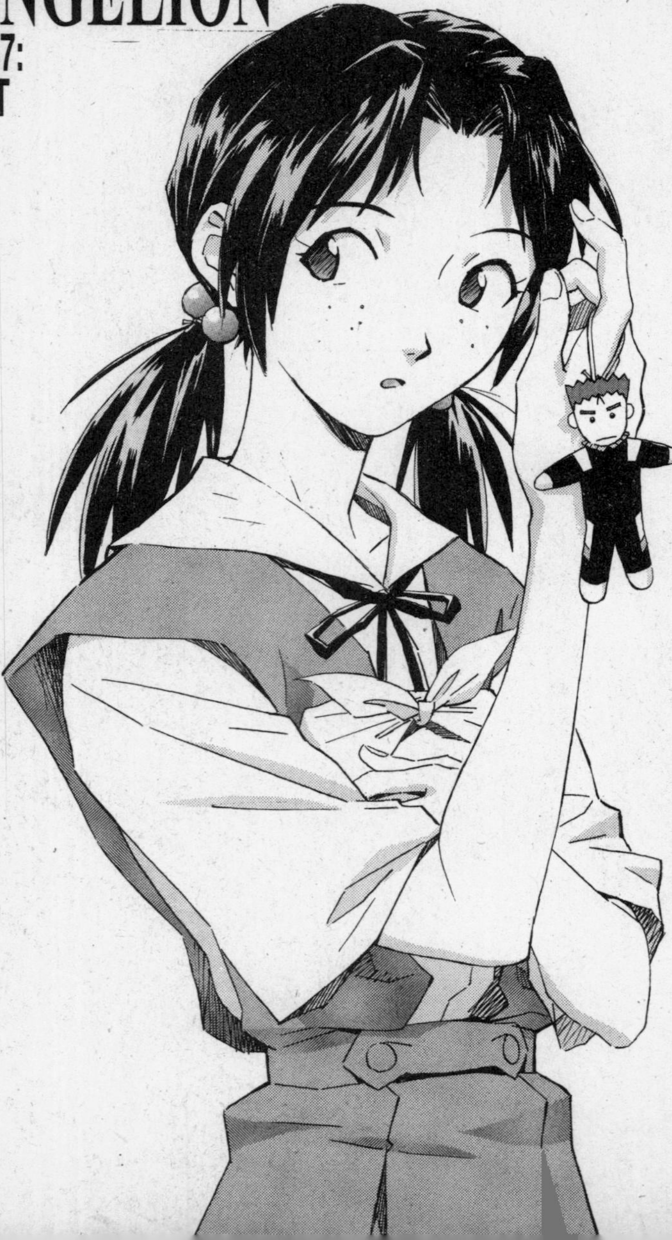

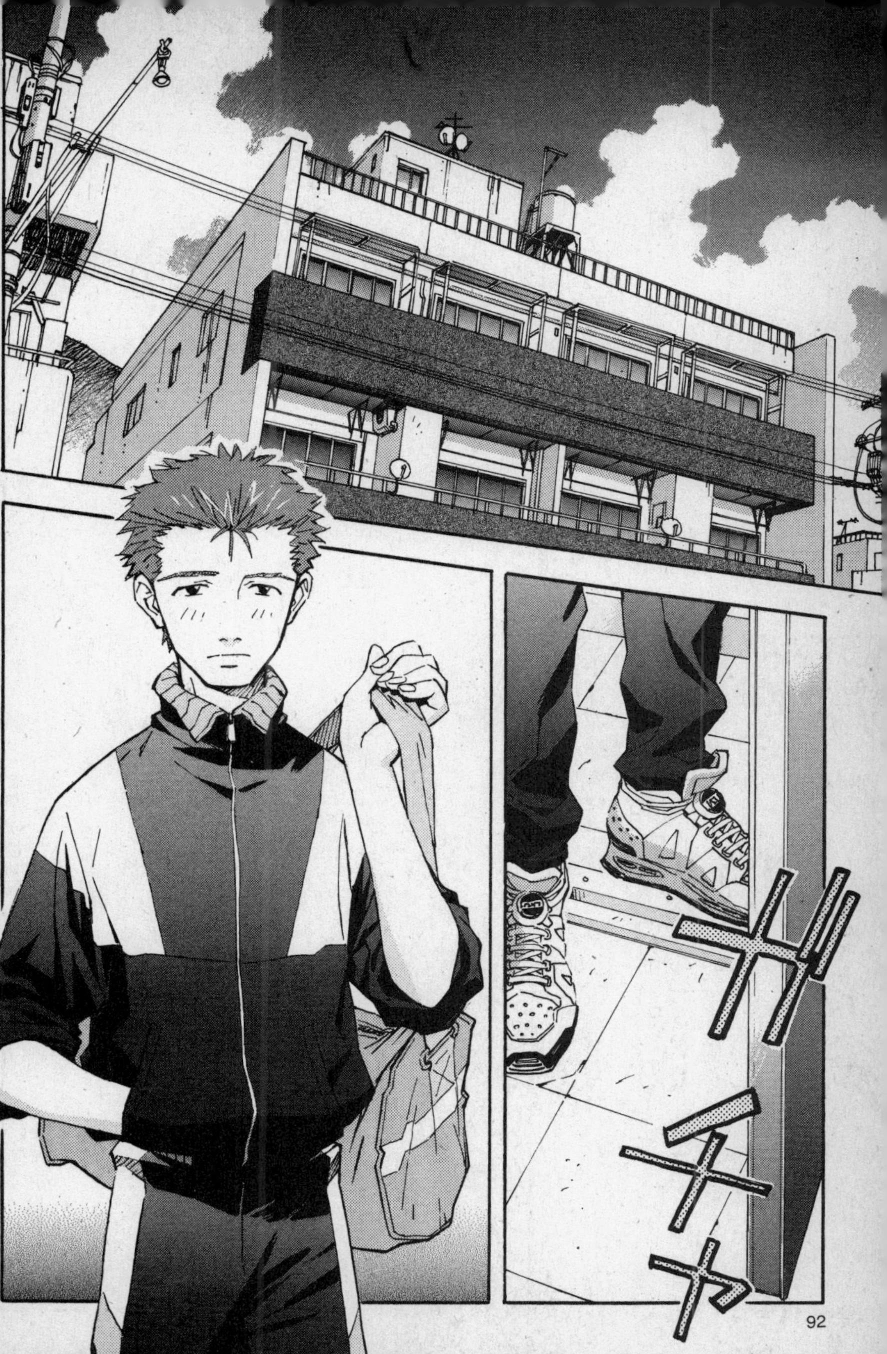

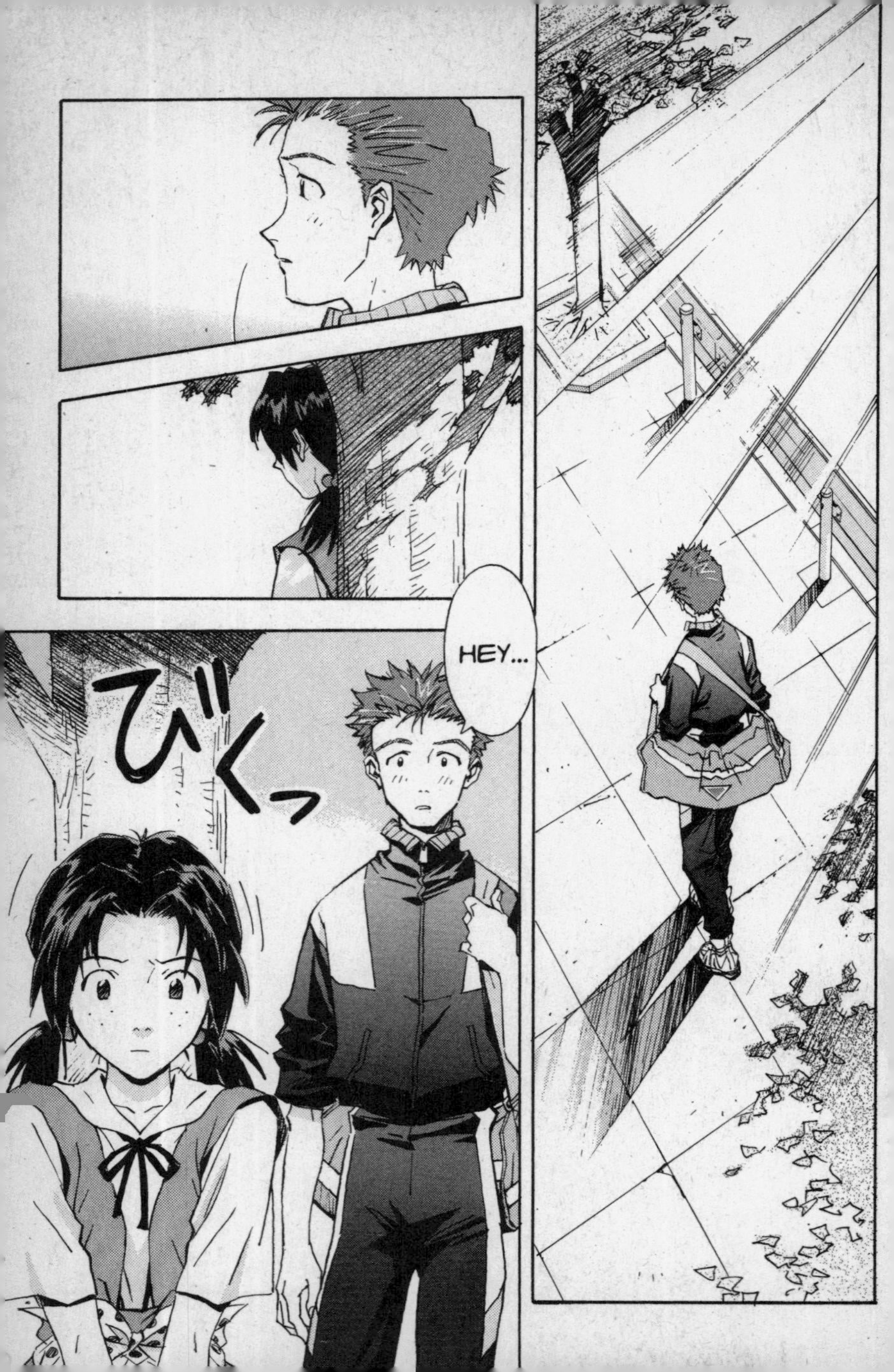
HEY...
びくっ

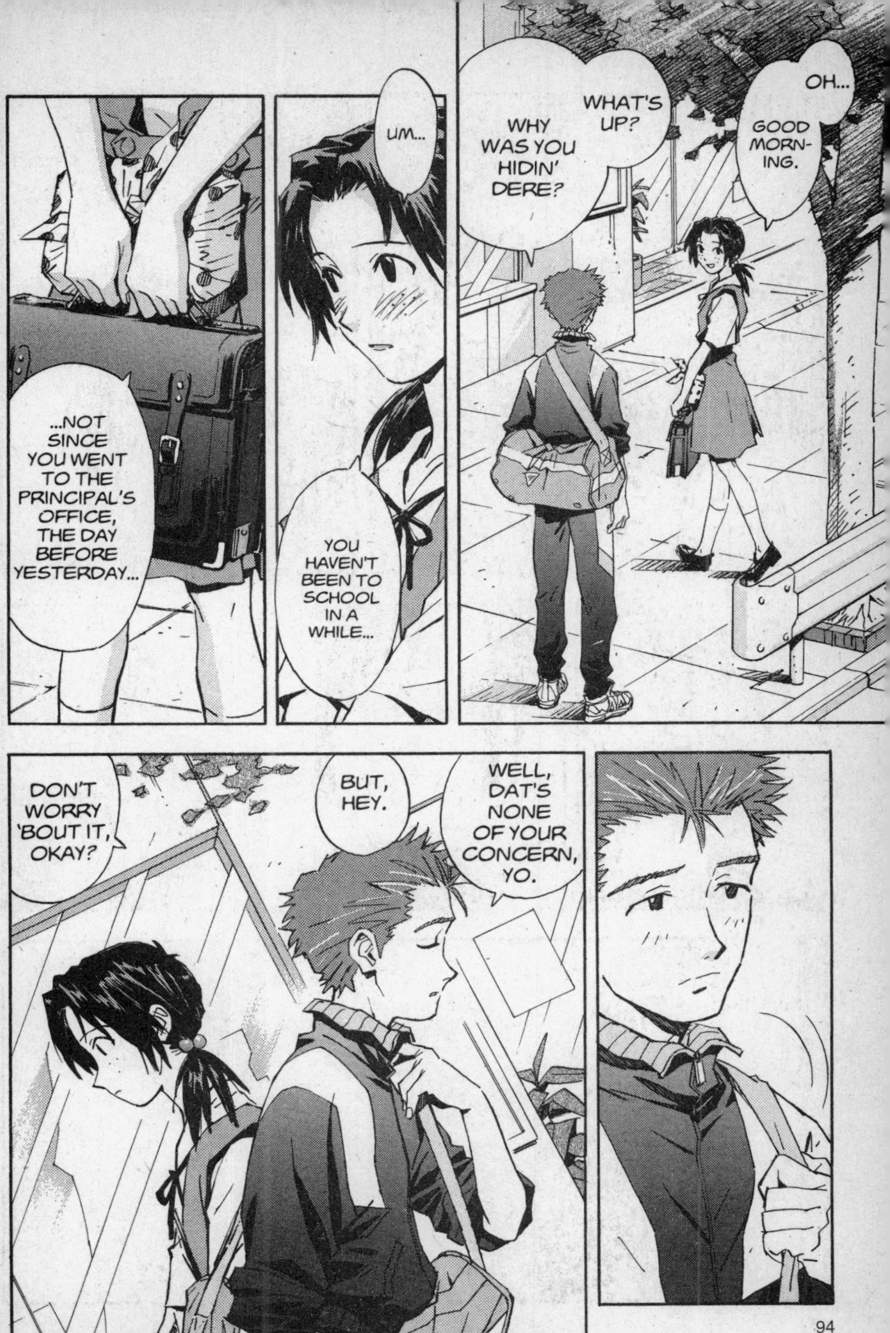
OH... GOOD MORNING.
WHAT'S UP? WHY WAS YOU HIDIN' DERE?
UM...
YOU HAVEN'T BEEN TO SCHOOL IN A WHILE...
...NOT SINCE YOU WENT TO THE PRINCIPAL'S OFFICE, THE DAY BEFORE YESTERDAY...
WELL, DAT'S NONE OF YOUR CONCERN, YO.
BUT, HEY.
DON'T WORRY 'BOUT IT, OKAY?

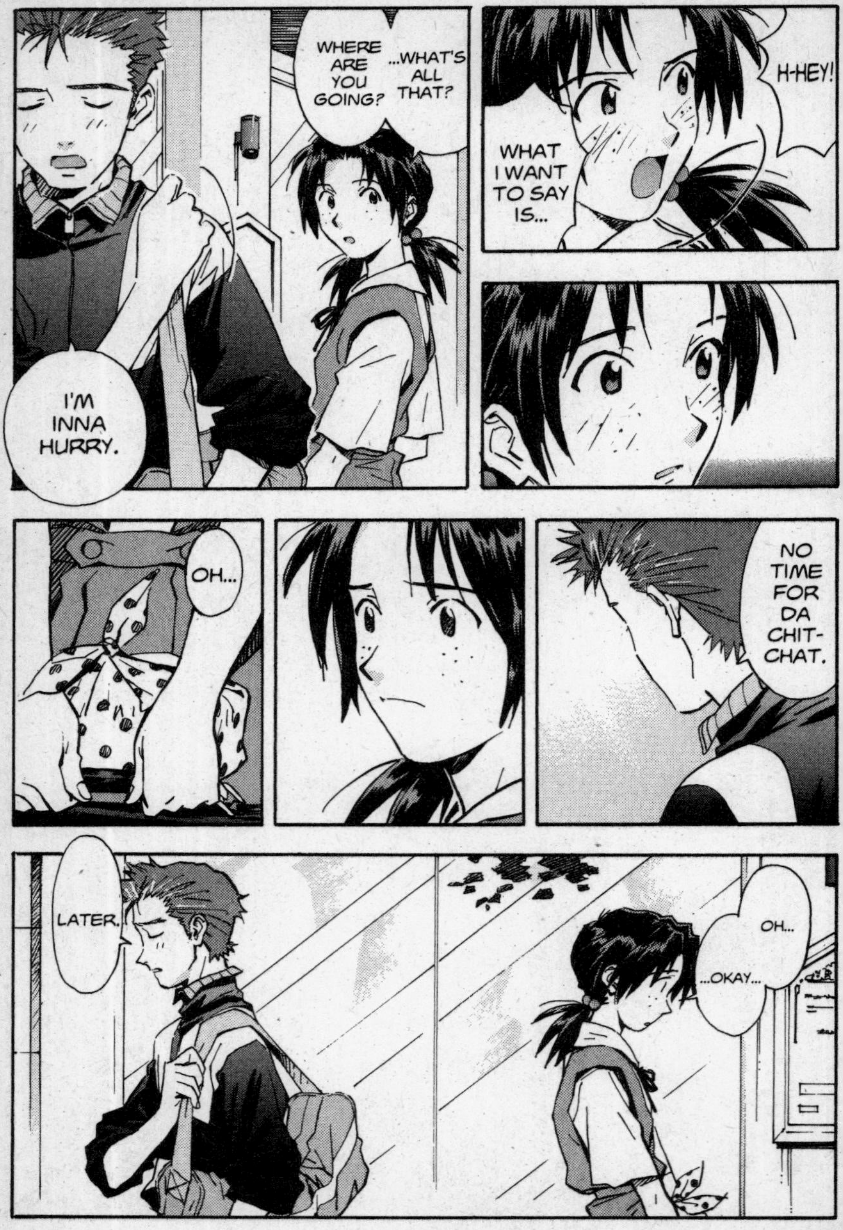
WHERE ARE YOU GOING?
...WHAT'S ALL THAT?
I'M INNA HURRY.
H-HEY!
WHAT I WANT TO SAY IS...
OH...
NO TIME FOR DA CHIT-CHAT.
LATER.
OH...
...OKAY...

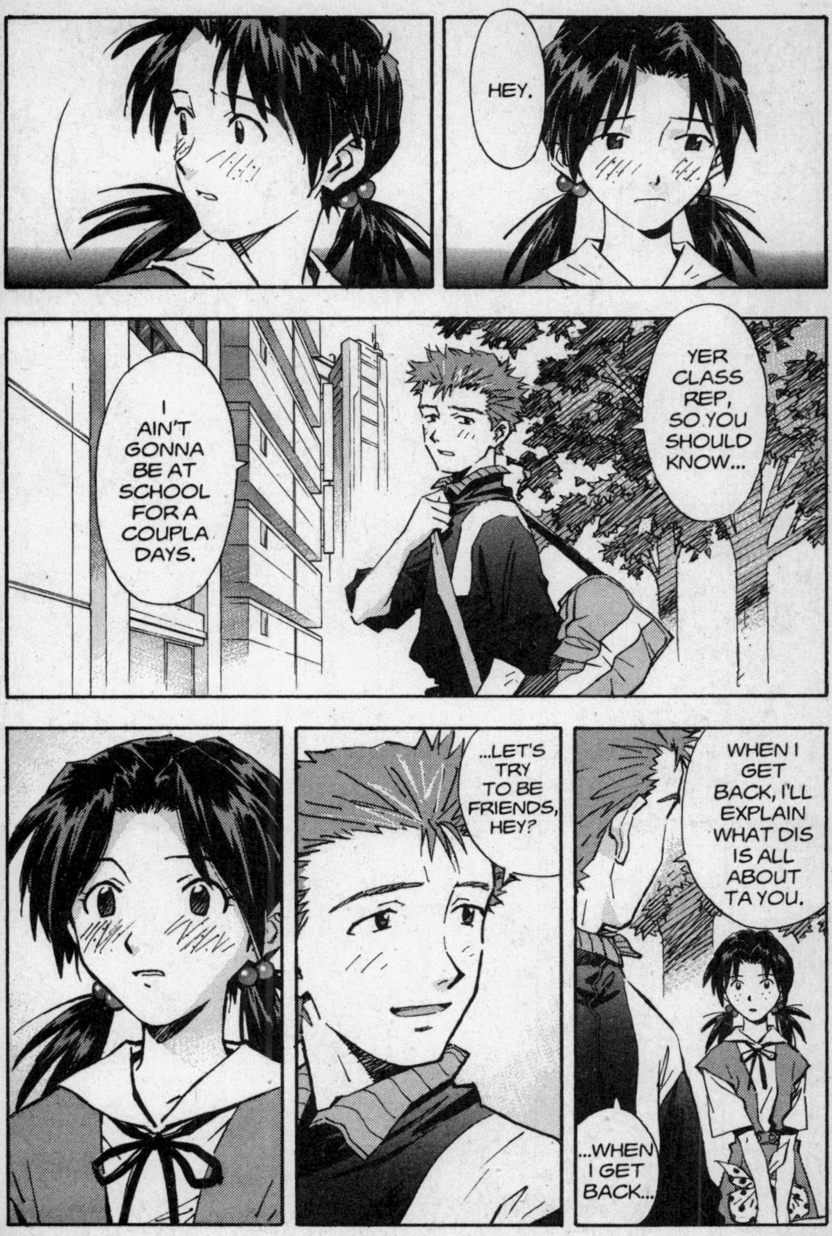
HEY.
YER CLASS REP, SO YOU SHOULD KNOW...
I AIN'T GONNA BE AT SCHOOL FOR A COUPLA DAYS.
WHEN I GET BACK, I'LL EXPLAIN WHAT DIS IS ALL ABOUT TA YOU.
...WHEN I GET BACK...
...LET'S TRY TO BE FRIENDS, HEY?

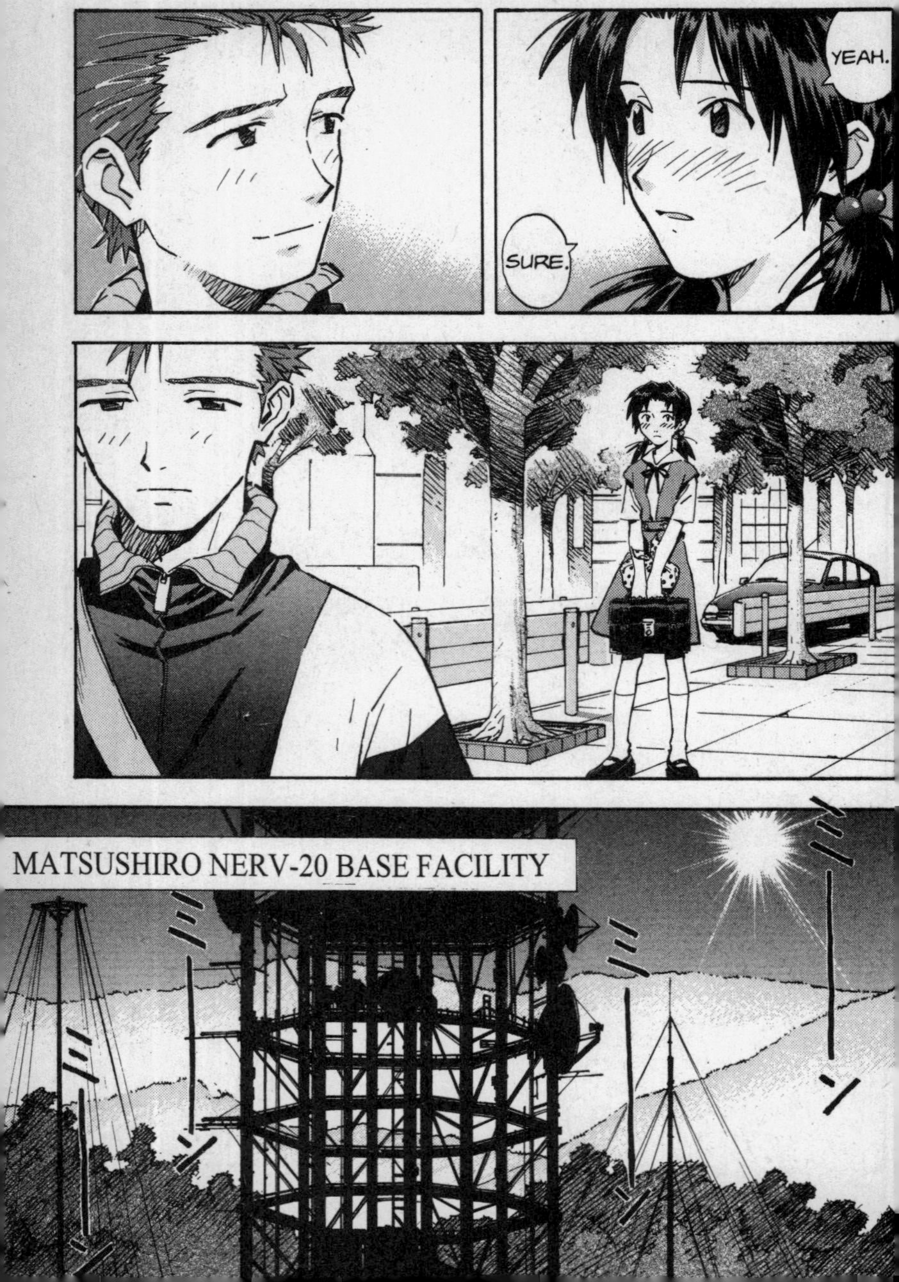
YEAH.
SURE.
MATSUSHIRO NERV-20 BASE FACILITY

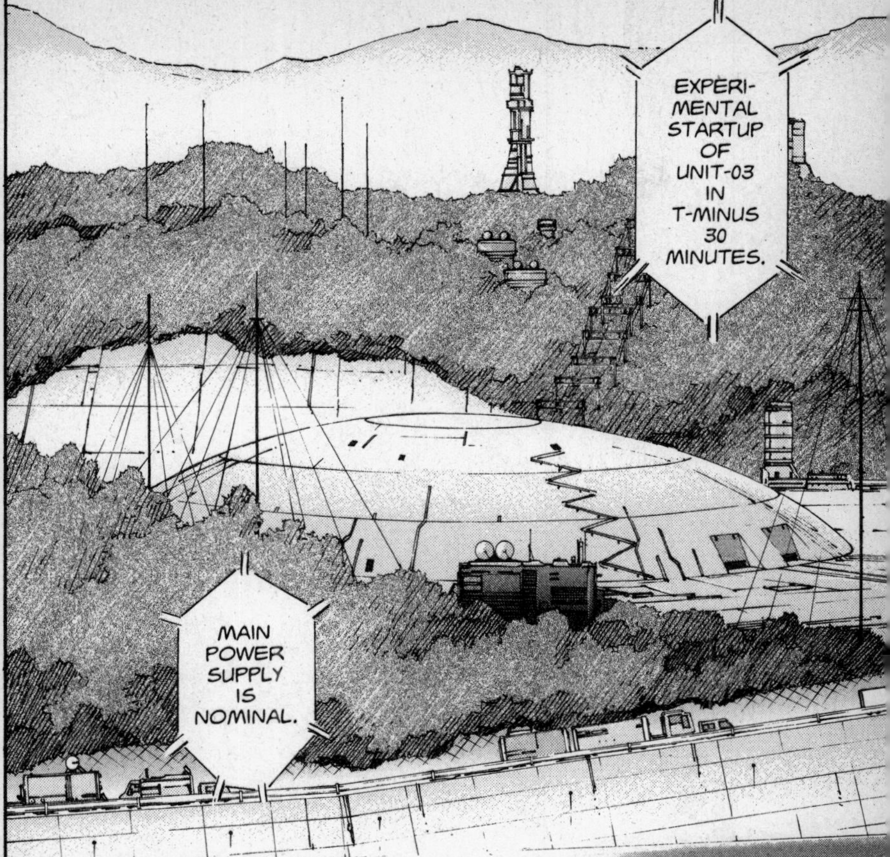
EXPERI-
MENTAL
STARTUP
OF
UNIT-03
IN
T-MINUS
30
MINUTES.
MAIN
POWER
SUPPLY
IS
NOMINAL.
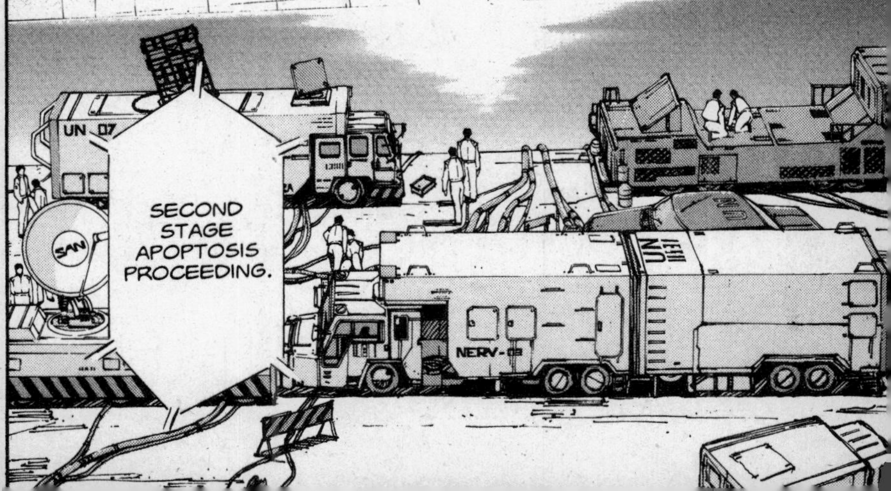
UN 07
SECOND
STAGE
APOPTOSIS
PROCEEDING.
NERV-03

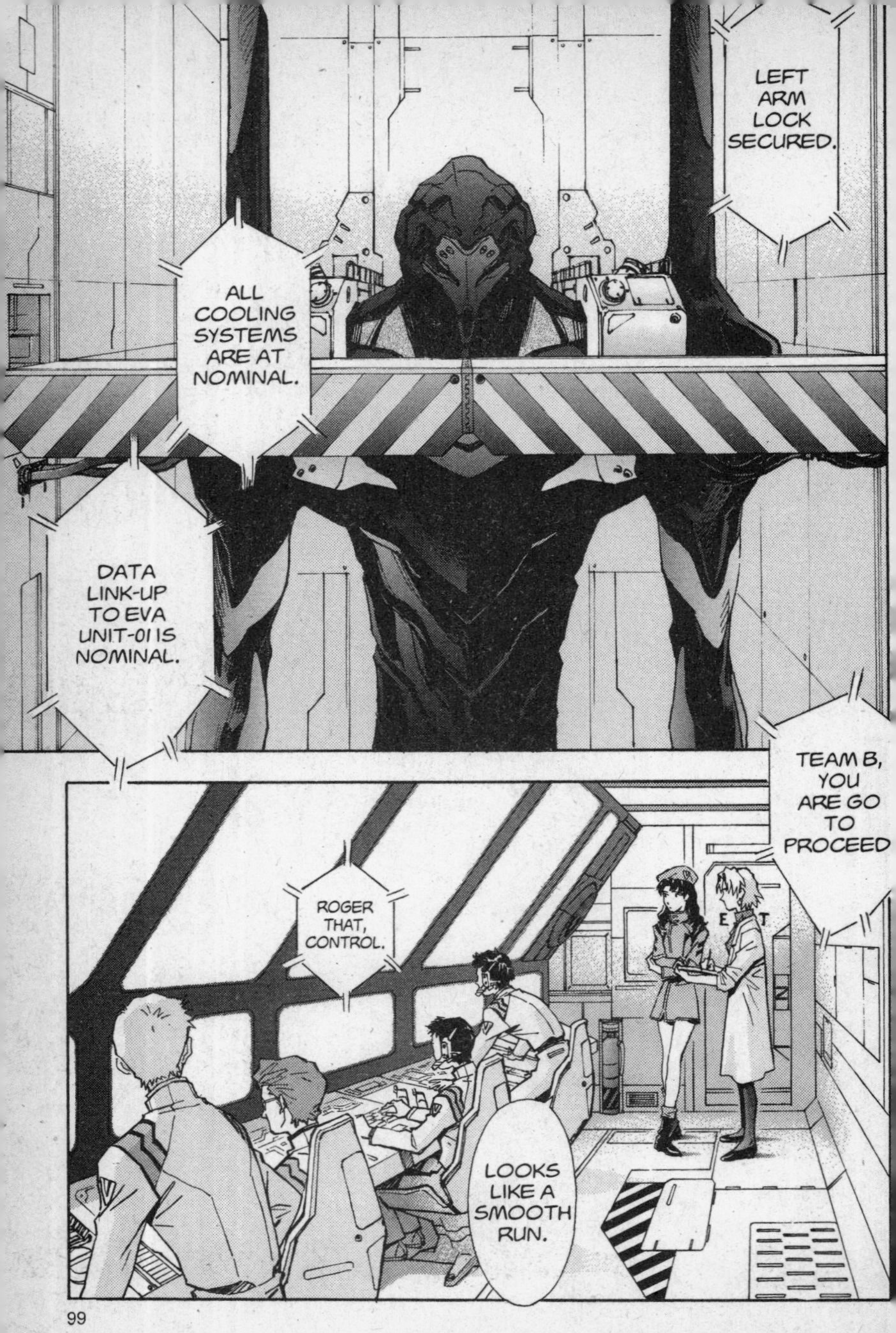
LEFT ARM LOCK SECURED.
ALL COOLING SYSTEMS ARE AT NOMINAL.
DATA LINK-UP TO EVA UNIT-01 IS NOMINAL.
TEAM B, YOU ARE GO TO PROCEED
ROGER THAT, CONTROL.
LOOKS LIKE A SMOOTH RUN.

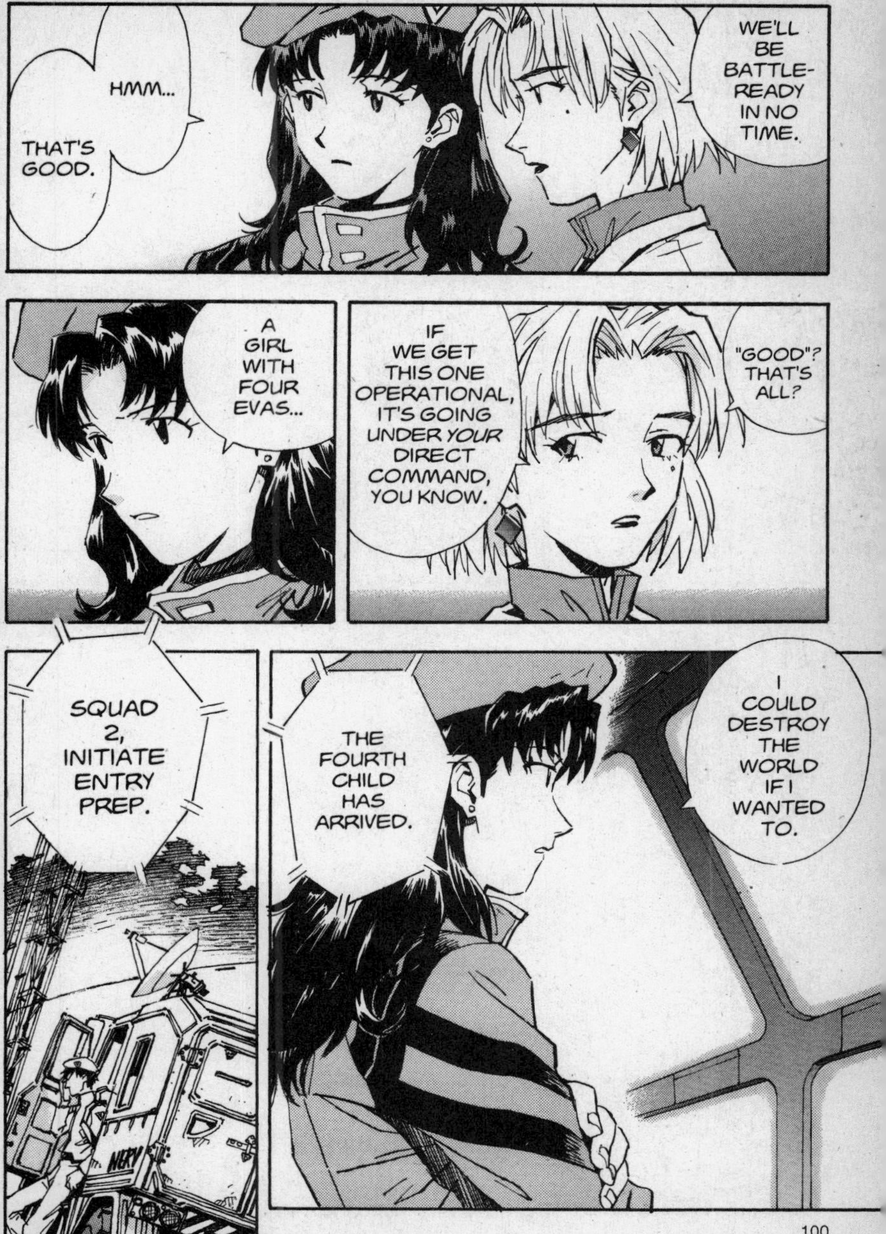
WE'LL BE BATTLE-READY IN NO TIME.
HMM...
THAT'S GOOD.
"GOOD"? THAT'S ALL?
IF WE GET THIS ONE OPERATIONAL, IT'S GOING UNDER *YOUR* DIRECT COMMAND, YOU KNOW.
A GIRL WITH FOUR EVAS...
I COULD DESTROY THE WORLD IF I WANTED TO.
THE FOURTH CHILD HAS ARRIVED.
SQUAD 2, INITIATE ENTRY PREP.
NERV

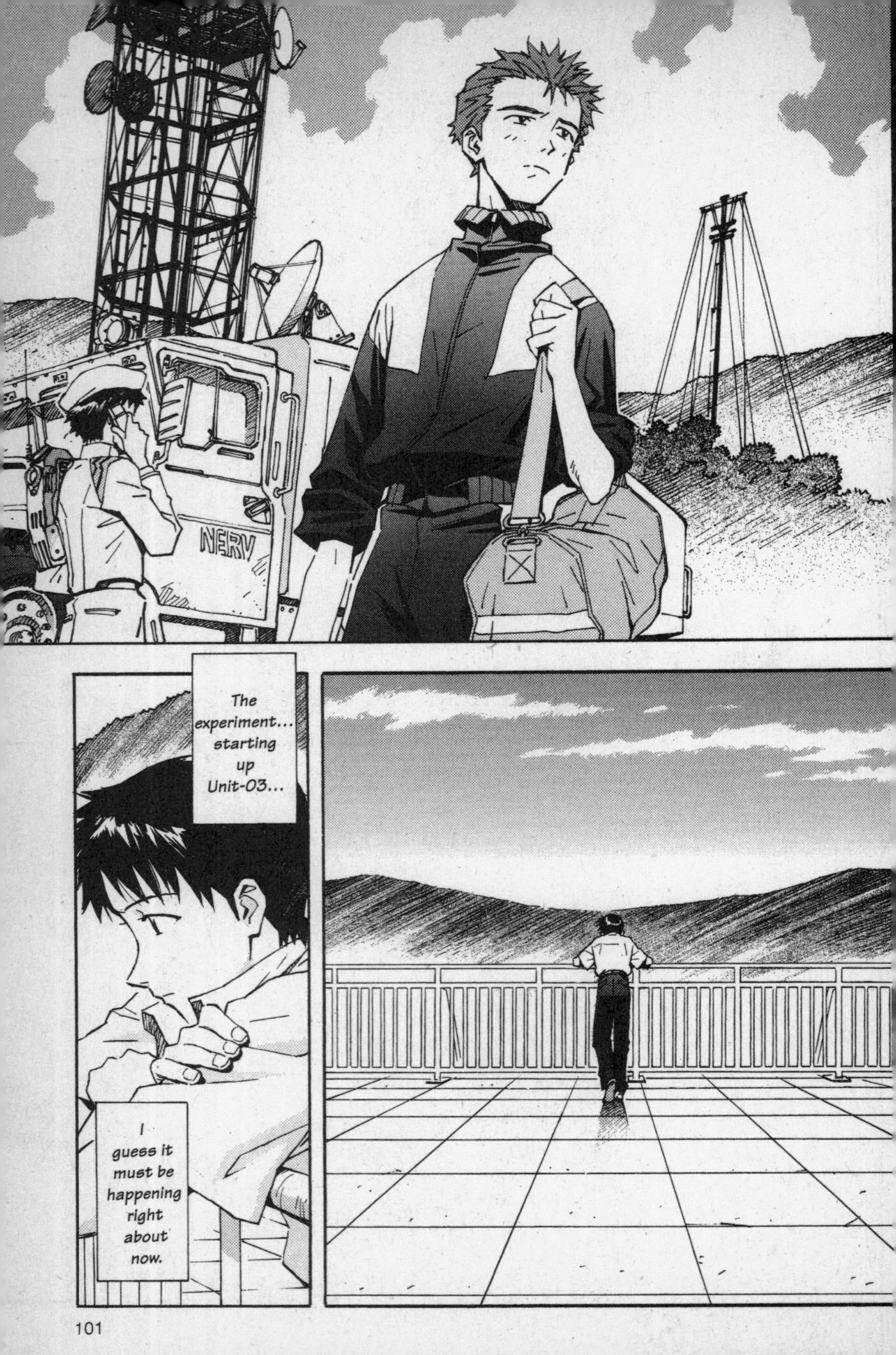
The experiment... starting up Unit-03...
I guess it must be happening right about now.

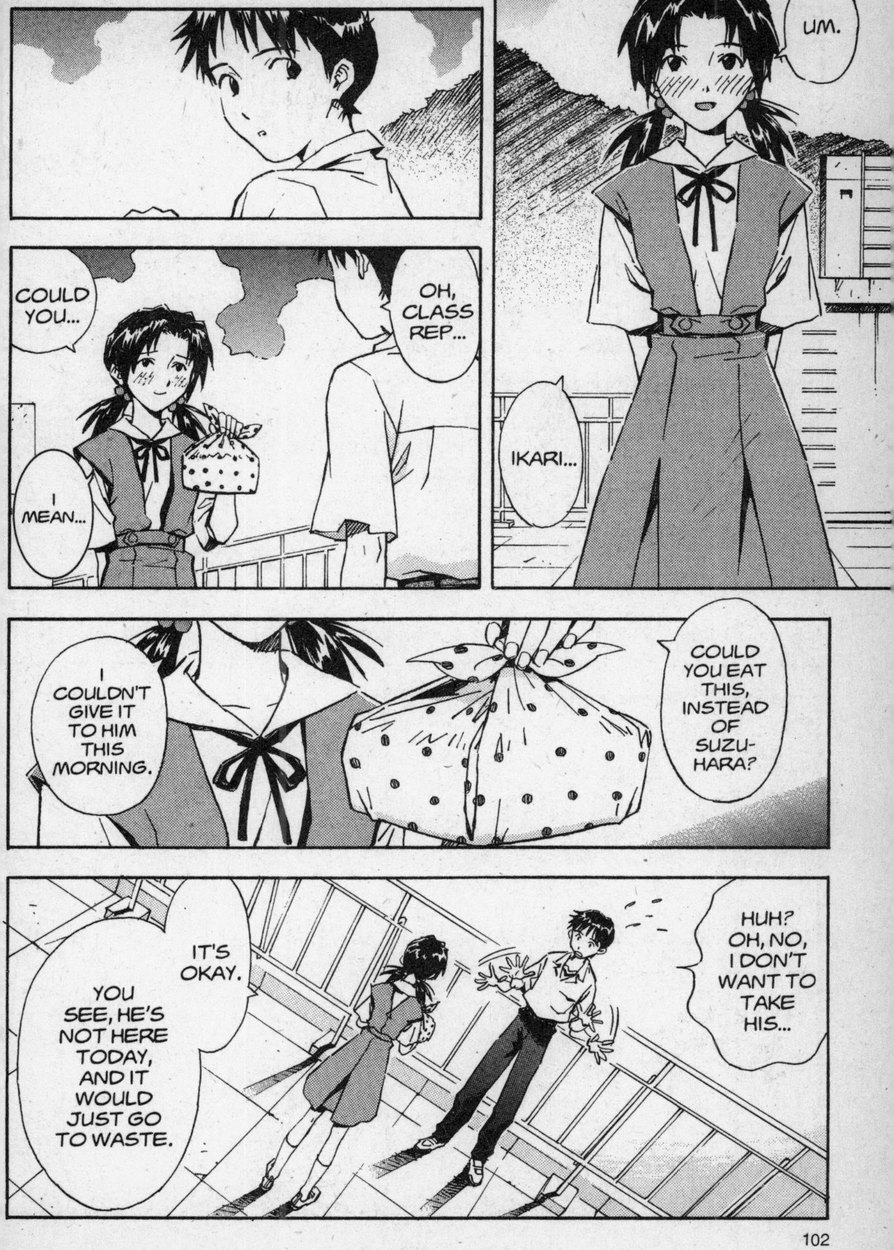
UM.
IKARI...
OH, CLASS REP...
COULD YOU...
I MEAN...
COULD YOU EAT THIS, INSTEAD OF SUZU-HARA?
I COULDN'T GIVE IT TO HIM THIS MORNING.
HUH? OH, NO, I DON'T WANT TO TAKE HIS...
IT'S OKAY.
YOU SEE, HE'S NOT HERE TODAY, AND IT WOULD JUST GO TO WASTE.

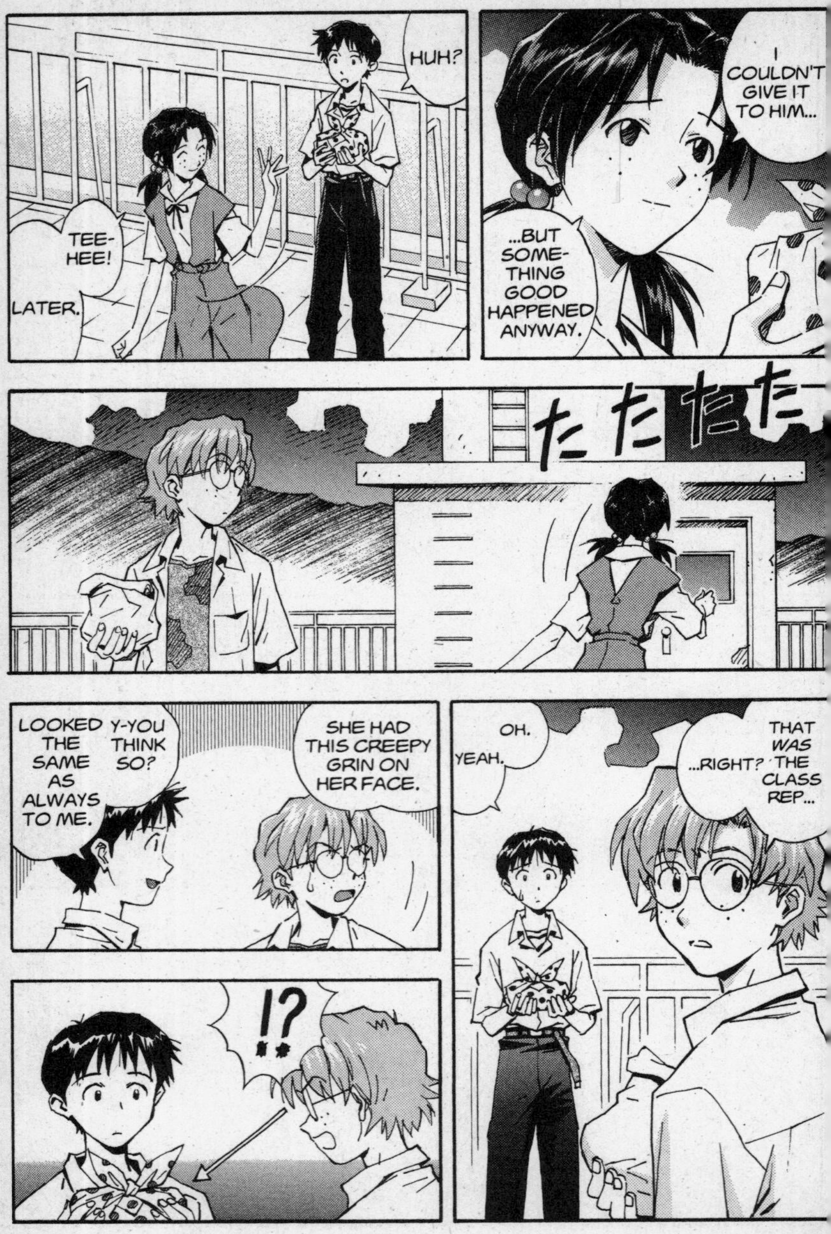
I COULDN'T GIVE IT TO HIM...
...BUT SOMETHING GOOD HAPPENED ANYWAY.
HUH?
TEE-HEE!
LATER.
たたたた
THAT WAS THE CLASS REP...
...RIGHT?
OH.
YEAH.
SHE HAD THIS CREEPY GRIN ON HER FACE.
Y-YOU THINK SO?
LOOKED THE SAME AS ALWAYS TO ME.
!?

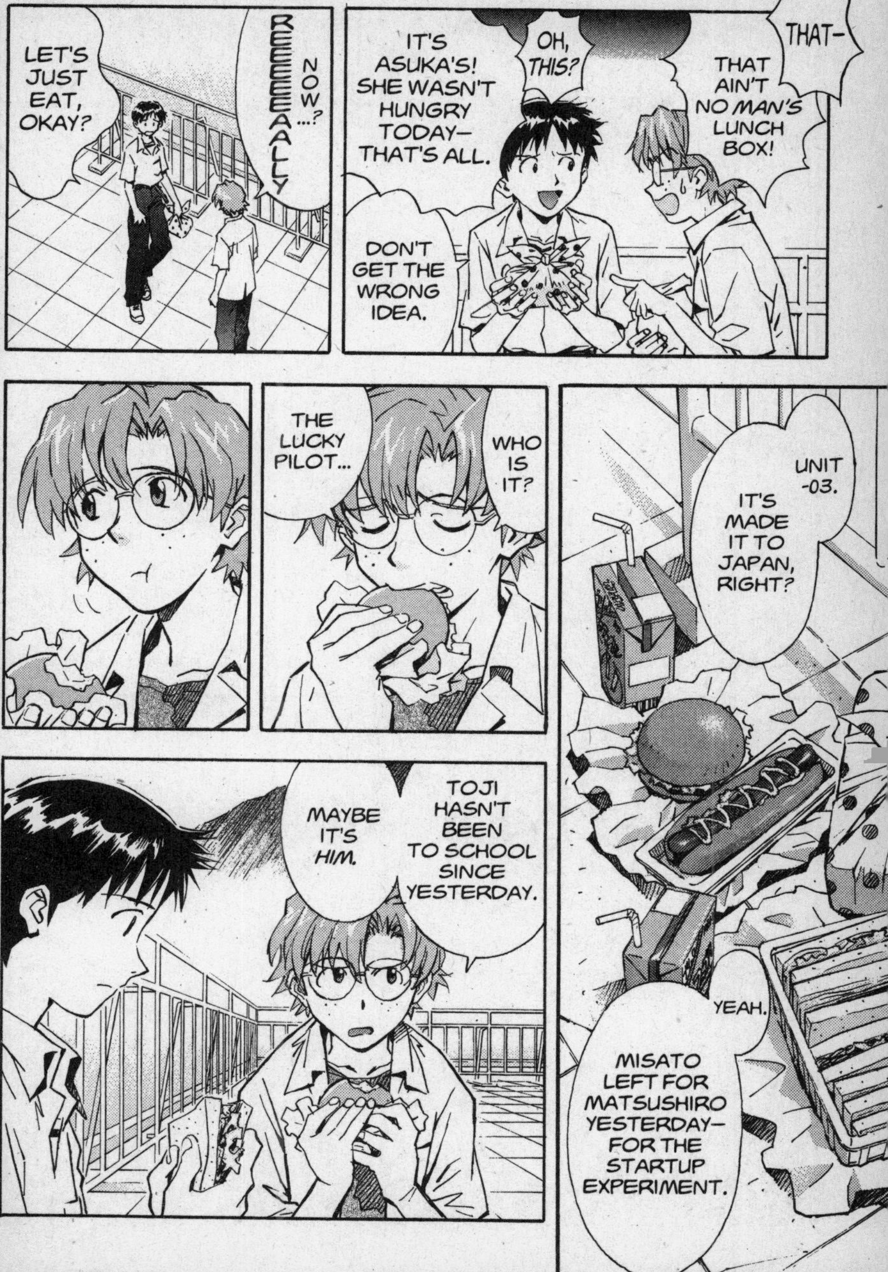
THAT-
THAT AIN'T NO MAN'S LUNCH BOX!
OH, THIS?
IT'S ASUKA'S! SHE WASN'T HUNGRY TODAY— THAT'S ALL.
DON'T GET THE WRONG IDEA.
REEEEEAALLY NOW...?
LET'S JUST EAT, OKAY?
UNIT -03.
IT'S MADE IT TO JAPAN, RIGHT?
YEAH.
MISATO LEFT FOR MATSUSHIRO YESTERDAY— FOR THE STARTUP EXPERIMENT.
THE LUCKY PILOT...
WHO IS IT?
TOJI HASN'T BEEN TO SCHOOL SINCE YESTERDAY.
MAYBE IT'S HIM.

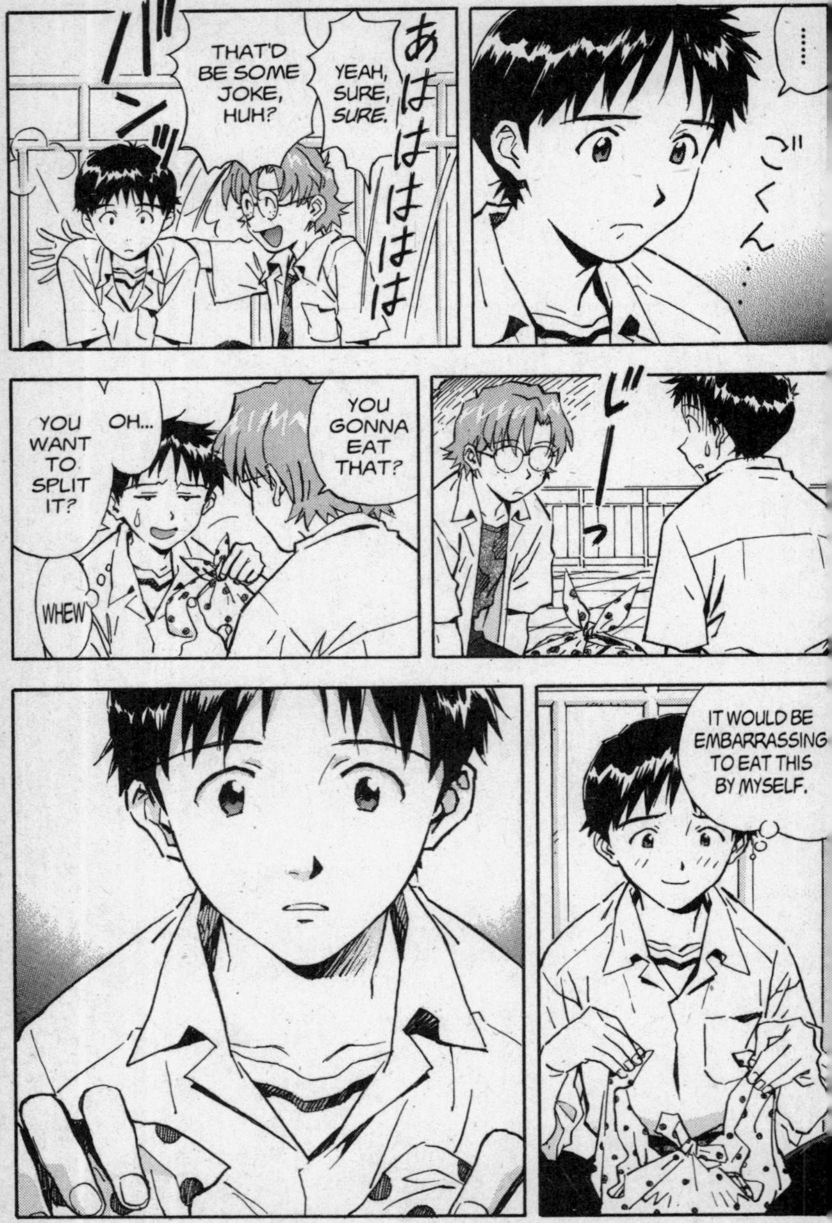
……
ごくん…
あははははは
YEAH, SURE, SURE.
THAT'D BE SOME JOKE, HUH?
バンッ
ジーっ
YOU GONNA EAT THAT?
OH... YOU WANT TO SPLIT IT?
WHEW
IT WOULD BE EMBARRASSING TO EAT THIS BY MYSELF.

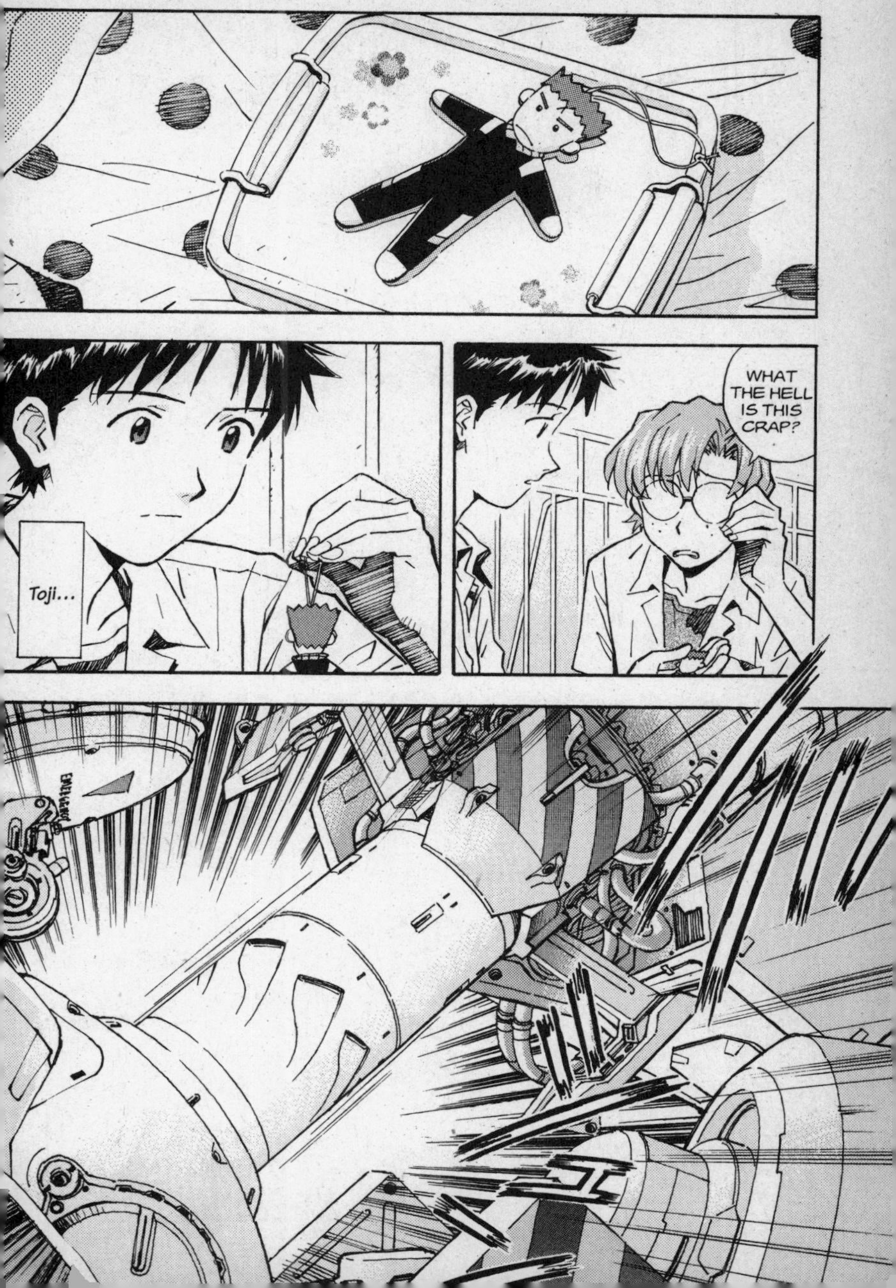
WHAT THE HELL IS THIS CRAP?
Toji...

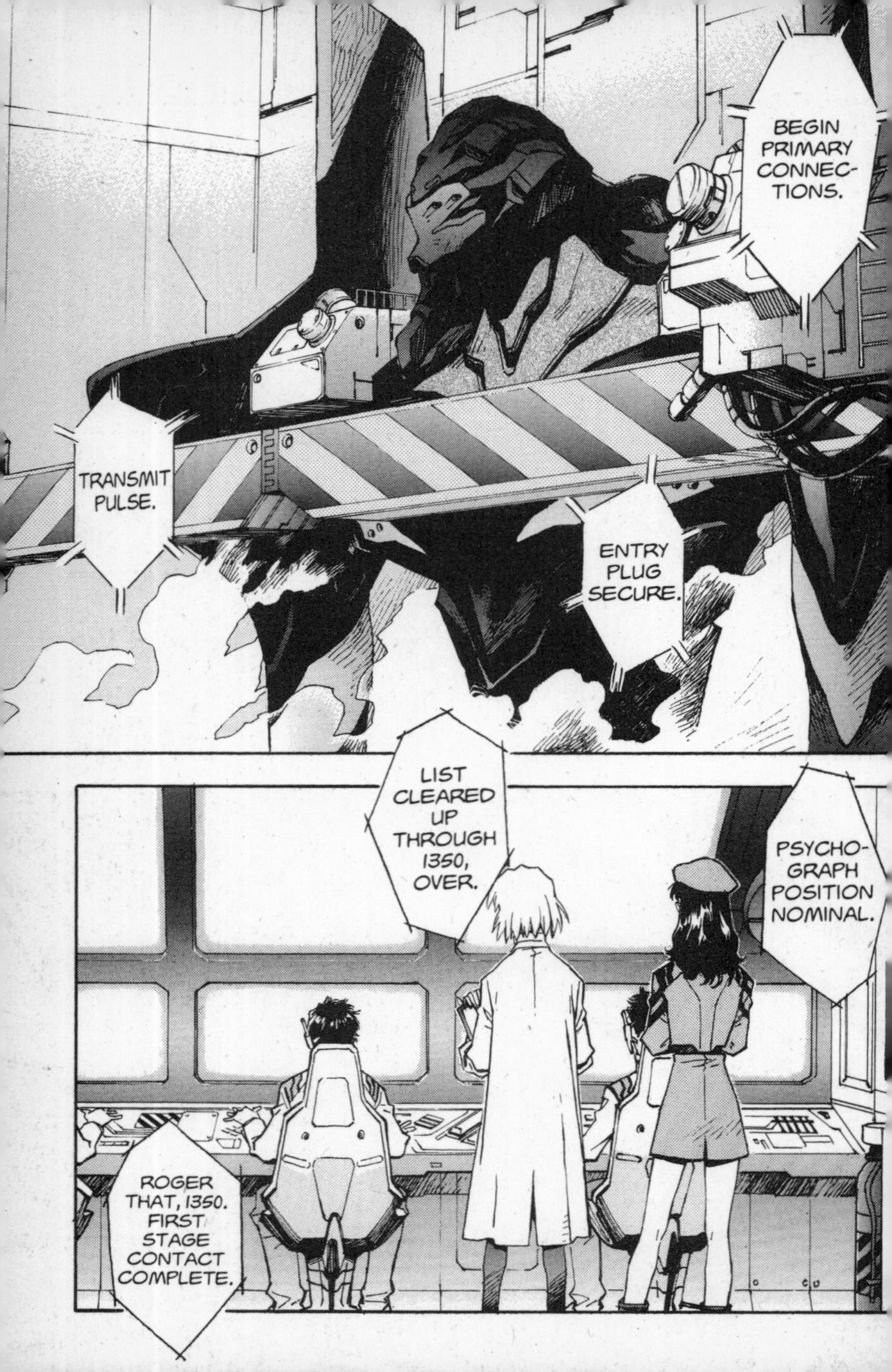
BEGIN PRIMARY CONNECTIONS.
ENTRY PLUG SECURE.
TRANSMIT PULSE.
PSYCHO-GRAPH POSITION NOMINAL.
LIST CLEARED UP THROUGH 1350, OVER.
ROGER THAT, 1350. FIRST STAGE CONTACT COMPLETE.

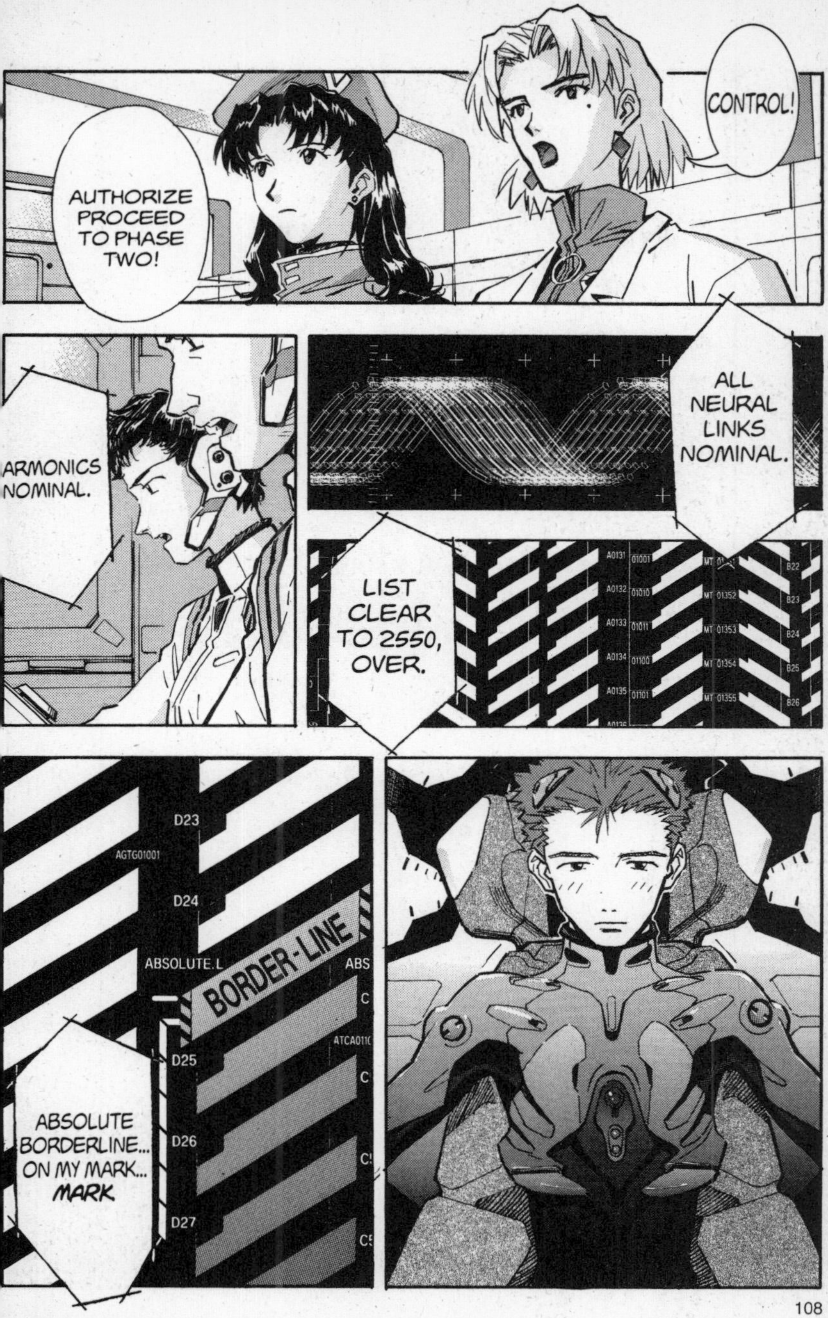
CONTROL!
AUTHORIZE PROCEED TO PHASE TWO!
ALL NEURAL LINKS NOMINAL.
LIST CLEAR TO 2550, OVER.
ARMONICS NOMINAL.
D23
AGTG01001
D24
BORDER-LINE
ABSOLUTE.L
D25
D26
D27
ABSOLUTE BORDERLINE... ON MY MARK... *MARK*

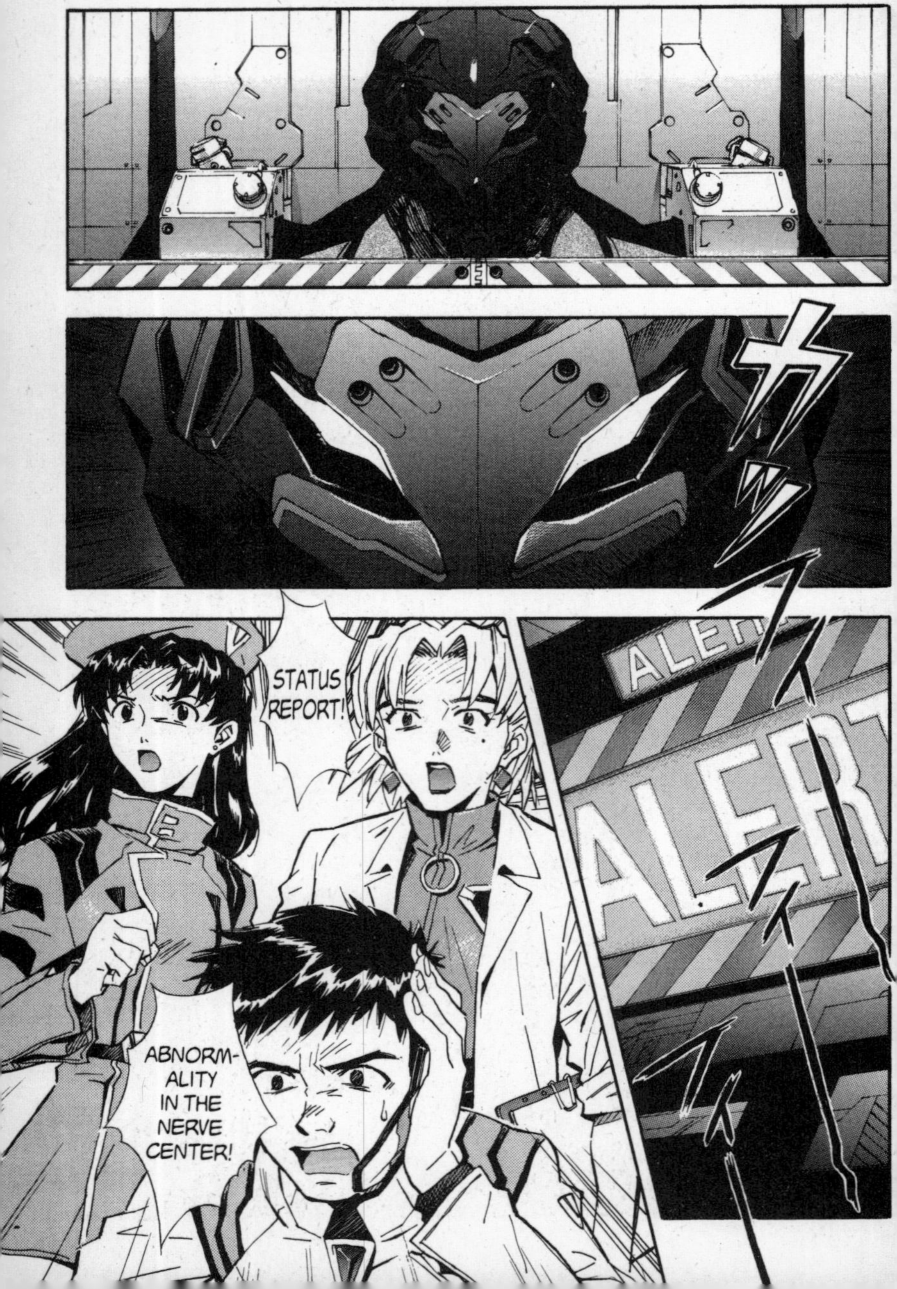
ガッ
STATUS REPORT!
ABNORM-
ALITY
IN THE
NERVE
CENTER!

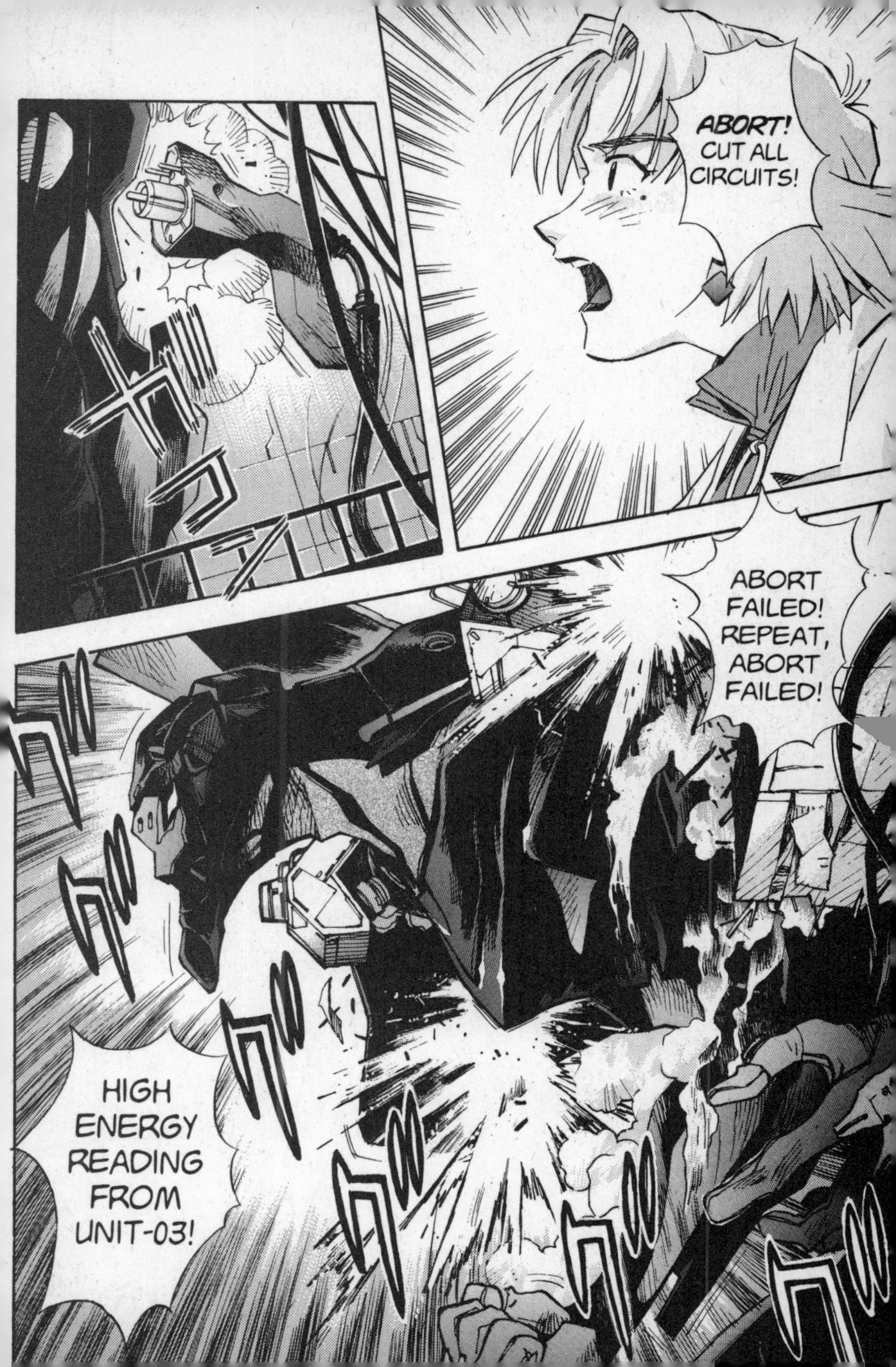
ABORT! CUT ALL CIRCUITS!
ABORT FAILED! REPEAT, ABORT FAILED!
HIGH ENERGY READING FROM UNIT-03!

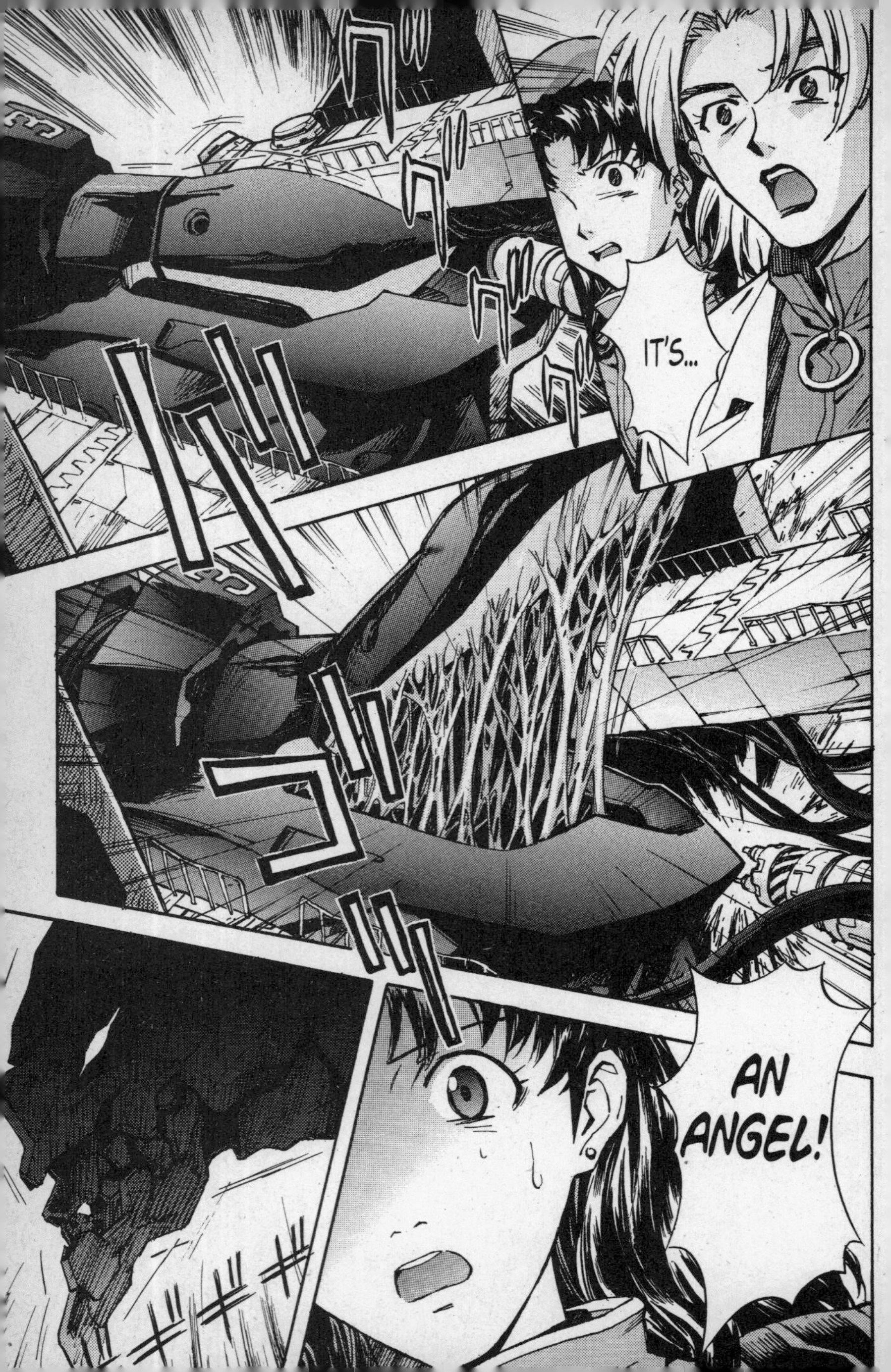
IT'S...
AN ANGEL!

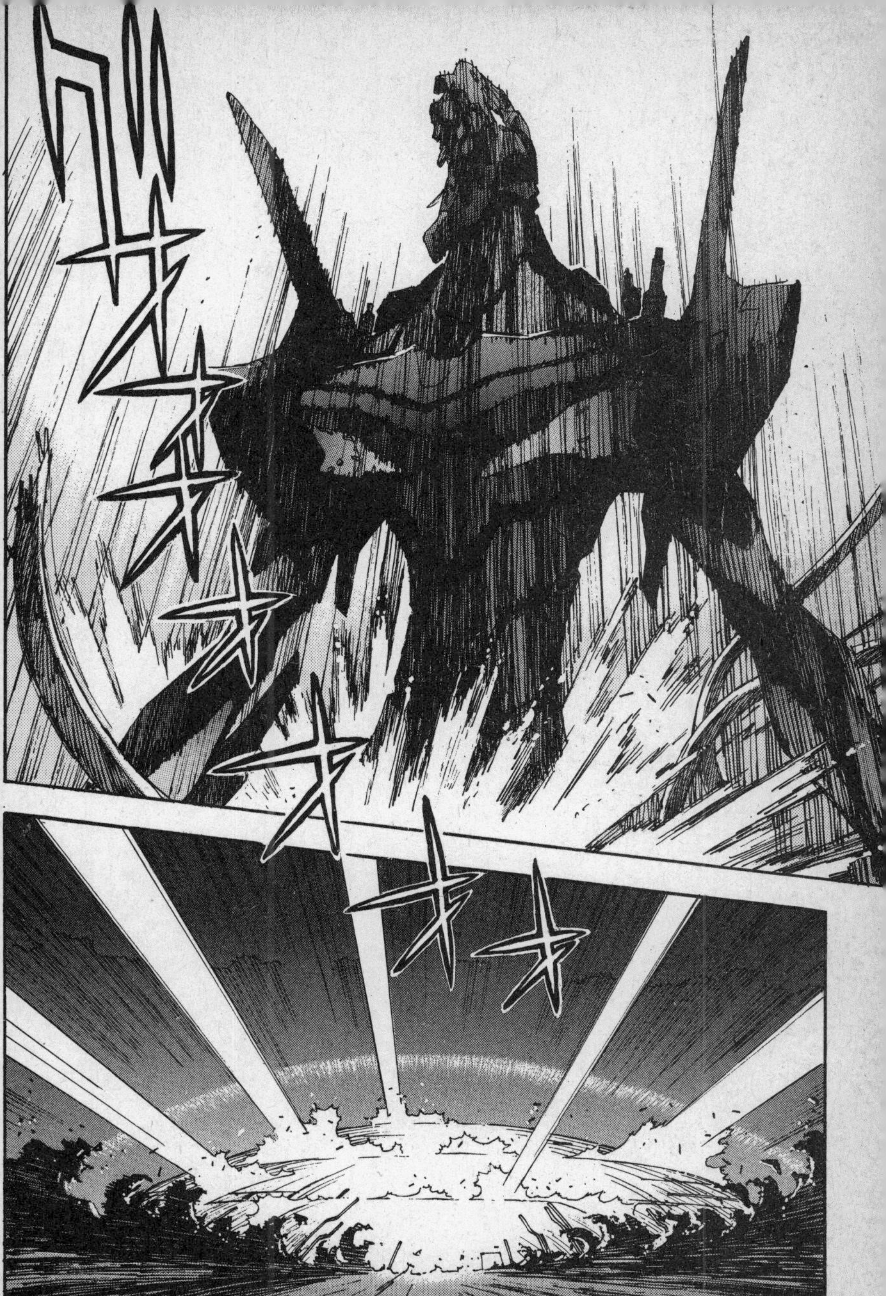

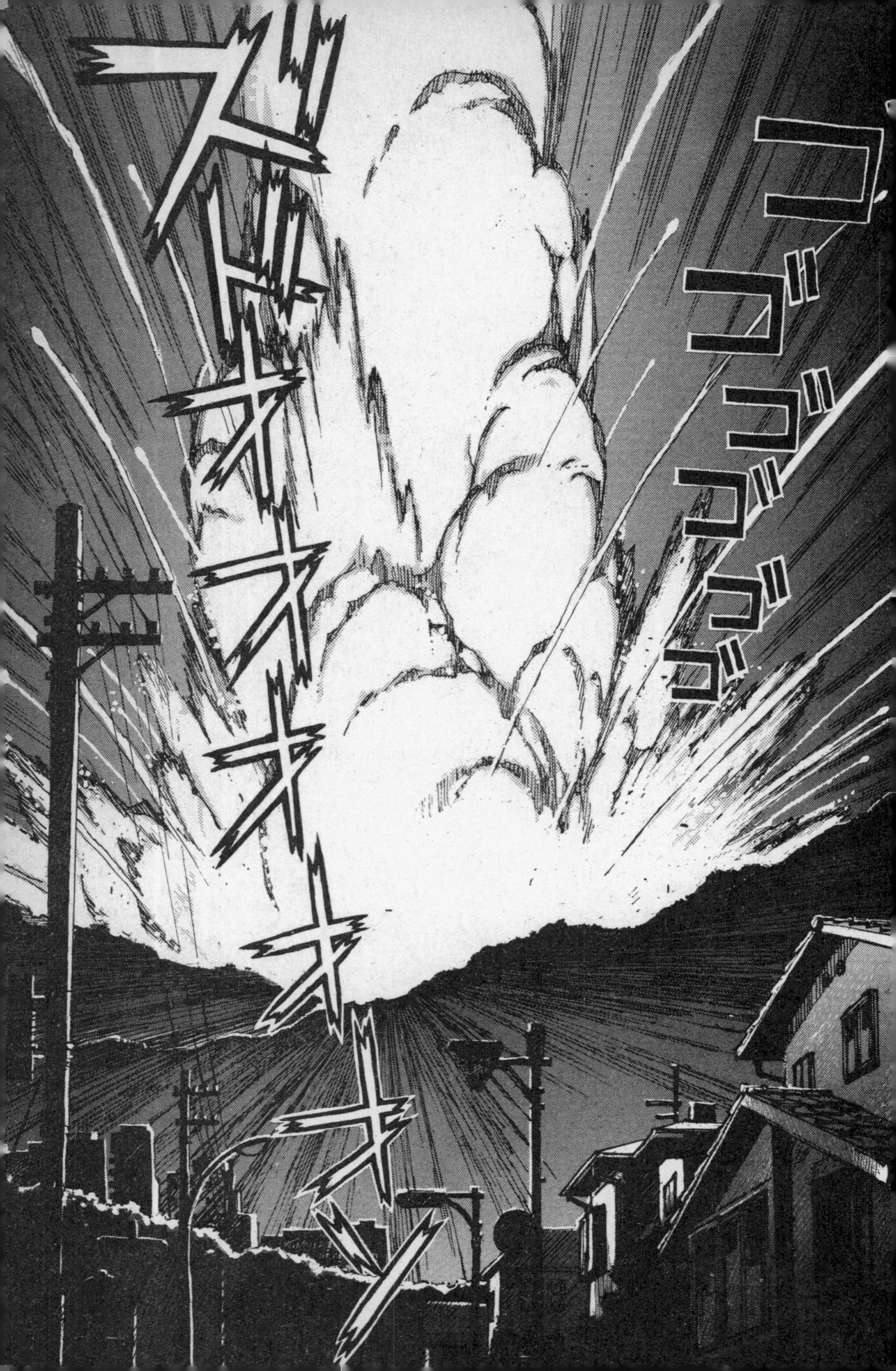
ゴゴゴゴゴ
ブゴオオオオオオン

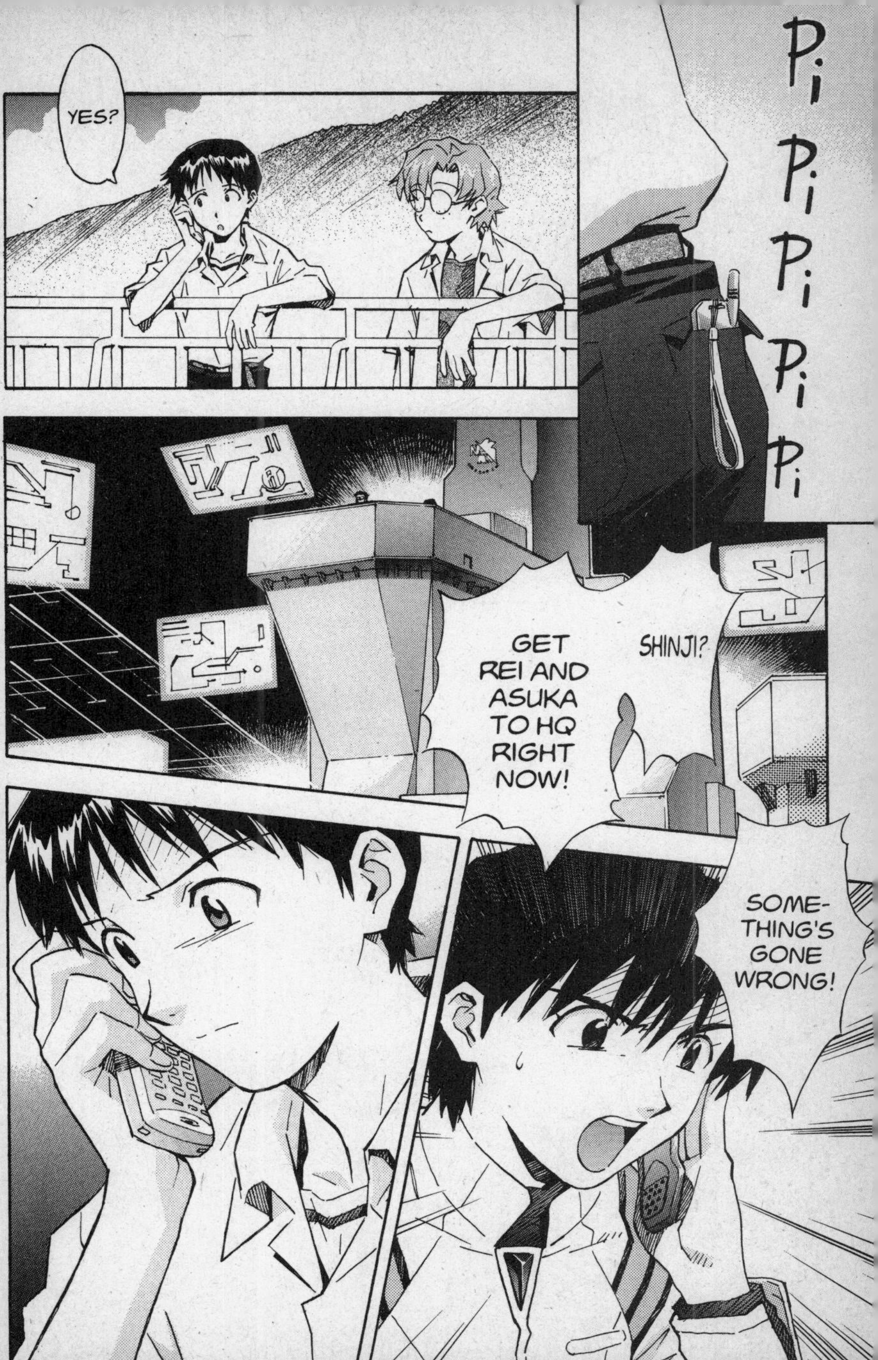
Pi Pi Pi Pi Pi Pi
YES?
SHINJI?
SOME-THING'S GONE WRONG!
GET REI AND ASUKA TO HQ RIGHT NOW!

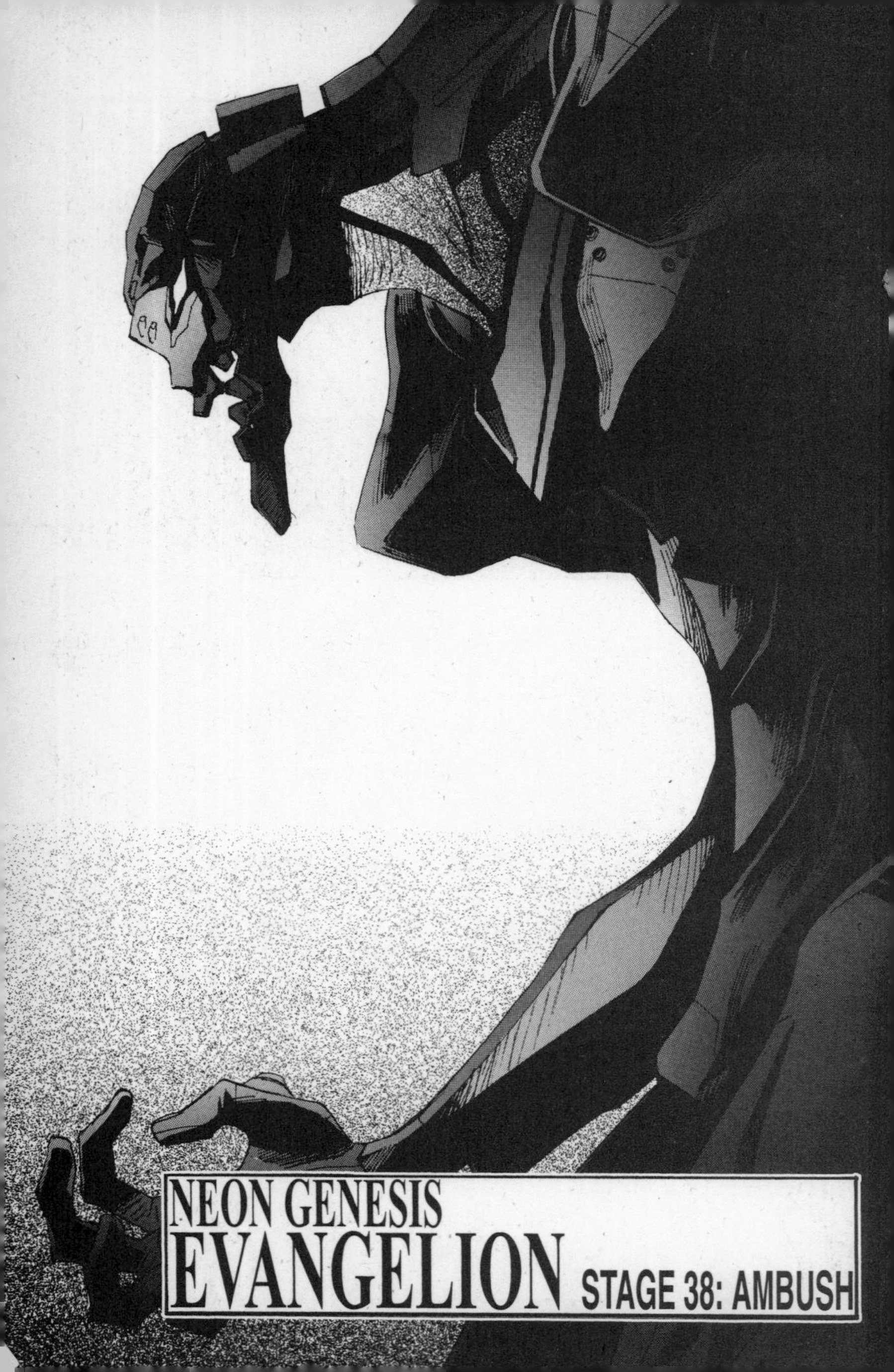

NEON GENESIS EVANGELION

STAGE 38: AMBUSH

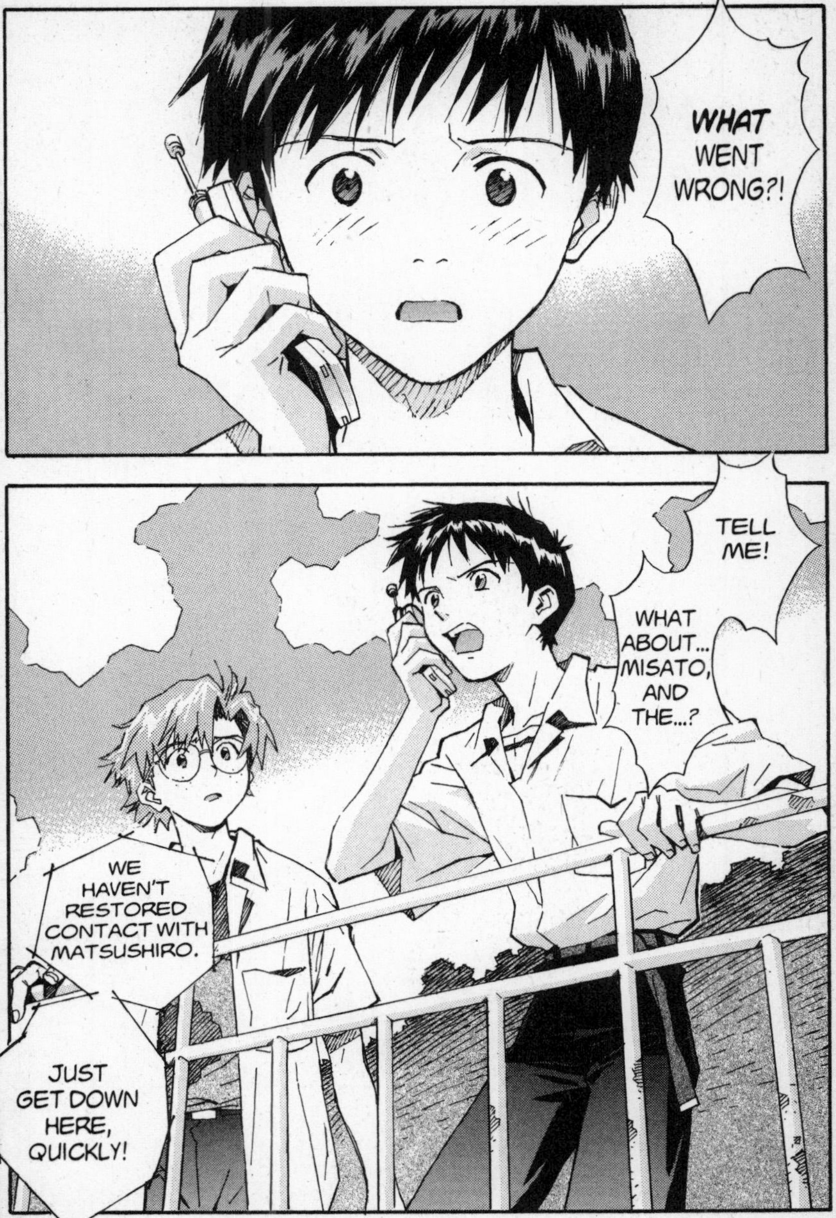
WHAT WENT WRONG?!
TELL ME!
WHAT ABOUT... MISATO, AND THE...?
WE HAVEN'T RESTORED CONTACT WITH MATSUSHIRO.
JUST GET DOWN HERE, QUICKLY!

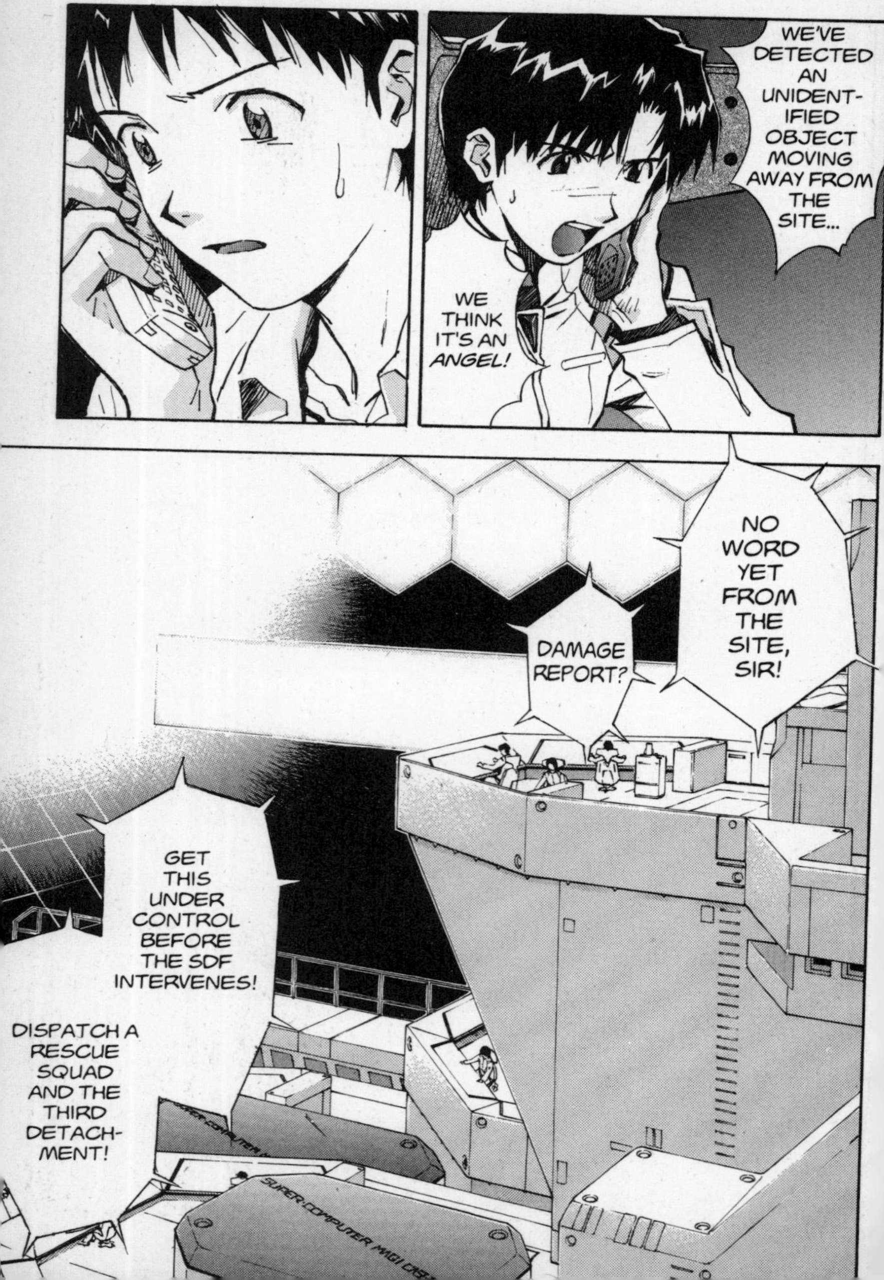
WE'VE DETECTED AN UNIDENT-IFIED OBJECT MOVING AWAY FROM THE SITE...
WE THINK IT'S AN ANGEL!
DAMAGE REPORT?
NO WORD YET FROM THE SITE, SIR!
GET THIS UNDER CONTROL BEFORE THE SDF INTERVENES!
DISPATCH A RESCUE SQUAD AND THE THIRD DETACH-MENT!

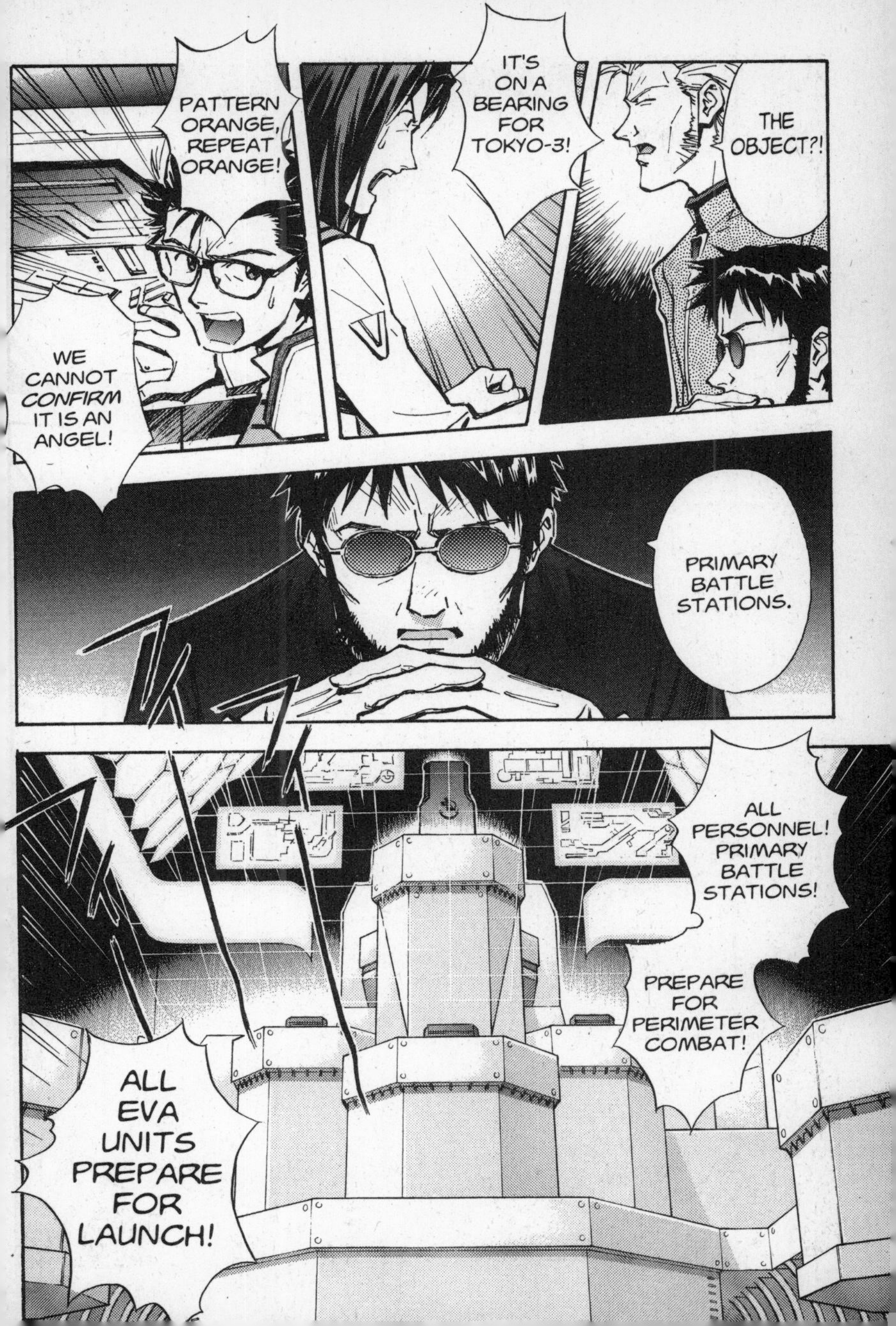
THE OBJECT?!
IT'S ON A BEARING FOR TOKYO-3!
PATTERN ORANGE, REPEAT ORANGE!
WE CANNOT CONFIRM IT IS AN ANGEL!
PRIMARY BATTLE STATIONS.
ALL PERSONNEL! PRIMARY BATTLE STATIONS!
PREPARE FOR PERIMETER COMBAT!
ALL EVA UNITS PREPARE FOR LAUNCH!

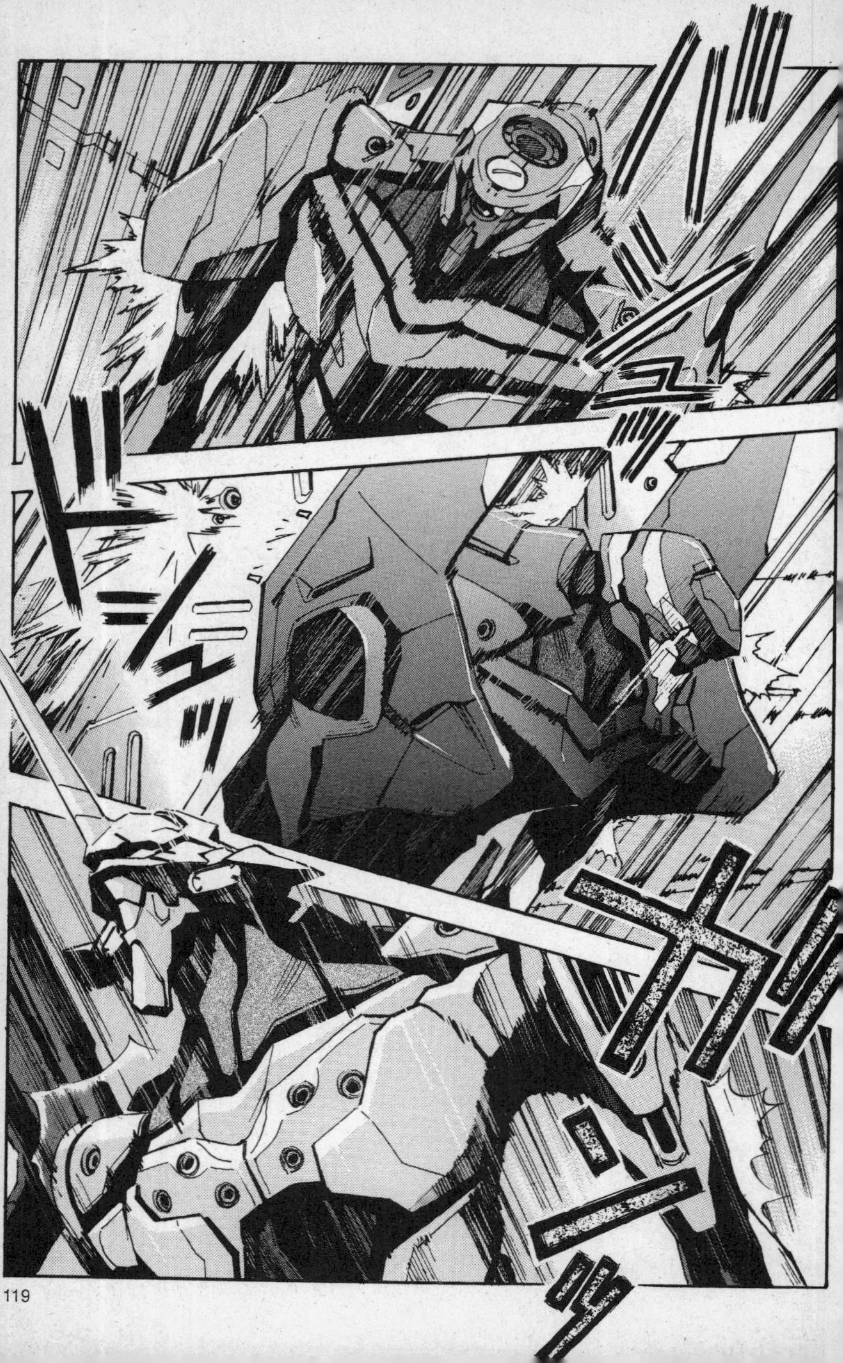

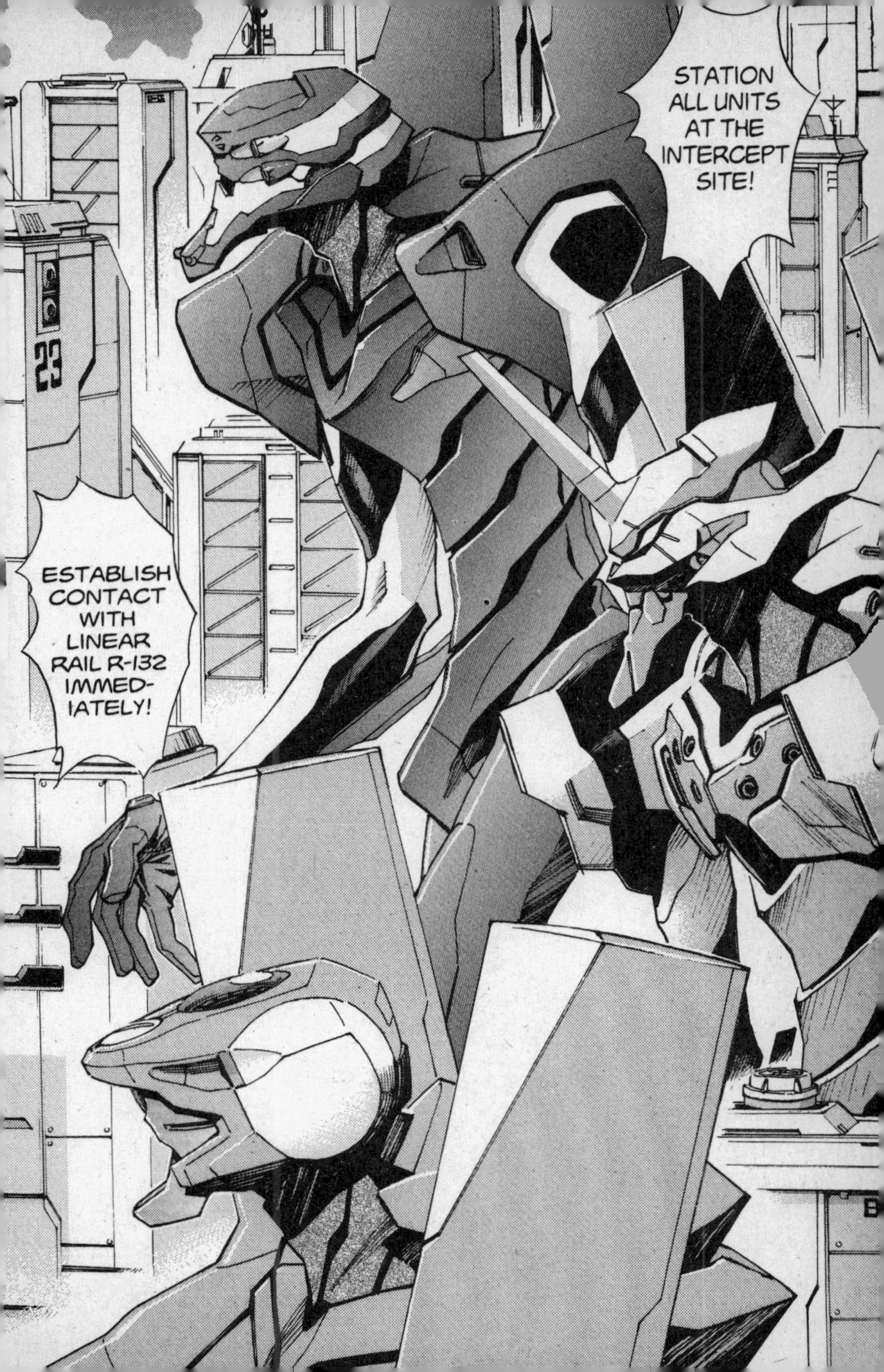
STATION ALL UNITS AT THE INTERCEPT SITE!
ESTABLISH CONTACT WITH LINEAR RAIL R-132 IMMED-IATELY!
23

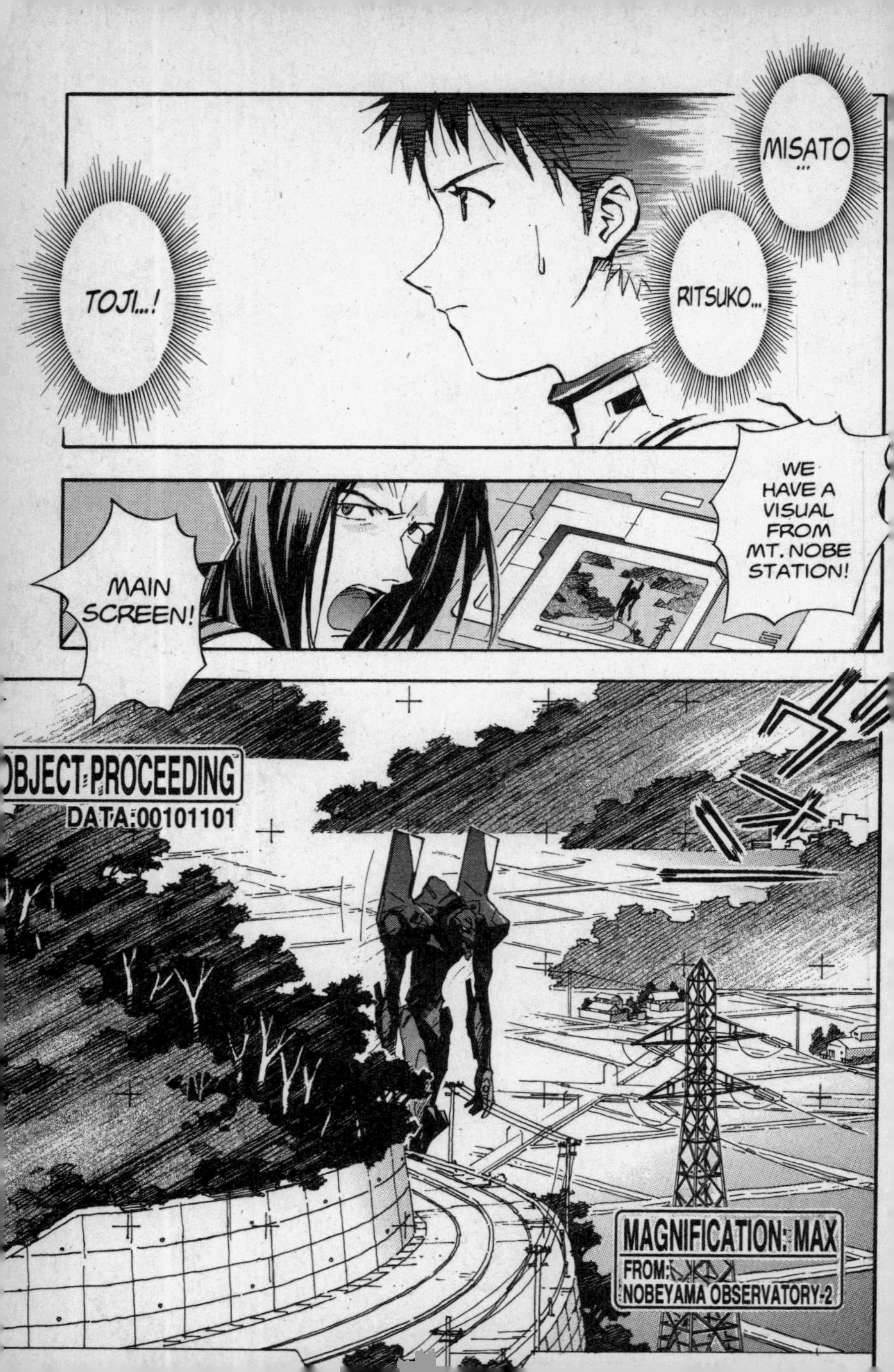
MISATO...
RITSUKO...
TOJI...!
WE HAVE A VISUAL FROM MT. NOBE STATION!
MAIN SCREEN!
OBJECT PROCEEDING
DATA:00101101
MAGNIFICATION: MAX
FROM:
NOBEYAMA OBSERVATORY-2

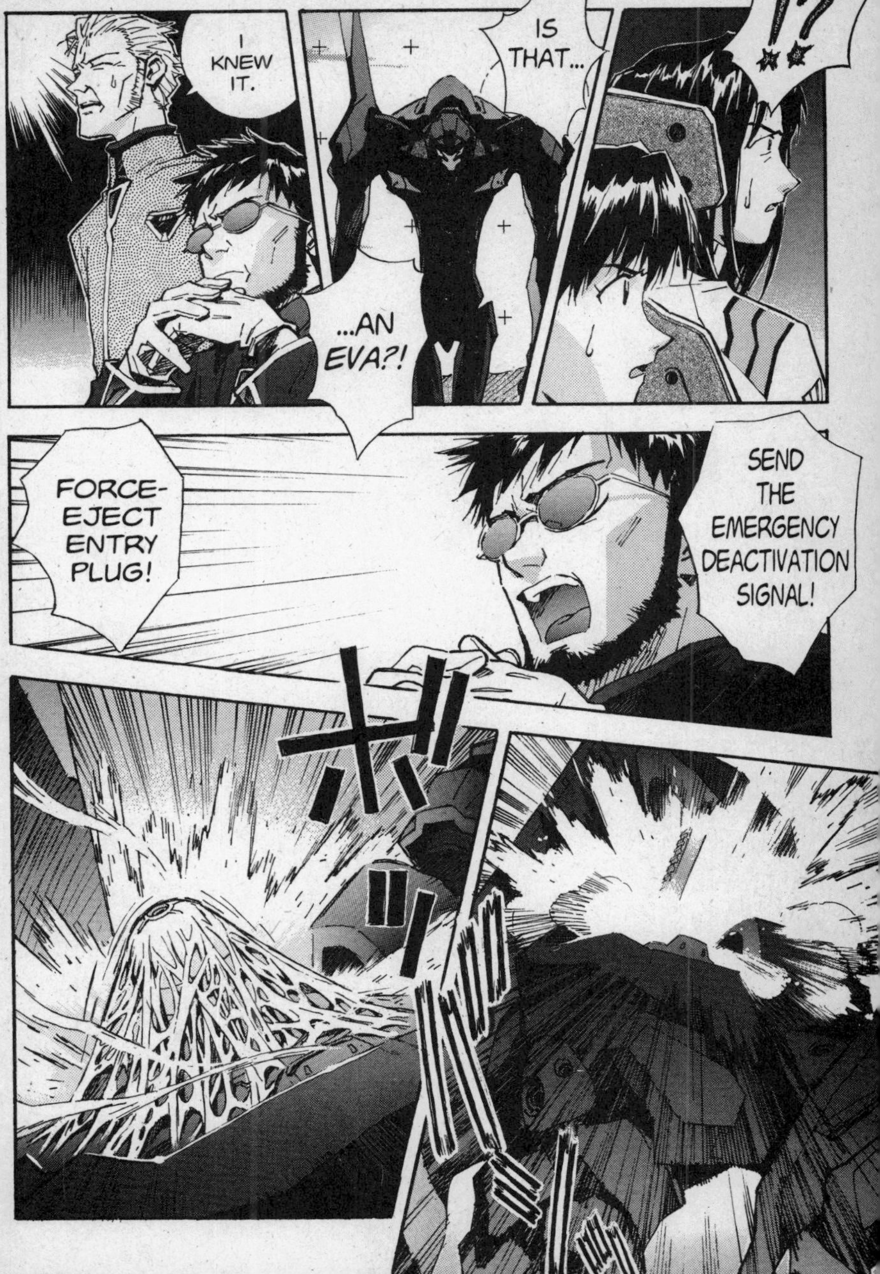
!?
IS THAT...
...AN EVA?!
I KNEW IT.
SEND THE EMERGENCY DEACTIVATION SIGNAL!
FORCE-EJECT ENTRY PLUG!

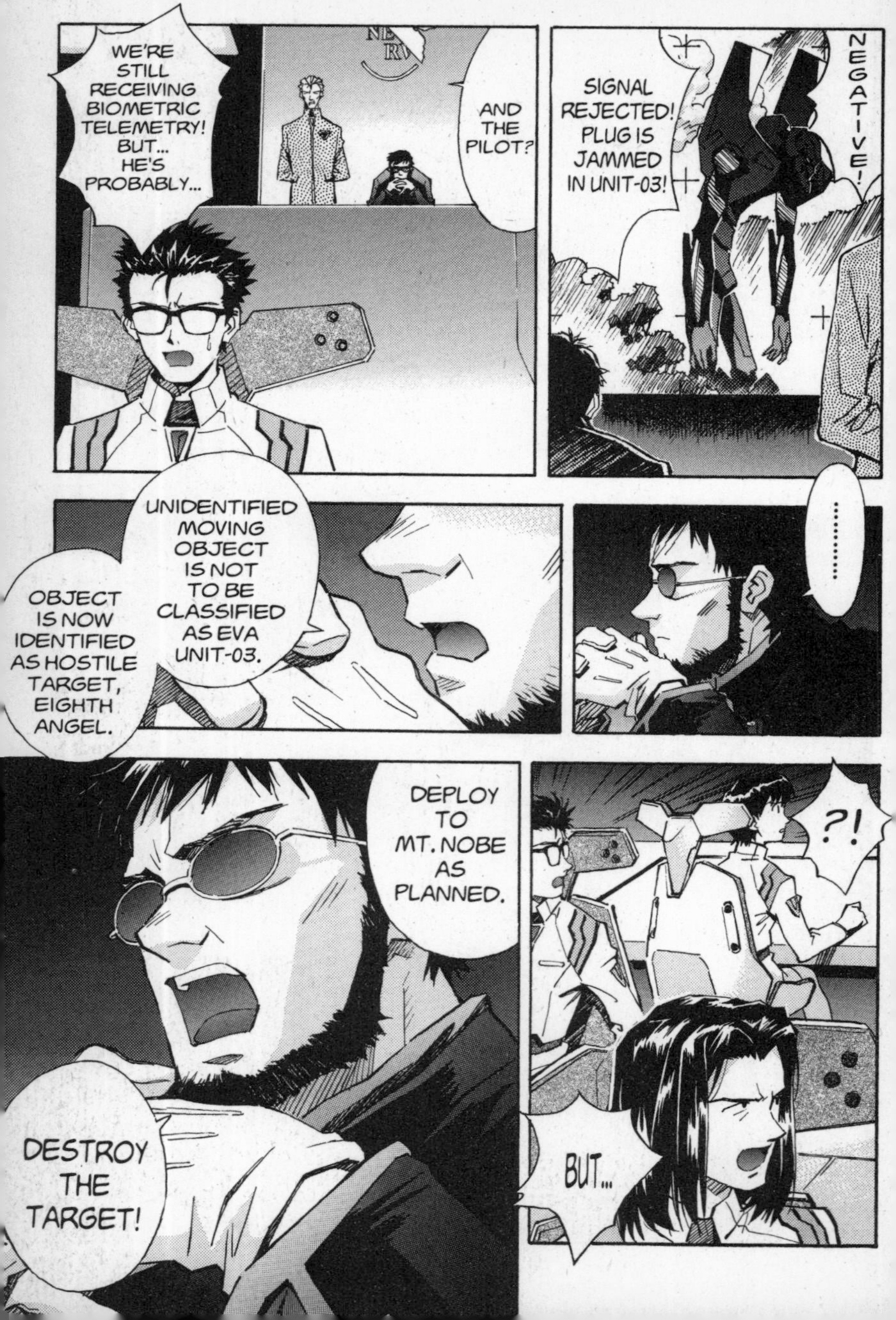
NEGATIVE!
SIGNAL REJECTED! PLUG IS JAMMED IN UNIT-03!
AND THE PILOT?
WE'RE STILL RECEIVING BIOMETRIC TELEMETRY! BUT... HE'S PROBABLY...
......
UNIDENTIFIED MOVING OBJECT IS NOT TO BE CLASSIFIED AS EVA UNIT-03.
OBJECT IS NOW IDENTIFIED AS HOSTILE TARGET, EIGHTH ANGEL.
?!
BUT...
DEPLOY TO MT. NOBE AS PLANNED.
DESTROY THE TARGET!

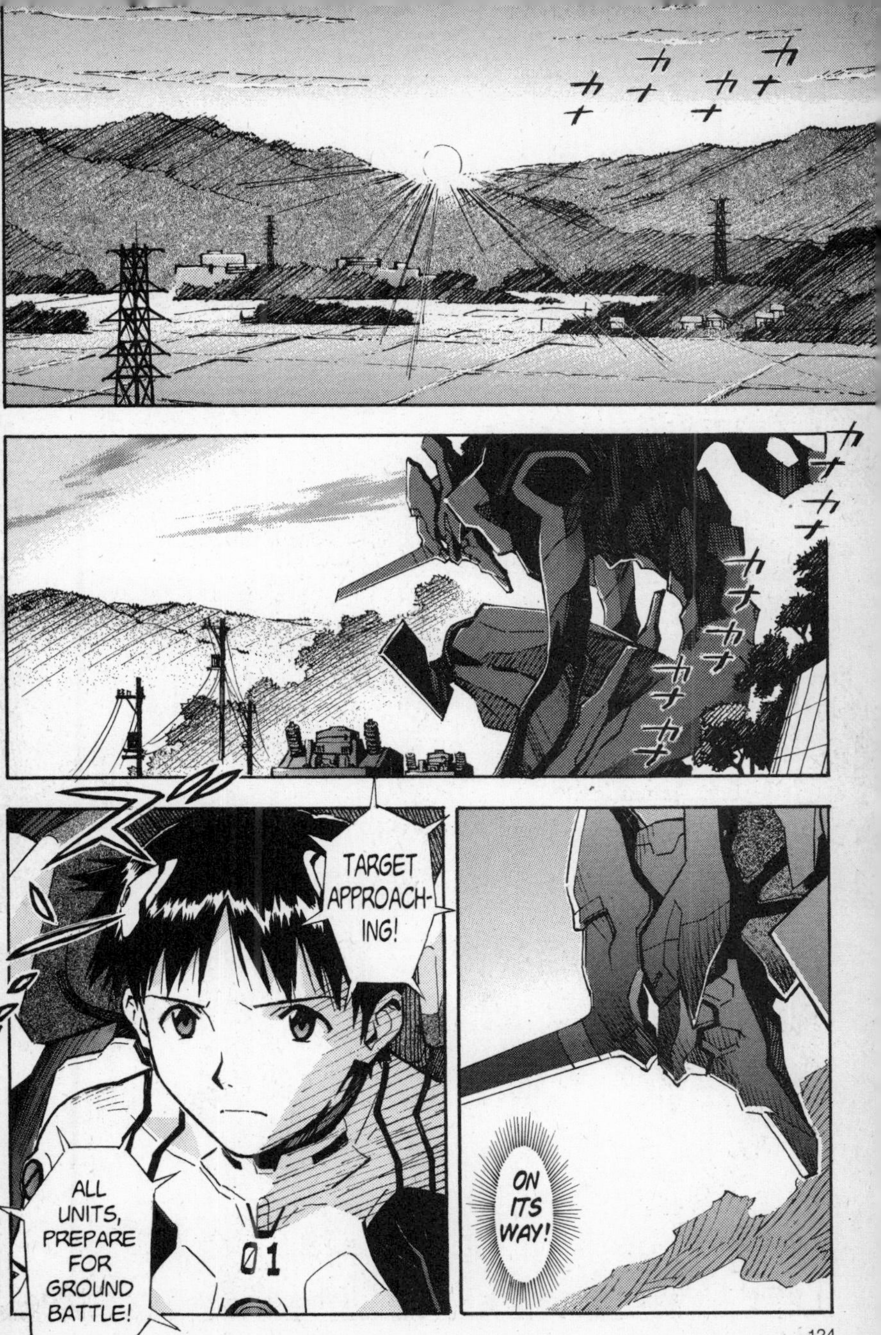
TARGET APPROACH-ING!
ON ITS WAY!
ALL UNITS, PREPARE FOR GROUND BATTLE!

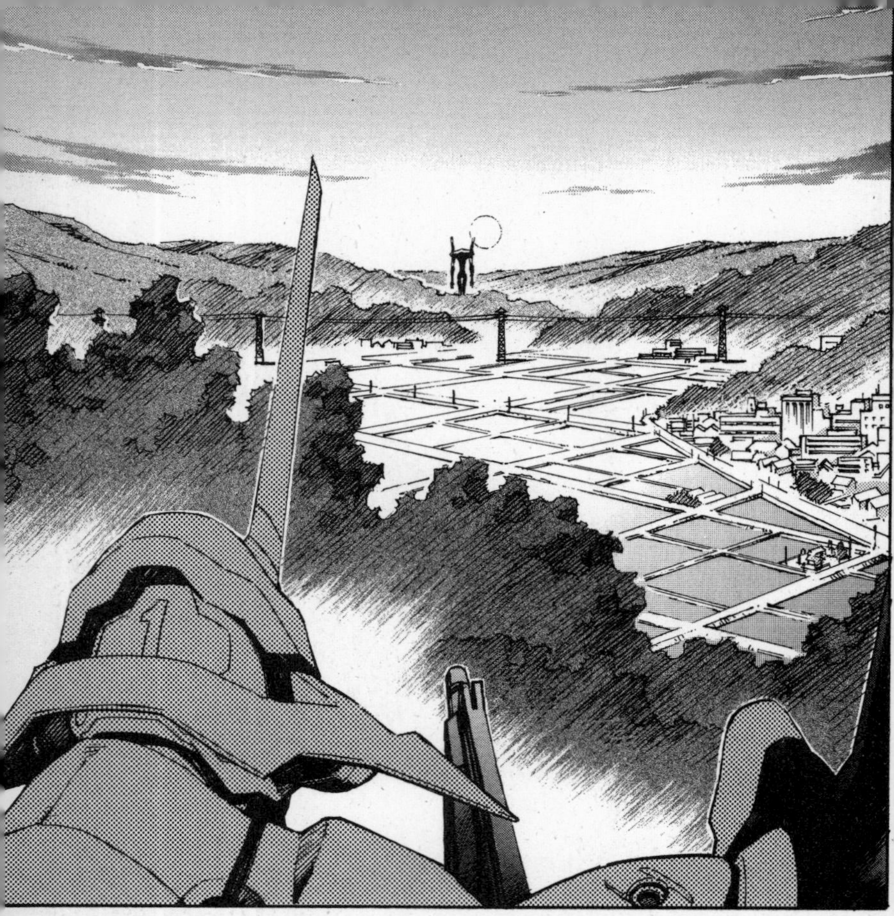
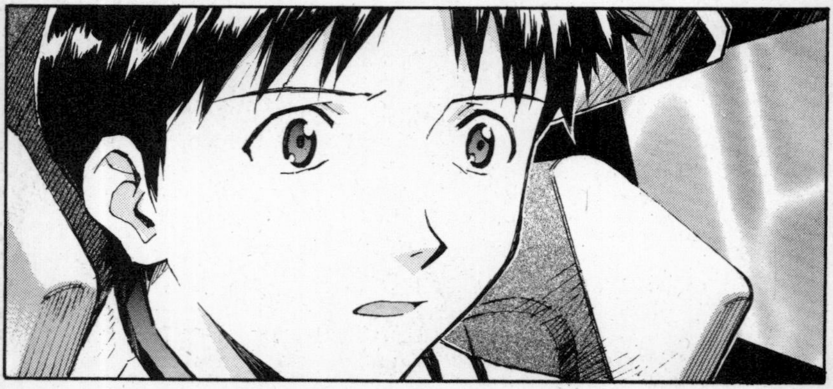

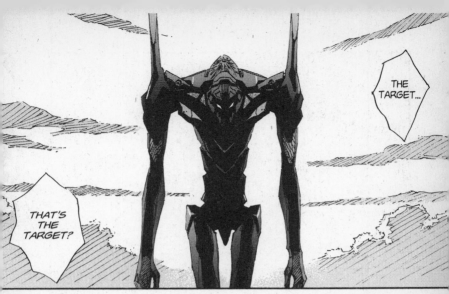

THE TARGET...

THAT'S THE TARGET?

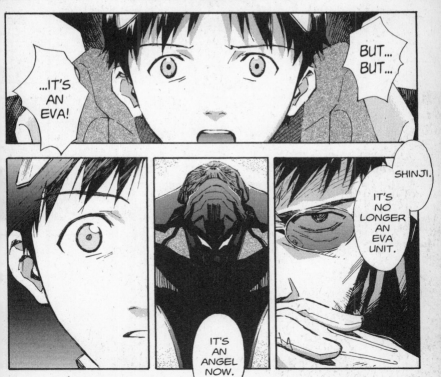

BUT... BUT...

...IT'S AN EVA!

SHINJI.

IT'S NO LONGER AN EVA UNIT.

IT'S AN ANGEL NOW.

126

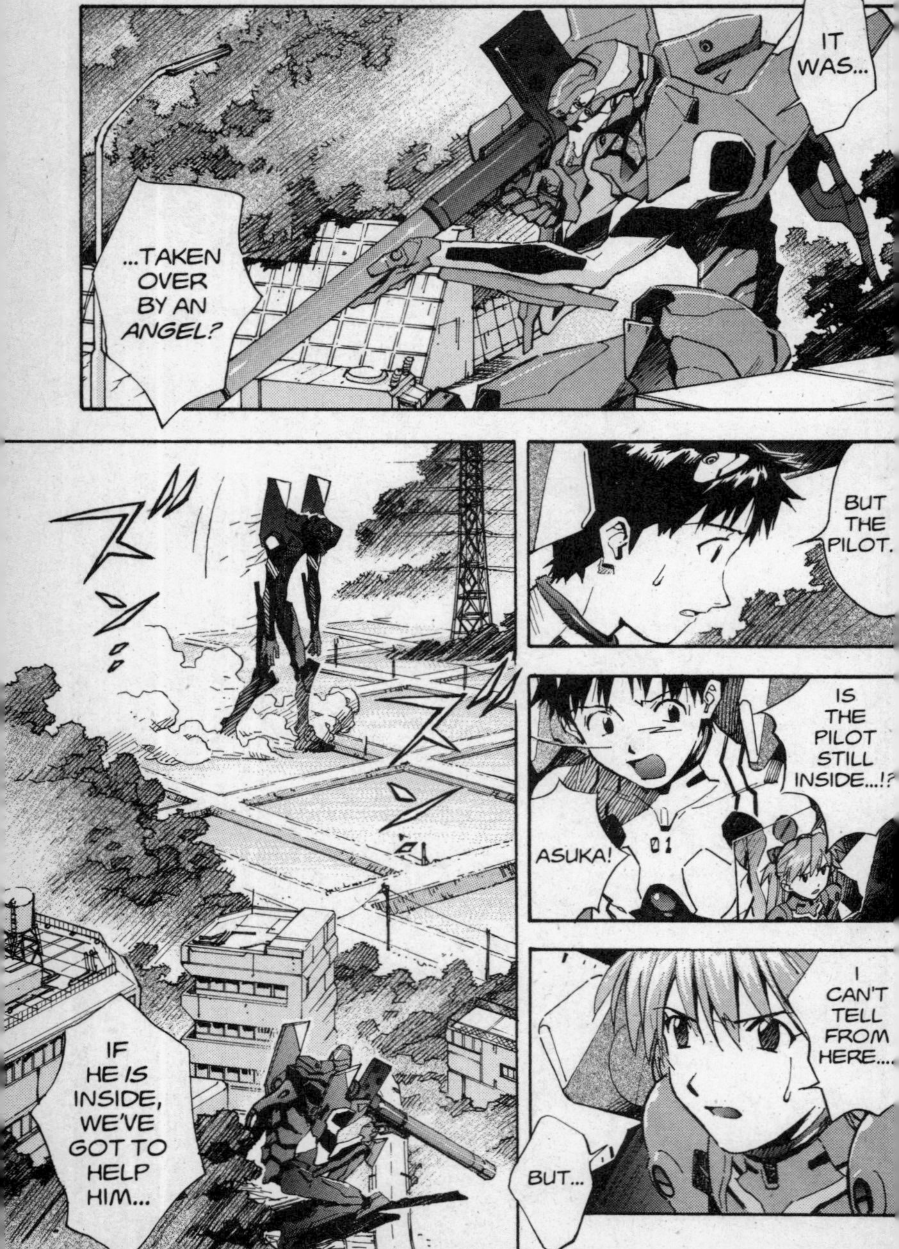
IT WAS...
...TAKEN OVER BY AN ANGEL?
BUT THE PILOT.
IS THE PILOT STILL INSIDE...!?
ASUKA!
01
I CAN'T TELL FROM HERE....
BUT...
IF HE IS INSIDE, WE'VE GOT TO HELP HIM...

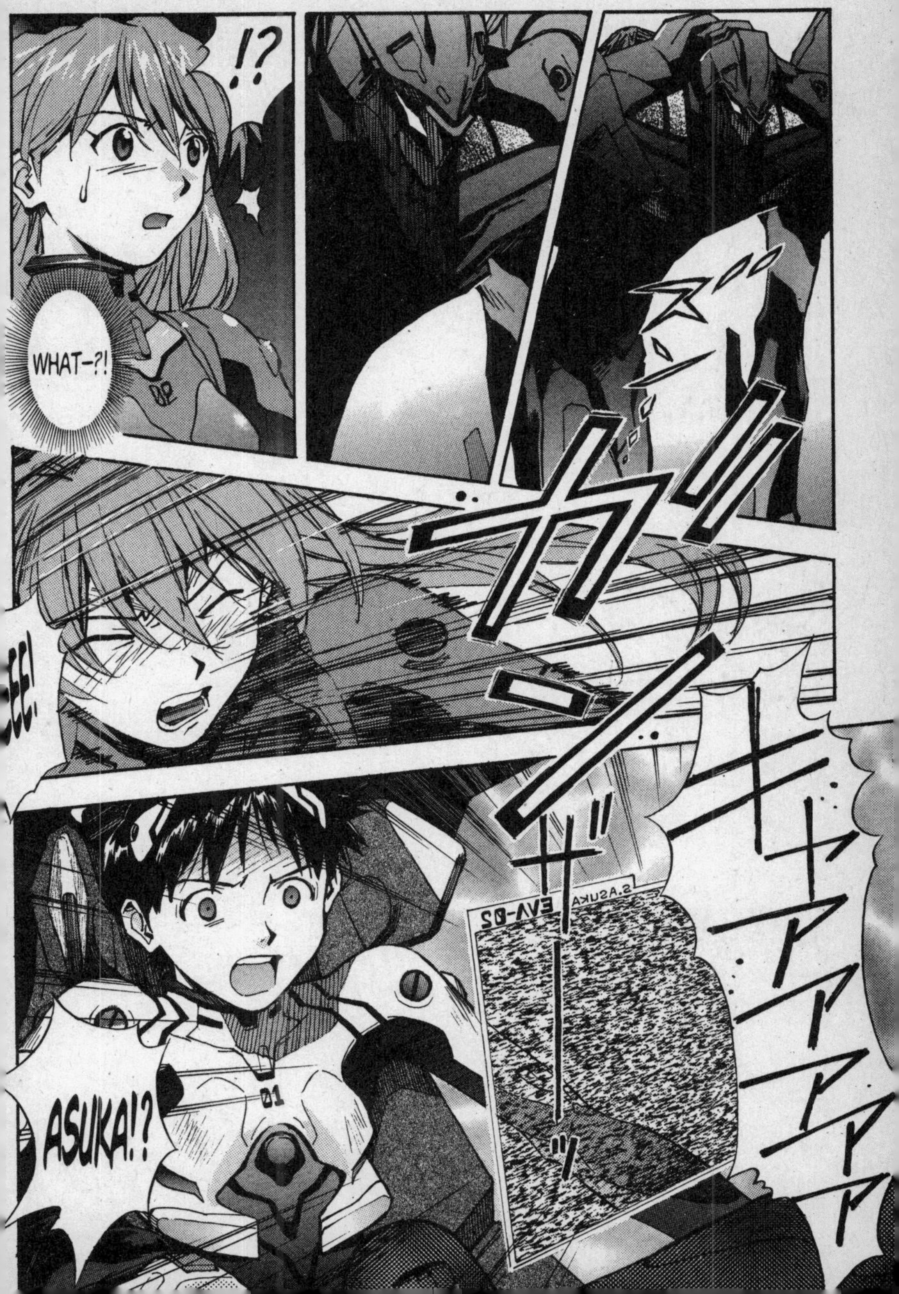
!?
WHAT-?!
EEE!
S.ASUKA
EVA-02
ASUKA!?

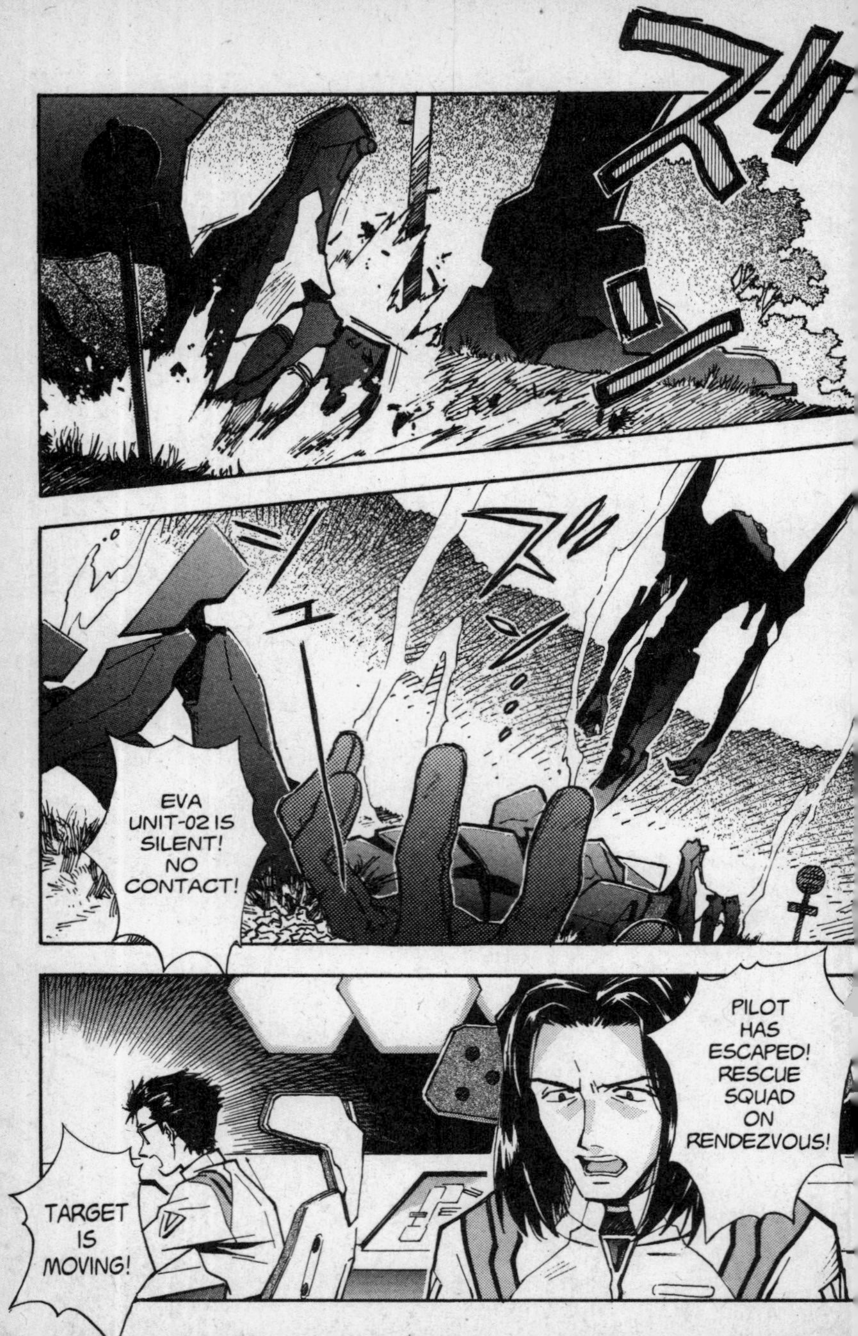
EVA UNIT-02 IS SILENT! NO CONTACT!
PILOT HAS ESCAPED! RESCUE SQUAD ON RENDEZVOUS!
TARGET IS MOVING!

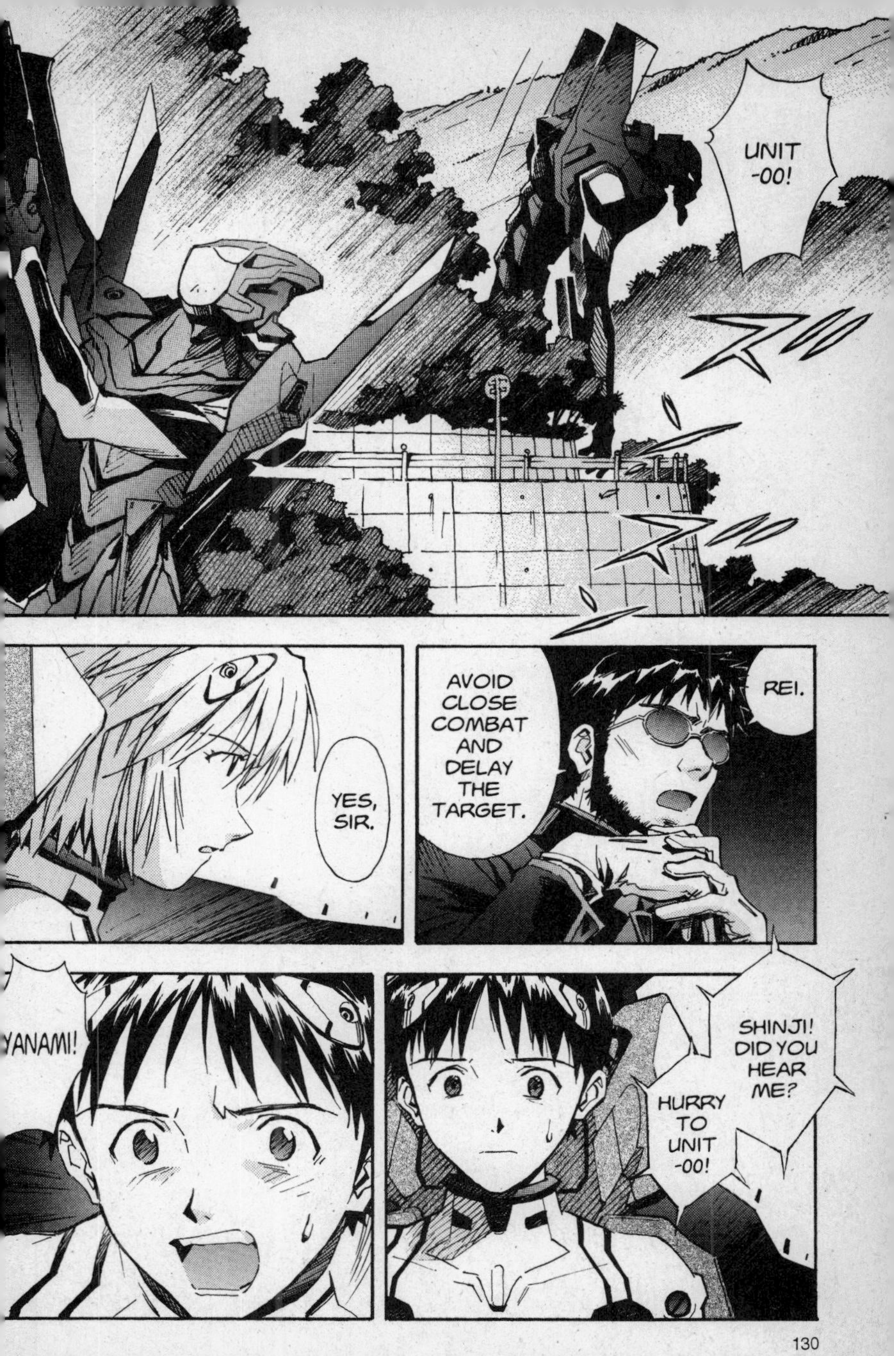
UNIT -00!
REI.
AVOID CLOSE COMBAT AND DELAY THE TARGET.
YES, SIR.
SHINJI! DID YOU HEAR ME?
HURRY TO UNIT -00!
YANAMI!

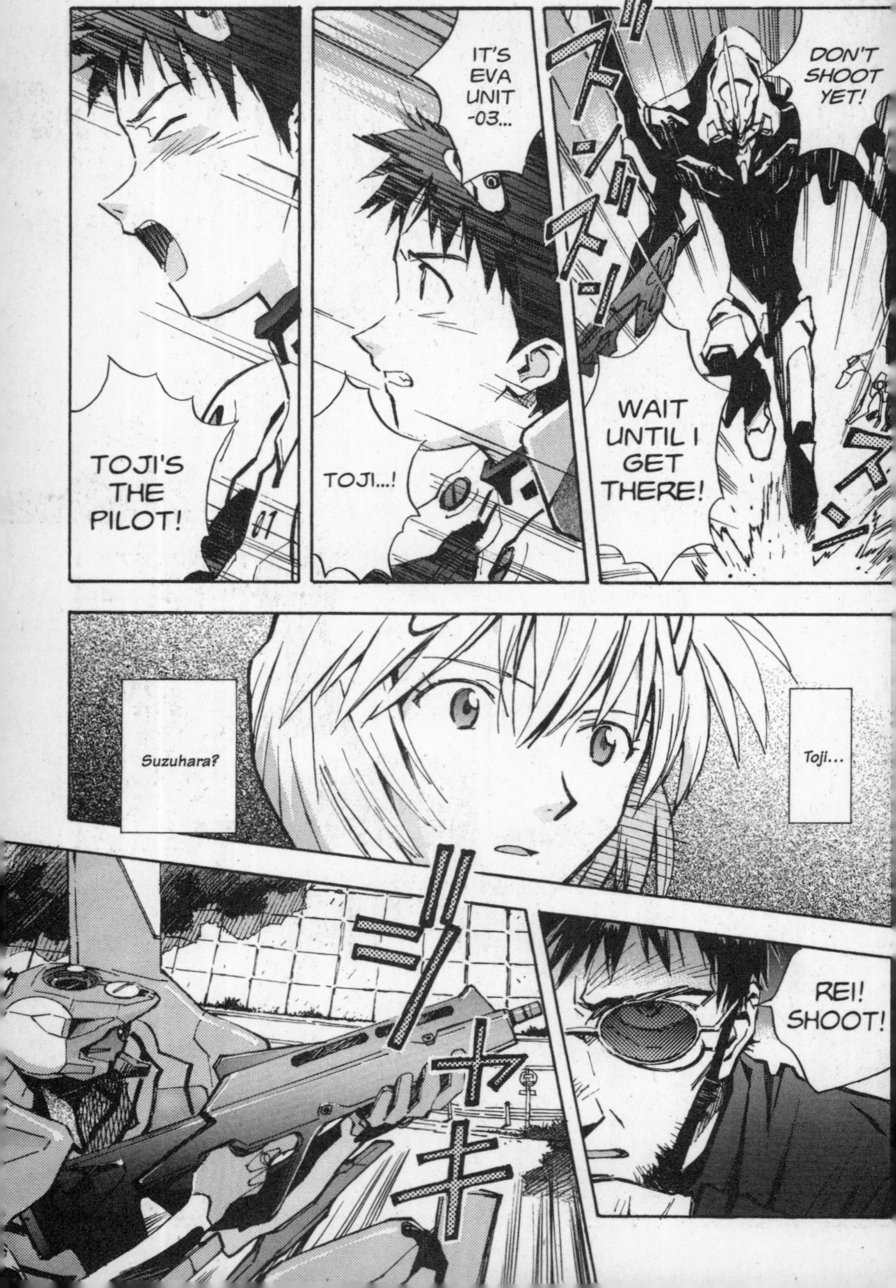
DON'T SHOOT YET!
WAIT UNTIL I GET THERE!
IT'S EVA UNIT -03...
TOJI...!
TOJI'S THE PILOT!
Toji...
Suzuhara?
REI! SHOOT!

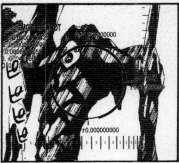

±0.000000000

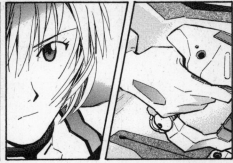

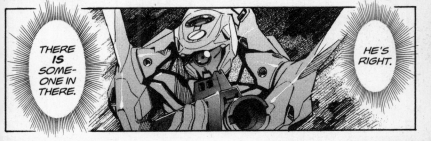

THERE
IS
SOME-
ONE IN
THERE.

HE'S
RIGHT.

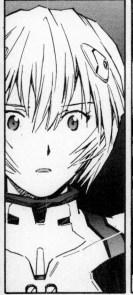

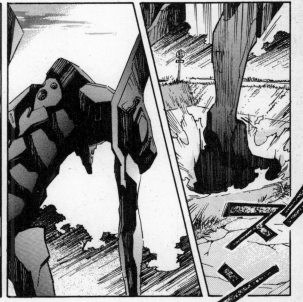

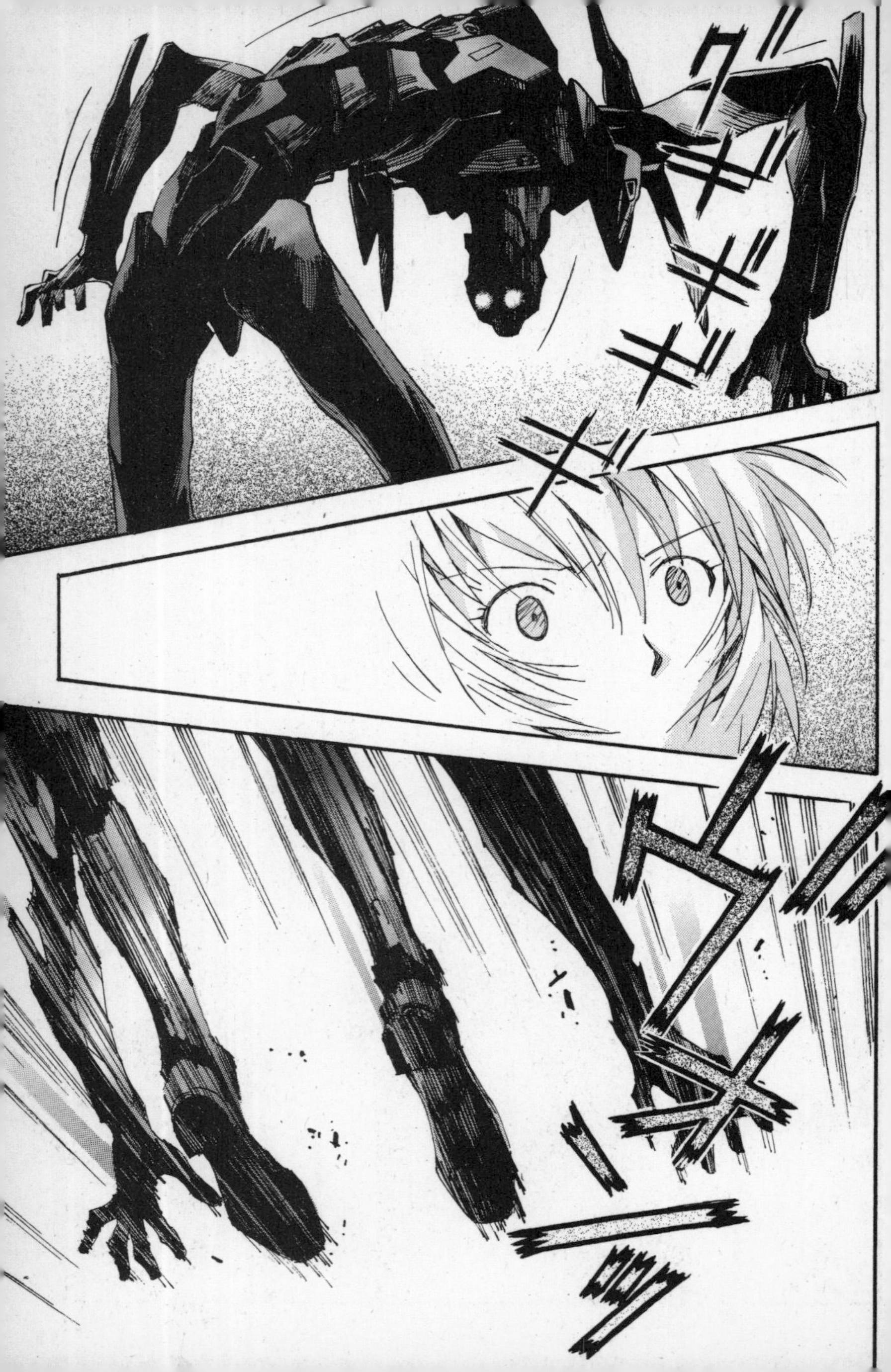
グギギギギ

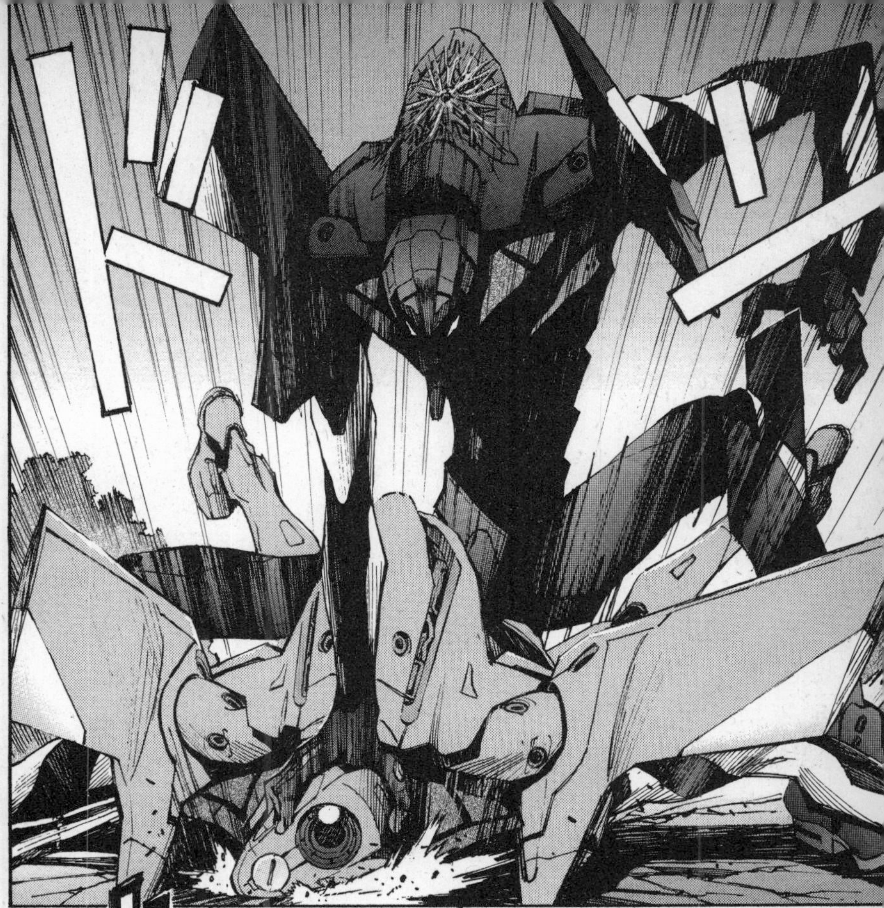

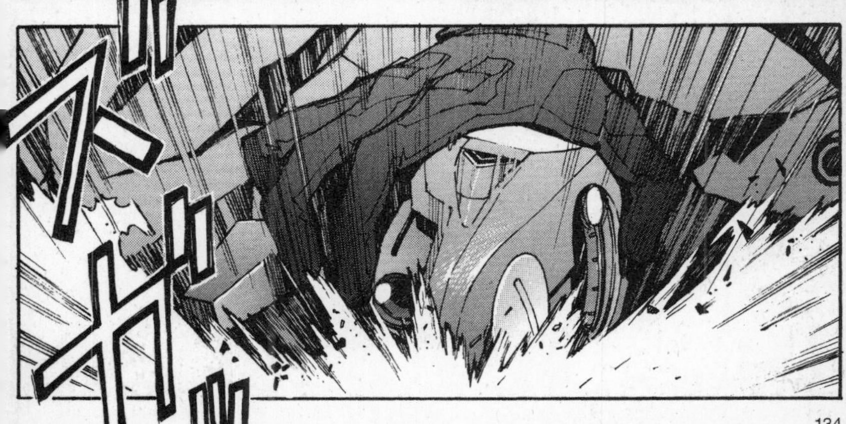

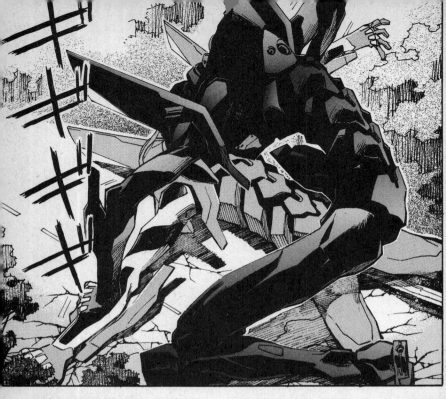

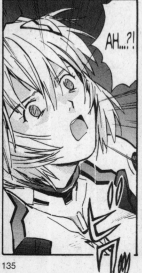

AH...?!

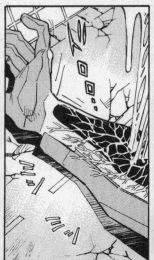

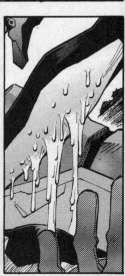

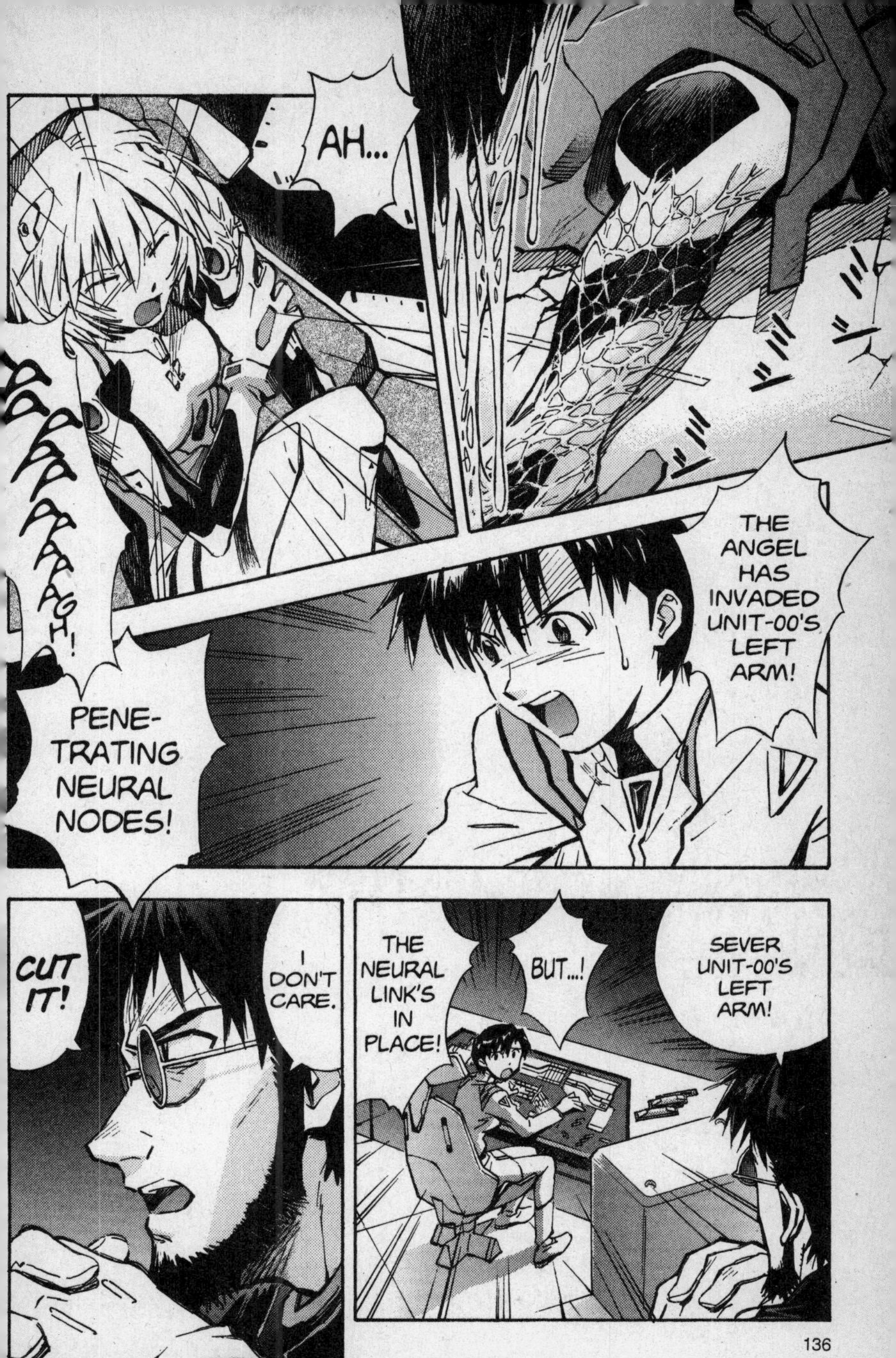
AH...
AAAAAAAAAAAAAAAGH!
THE ANGEL HAS INVADED UNIT-00'S LEFT ARM!
PENE-TRATING NEURAL NODES!
SEVER UNIT-00'S LEFT ARM!
BUT...!
THE NEURAL LINK'S IN PLACE!
I DON'T CARE.
CUT IT!

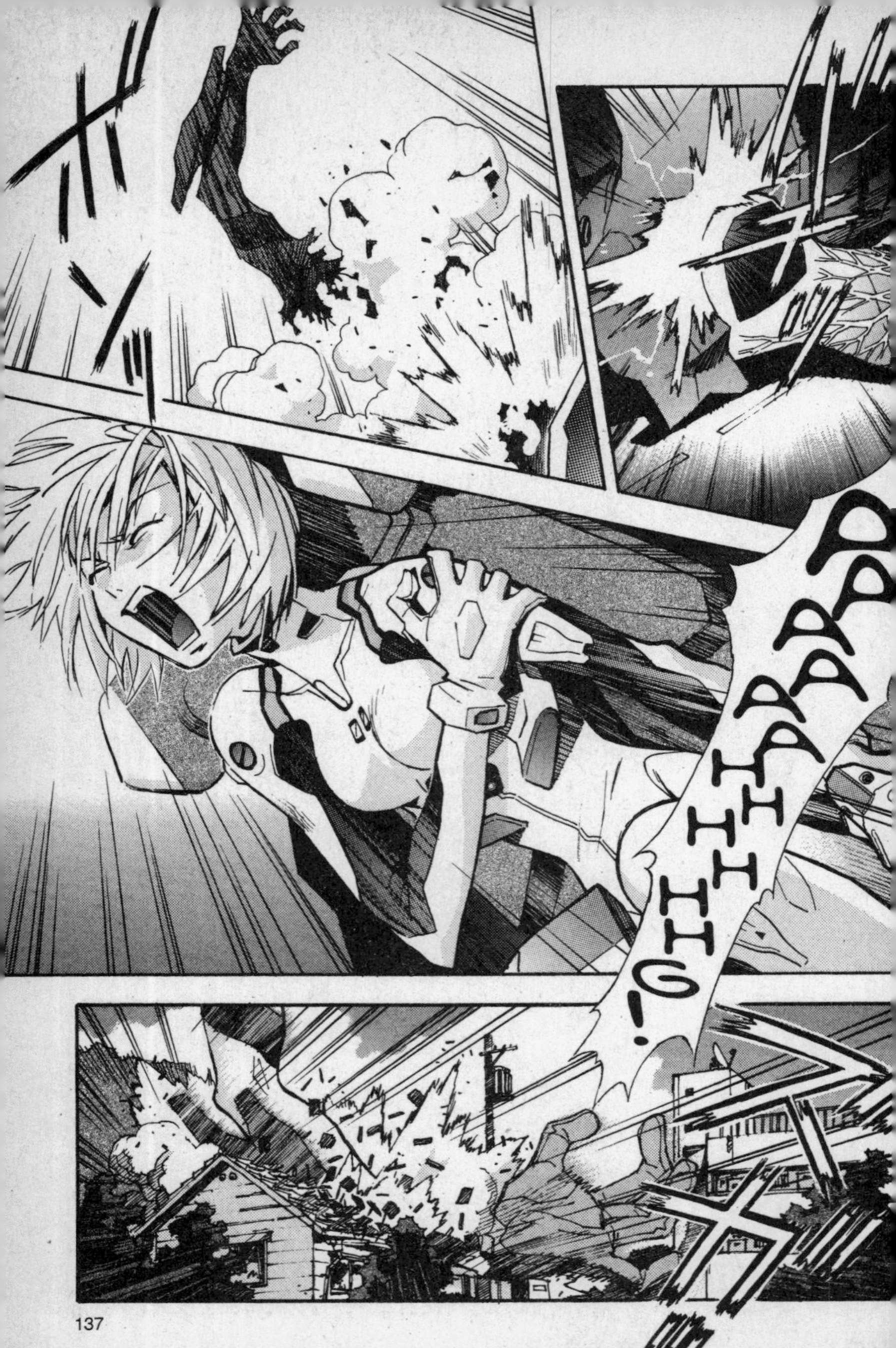
AAAAAAHHHHHHG!

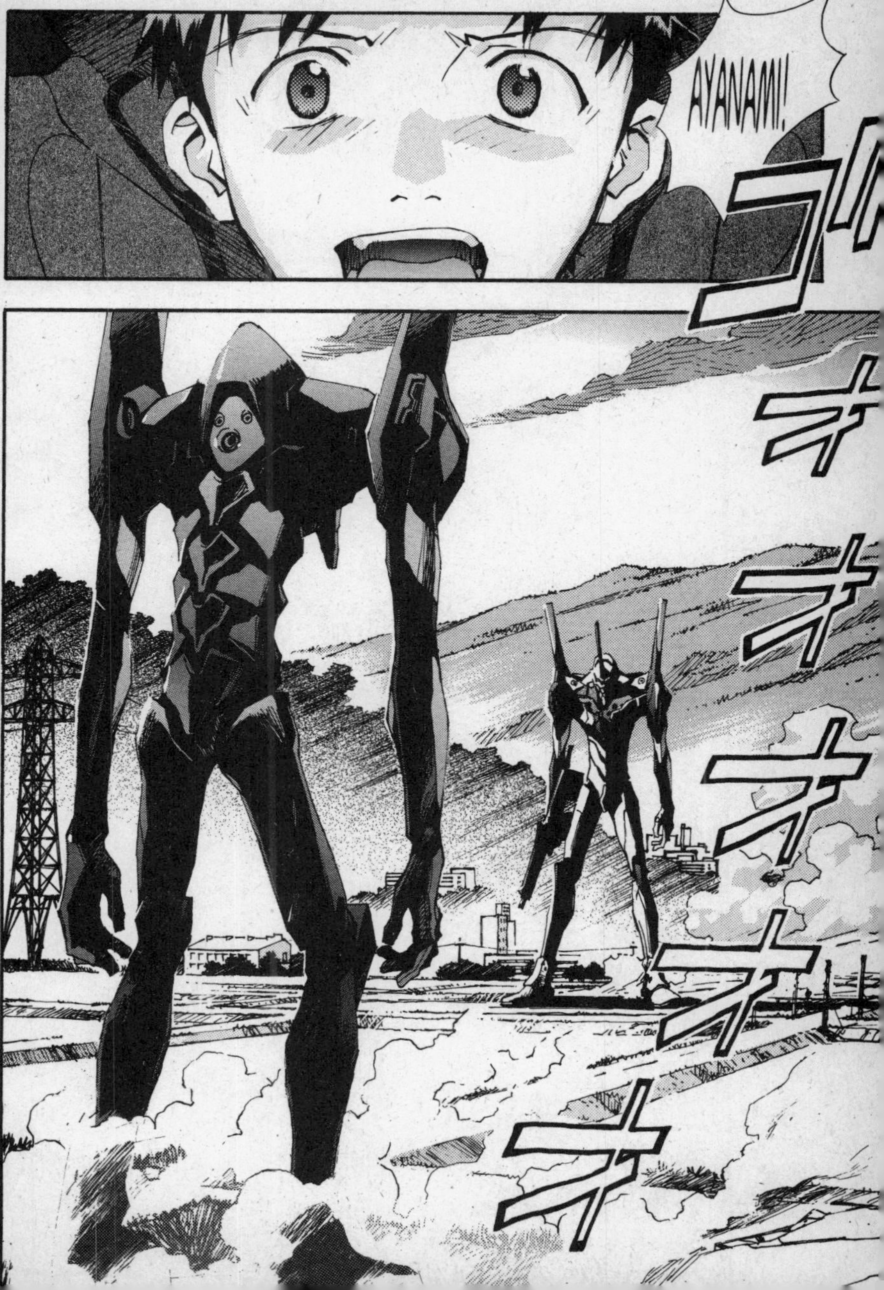
AYANAMI!
ゴォオオオオ

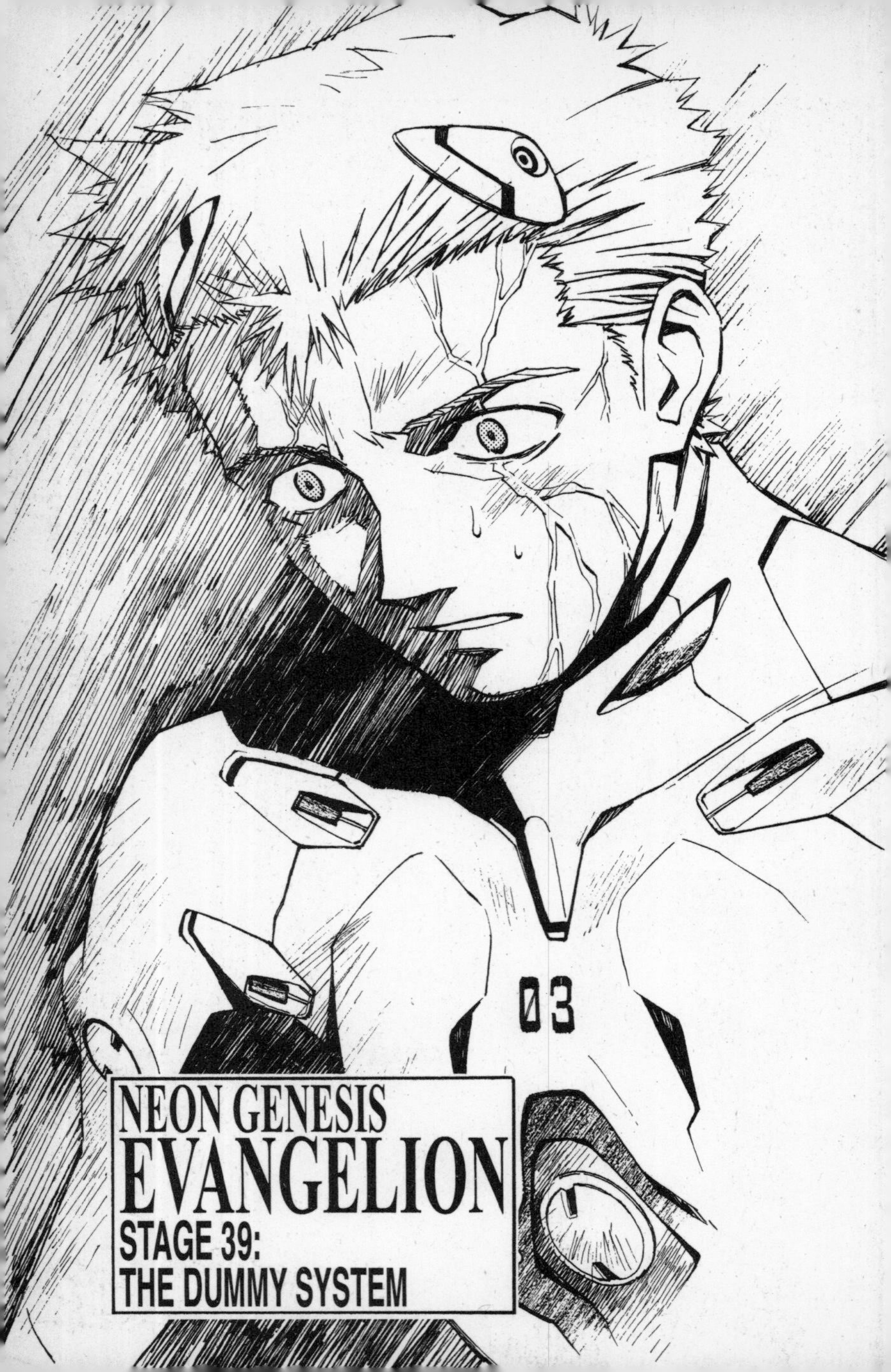
03
NEON GENESIS
EVANGELION
STAGE 39:
THE DUMMY SYSTEM

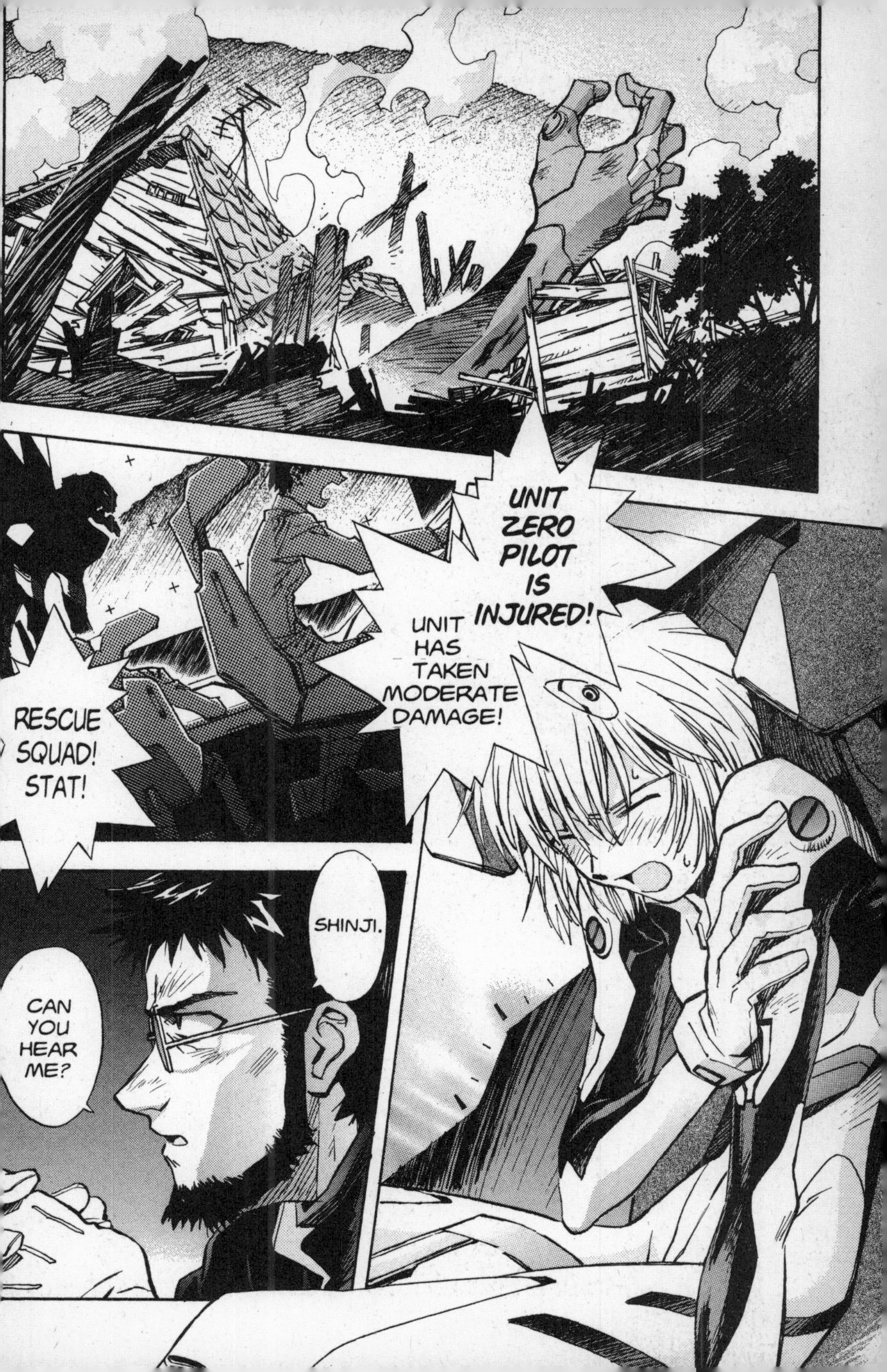
UNIT ZERO PILOT IS INJURED!
UNIT HAS TAKEN MODERATE DAMAGE!
RESCUE SQUAD! STAT!
SHINJI.
CAN YOU HEAR ME?

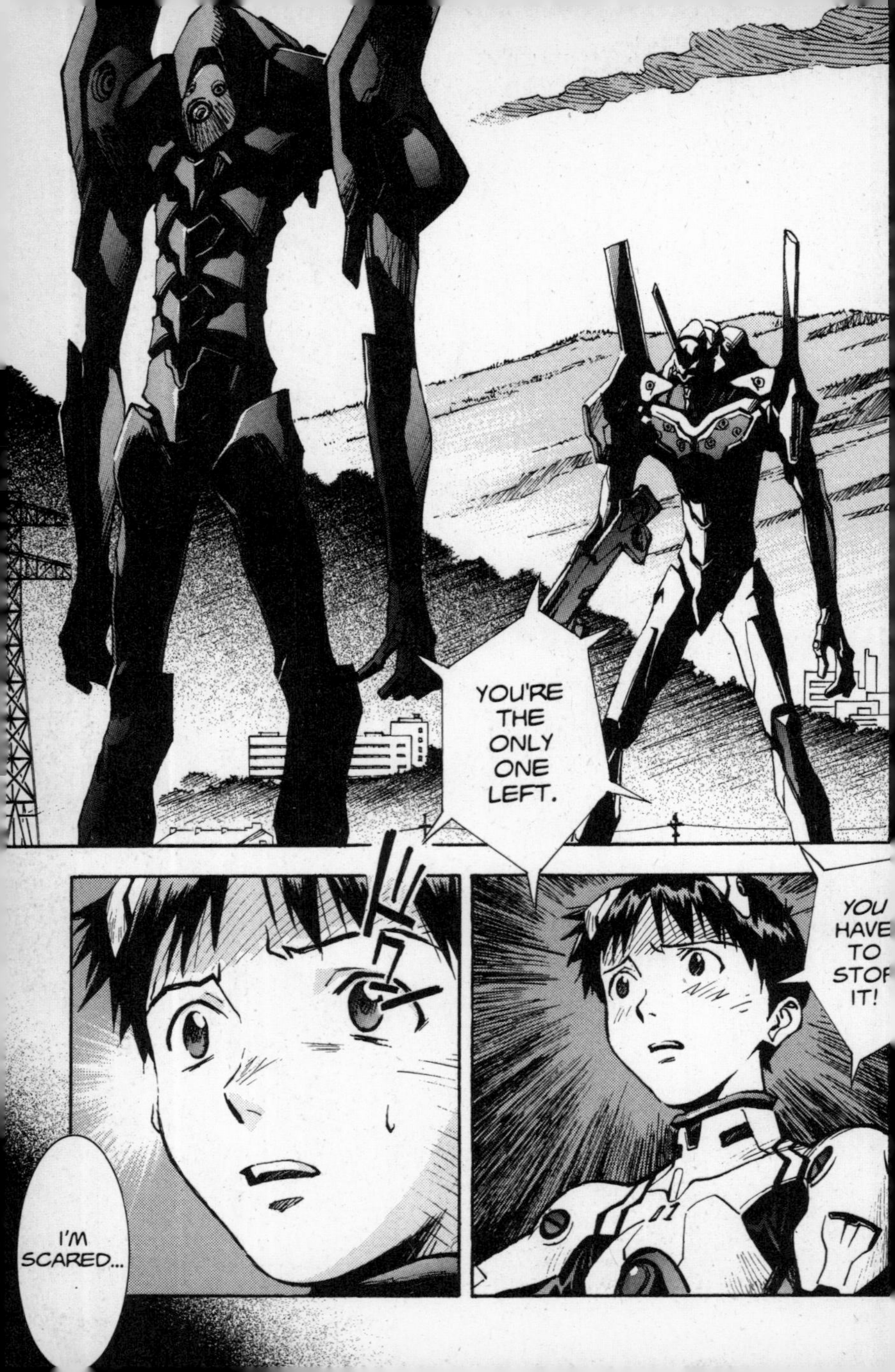
YOU'RE THE ONLY ONE LEFT.
YOU HAVE TO STOP IT!
I'M SCARED...

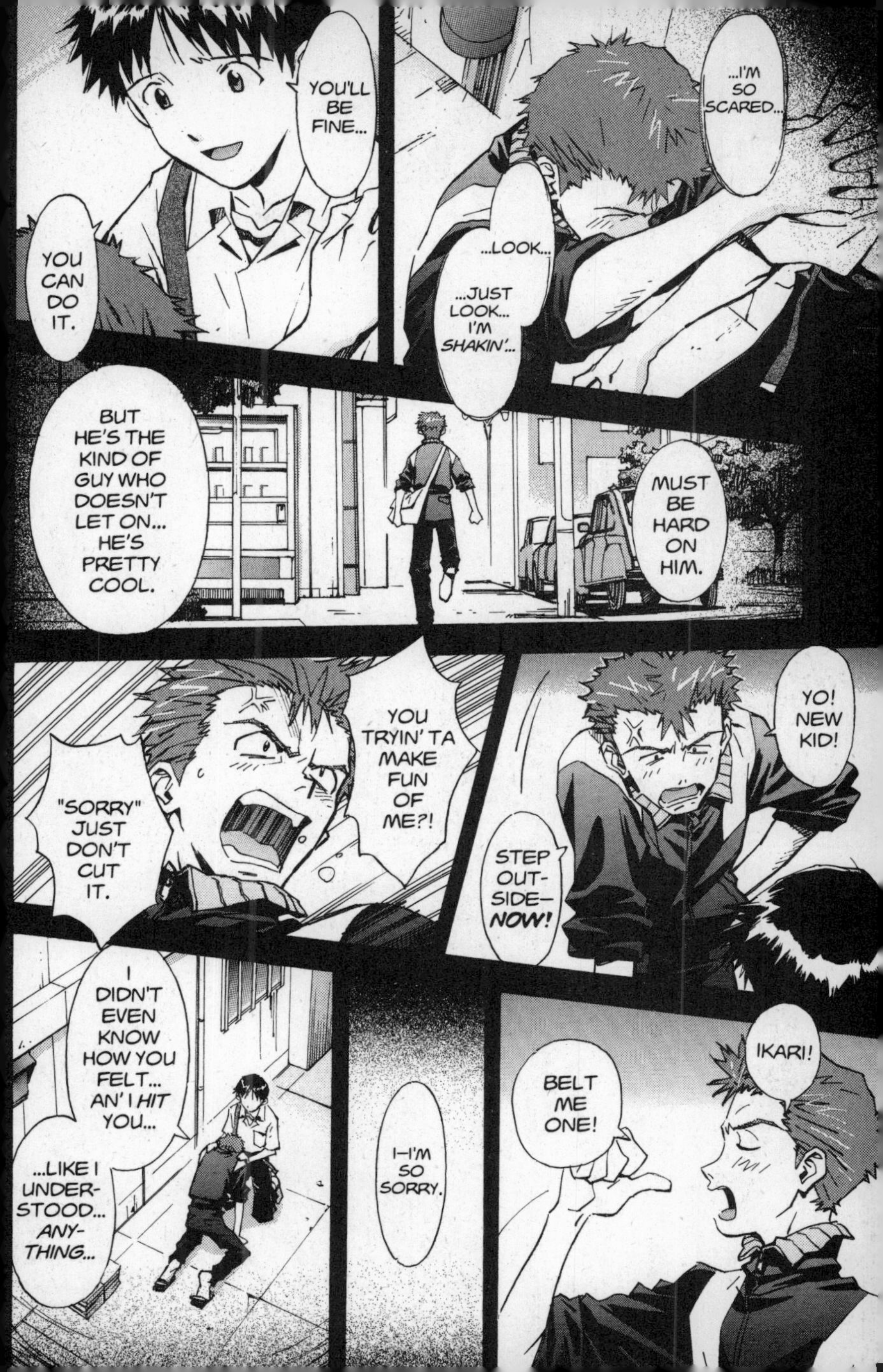
...I'M SO SCARED...
...LOOK...
...JUST LOOK... I'M *SHAKIN'*...
YOU'LL BE FINE...
YOU CAN DO IT.
MUST BE HARD ON HIM.
BUT HE'S THE KIND OF GUY WHO DOESN'T LET ON... HE'S PRETTY COOL.
YO! NEW KID!
STEP OUT-SIDE—*NOW!*
YOU TRYIN' TA MAKE FUN OF ME?!
"SORRY" JUST DON'T CUT IT.
IKARI!
BELT ME ONE!
I-I'M SO SORRY.
I DIDN'T EVEN KNOW HOW YOU FELT... AN' I *HIT* YOU...
...LIKE I UNDER-STOOD... ANY-*THING*...

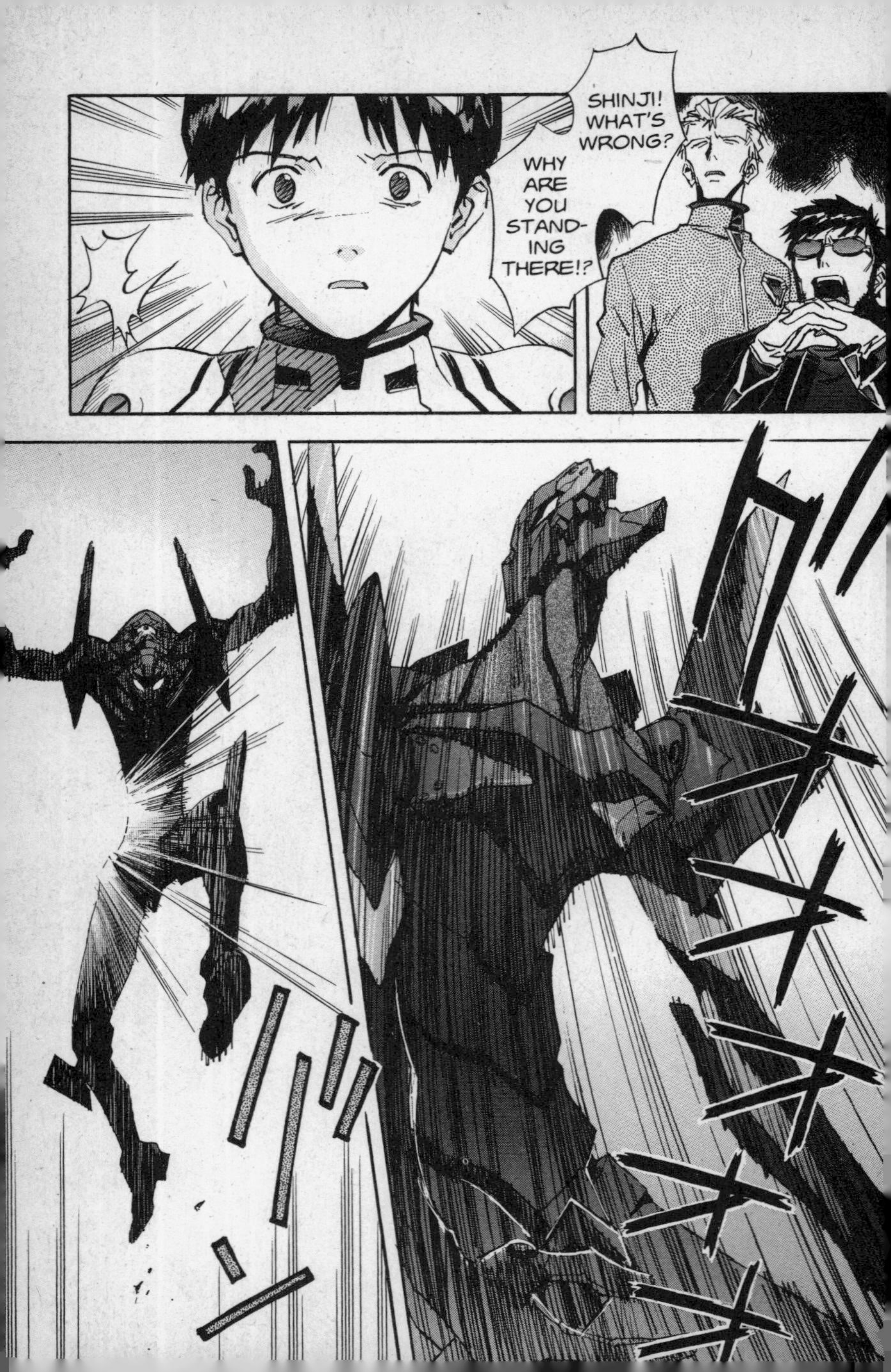
SHINJI! WHAT'S WRONG?
WHY ARE YOU STANDING-ING THERE!?

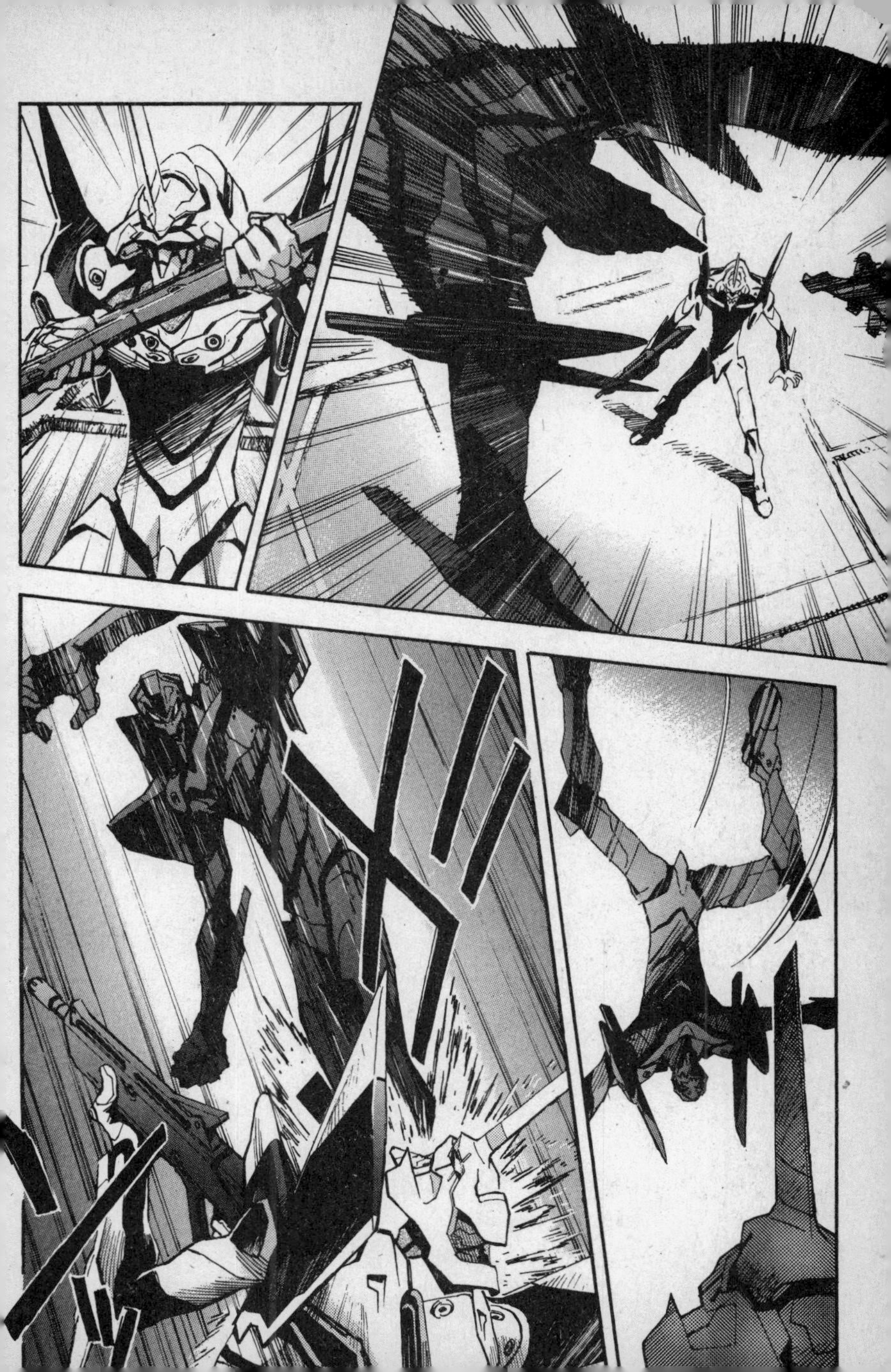

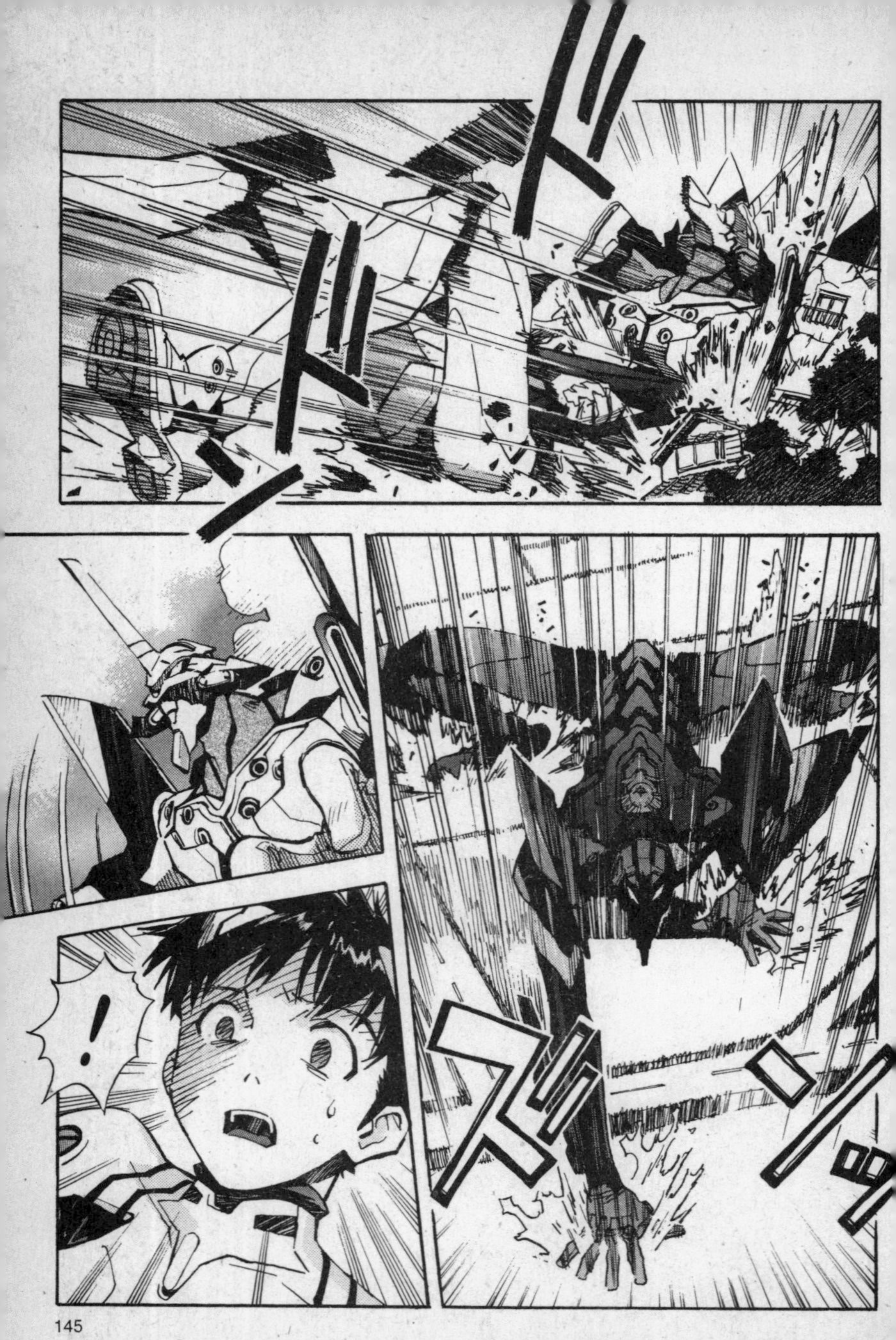
!

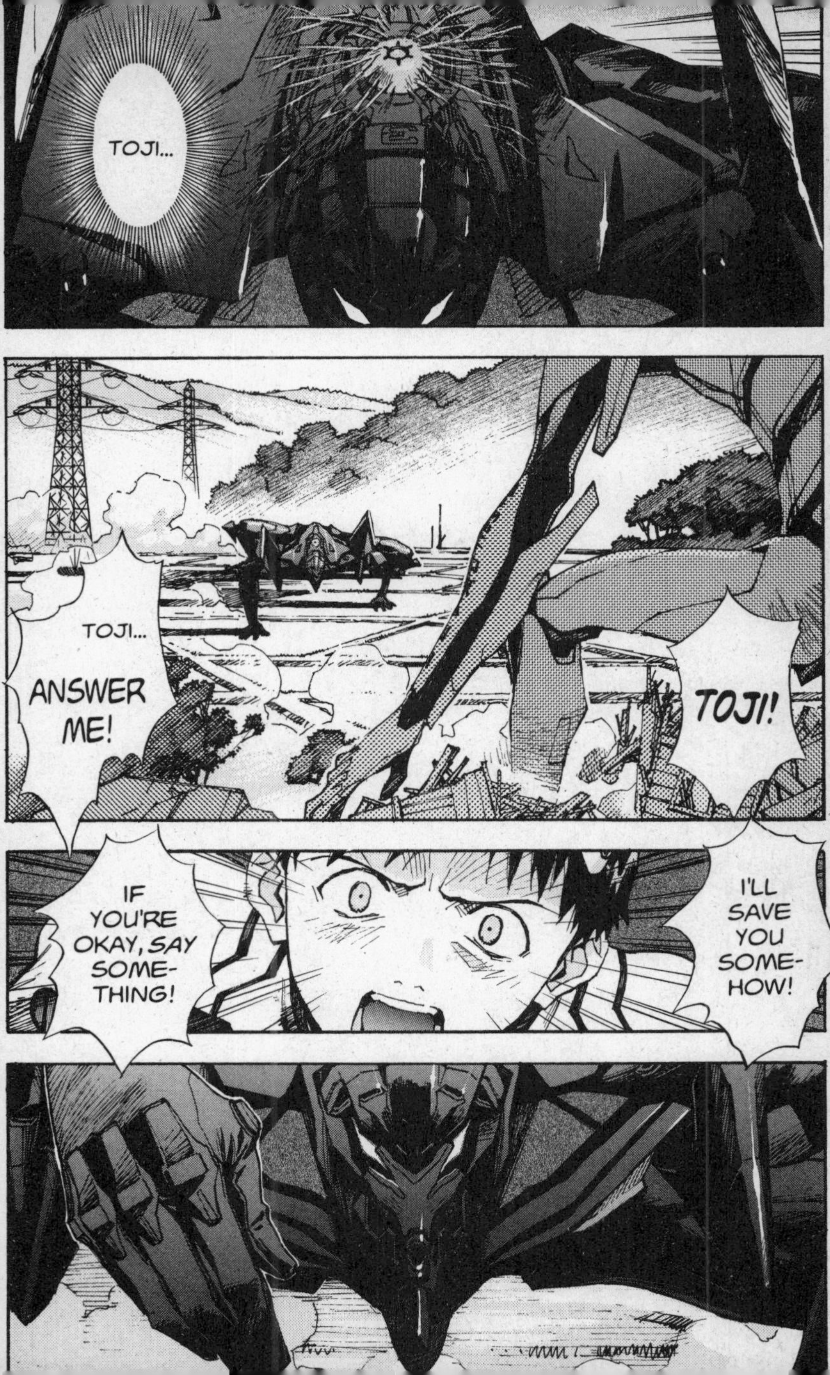
TOJI...
TOJI!
TOJI... ANSWER ME!
I'LL SAVE YOU SOME-HOW!
IF YOU'RE OKAY, SAY SOME-THING!

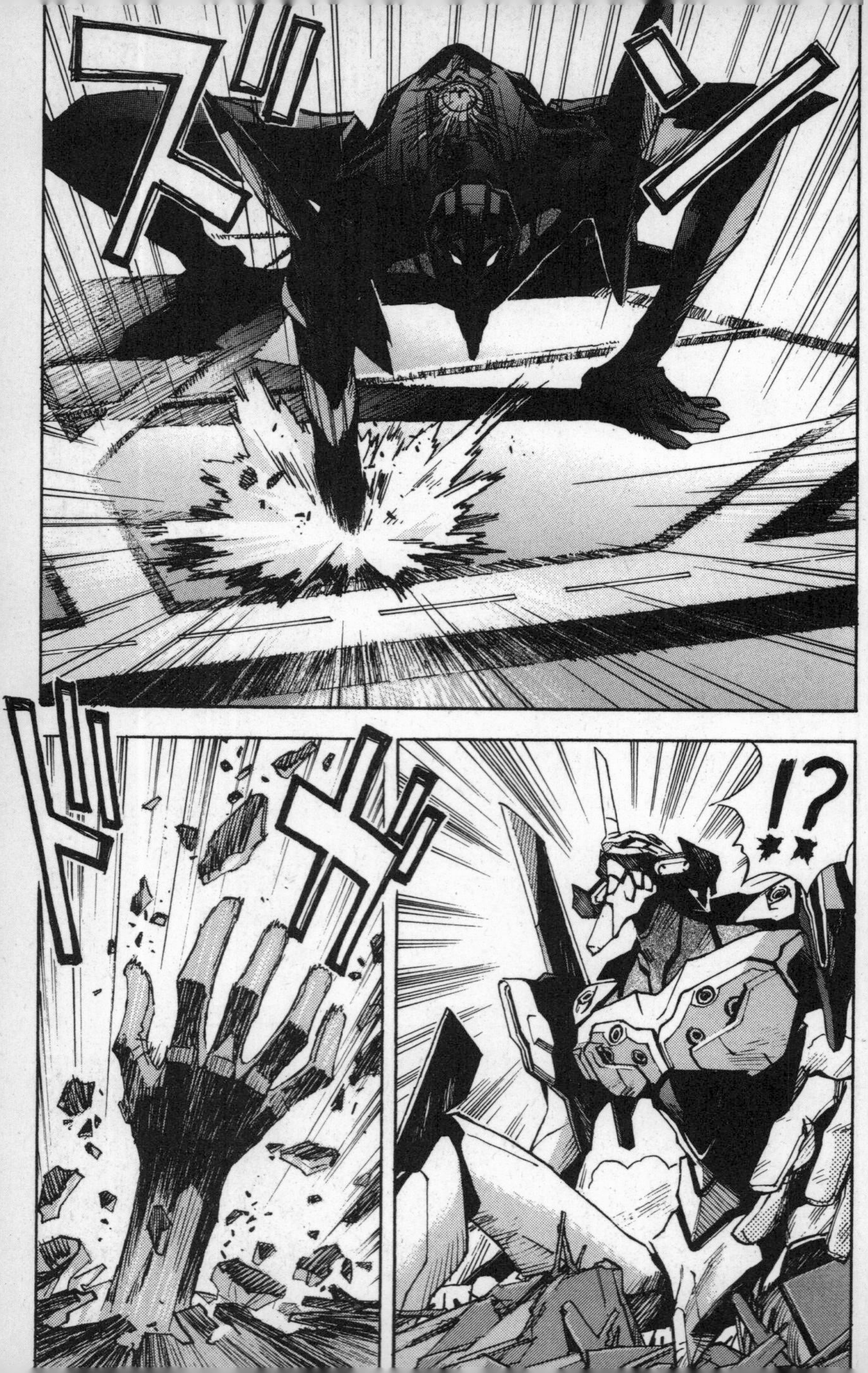
!?

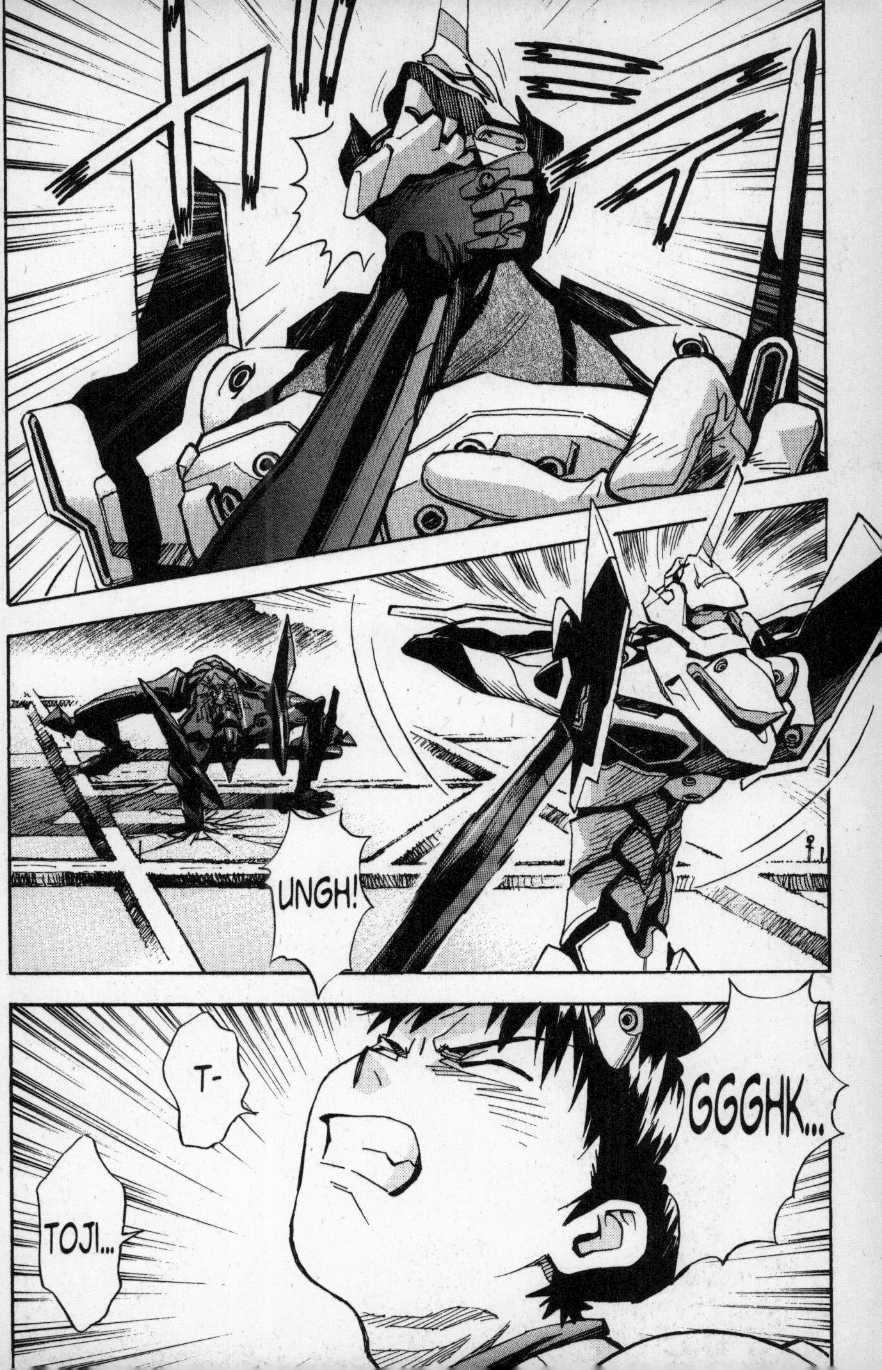
UNGH!
GGGHK...
T-
TOJI...

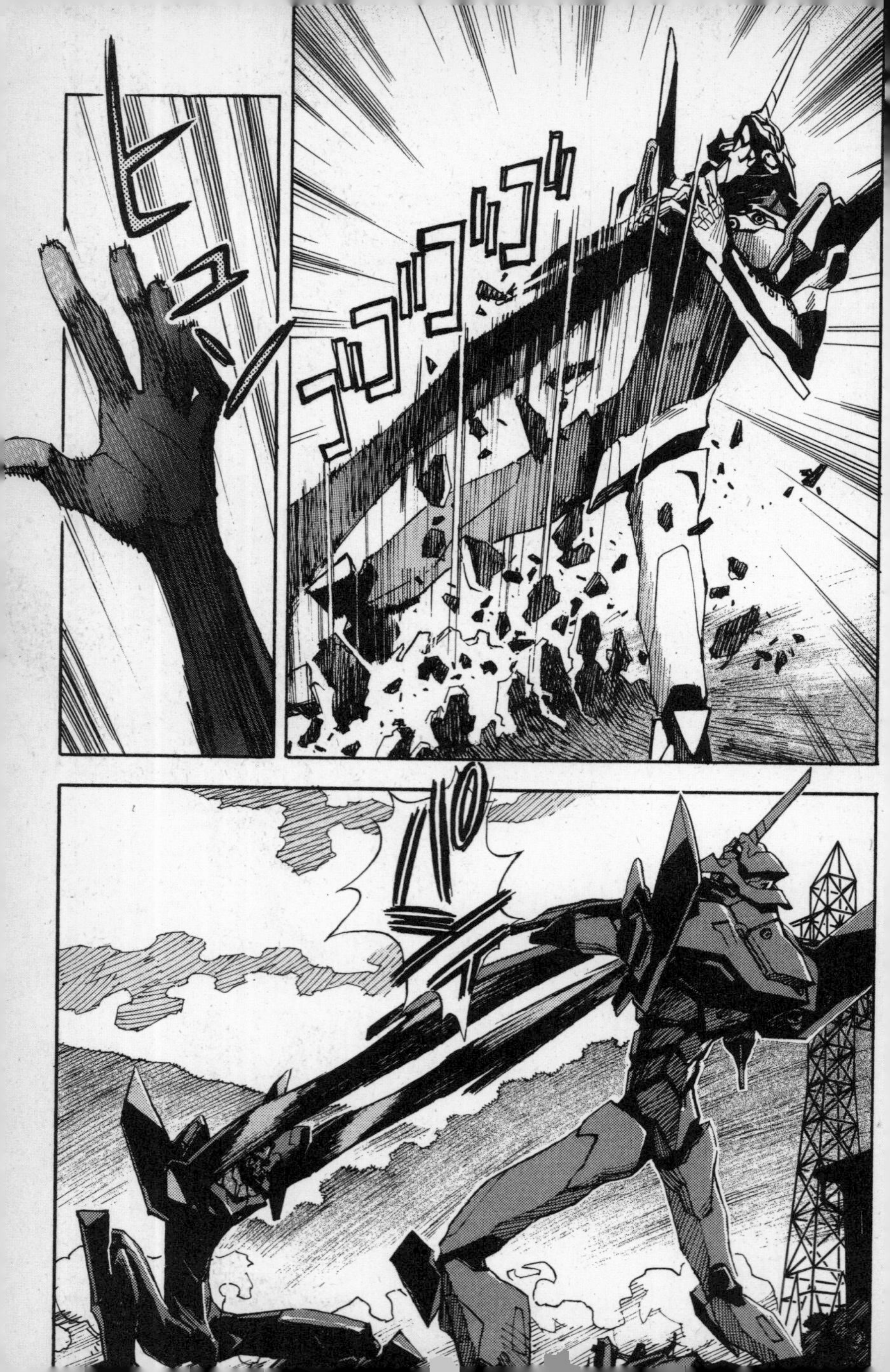
ゴゴゴゴゴゴ
ヒュン
パン

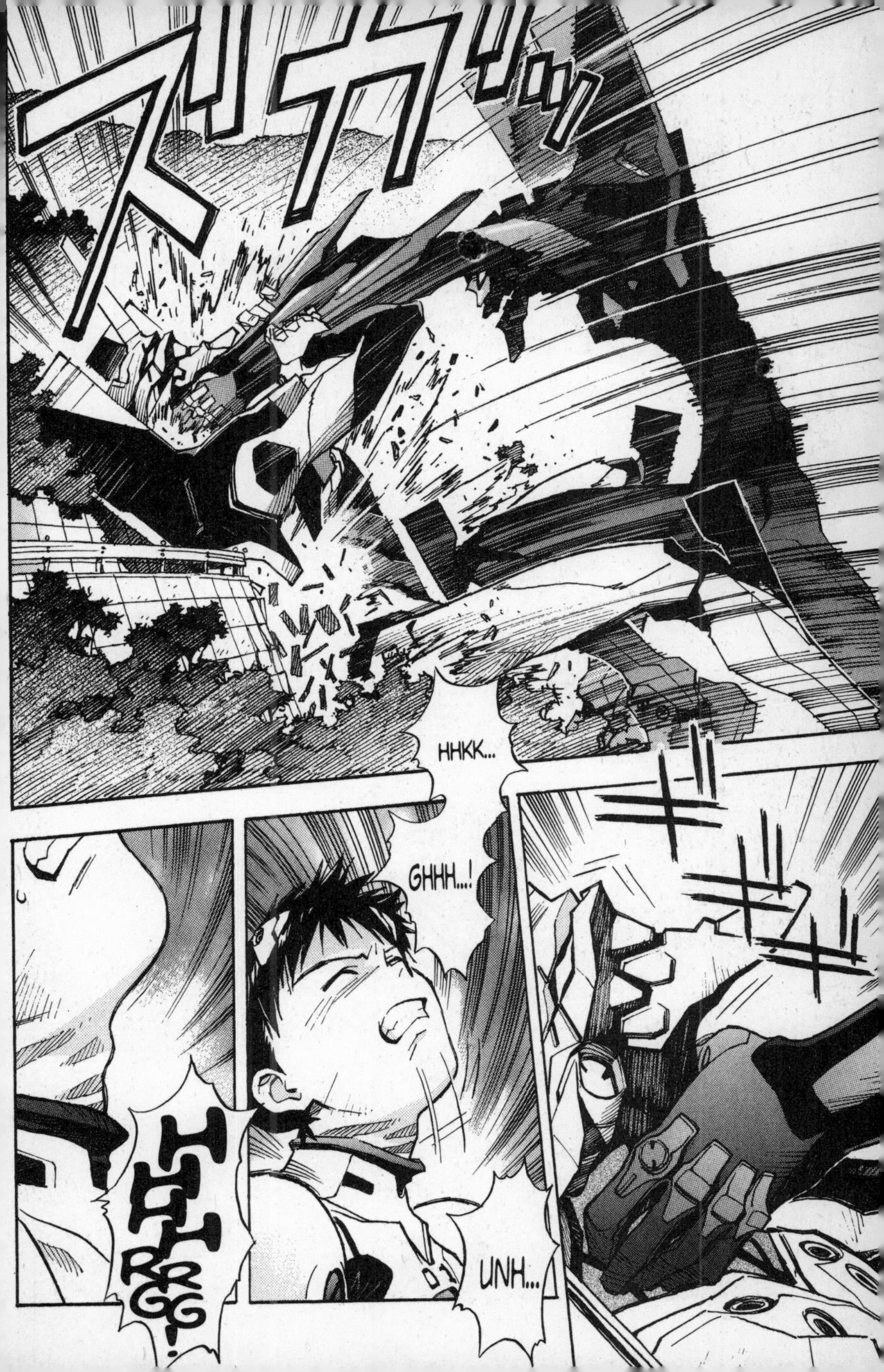
HHKK...
GHHH...!
UNH...
HHHRRGG!

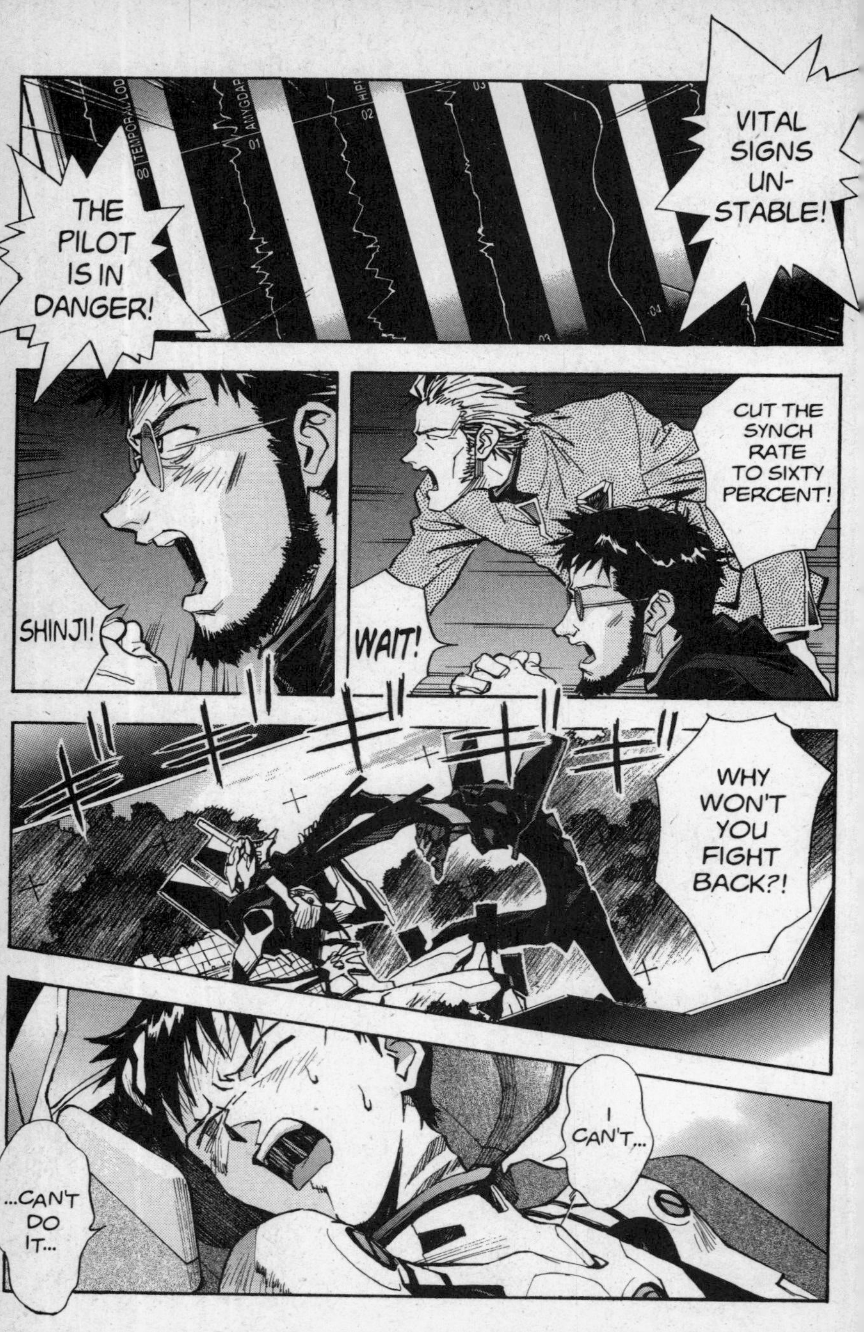
VITAL SIGNS UN-STABLE!
THE PILOT IS IN DANGER!
CUT THE SYNCH RATE TO SIXTY PERCENT!
WAIT!
SHINJI!
WHY WON'T YOU FIGHT BACK?!
I CAN'T...
...CAN'T DO IT...

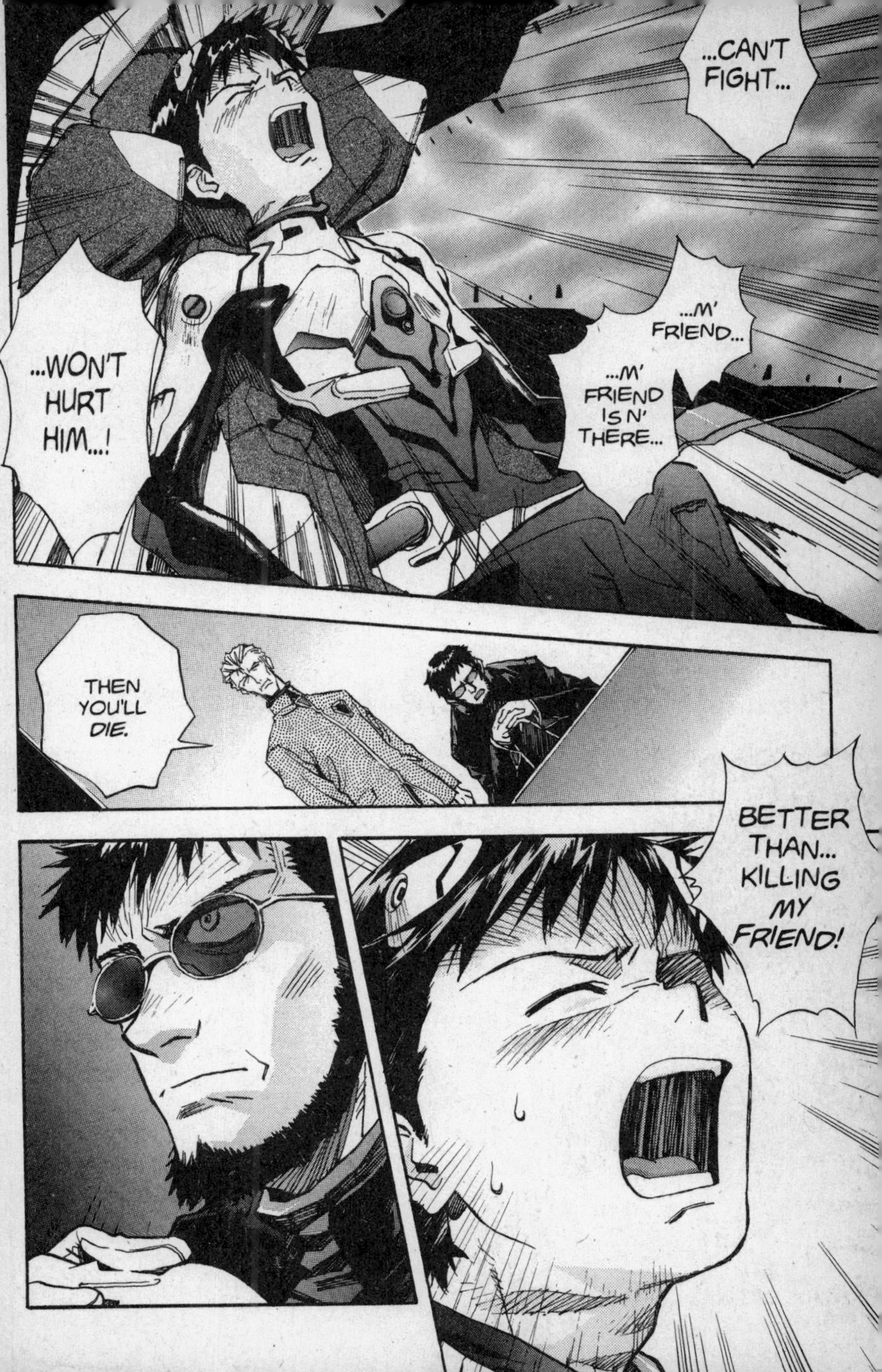
...CAN'T FIGHT...
...M' FRIEND...
...M' FRIEND IS N' THERE...
...WON'T HURT HIM...!
THEN YOU'LL DIE.
BETTER THAN... KILLING MY FRIEND!

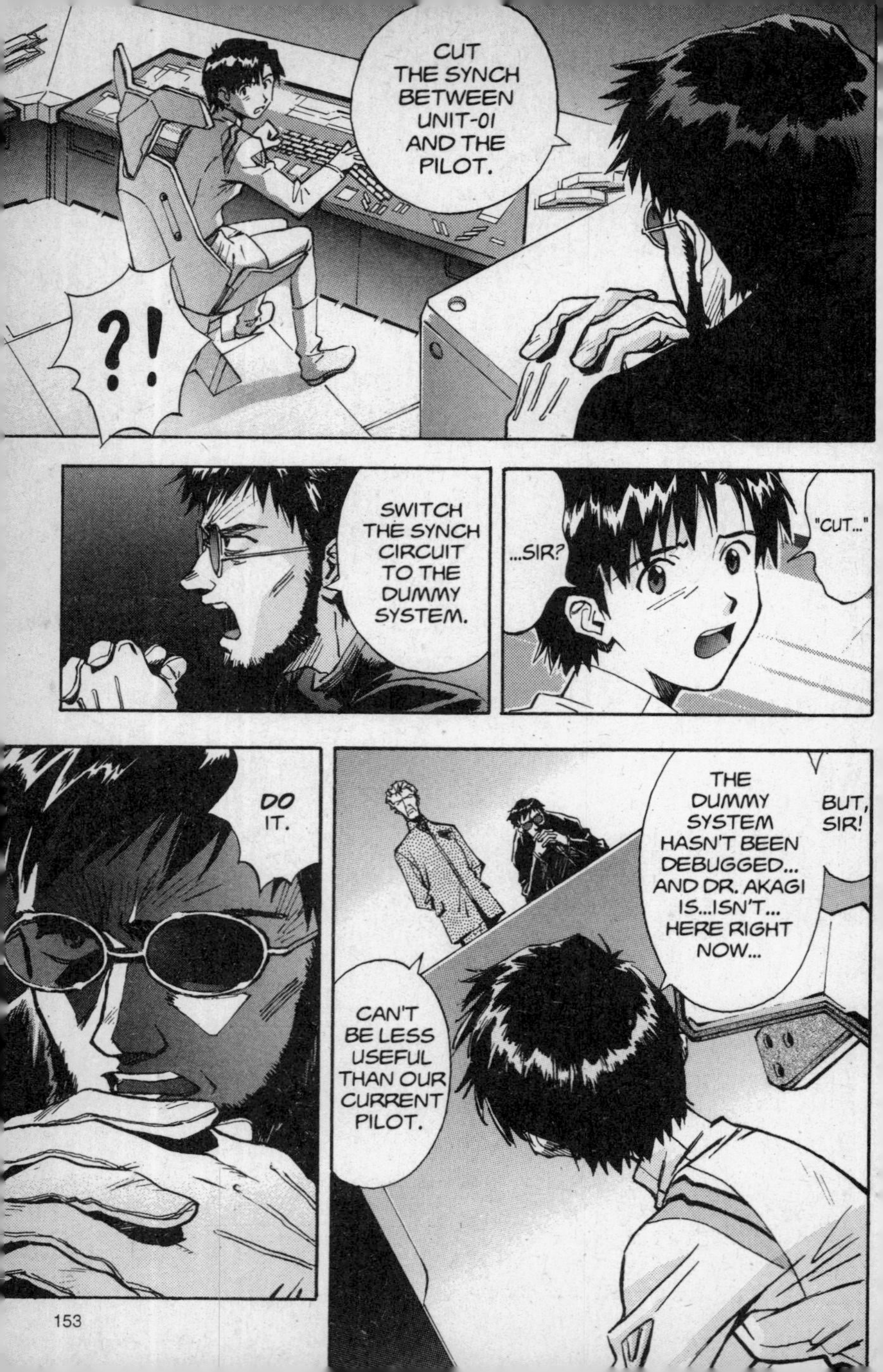
CUT THE SYNCH BETWEEN UNIT-01 AND THE PILOT.
?!
"CUT..."
...SIR?
SWITCH THE SYNCH CIRCUIT TO THE DUMMY SYSTEM.
BUT, SIR!
THE DUMMY SYSTEM HASN'T BEEN DEBUGGED... AND DR. AKAGI IS...ISN'T... HERE RIGHT NOW...
CAN'T BE LESS USEFUL THAN OUR CURRENT PILOT.
DO IT.

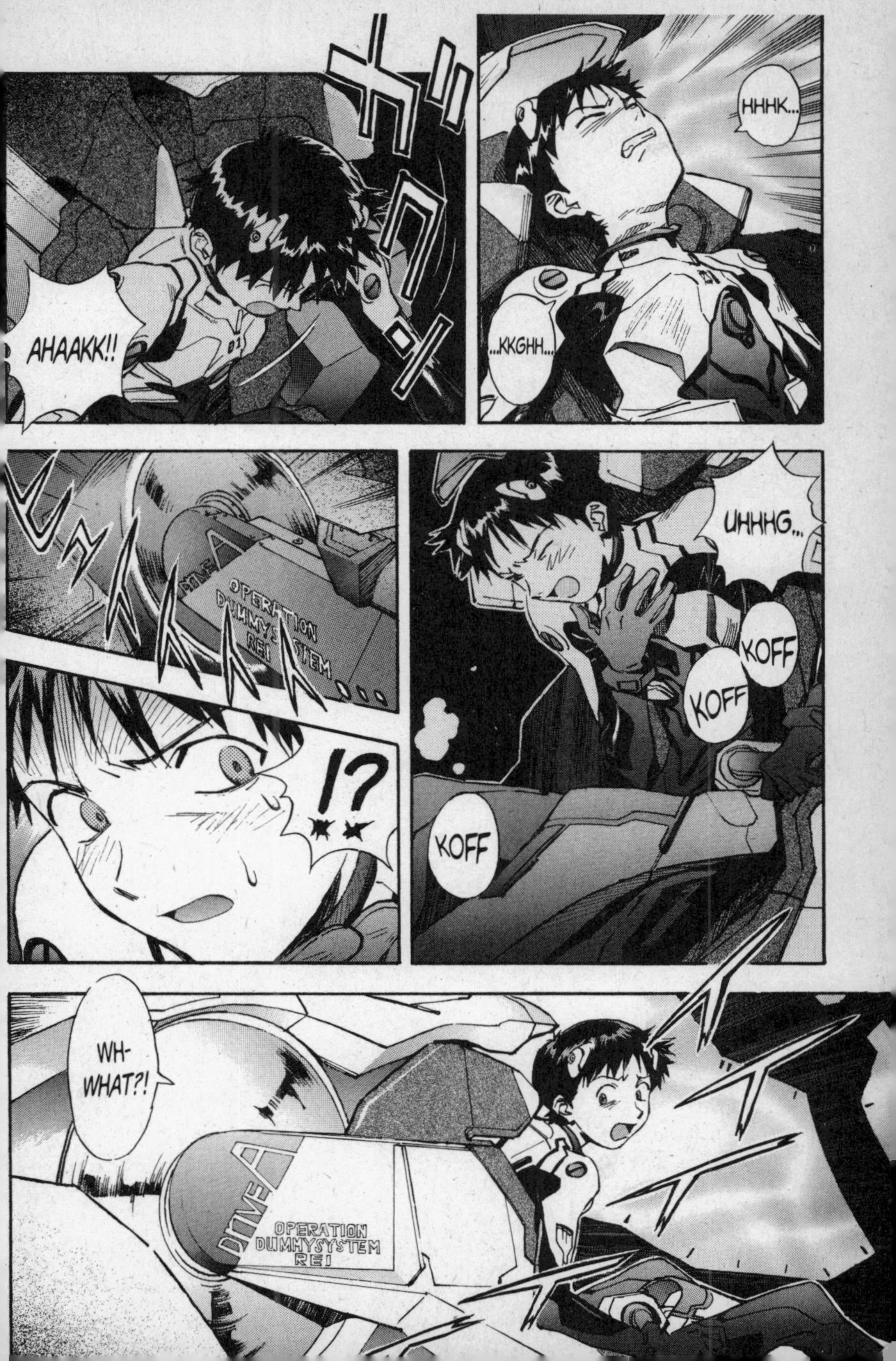
HHHK...
...KKGHH...
AHAAKK!!
UHHHG...
KOFF
KOFF
KOFF
OPERATION
DUMMYSYSTEM
REI
...
!?
WH-
WHAT?!
OPERATION
DUMMYSYSTEM
REI

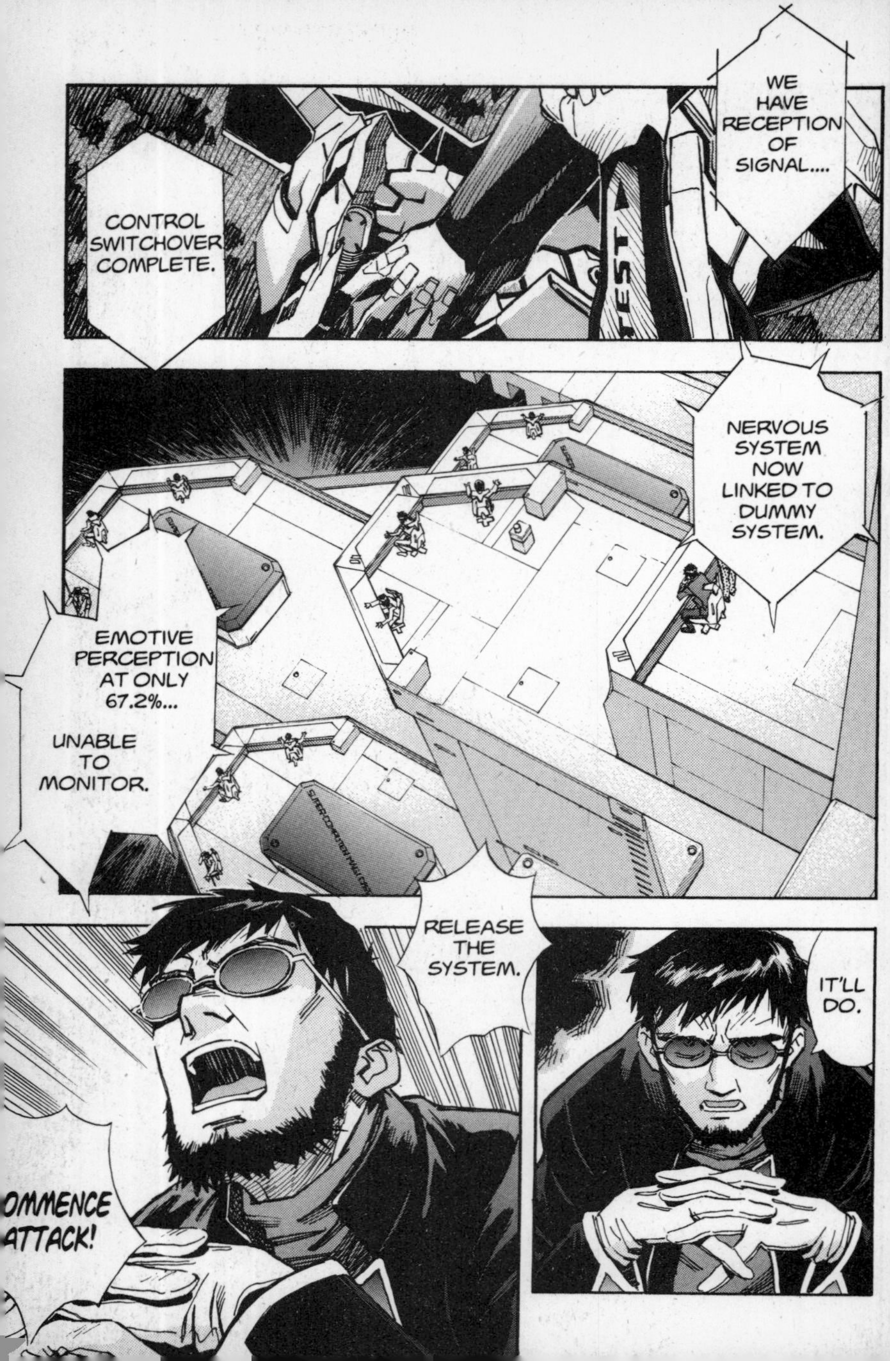
WE HAVE RECEPTION OF SIGNAL....
CONTROL SWITCHOVER COMPLETE.
NERVOUS SYSTEM NOW LINKED TO DUMMY SYSTEM.
EMOTIVE PERCEPTION AT ONLY 67.2%...
UNABLE TO MONITOR.
IT'LL DO.
RELEASE THE SYSTEM.
OMMENCE ATTACK!

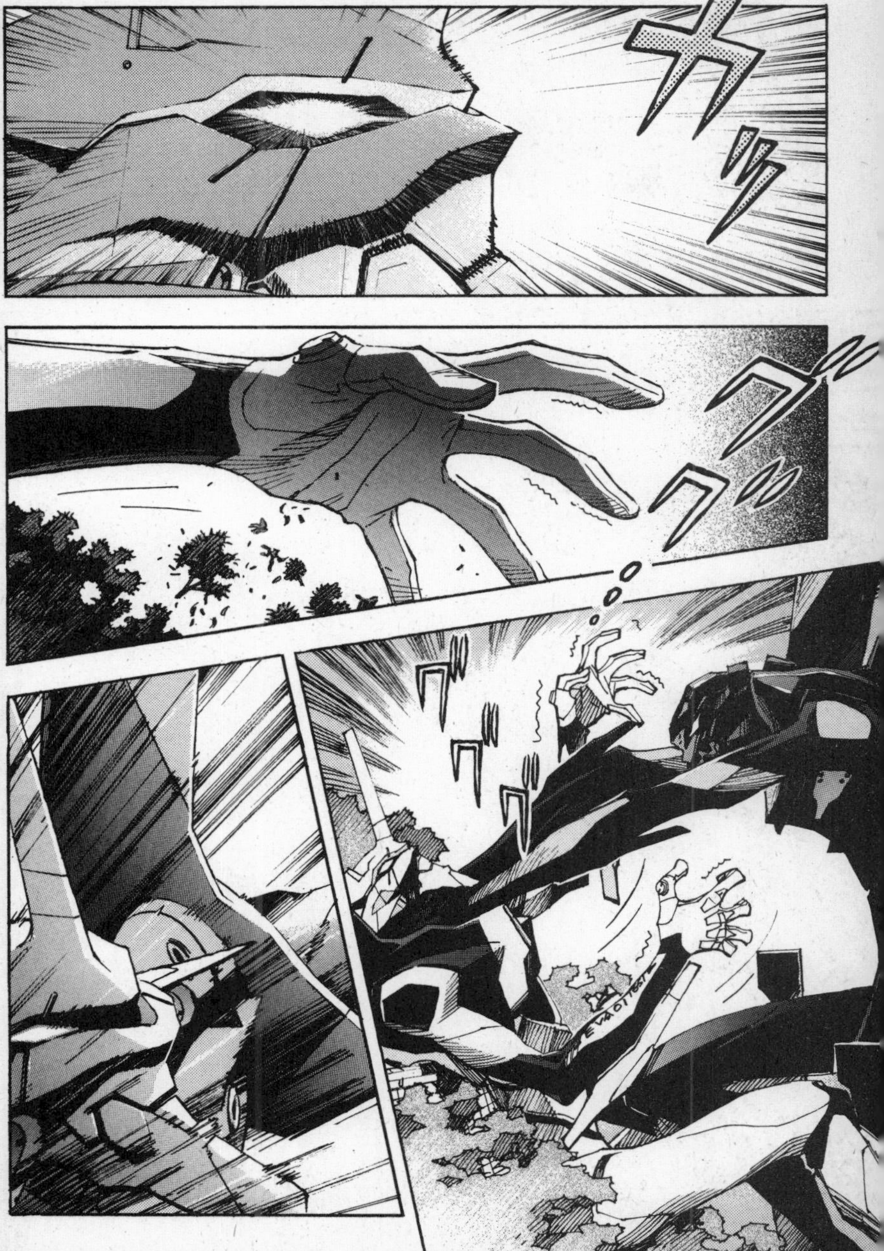
カッ
ググ

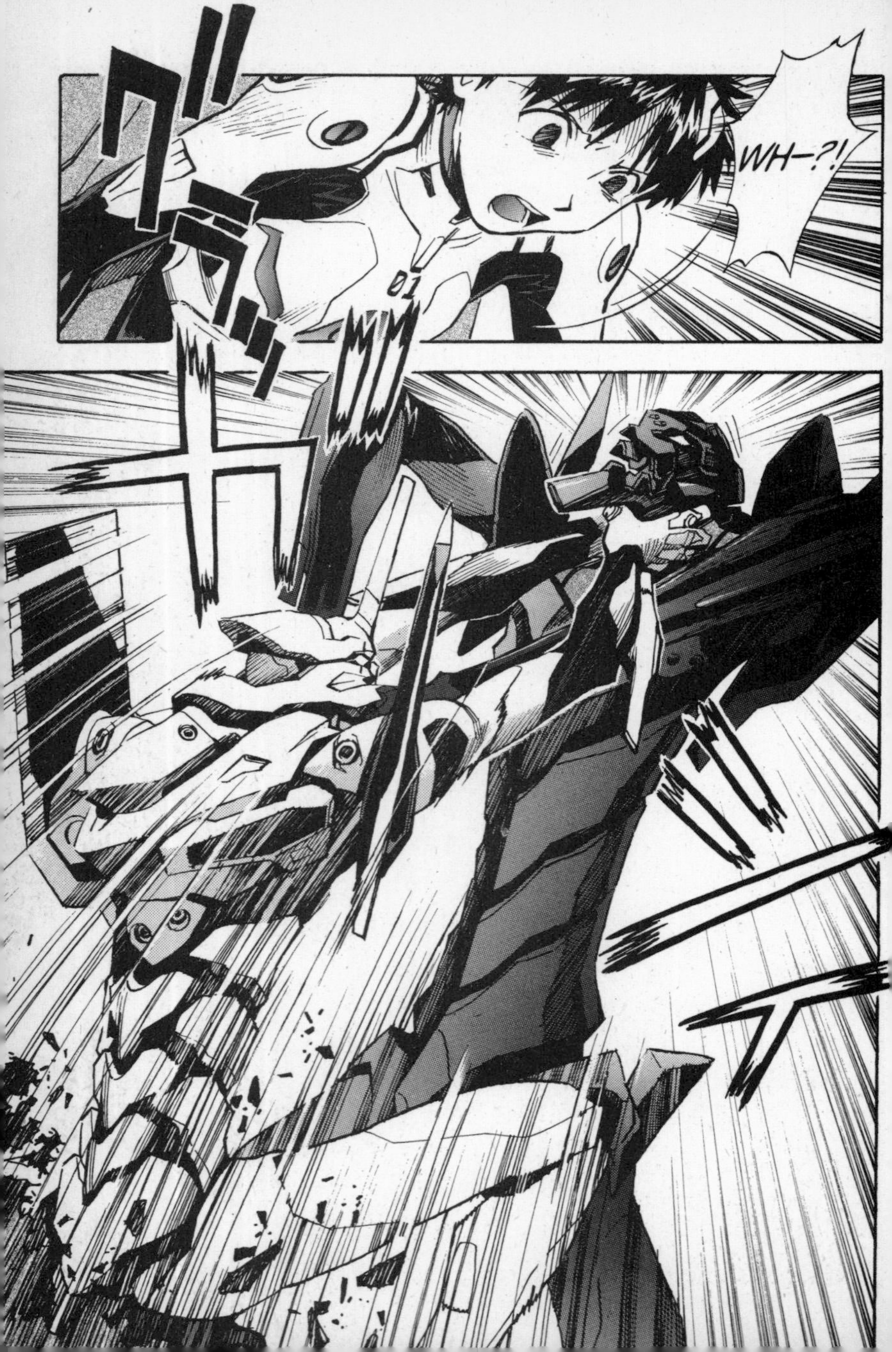
WH–?!

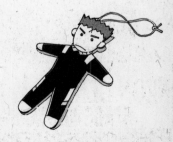

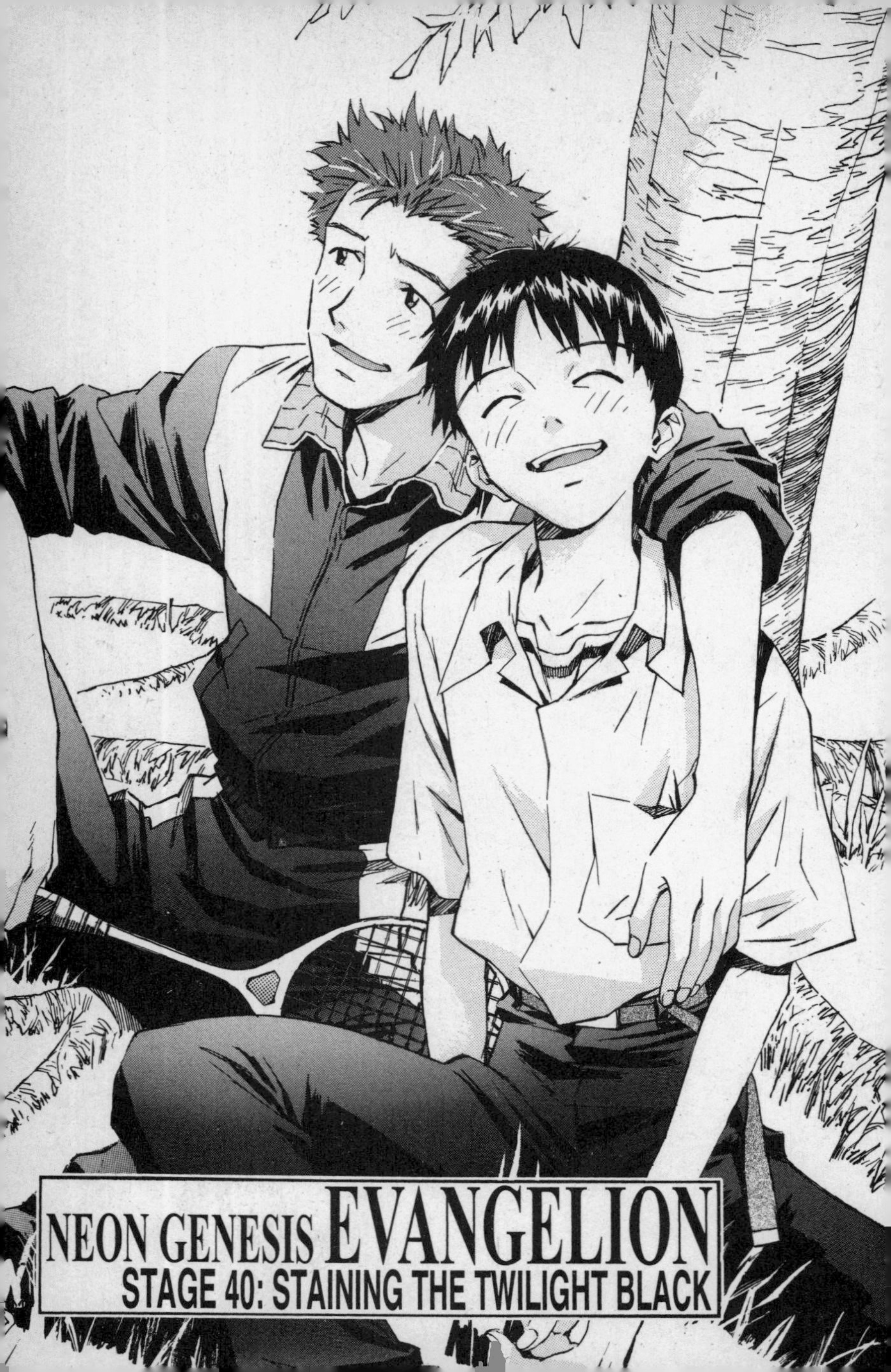
NEON GENESIS EVANGELION
STAGE 40: STAINING THE TWILIGHT BLACK

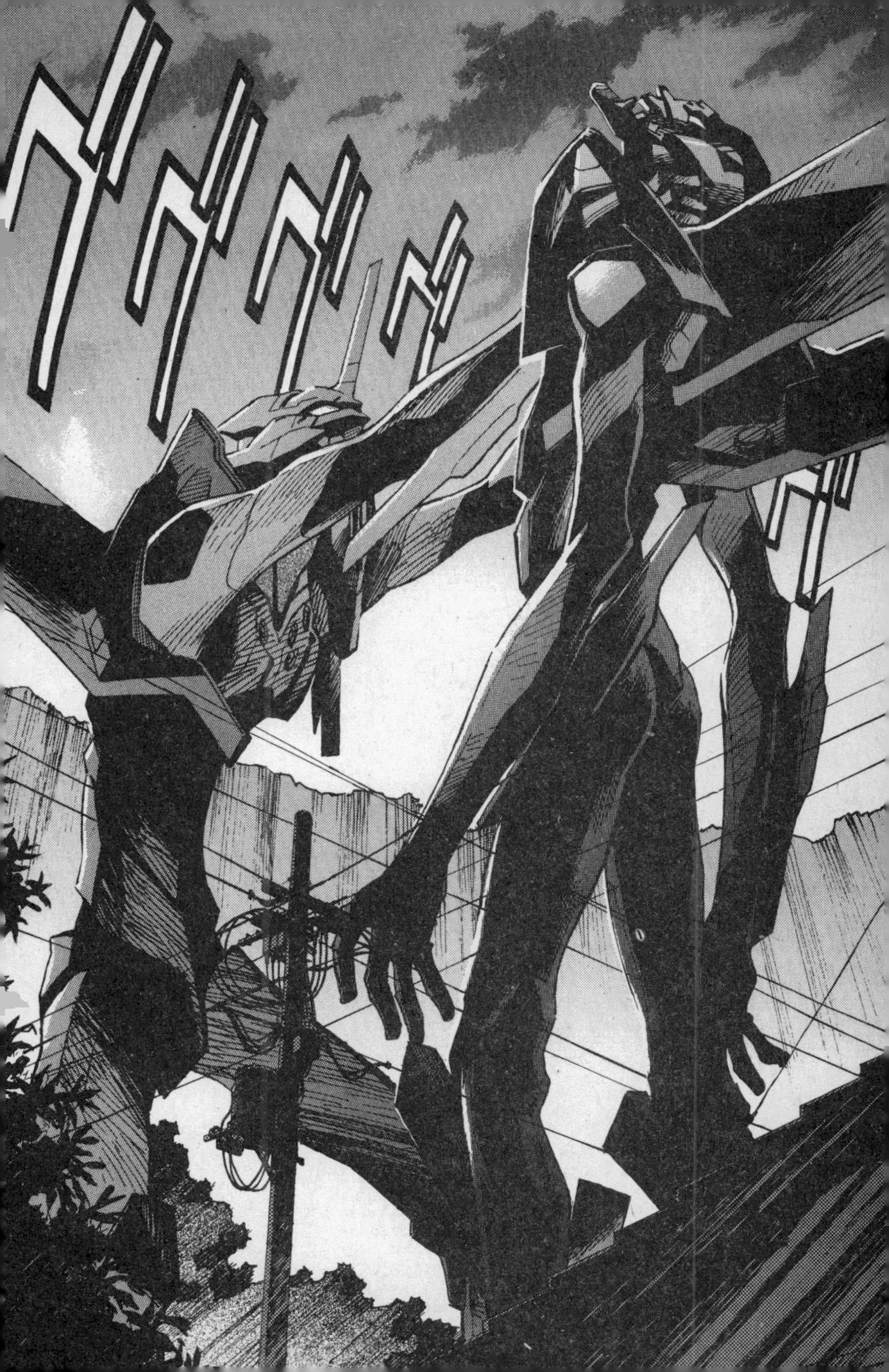

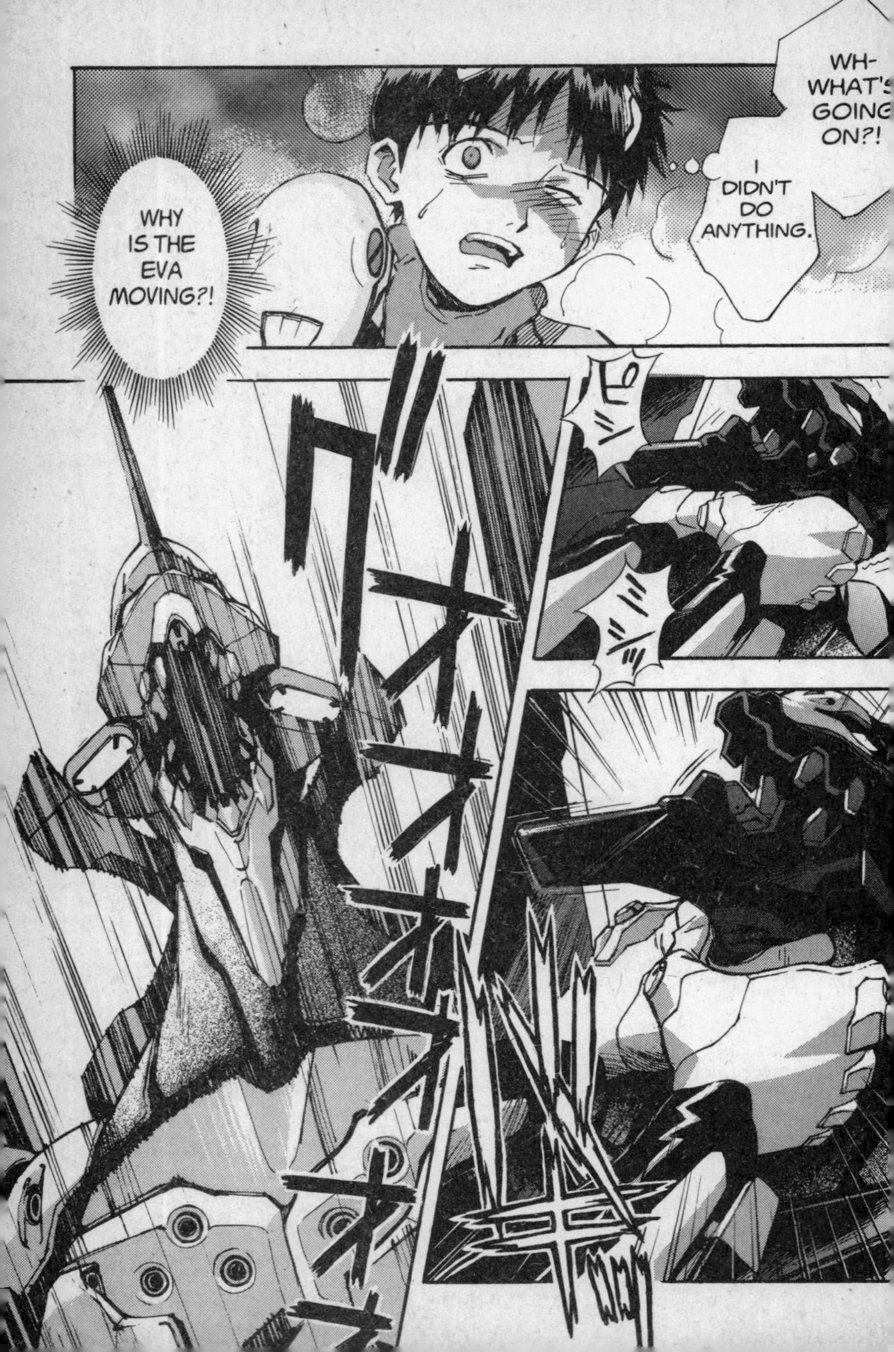
WH- WHAT'S GOING ON?!
I DIDN'T DO ANYTHING.
WHY IS THE EVA MOVING?!

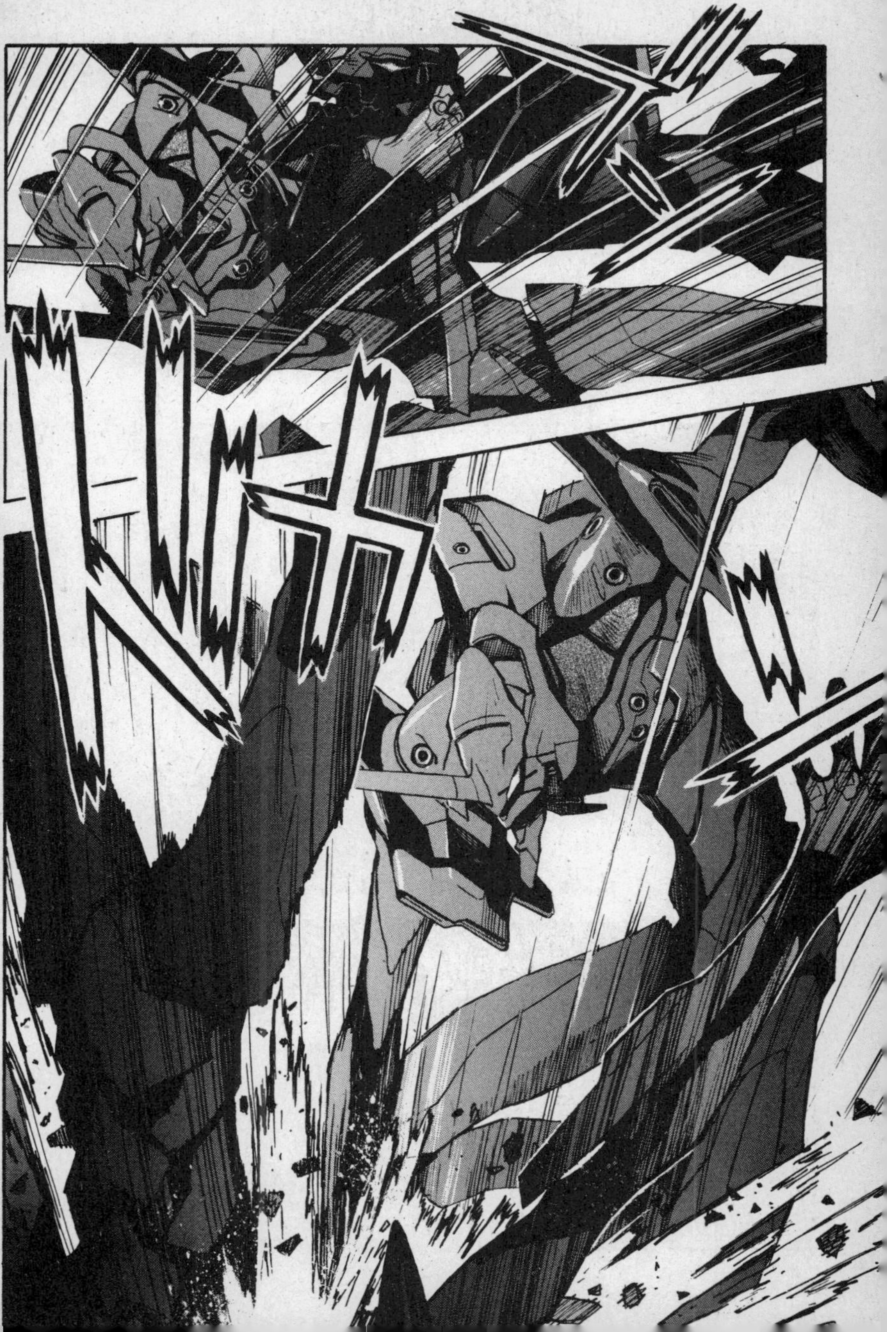

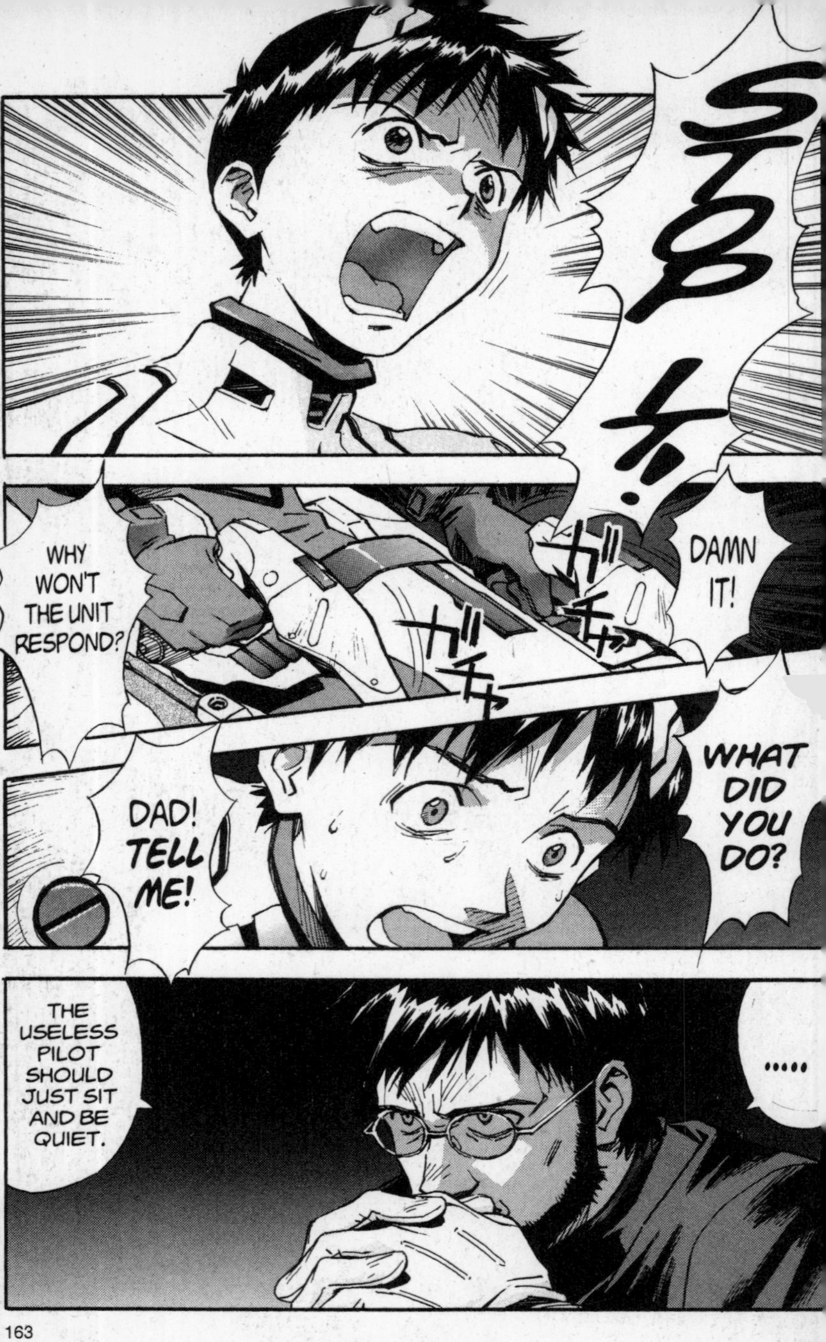
STOP IT!!
DAMN IT!
ガチャ
ガチャ
WHY WON'T THE UNIT RESPOND?
WHAT DID YOU DO?
DAD! TELL ME!
.....
THE USELESS PILOT SHOULD JUST SIT AND BE QUIET.

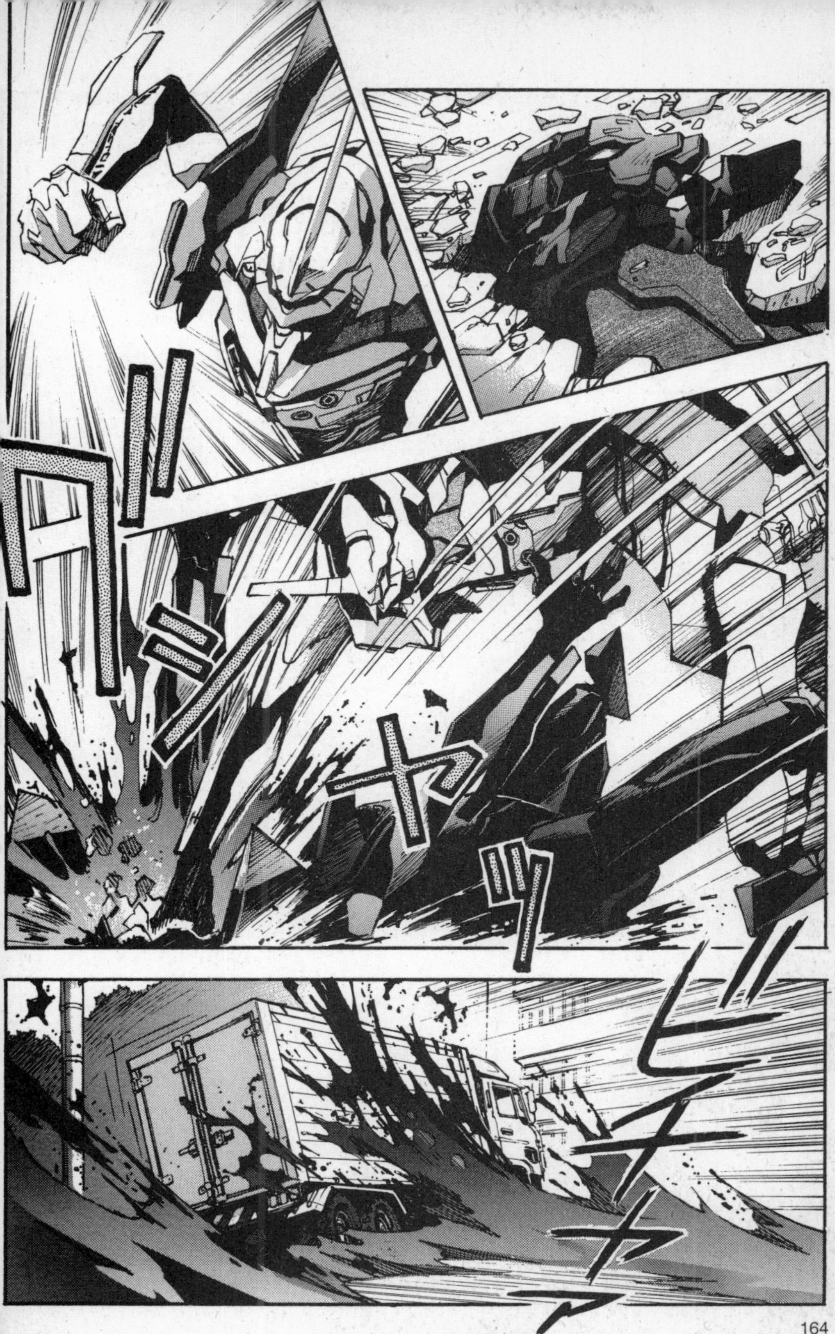

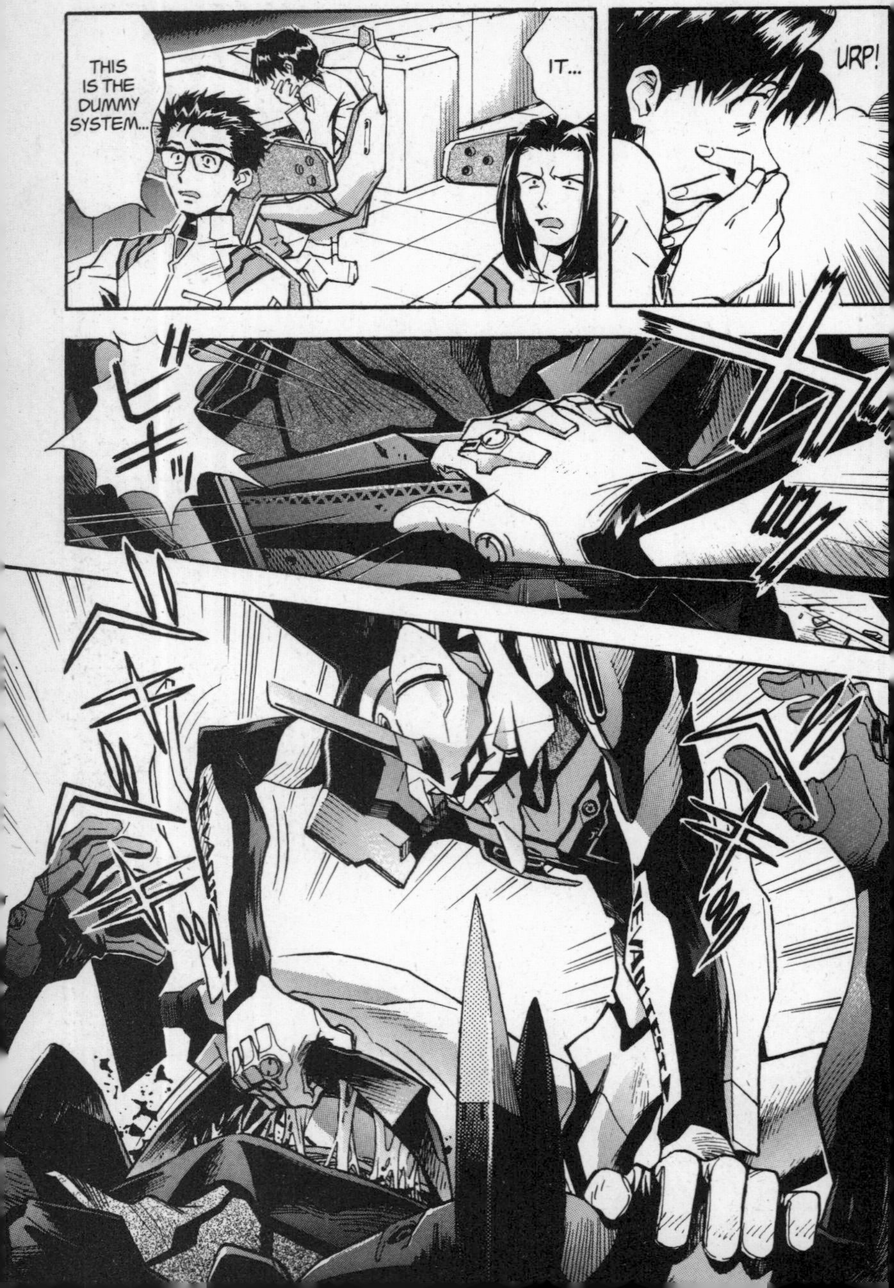
URP!
IT...
THIS IS THE DUMMY SYSTEM...

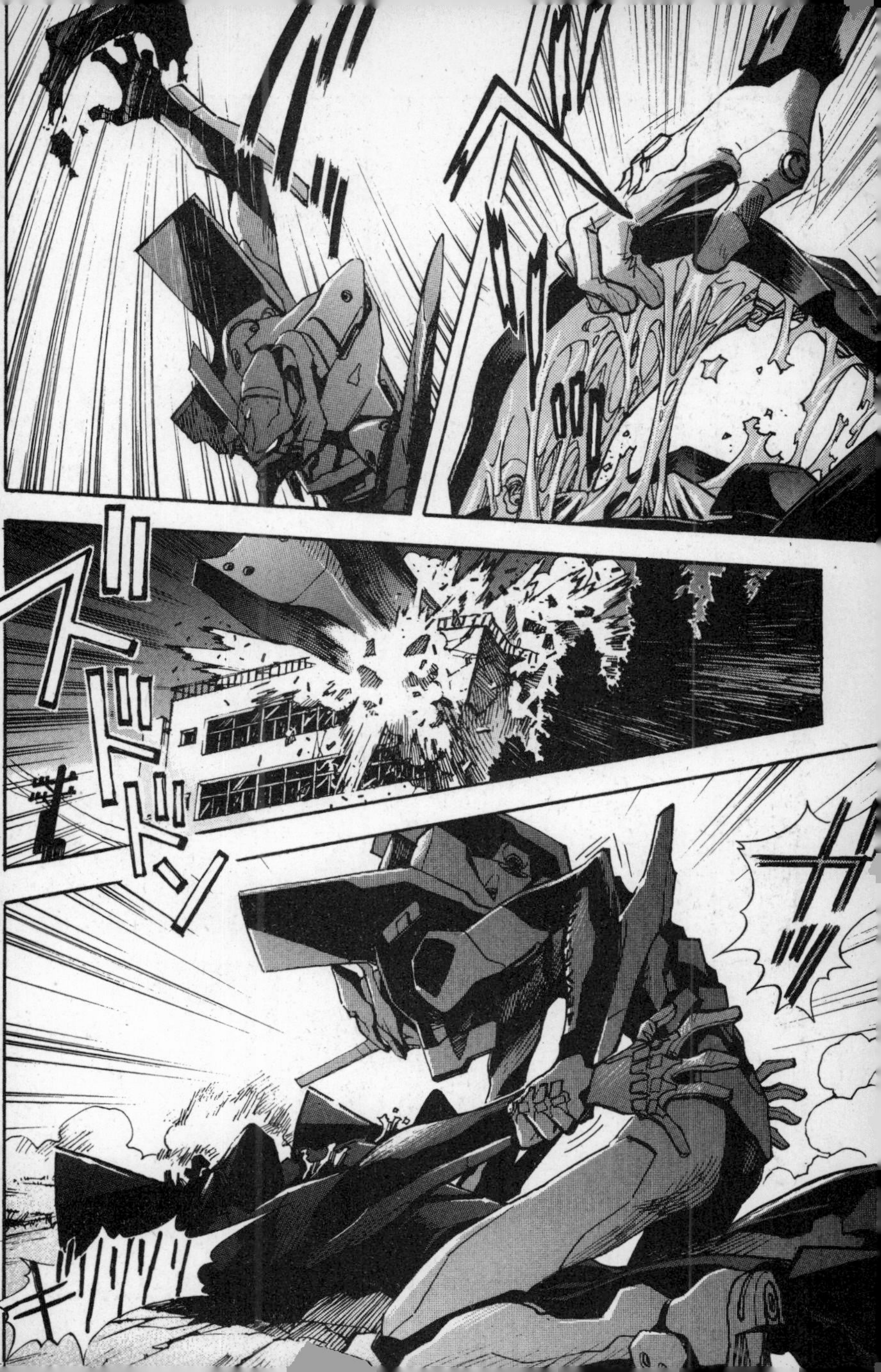
ズドドドン
ガッ

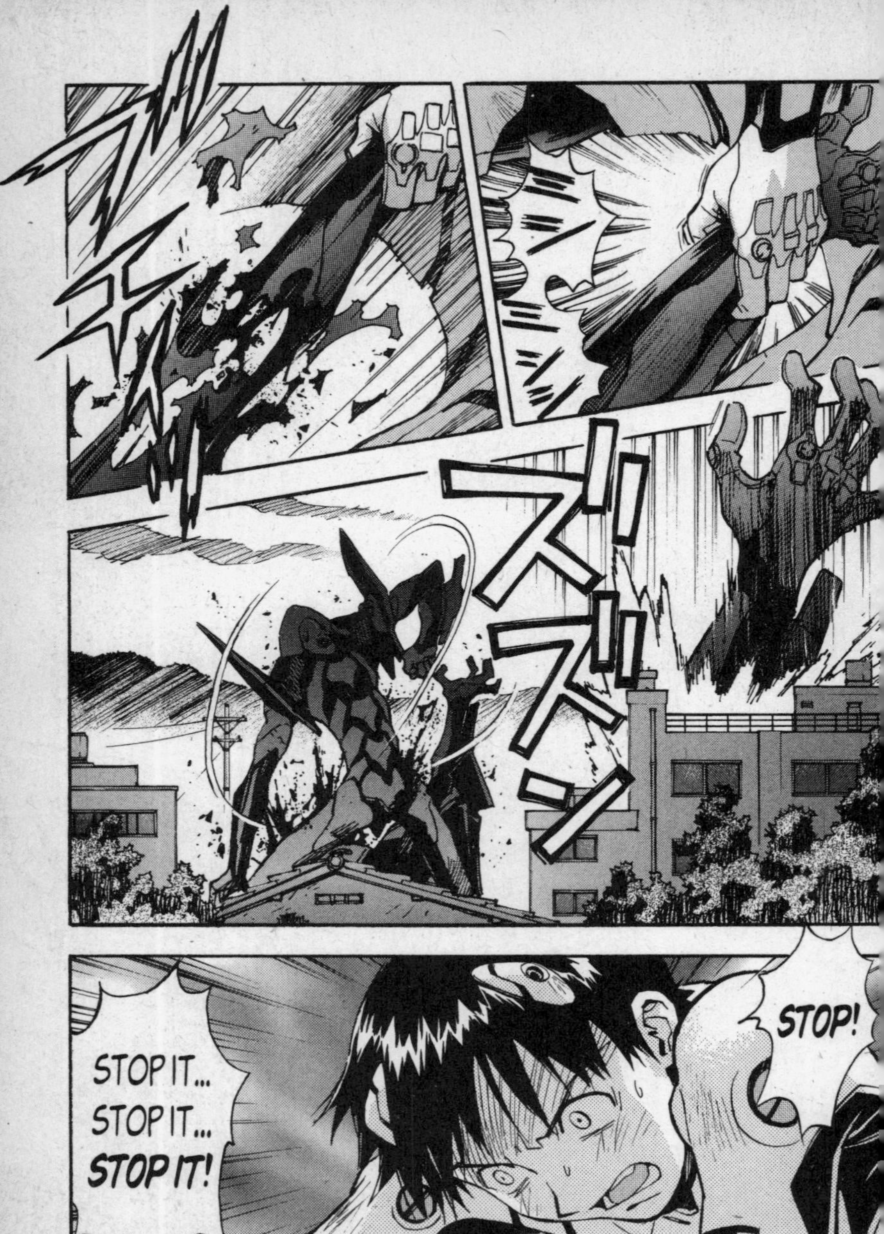
STOP!
STOP IT...
STOP IT...
STOP IT!

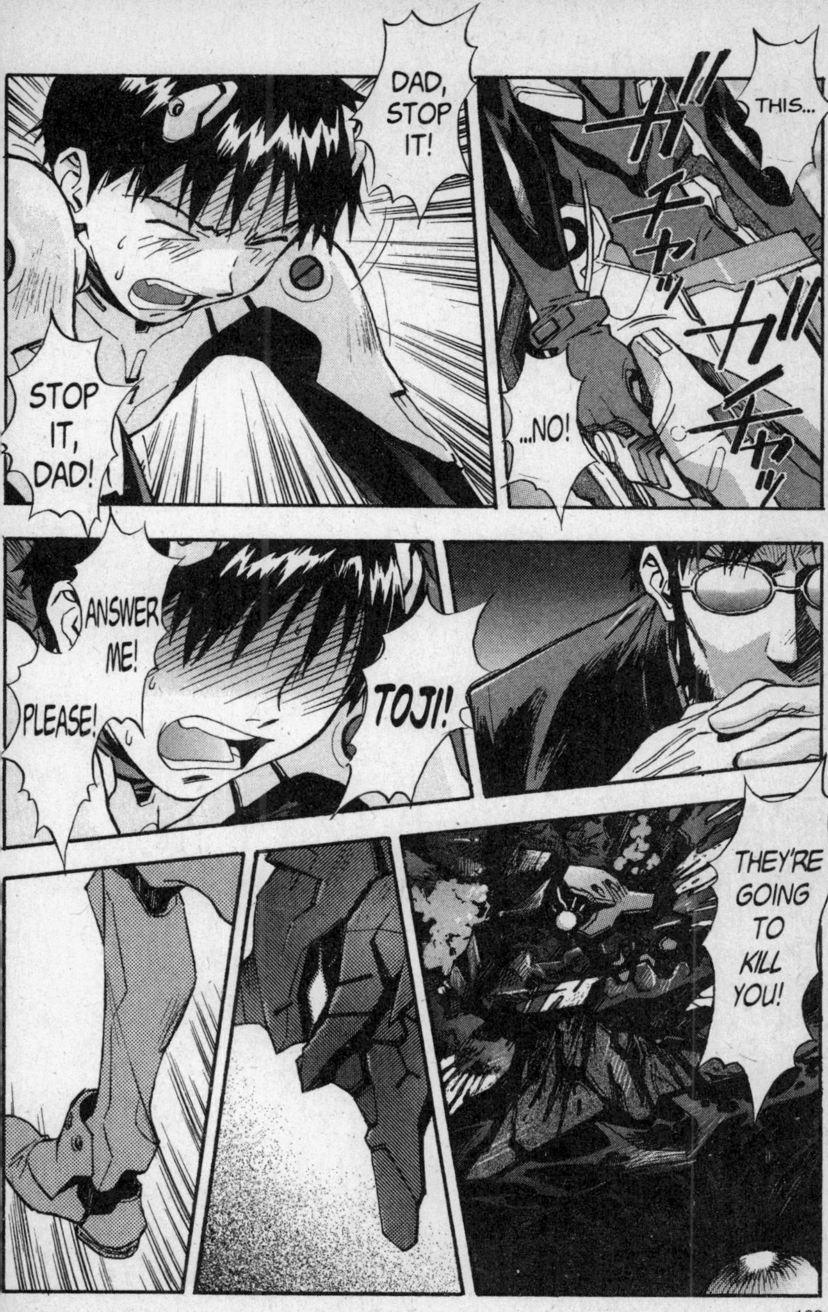
THIS...
...NO!
DAD, STOP IT!
STOP IT, DAD!
ANSWER ME!
TOJI!
PLEASE!
THEY'RE GOING TO KILL YOU!

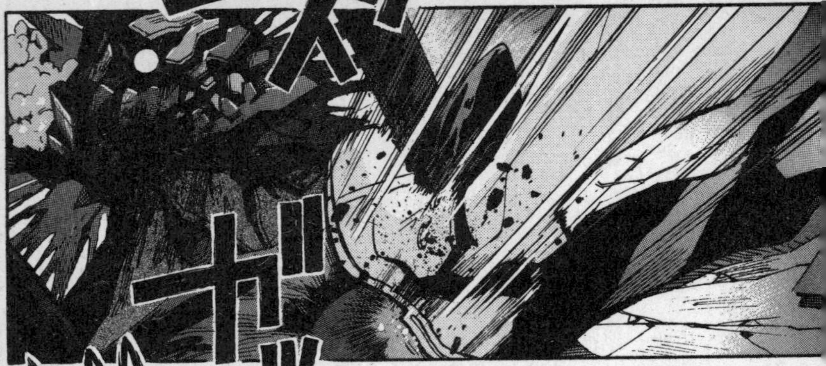
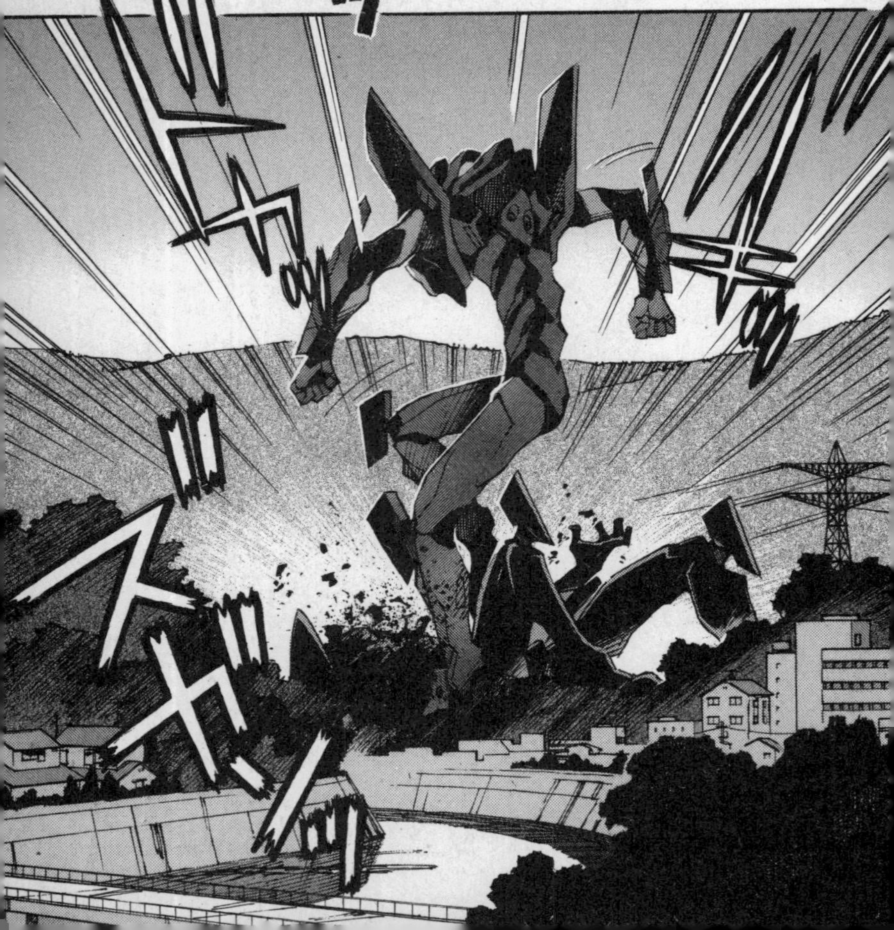

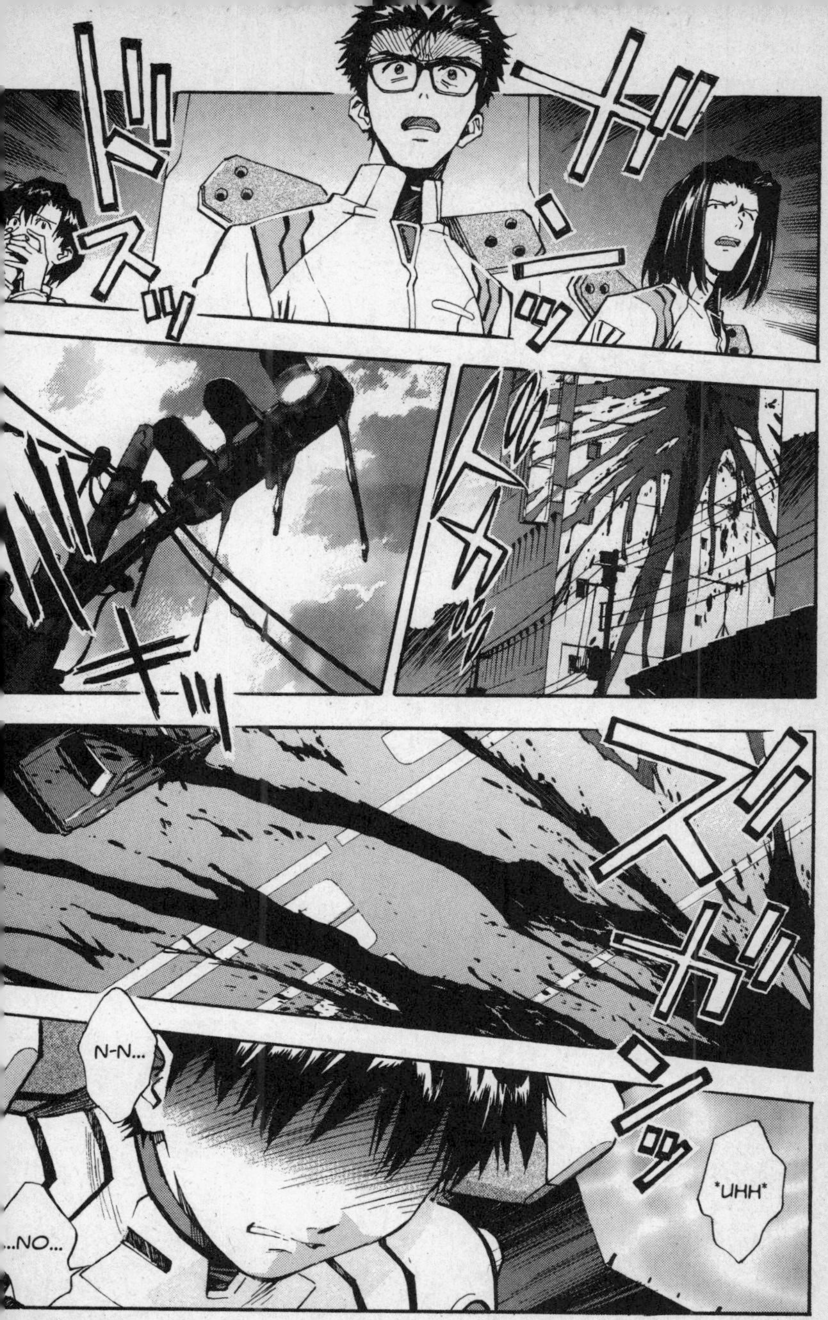
N-N...
...NO...
UHH

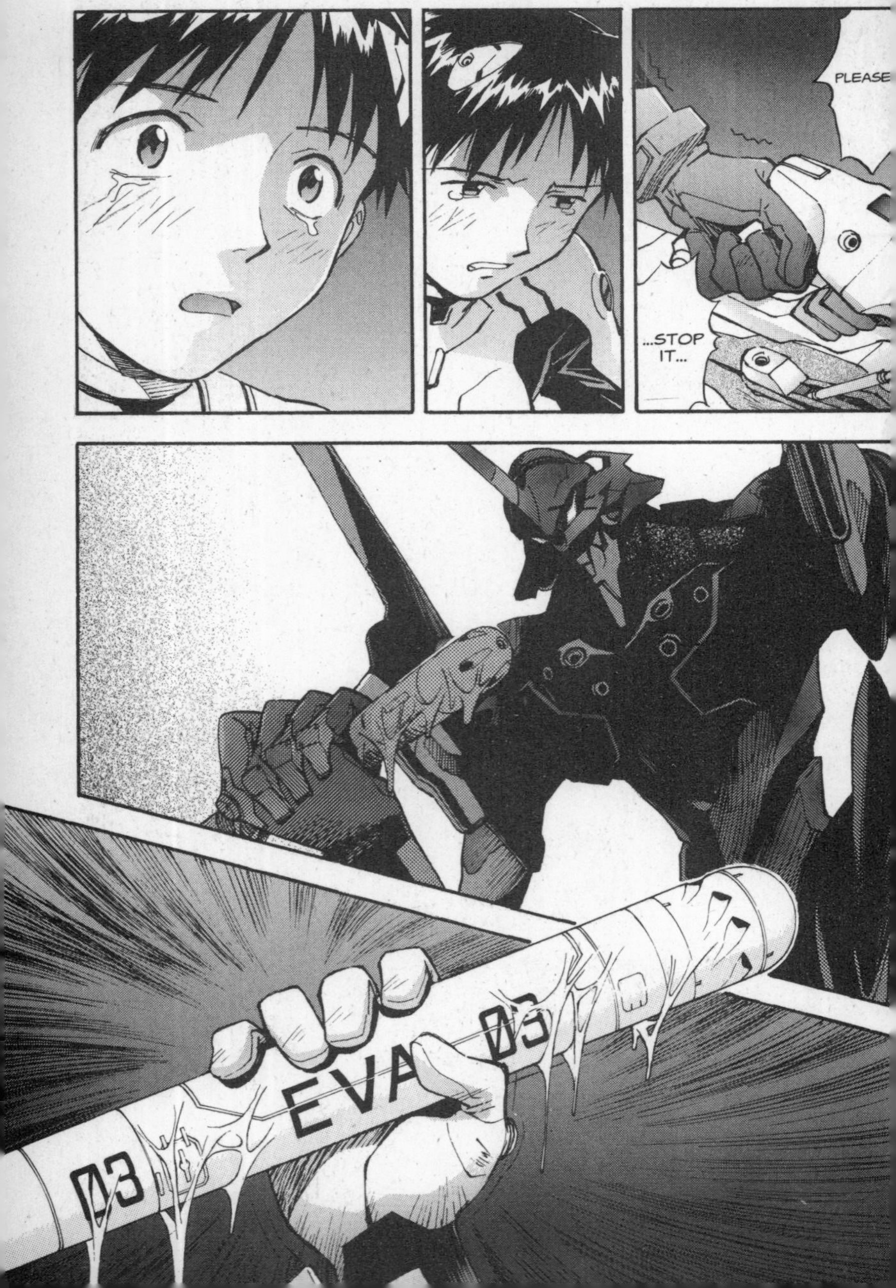
PLEASE
...STOP IT...
EVA 03
03

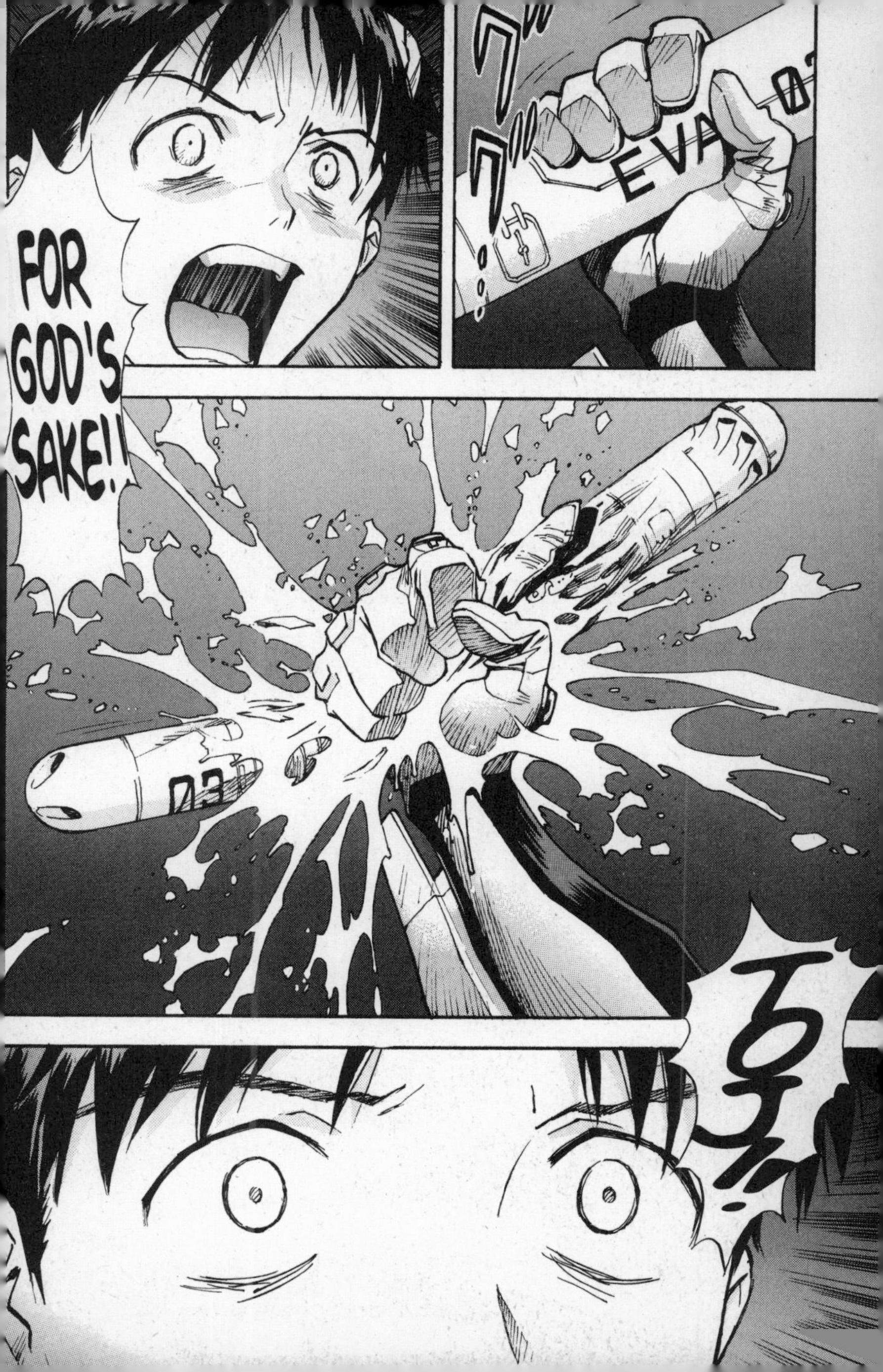
EVA
FOR GOD'S SAKE!!
03

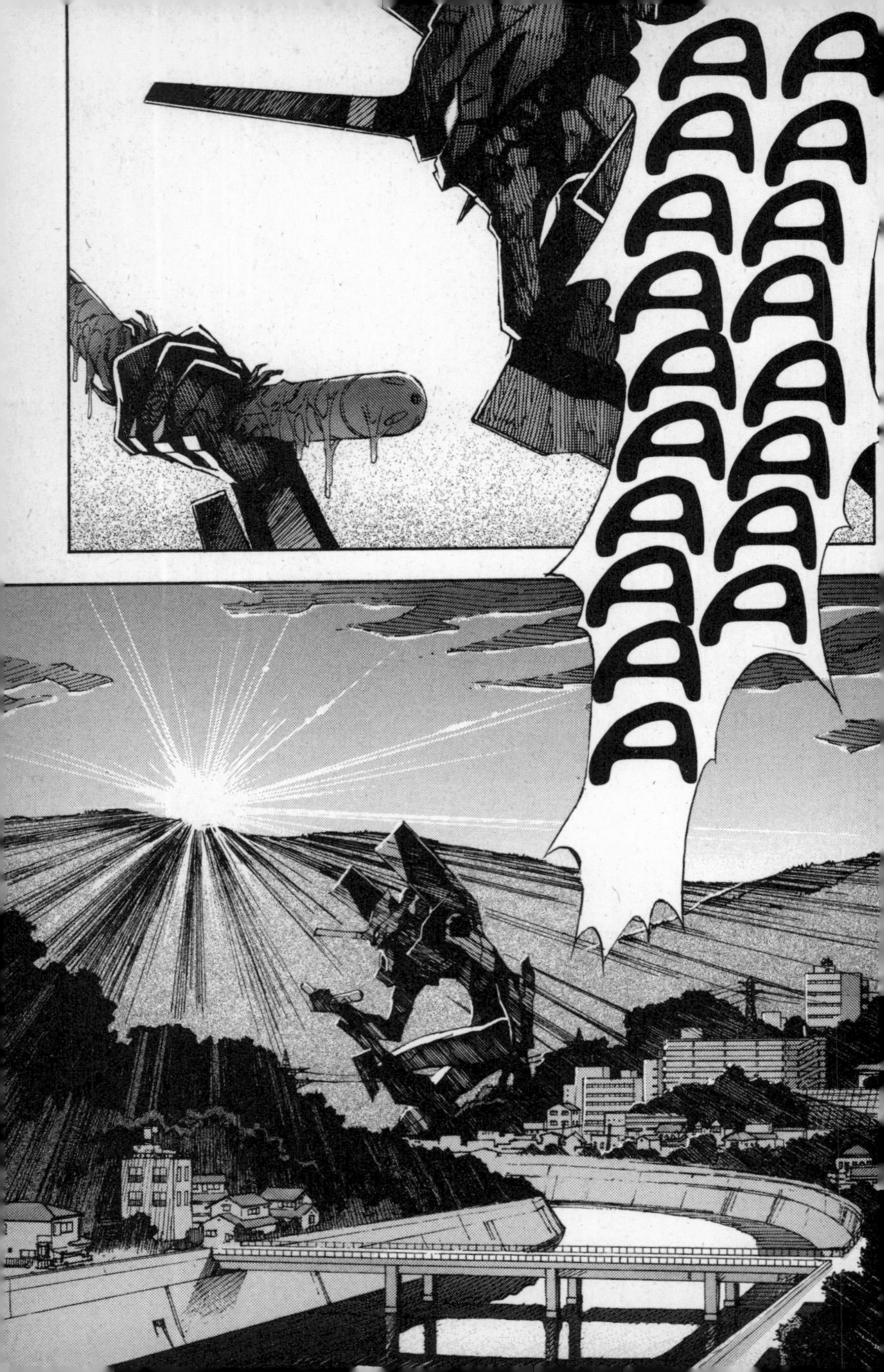
AAAAAAAAAAAAAAAAAAAAA

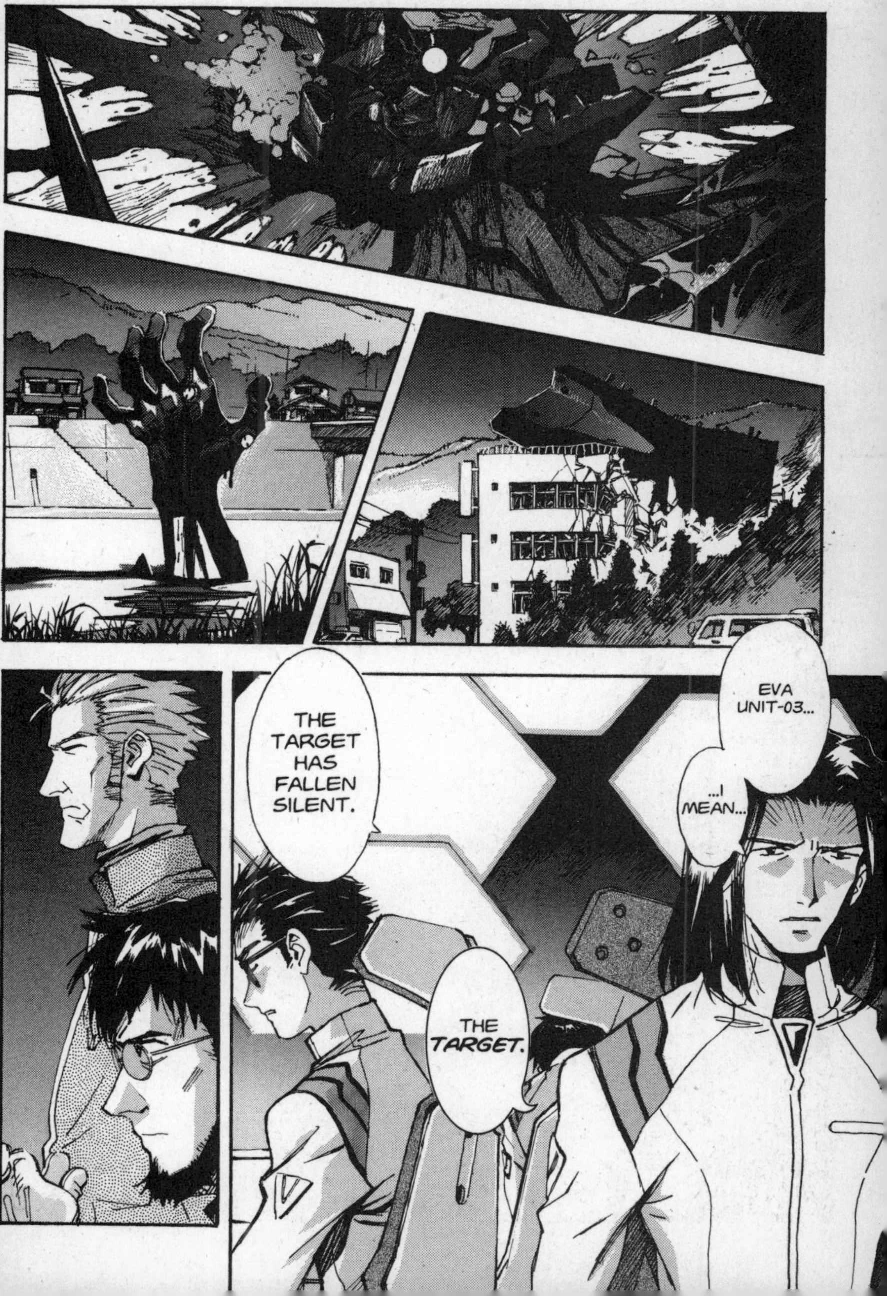

EVA UNIT-03...
...I MEAN...
THE TARGET HAS FALLEN SILENT.
THE *TARGET*.

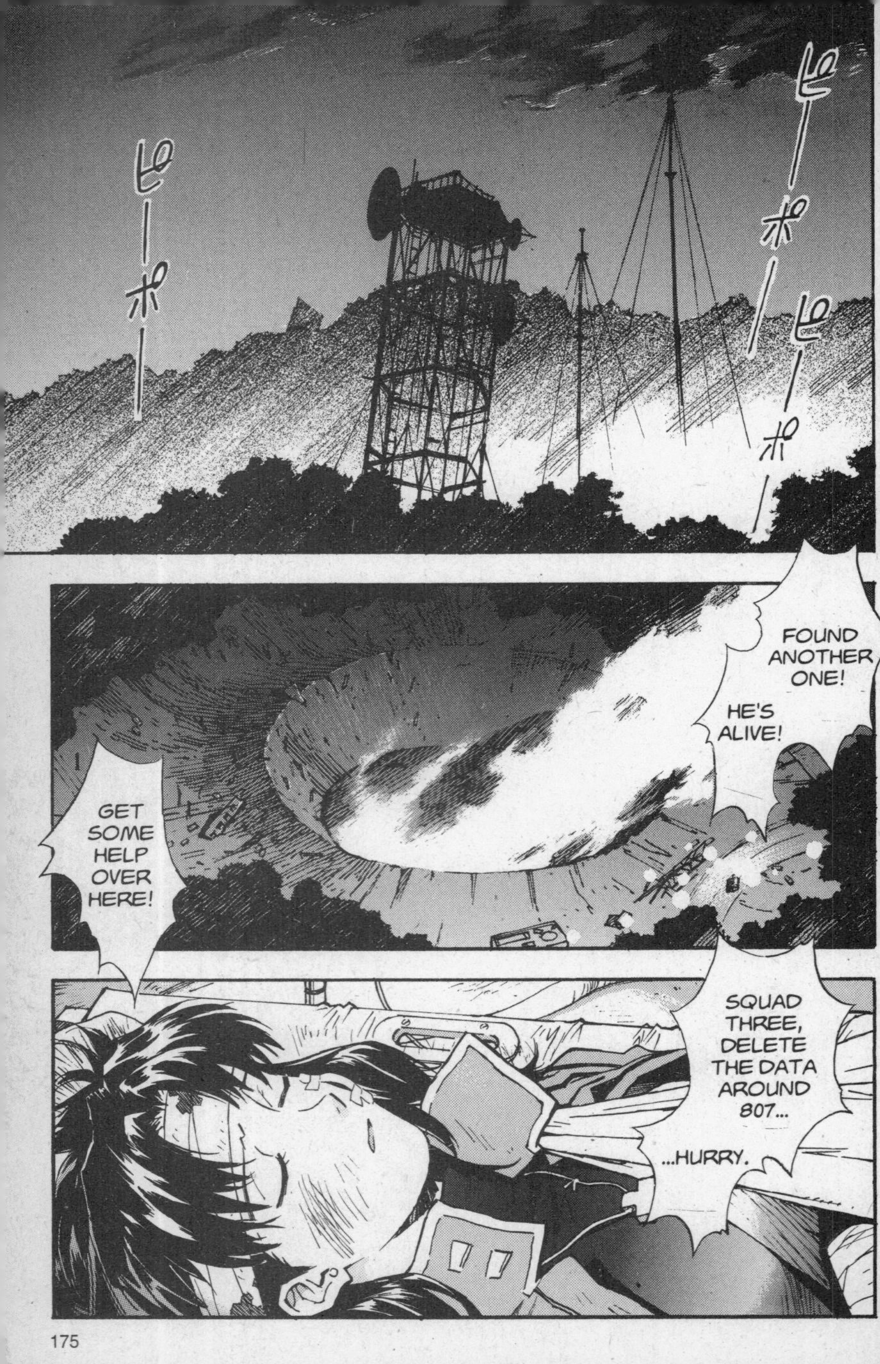
ピーポーピーポー
ピーポー
FOUND ANOTHER ONE!
HE'S ALIVE!
GET SOME HELP OVER HERE!
SQUAD THREE, DELETE THE DATA AROUND 807...
...HURRY.

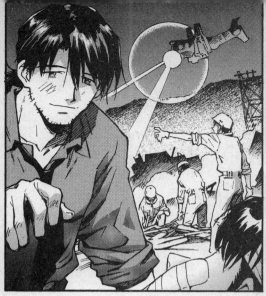

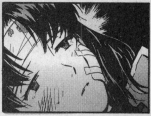

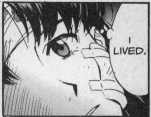

I LIVED.

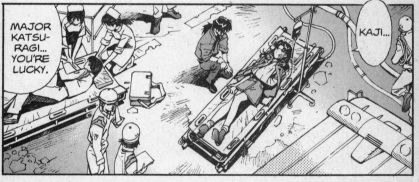

MAJOR KATSU-RAGI... YOU'RE LUCKY.

KAJI...

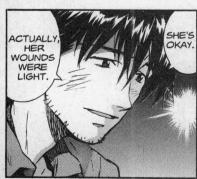

ACTUALLY, HER WOUNDS WERE LIGHT.

SHE'S OKAY.

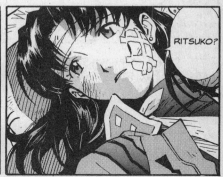

RITSUKO?

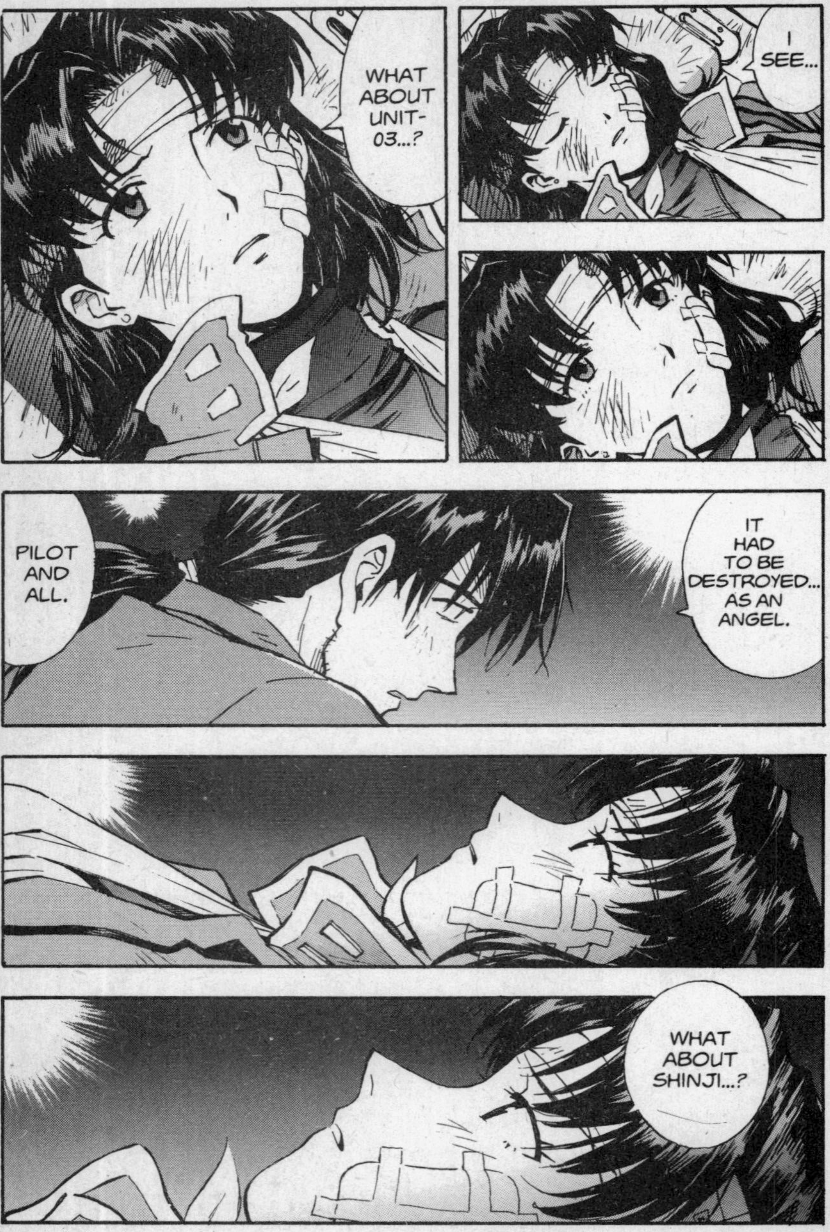
I SEE...
WHAT ABOUT UNIT-03...?
IT HAD TO BE DESTROYED... AS AN ANGEL.
PILOT AND ALL.
WHAT ABOUT SHINJI...?

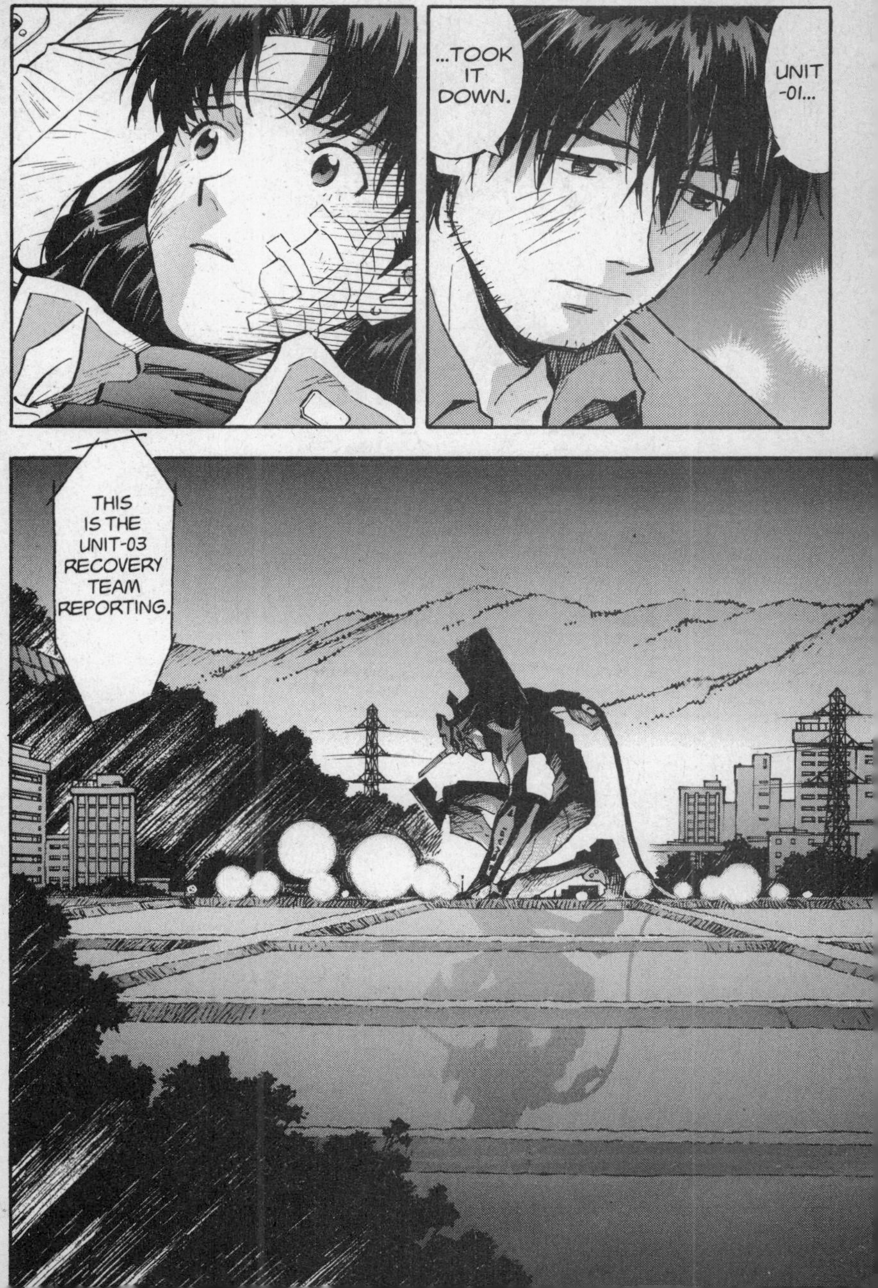
UNIT -01...
...TOOK IT DOWN.
THIS IS THE UNIT-03 RECOVERY TEAM REPORTING.

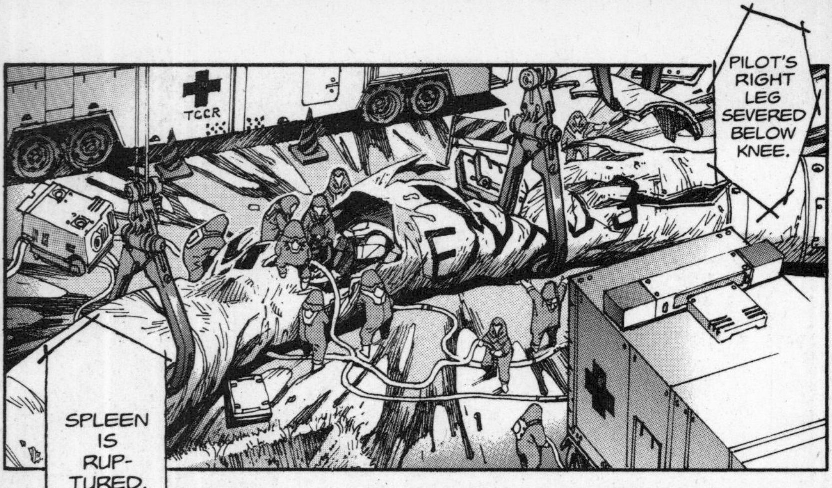
PILOT'S RIGHT LEG SEVERED BELOW KNEE.
SPLEEN IS RUP-TURED.
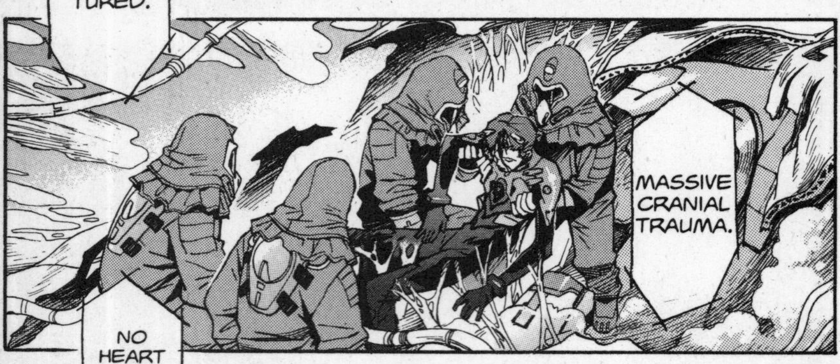
MASSIVE CRANIAL TRAUMA.
NO HEART SOUNDS.
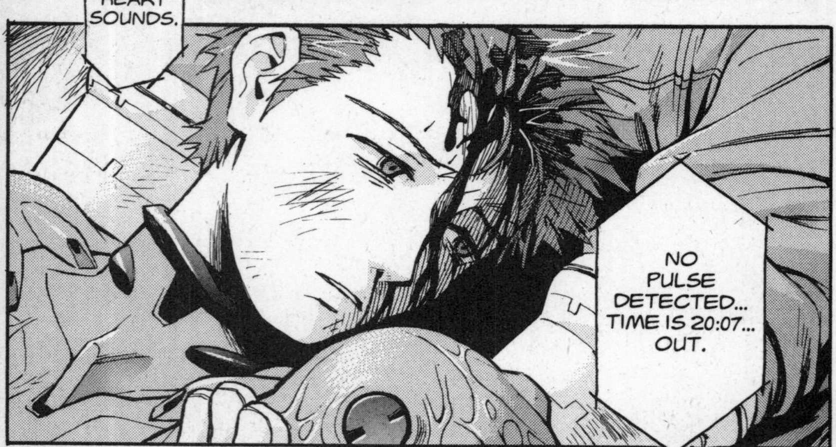
NO PULSE DETECTED... TIME IS 20:07... OUT.

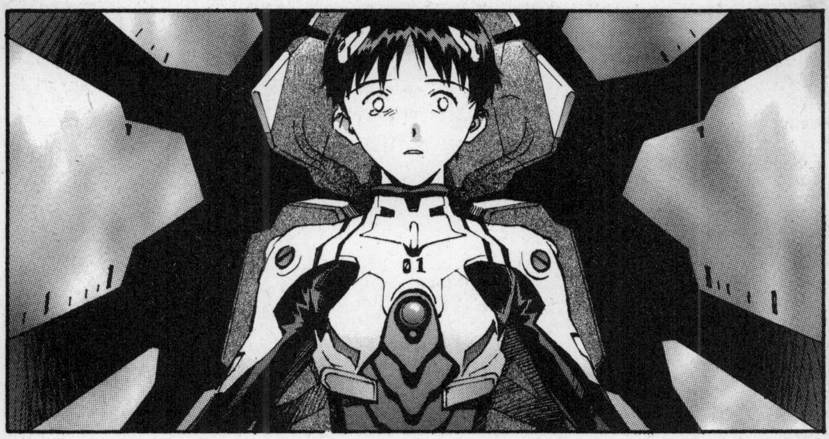
01
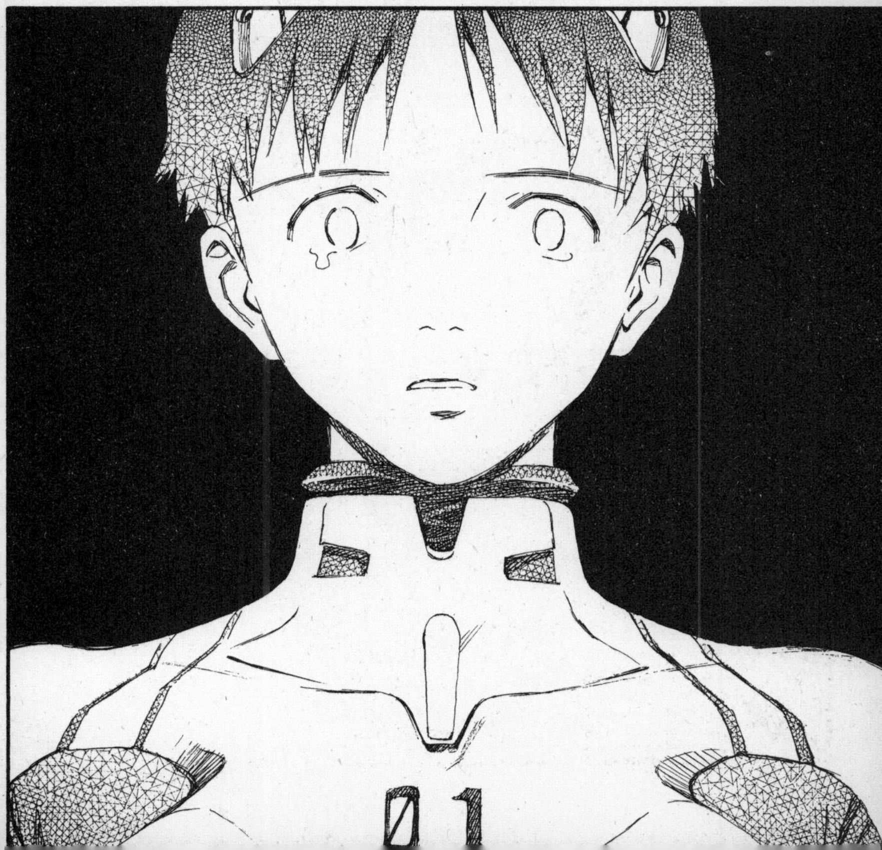
01

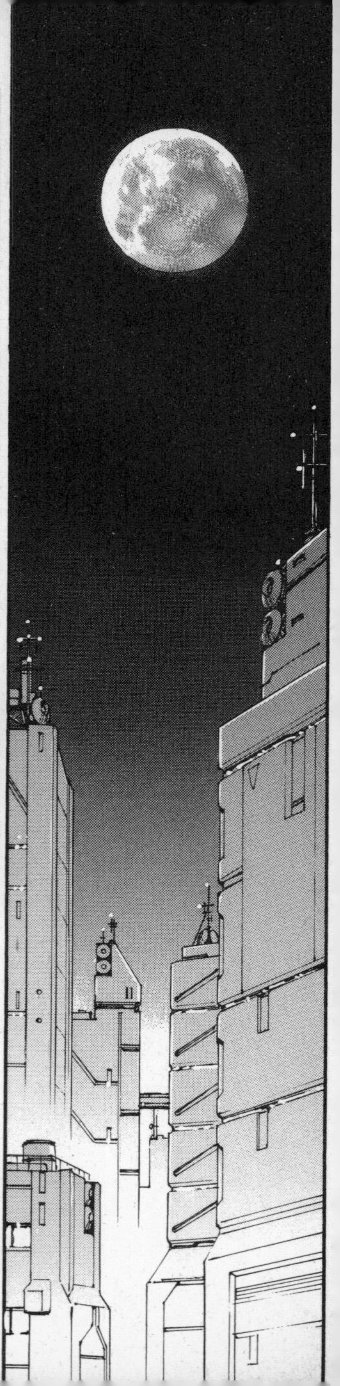

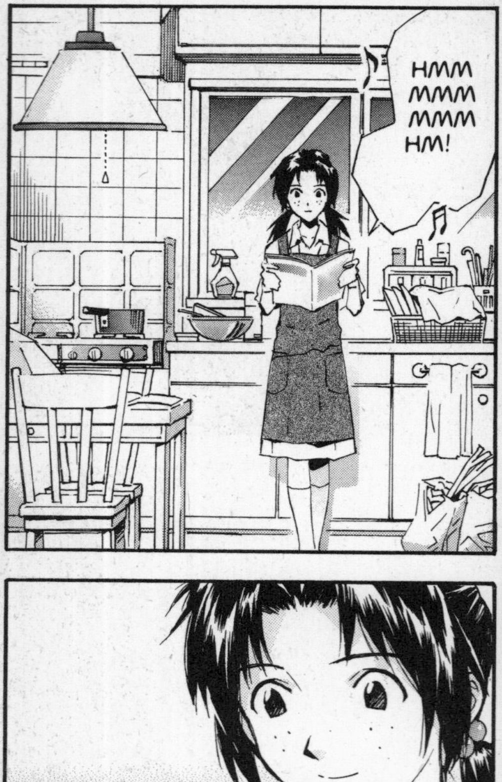
HMM MMM MMM HM!
I'LL GO WITH THIS ONE!
PER-FECT!
744kcal
20分

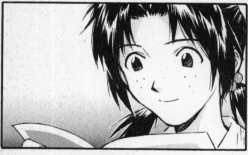

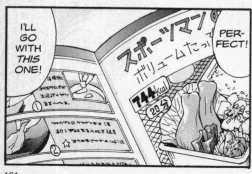

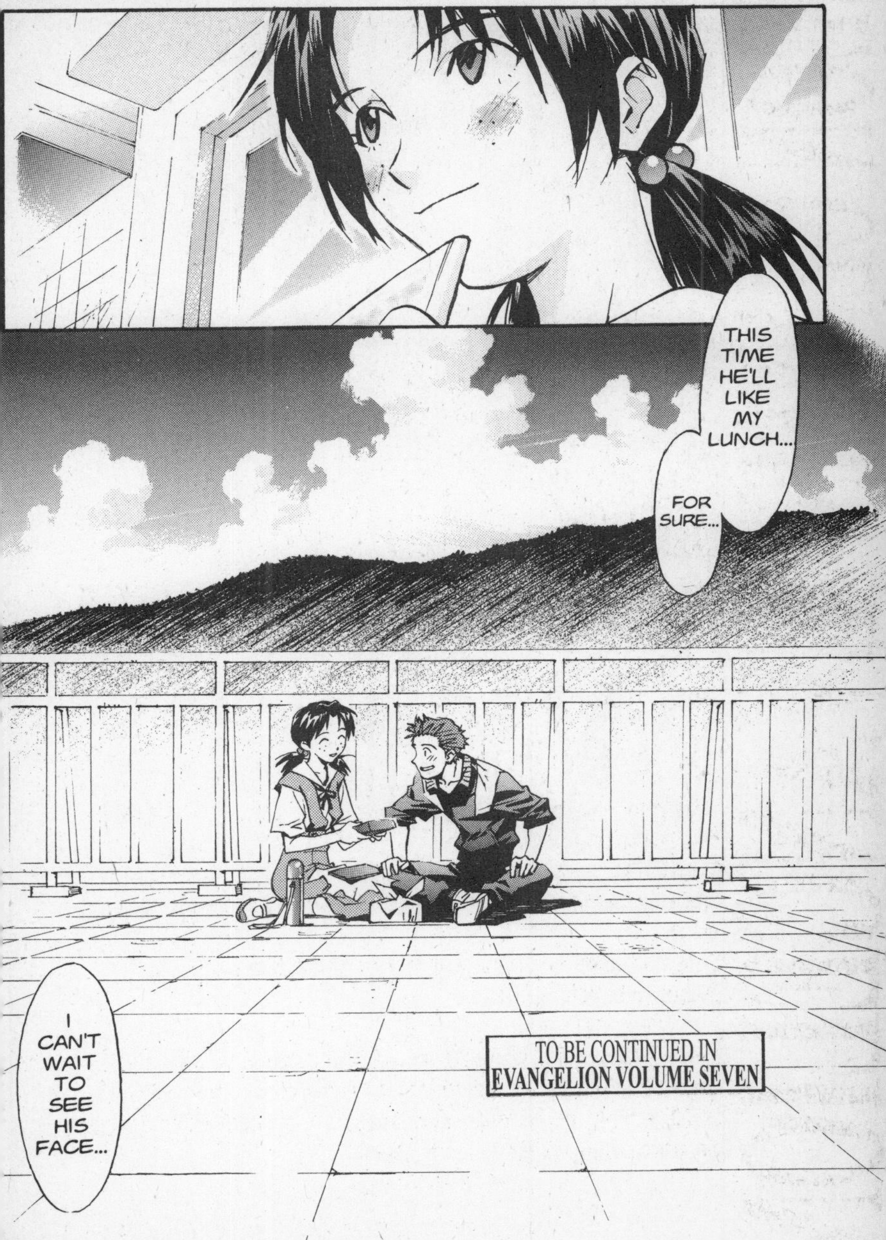
THIS TIME HE'LL LIKE MY LUNCH...
FOR SURE...
I CAN'T WAIT TO SEE HIS FACE...
TO BE CONTINUED IN EVANGELION VOLUME SEVEN

NEON GENESIS EVANGELION

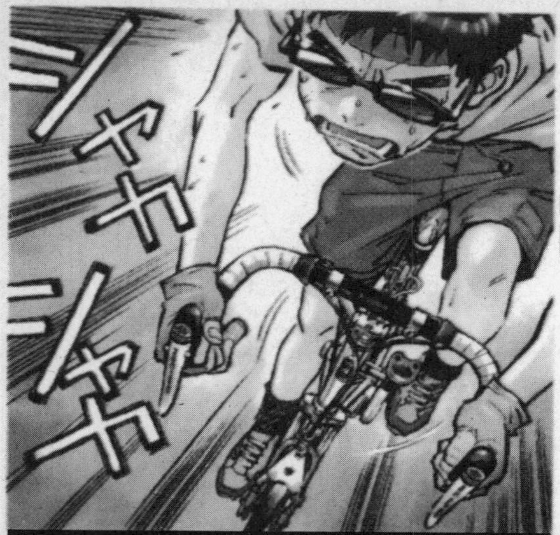

YOSHIYUKI SADAMOTO

YOSHIYUKI SADAMOTO

WRITER AND ARTIST

I've gotten into bicycling lately.
Not racing, you understand... just wandering around the neighborhood. When I think about it, the bike I got as a kid was probably the first time in my life I ever received a "modern convenience."
So is this some sort of back-to-basics? I don't know.
Or am I just getting old?

...Still, it feels good to my 38 year-old self, those innocent memories and emotions evoked: the joy of ownership, combined with the primitive thrill of a pedal-powered engine. If only any of this struggle affected my weight in the slightest.

SOUND EFFECTS GLOSSARY

Welcome to the sound effects glossary for Volume Six of *Neon Genesis Evangelion*! Japanese is written with a combination of *kanji*—Chinese ideograms, borrowed and modified—and *kana*, phonetic characters. There are two kinds of *kana*: *katakana* and *hiragana*. *Hiragana*, written in a cursive style, is very important in indicating grammar in Japanese.

However, when it comes to manga sound FX, we're mostly concerned with *katakana*. These are written in a more angular style, and their uses include spelling out foreign words, and giving emphasis in ads and signs (sort of like writing in block letters). It's in this role of emphasis that *katakana* are used as sound FX, and almost all of *Evangelion*'s FX (and manga in general) so use it. Sometimes, however, *hiragana* is used instead—in cases where, for some reason, it would seem more "natural" to a Japanese speaker to write out that particular FX.

Here's how this glossary works: 13.4 simply means the sound FX that's on page 13 in panel 4; when a third number gets added—as in 55.6.1 for instance—it means there's more than one FX in the panel. The order all FX are listed, of course, is the Japanese reading order, right-to-left: so 30.1 is the upper right (not upper left) panel of page 30; and 55.6.2 is to the left (not the right) of 55.6.1. In situations where you have multiple FX in a panel, but they're at different heights, the numbering goes clockwise. Note that a hyphen is sometimes used in such instances as 90.1-2 where an FX is perceived to stretch over more than one panel.

After each line's number and FX, you get the literal *kana* reading followed by the description of what the FX stands for in brackets. Sometimes this will be symbolized by an attempt to give an English equivalent of the sound FX, and sometimes just a description of the sound will be given.

Note, however, that some of the FX the artist draws in *Evangelion* aren't literally representing sounds; instead they represent the "sound" Japanese sometimes give to things that don't really have sounds—attitudes, emotional states. In the West the difference between these two kinds of FX is described by the words *onomatopoeia* vs. *mimesis*; in Japan, the equivalent concepts are *giseigo* and *gitaigo*.

One final note: Japanese vowels (they learn them as "AIUEO" rather than "AEIOU") have a regular pronunciation, like those in Spanish. "A" is said *ah*, "I" is *eee*, "U" is *ooh*, "E" is *eh*, and "O" is *oh*.

13.4 —— FX: zaa [zzt]

16.4 —— FX: miin miin miin miin [cicadas]

20.2 —— FX: Uooo! Yappa AK-47 kakkoeee! Chikushyooo hosshii! ["Ooh! AK-47s are sooo cool! I want one!" Note the 'eh,' not 'ee' pronunciation of e in Japanese; so what Kensuke is doing is pronouncing kakko ii in the more 'manly' fashion kakkoeee—said kahk'koh-ehhhhh.]

30.1 —— FX: pako [wap]

32.3 —— FX: den zudedede [slam whamamam]

36.3 —— FX: Gatten shite itadake-mashita deshoo ka? ["Do you get it now?"]

37.1 —— FX: Gatten! Gatten! Gatten! ["I got it!" "I got it!" "I got it!"]

37.2 —— FX: pi [clik]

38.1 —— FX: Geee! [gack]

40.3 —— FX: kata kata [clacketa]

40.5 —— FX: kata kata [clacketa]

41.3 —— FX: katata katata [clacketa clacketa]

49.2 —— FX: gaa [grr/mreow]

50.3 —— FX: pon [pat]

52.4 —— FX: biku [urk]

55.3 —— FX: kächan [clink]

55.6.1 —— FX: pi [eep]

55.6.2 —— FX: gaton [clunk]

56.5 —— FX: pi [eep]

56.6 —— FX: gaton [clunk]

57.2 —— FX: kakyo [ckrish- opening can]

59.1 —— FX: miin miin miin [cicadas]

60.3 —— FX: ba [grab]

61.1 —— FX: keho [koff]

61.2 —— FX: shuyuun [sniff]

68.2 —— FX: suu [breath]

68.4 —— FX: gofa [door]

69.1 —— FX: kacha kacha [clacketa clacketa]

69.4 —— FX: pi [clik]

72.1 —— FX: shuru [shwip- ribbon]

76.4.1 —— FX: gata [clunk]

76.4.2 —— FX: pi [eep]

78.1 —— FX: kacha [clink]

79.1 —— FX: zaa [fshh- water]

79.3 —— FX: kacha kacha [clink clatter- dishes]

87.4 —— FX: suu [sliding door]

87.5 —— FX: pisha [slam]

88.6 —— FX: pon [pat]

89.2 —— FX: gachan [clik]

89.4 —— FX: goo [roarr]

90.1-2 —— FX: goo [roarr]

90.2 —— FX: uoo [whoo]

92.2 —— FX: gacha [chk- door]

93.4 —— FX: biku [urk]

97.4 —— FX: miin miin miin miin [cicadas]

103.3 —— FX: tatata [running]

105.1 —— FX: gokun [gulp]

105.2.1 —— FX: ahahaha

105.2.2 —— FX: ban [smack]

105.3 —— FX: jii [stare]

106.4 —— FX: bashun [fshoom]

109.2 —— FX: ka [flash]

109.3 —— FX: fii fii fii [alarm]

110.2 —— FX: gakon [klang]

110.3 —— FX: gugugu [straining]

111.2 —— FX: gugugu [straining]

111.2-4 —— FX: bago [crack]

111.5 —— FX: gigigi [creeak]

112.1-2 —— FX: guoo [grrraugh]

135.4 — FX: biku [gasp]

136.1 — FX: mishi mishi [crackle]

137.1 — FX: bachi [zzak/snap]

137.2 — FX: bon [boom]

137.4 — FX: zuga [crash]

138.1-2 — FX: goo [whoo]

141.3 — FX: dokun [ba-bump]

143.3 — FX: guooo [graaurr]

143.4 — FX: ban [leap]

144.4 — FX: gan [whack]

145.1 — FX: dodon [slam]

145.2 — FX: zun [thud]

147.1 — FX: zun [thunk]

147.3 — FX: doga [crash]

148.1 — FX: gashi [glomp]

149.1 — FX: gogogo [crumble]

149.2 — FX: hyun [whoosh]

149.3 — FX: pashi [wpsh]

150.1 — FX: zuga [slam]

150.2 — FX: gigigi [rrk- strangulation]

151.4 — FX: gigigi [rkkk]

154.2 — FX: gakun [oof]

154.4 — FX: hyuii [whirr]

154.6 — FX: iii [whirr]

156.1 — FX: ka [flash]

156.2 — FX: gugu [rrk- raising arm]

156.3 — FX: gugugu [rrk]

157.1 — FX: gura [lurch]

157.2 — FX: gashi [glomp]

160.1 — FX: gugugu [rrkk]

161.2.1 — FX: pishi [crack]

161.2.2 — FX: mishi [creak]

161.3 — FX: baki [snap]

113.1.1 — FX: gogogo [rumble]

113.1.2 — FX: zudoon [kaboom]

114.1 — FX: pi pi pi [cell phone]

118.5 — FX: fii fii fii [alarm]

119.1 — FX: bashu [bwoosh]

119.2 — FX: doshu [doosh]

119.3 — FX: gan [klang]

121.3 — FX: von [vmm]

122.5 — FX: bashi [wpsh]

122.6 — FX: bo [bom]

124.1 — FX: kana kana kana [another species of cicada]

124.2 — FX: kana kana kana [cicadas]

124.4 — FX: zun [thm]

127.5 — FX: zun zun [thm thm]

128.1 — FX: zun [thm].

128.4 — FX: gan [wham]

128.5 — FX: zaa [sskt- static]

129.1 — FX: zun [thud]

129.2.1 — FX: zun zun [thm thm]

129.2.2 — FX: shuu [fssht]

130.1 — FX: zun zun [thm thm]

131.1 — FX: zun zun zun [dm dm dm]

131.6 — FX: jaki [chk]

132.3 — FX: pipipi [eep eep]

132.5 — FX: zun [thm]

133.1 — FX: gugigigi [creeak]

133.3 — FX: guon [leap]

134.1 — FX: don [slam]

134.2 — FX: zuga [wham]

135.1 — FX: gigigi [creeak]

135.3.1 — FX: dororo [gloop]

135.3.2 — FX: mishi mishi [crackle]

161.4 — FX: guoo [graaugh]

162.1 — FX: bun [fling]

162.2 — FX: dokan [slam]

163.2 — FX: gacha gacha [clacka clacka]

164.2-3 — FX: gusha [smash]

164.4 — FX: bichaa [splorch]

165.3.1 — FX: ga [grip]

165.3.2 — FX: biki [creak]

165.4 — FX: beki beki beki [rip crack]

166.1 — FX: beri [rrip]

166.2 — FX: ba [toss]

166.3-4 — FX: zudodon [crash]

166.4.1 — FX: ga [grip]

166.4.2 — FX: giriri [rrkk]

167.1 — FX: mishi mishishi [creak crack]

167.2 — FX: buchi [rrip]

167.3 — FX: zuzun [crash]

168.1 — FX: gacha gacha [clacka clacka]

169.1 — FX: zuga [stomp]

169.2 — FX: baki doka zugan [smash stomp crunch]

170.1 — FX: gan dosu [wham thud]

170.2 — FX: doka [whack]

170.3 — FX: baki [crack]

170.4-5 — FX: zugan [crunch]

172.1 — FX: gugu [squeeze]

175.1 — FX: piipoo piipoo piipoo
[weeoo weeoo- ambulance]

181.4 — FX: [magazine] Sportsman no Volume Tappuri
[lit. "A whole lot of volume (i.e., a hearty
meal) for the sportsman."]

183 — FX: shaka shaka [zoom zoom- mad pedaling]

SPECIAL BONUS DOSSIER SECTION

NEON GENESIS EVANGELION

VOLUME SIX

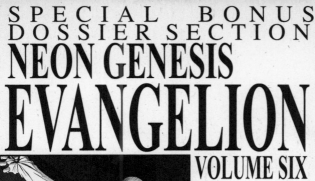

SECRETS OF EVANGELION

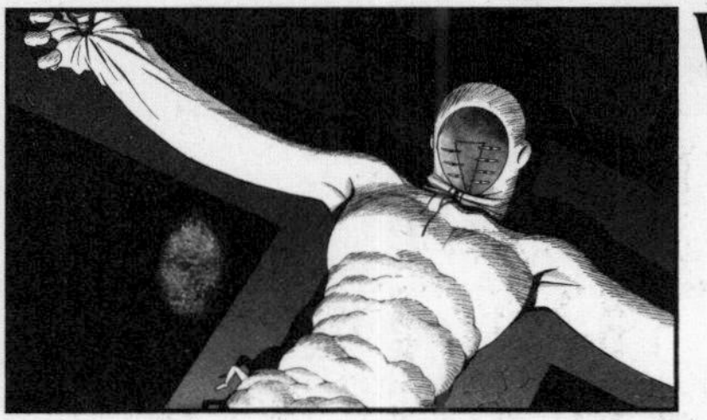

ADAM:

Two different-appearing entities, which may or may not be one and the same, have been referred to by this name at this point in events: a.) an object several cm in length resembling a human embryo, carried by Ryoji Kaji in "suspended animation" within a case and delivered to Gendo Ikari, an object described as "the key to the Instrumentality Project" and "the first human being;" and, b.) several weeks later: a giant, humanoid figure hanging from a cross in NERV's ultimate-level classified facility, the deep subterranean hangar known as Terminal Dogma. Upon first witnessing this figure, Major Katsuragi characterized Adam as "the First Angel;" Kaji added "This is also 'Project-E'."

The appearance of the figure described in b.) is that of a sexually indistinct human, white, hairless, almost blubbery. Its wrists are affixed to the cross by bolts or screws. Where its face would be, is a mask, possibly physically driven into the figure (a dark liquid can be observed oozing from where the mask meets the neck). On the mask is the sigil of **SEELE** (see below). The "body" is missing its presumed lower half, as if severed at the waist, but close inspection shows many smaller (that is, human-sized) pelvises and legs dangling from the blobby terminus of the figure. A paler, serum-like liquid runs down from the figure down to the bottom of the cross.

Kaji told Shinji that his mother, Dr. Yui Ikari, who vanished during the initial creation of the Evangelion series, solved the "primary problem" or "'Eva,' born from 'Adam.'" In an action related to the "Adam Project," Unit-00 pilot Rei Ayanami drove the **Spear of Longinus** (see below) into the body of Adam, where it currently resides at this point in events.

20th-century rabbi Z'ev ben Shimon Halevi, a student of Kabbalah (an ancient tradition with Judaism that seeks the mystical and esoteric rationale behind Creation) explained the Kabbalistic theory that the **Systema Sephiroticum** (see below)—a representation of which is on the floor and ceiling of Gendo Ikari's office—represents the model, map, schematic and code for the totality of Creation and, simultaneously, also the diagram for the body of the primal human being, "Adam Kadmon." In the process of Creation, Adam Kadmon, says Rabbi Halevi, is "the first of four reflections of God to become manifest as existence extends from Divinity to Materiality, before returning to merge again at the end of time." The Adam created in the book of Genesis is based on this model of Adam Kadmon; Halevi relates that while mainline Judaism "has it that Adam was created last of all creatures so that he would be humble, the Kabbalistic view is that all other creatures without exception—even the angels and archangels—are based on Adam (Kadmon) but were left incomplete: only the Adam (of Genesis) was a complete image of the Divine. This fact accounts for the myth of jealousy and discord among the angelic hosts..."

SECRETS OF EVANGELION

SPECIAL
BONUS
DOSSIER
SECTION

NEON GENESIS EVANGELION

VOLUME SIX

ALBINISM:

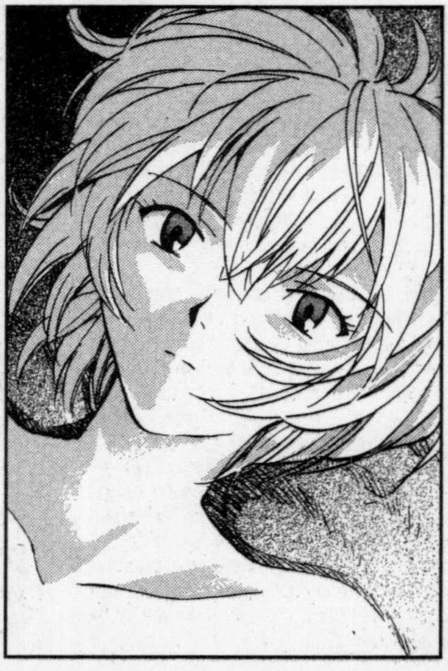

One explanation that has been offered for the unusual appearance of the First Child, Rei Ayanami. Albinism is a genetic defect; the hereditary inability to produce the pigment melanin, which, in different combinations, is what gives human skin, eyes, and hair their different colors. Rei's blue-white hair, pale skin, and red eyes (the red color of the underlying retina) are all highly symptomatic of albinism. There has been the strong suggestion that the Children are either the product of genetic experimentation or have certain "natural" genetic characteristics. If this is true, then Ayanami's presumed albinism could be either an "acceptable side effect" or "acceptable defect," considering the overall importance of her job. It is interesting to note, however, that while albinism necessarily results in sensitive skin and eyes, Ayanami appears to wear no special protection for either. She has been observed to be taking some sort of medication, however.

SPECIAL BONUS DOSSIER SECTION

NEON GENESIS EVANGELION VOLUME SIX

SECRETS OF EVANGELION

MARDUK AGENCY:

Like NERV itself, the even more obscure Marduk Agency is supposedly an organization established by the United Nations' secret Instrumentality of Man Committee, under its chairman, Lorenz Kiel. The founding date of the Marduk Agency is unknown. The purpose of Marduk is to find and identify those 14 year-old "Children" able to "synchronize" with and hence pilot the Evangelion units. At this point in events, four have been found: in order, the First, Rei Ayanami; the Second, Asuka Langley Soryu; the Third, Shinji Ikari, and the Fourth, Toji Suzuhara. Records indicate that the Marduk Agency is a vast concern, with connections to a family of 108 international enterprises. However, NERV's Ryoji Kaji, acting as a double agent for the Japanese Ministry of the Interior, maintains that he has evidence that Marduk is nothing but a vast series of blinds, and the truth about the selection process lies not with Marduk, but with the school all the Children attend.

"Marduk" was the ruler of the gods worshipped by ancient Babylon, the city-state whose armies in 586 B.C. destroyed the original Temple of Solomon in Jerusalem, and then exiled the Jews from their homeland during the forty-eight-year "Babylonian Captivity." This otherwise obscure detail may connect to the Instrumentality of Man Committee. The "Dead Sea Scrolls" consulted by the Committee for their prophecies are believed by many scholars to have been written by the Essene community of Jews—a community which is thought to have had its origins during the Babylonian Captivity (see also **SEELE**, below).

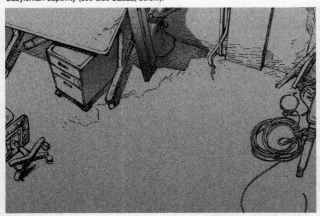

SECRETS OF EVANGELION

SPECIAL BONUS DOSSIER SECTION

NEON GENESIS EVANGELION

VOLUME SIX

POSITRONS:

One type of antimatter particle; the first variety of antimatter ever created in laboratory. Although postulated by noted 20th century physicist Paul Dirac as early as the 1930s, their manufacture, even in ultra-minute qualities, was not realized until the 1970s, when the breakthrough occurred at the giant accelerator spanning the Franco-Swiss borde CERN, the Conseil Européen pour la Recherche Nucléaire (European Organization for Nuclea Research). Positrons are the antimatter counterpart to the electrons that surround the nucle ordinary matter. Their potential as a weapon is clear when one realizes that while even the most efficient nuclear bombs only manage to release a small percentage of the energy con tained in their explosive mass, the intersection of matter and antimatter results in the total conversion to energy of both—a 200% efficient reaction.

The late Joe Bankhead, former USNS Electronics Tech 1st Class/Reactor Operator, commented upon the positron cannon employed by NERV against the Angel Rami Bankhead noted that while a stream of positrons might be a practical weapon in the vacuu of space, where normal matter in the path of the beam would be tenuous, a positron beam used in Earth's atmosphere would be "the equivalent of putting the barrel of your grenade launcher right up against a wall and then pulling the trigger…The matter/antimatter reactic in other words, would start to occur within nanometers once the positrons leave the (pre-sumed) magnetic containment field within the barrel. Boom." Bankhead added that in theor this could be prevented by surrounding the positron beam with some kind of generated neu nos, but that in his judgment it remained "a highly dubious prospect."

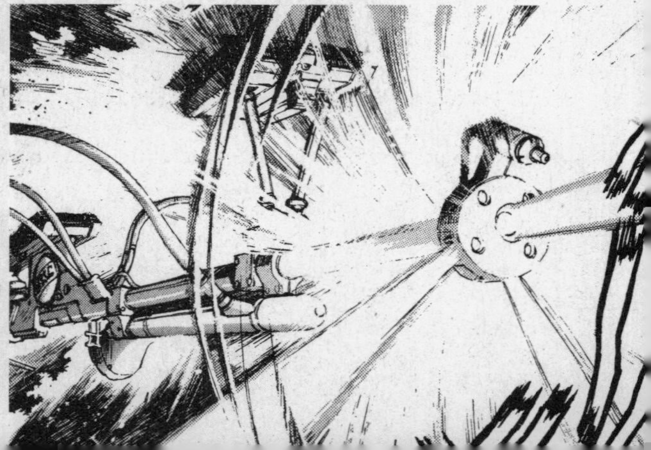

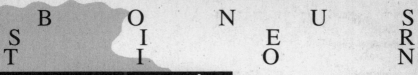
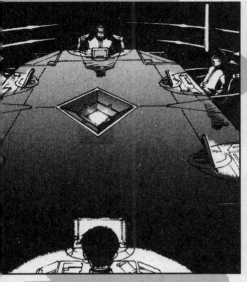

A great many of the Dead Sea Scrolls—important early Jewish historical and theological documents dating from circa 250 BC to circa 135 AD—are publicly known to scholars. However, the first of the Scrolls were unearthed under chaotic circumstances in 1947 and were restricted to a small group of scholars for many years thereafter; scholars also assume others remain hidden in private custody, if only for their priceless monetary value. All are factors lending mystery to these documents, and make SEELE's claim to possess secret Scrolls difficult to dismiss on its face.

In fact, even among the publicly-known Scrolls is a fragment of the earliest ever found version of the pseudoepigraphical Book of Enoch, a work not accepted as canonical by mainline Judaism or Christianity but of enduring interest to occultists. This particular fragment, 4Q201, has an odd resonance with the history of NERV, reading in part, "[They (the leaders) and all...of them took for themselves] wives from all that they chose and [they began to cohabit with them and to defile themselves with them]; and to teach them sorcery and [spells and the cutting of roots; and to acquaint them with herbs.] And they become pregnant by them and bo[re (great) giants three thousand cubits high ...]."

It has been suggested by Taliesin Jaffe that Kiel identifies himself and his committee with the personages described in the Old Testament book of the prophet Zechariah (see also **Spear of Longinus**, below) chapters 3, 4 and 8: "For behold the stone that I have laid before Joshua; upon one stone shall be seven eyes: behold, I will engrave the graving thereof, saith the LORD of hosts, and I will remove the iniquity of that land in one day...and he shall bring forth the headstone thereof with shoutings, crying, Grace, grace unto it. Moreover the word of the LORD came unto me, saying, The hands of Zerubbabel have laid the foundation of this house; his hands shall also finish it...they shall rejoice, and shall see the plummet in the hand of Zerubbabel with those seven; they are the eyes of the LORD, which run to and fro through the whole earth....In those days it shall come to pass, that ten men shall take hold out of all languages of the nations, even shall take hold of the skirt of him that is a Jew, saying, We will go with you: for we have heard that God is with you."

Zerubbabel, which means "Seed of Babylon" in Hebrew, was a lineal ancestor of Christ (Michelangelo depicted him in the Vatican's Sistine Chapel). He was a leader among the Jews who returned to Jerusalem from exile after the "Babylonian Captivity," and it was he who finished the rebuilding of the Temple of Solomon. Solomon's Temple, today a ruin except for its western, or "Wailing" Wall, was long regarded in esoteric traditions (notably Masonry) to be as close to a physical expression of the majesty, secrets, and perfection of God as human technology ever created. The Branch Davidians, an apocalyptic sect of the 1990s, also believed that the "latter-day Zerubbabel" was among them.

SECRETS OF EVANGELION

SPECIAL
D O S
S E C

NEON GENESIS EVANGELION
VOLUME SIX

SEELE:

German for "soul" (pronounced "ZAY-leh"), a committee variously shown to be of as few as five or as many as fifteen personages of apparently different ethnic or national origin, to whom Gendo and his sub-commander, Fuyutsuki, have been seen to report. "Seele" is the esoteric name of the (itself secret) Instrumentality of Man Committee of the United Nations. However, neither the existence of the Committee nor the name "Seele" are known to the general public; indeed, it is not known if anyone outside NERV is aware of their existence, and they appear a secret to many inside NERV as well. Also secret is the existence of the Instrumentality Project, the completion of which (and not defeating the Angels per se) Chairman Kiel has stated as NERV's primary objective. Adam, the crucified First Angel kept by NERV, bears a mask with marks resembling lunar craters above the sigil of SEELE—an inverted triangle with seven eyes.

The origins of SEELE and Kiel are unknown, although "Lorenz Kiel" is also a German name, as is both "NERV" and its precursor organization "GEHIRN." Although sometimes communicating only through a hologram, there is certainly evidence to suggest Kiel is an actual person, him having been photographed in a public gathering with Gendo Ikari in 2002. Kiel is a Caucasian and has the appearance of a man in late middle or early old age; he possibly has sensitive eyesight, as he, unlike the other members of SEELE, wears a slitted visor over his eyes, and wore wide dark glasses in the 2002 photo.

It is known for certain that Dr. Yui Ikari, and through her, Gendo, worked for SEELE in the year before the Second Impact. It is possible that SEELE is indeed an organization of ancient lineage and a hidden power in world history (indeed, Ryoji Kaji suggests this is in fact the case, saying they at least are certainly the progenitors of NERV); they may also be of more modern origins, and merely claim an unwarranted, exaggerated, or unproven antiquity to bolster their prestige or sense of mission, as has been the case with other secret societies such as the Masons and Rosicrucians. In any event, SEELE makes a convincing claim to have access to ancient knowledge, including knowledge of both the human past and future based on prophecies and revelations in certain secret "Dead Sea Scrolls" in their possession.

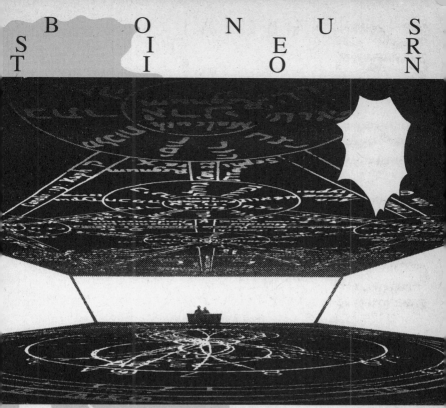

and has included not only figures regarded as mystics but philosophers such as the psychologist C.G. Jung. However, one of the earliest non-Jews known to seek occult knowledge from the Kabbalah was the mysterious Jesuit scholar Athanasius Kircher (1602-1680). He drew the particular diagrammatic interpretation of the Kabbalah that appears on the ceiling of Gendo's office, and gave it the Latin name "Systema Sephiroticum" (System of the Sephira). Kircher drew controversial, syncretic associations between Christian teaching and the Kabbalah, which had by this time already existed separately for centuries as a Jewish discipline. It is of course also important to bear in mind that the long history of Judaism has included within its own adherents a full range of interpretations of Kabbalah, no less than debate over everyday questions of morals, ethics, practices and beliefs, with differences that continue to the present day.

However, the pattern does accurately describe fundamental Jewish Kabbalistic beliefs: to wit, that the ten "sephirah," (the word, which is the original Hebrew, is an ancestor of the English "cipher") shown in the diagrams, are attributes of God, linked together by a complex pattern that serves also as a model, map, schematic and code for the totality of Creation; thereby, through its study, all knowledge of Creation and God can eventually be revealed and understood by human beings.

For this to happen, in Kabbalah, is in fact the purpose of existence itself, as Kabbalists believe that Creation—where One made many—occurred because "God wished to behold God," and therefore, "Face must behold Face." Only when our knowledge of Creation—including its experiences and possibilities as brought about by free will—is complete, will all existence be reunited with God.

SPECIAL
S   L
S   O
      E   S   C

NEON GENESIS
EVANGELION
VOLUME SIX

SYSTEMA SEPHIROTICUM:

Inscribed on the ceiling (and floor, in a different form) of Commander Ikari's office, are diagrams of Creation as conceived within the ancient Judaic mystical tradition known as Kabbalah. It is important to note that because of the antiquity and basic primacy of Judaism and Jewish writings within the Western (and also Islamic) theological tradition, historically, many non-Jews have attempted to adapt, or co-opt, such to their own systems of belief or practice. While this has often been done without malign intended, it has also often taken on an expression that could be characterized as anti-Semitic.

This occurred notoriously with the chief editor of the Dead Sea Scrolls research project himself, Harvard Divinity School's Dr. John Strugnell, who was dismissed from his position after voicing supersessionist views about Judaism in a November 9, 1990 interview with the Israeli newspaper HaAretz. Supersessionism is when believers in newer religions based on Judaism (for example, religions such as Christianity, founded c. 27 A.D. and Islam, founded 610 A.D., both of which regard the God with whom the Jewish patriarch Abraham made a covenant in c. 1850 B.C. as also being their God) express the idea that their new religion "supersedes," "completes," or "corrects" an original Judaism that is now irrelevant. Another extreme example of the co-opting of Jewish revelation to justify a movement or program are the views of present-day sects such as the Christian Identity movement, who seek to write Jews out of their own history, claiming that "White, Anglo-Saxon, Germanic and kindred people" were the actual people of Abraham's covenant and that modern Jews are somehow imposters.

This millennia-old interest in Jewish concepts and thought has included conventional religious practice as well as esoteric ritual,

SPECIAL BONUS DOSSIER SECTION

NEON GENESIS EVANGELION

VOLUME SIX

SECRETS OF EVANGELION

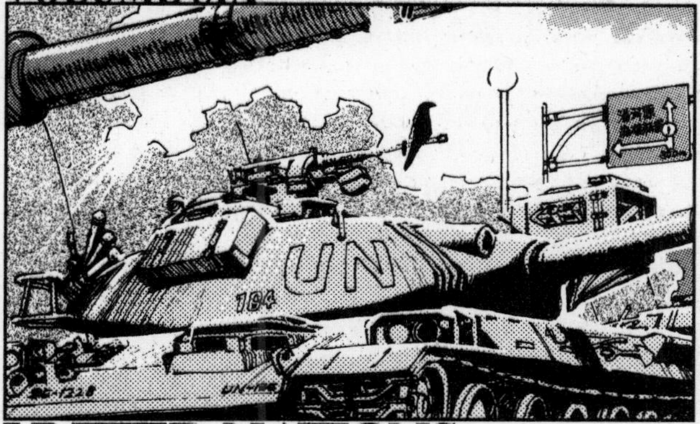
UN
194

UNITED NATIONS:

An international organization of sovereign states, established in the immediate aftermath of the Second World War in 1945 with its headquarters in New York City. Originally composed of the victorious Allied Powers, the chartered purpose of the UN was to promote world peace, security and cooperation in the post-war world, and the organization had come to include nearly all countries by the end of the century. The discovery of the Dead Sea Scrolls took place against the backdrop of the UN partition of Israel and Palestine as separate entities, and it was a member of the United Nations Truce Supervision Organization, Captain Philippe Lippens, who brought in Roland de Vaux, director of the Ecole Biblique, a French Catholic theological school in Arab East Jerusalem, to oversee research on the Scrolls; he remained director of the project until his death in 1971. It was de Vaux who discovered the fragments of the Book of Enoch in 1952.

The Antarctic Treaty of 1959, which suspended the claims of any individual nation to that continent, opening it up to extensive research, was written to "further the purposes and principles embodied in the Charter of the United Nations." It was the United Nations that investigated and published the official explanation of the Second Impact in 2002, claiming it resulted from a meteor strike. The UN gained in the aftermath of that catastrophe a heretofore unseen level of power and influence that made it, for the first time, an agency capable—if it deemed so necessary—of action independent of the major surviving world governments. Of those governments, that of Japan appears the most susceptible to UN influence (although the mistrust and rivalry between the two organizations is also evident). The headquarters of the 21st century United Nations is in fact now in Japan's own capital of Tokyo-2, formerly called Matsumoto City.

SECRETS OF EVANGELION

SPECIAL BONUS DOSSIER SECTION

NEON GENESIS EVANGELION

SPEAR OF LONGINUS:

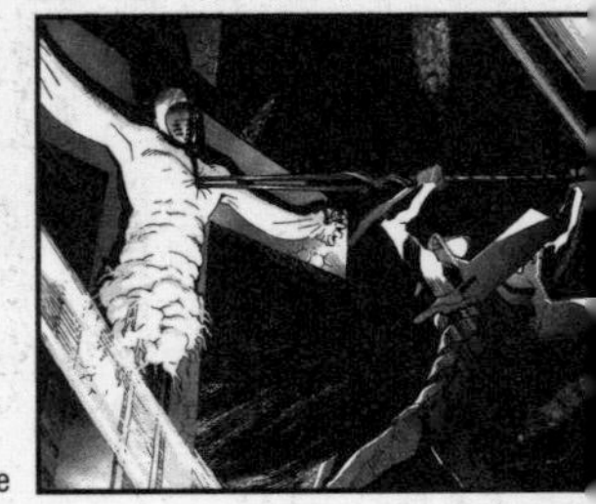

In the account of the Crucifixion given in John 19:34, we are told that after Christ died, "one of the soldiers with a spear pierced his side, and forthwith there came out blood and water," an act interpreted by John to be a fulfillment of a description of the Messiah as given by the prophet Zechariah (Zechariah 12:10). In the apocryphal Gospel of Nicodemus, it is said that this Roman soldier's name was Longinus and—perhaps significantly—that Longinus pierced the living, not the dead Christ. Longinus is regarded as a saint and martyr by both the Catholic and Orthodox churches; he is said to have been converted to Christianity by the experience. His supposed name ("Longinus" may simply be taken from the Latin word for "lance," as this relic is also known), his biographical origins, and the true location, if extant, of his Spear are shrouded in uncertainty.

In previous centuries the Spear has been variously claimed to reside in Rome, Vienna, and Cracow. However, according to a discussion (recorded by classified UN documentary footage, and recovered by Brendan Jamieson) amongst scientists of the Katsuragi Expedition that first discovered **Adam** beneath their base at Mt. Markham on the Shackleton Coast of Antarctica, the Spear was found in the Dead Sea itself. It was subsequently delivered to the base's dock the week of August 7, 2000. The Second Impact occurred on September 13 during the experimental insertion of the Spear into Adam; the UN scientists attempted to pull it back after "the planned limit values" were exceeded. The Spear, however, continued to sink into Adam, whose A.T. Field released itself in an explosion causing massive tsunami, climactic change, and subsequent civil strife that led to the death of 50% of humanity within the next year. The Spear was recovered and brought to Tokyo-3 in 2015 by an expedition to Antarctica led personally by Gendo Ikari and his second-in-command, Kozo Fuyutsuki.

The lore surrounding the Spear has extended into modern times, as it is maintained by some that Hitler's interest in the occult included this relic. From the gigantic dimensions (the length of an aircraft carrier) of the "Spear" recovered by NERV, it is evident that it cannot literally have been a weapon wielded by any human being. Neither does the "Spear"'s design, that of a military fork whose tines emerge from the unwinding of a progressively tightened double helix, resemble any Roman weapon known to have been in use during the 1st century A.D. NERV, however, and its putative overseer SEELE, are organizations steeped in symbolism and seeking an esoteric meaning behind the plain text of scripture and prophecy. The association of the Spear with the structure of DNA may have been quite literal; one of the very last remarks recorded in the UN footage, mere seconds before the Second Impact, is "The genes implanted into Adam have already achieved physical merging."

Taking that into account, as well as the uncertainty regarding the relic itself, speculation suggests one or more of the following: a.) the Spear is an authentic relic whose suprahuman origins, like those of the Angels, were revealed only through secret revelations to which SEELE and NERV have access, b.) "Spear of Longinus" is a code name, chosen for its mythological associations in the manner of the names given to many modern military weapons, or even c.) the Spear contains encased *within it* the actual artifact; interestingly, one of the massive pillars over the high altar of the Vatican is said to contain the Spear.

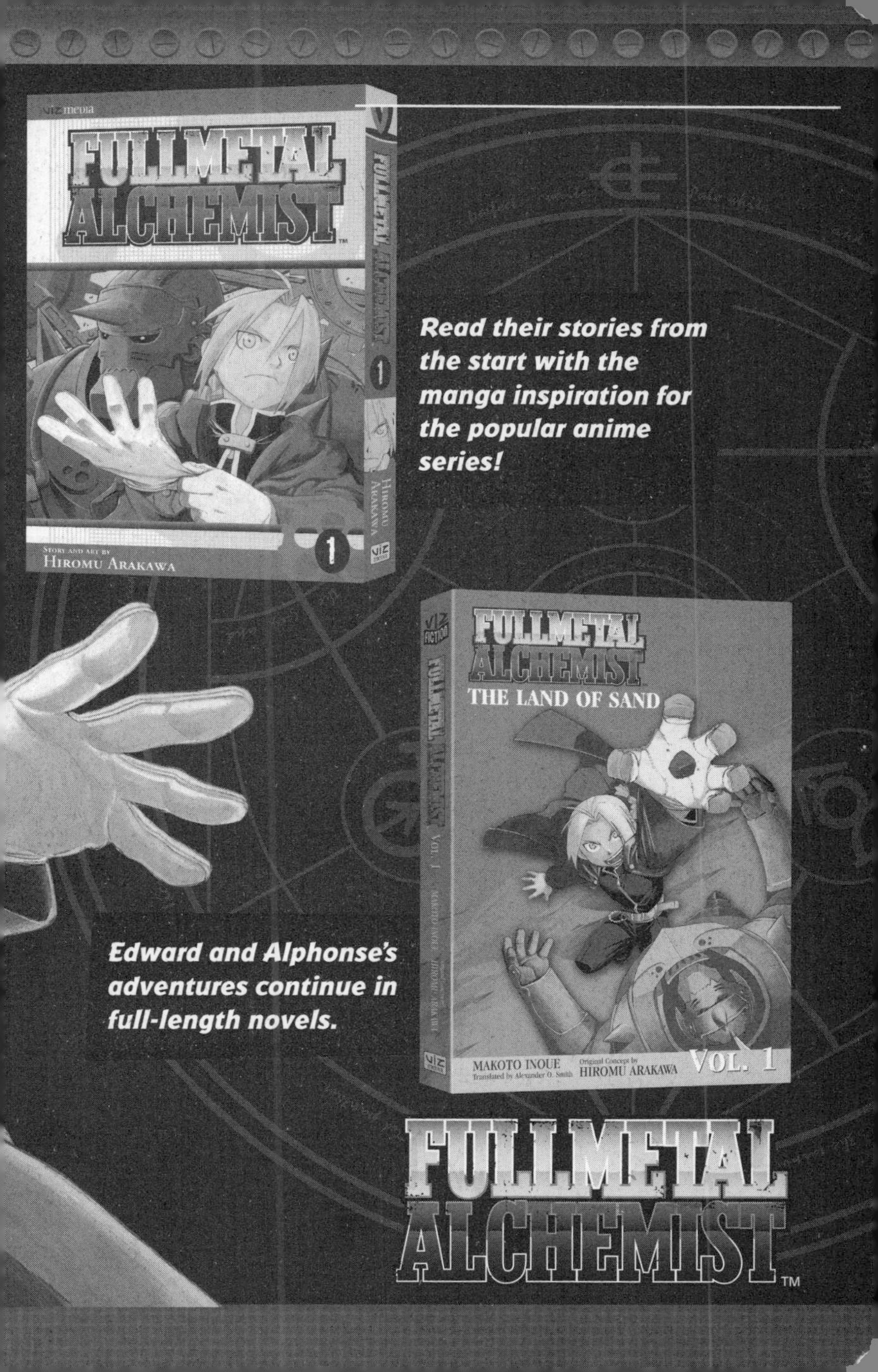
VIZ media
FULLMETAL ALCHEMIST
1
HIROMU ARAKAWA
STORY AND ART BY
HIROMU ARAKAWA
Read their stories from the start with the manga inspiration for the popular anime series!
VIZ FICTION
FULLMETAL ALCHEMIST
THE LAND OF SAND
VOL. 1
MAKOTO INOUE
Translated by Alexander O. Smith
Original Concept by
HIROMU ARAKAWA
VOL. 1
Edward and Alphonse's adventures continue in full-length novels.
FULLMETAL ALCHEMIST™

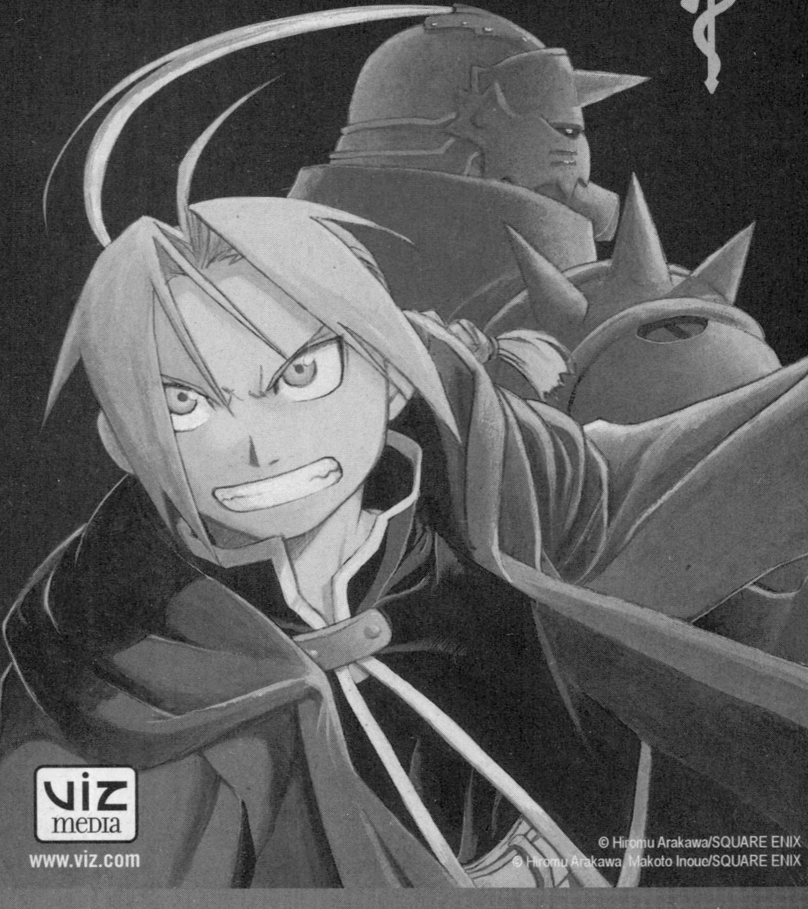

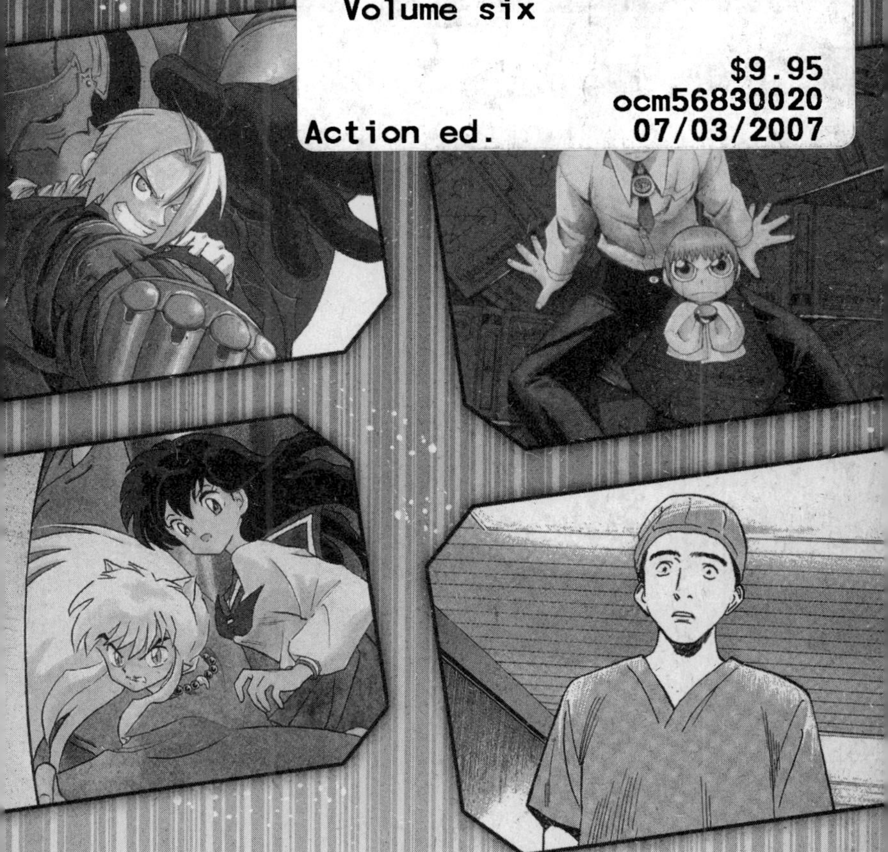

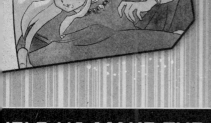